The Evolution of American Urban Society

Howard P. Chudacoff
Brown University

Judith E. Smith
University of Massachusetts, Boston

PEARSON
Prentice Hall

Upper Saddle River, NJ 07458

Library of Congress Cataloging-in-Publication Data

Chudacoff, Howard P.
   The evolution of American urban society / Howard P. Chudacoff, Judith E. Smith.-- 6th ed.
   p. cm.
   Includes bibliographical references and index.
   ISBN 0-13-189824-8
   1. Cities and towns--United States--History. 2. Urbanization--United States. 3. United
   States--Social conditions. I. Smith, Judith E., 1948- II. Title.

   HT123.C49 2005
   307.76'0973--dc22   2004053383

Editorial Director: Charlyce Jones Owen
Executive Editor: Charles Cavaliere
Associate Editor: Emsal Hasan
Editorial Assistant: Shannon Corliss
Executive Marketing Manager: Heather Shelstad
Marketing Assistant: Jennifer Bryant
Managing Editor: Joanne Riker
Production Liaison: Marianne Peters-Riordan
Manufacturing Buyer: Tricia Kenny
Cover Design: Bruce Kenselaar
Cover Photo: Courtesy of the Library of Congress
Image Permission Coordinator: Nancy Seise
Composition/Full-Service Project Management: Lithokraft/Marty Sopher
Printer/Binder: Phoenix Color Corp.
Cover Printer: Phoenix Color Corp.

Credits and acknowledgments borrowed from other sources and reproduced, with permission, in this textbook appear on appropriate page.

Pearson Education LTD., London
Pearson Education Singapore, Pte. Ltd
Pearson Education, Canada, Ltd
Pearson Education–Japan
Pearson Education Australia PTY,
   Limited

Pearson Education North Asia Ltd
Pearson Educación de Mexico,
   S.A. de C.V.
Pearson Education Malaysia, Pte. Ltd
Pearson Education, Upper Saddle River,
   New Jersey

10 9 8 7 6 5 4 3 2 1
ISBN 0-13-189824-8

Contents

Photo Credits   312

Index   314

Preface

Since 1975, when *The Evolution of American Urban Society* was first published, American cities and the scholarship about the history of American cities have undergone consequential changes. Yet at the same time, there have been vital consistencies in both urban life and the scholarly focus on how American urban society has evolved. Throughout almost three decades, the authors of this book have maintained their focus on the social history of urban life, with special attention to the unfolding political and economic processes that have shaped the development of cities and the lives of urban dwellers. Equally important have been the ways that the actions of urban dwellers—the powerful and the ordinary—have influenced the course of urban history.

For this, the sixth edition of *The Evolution of American Urban Society*, we have updated the scholarship and bibliographies for each chapter, paying particular attention to issues of race, ethnicity, gender, the built environment, regional differentials, and emerging cultural forms such as rock and rap music. Wherever possible, we have added perspectives on the environmental impact of cities and suburbs. The chapters on the post-World War II cities offer new attention to the new racial and ethnic mix produced by the most recent immigration trends and to the re-institutionalization of segregation resulting from public housing development and highway policies. As well, we have tried to be sensitive to the effects of concentrated poverty in inner-city neighborhoods and the costs of hardening barriers between city and suburb. The final chapter has been expanded to take into account issues relating to the presidential administration of George W. Bush and to the consequences of the terrorist attacks of September 11, 2001.

Once again, we owe special thanks to Pembroke Herbert for her valuable picture research and to Jim O'Brien for his efficient indexing. We also wish to acknowledge the insightful critiques offered by Mark Newman, National Louis University; Abel Bartley, University of Akron; Anne Brophy, Georgia State University; George Lubick, Northern Arizona University; and Jacob Judd, CUNY/Lehman College. Howard Chudacoff thanks Nancy Fisher Chudacoff for guidance and inspiration, and Judith Smith thanks Larry Blum, and Ben, Sarah, and Laura Blum-Smith for their insights and support.

*To my father, Irving Chudacoff,
and to the memory of my mother,
Mildred Chudacoff, and my grandparents,
Jenny and William Saferstein*

*To my mother, Beth K. Smith,
and to the memory of my father, Edward A. Smith
and my grandparents, James and Sarah Smith,
and J. Harry and Sadie Kulakofsky*

1

Urban America in the Colonial Age, 1600–1776

URBAN BEGINNINGS

The history of city building on the North American continent preceded the arrival of the Europeans. Indian tribes in the Mississippi Valley built a settlement known as Cahokia, estimated to have had a population of thirty-five thousand long before whites settled the area. Artifacts recovered at Cahokia indicate the existence of far-flung trading networks, specialization of crafts, and clustered housing and markets, although by the time of European colonization this urban civilization had largely disappeared. Similarly, archaeological evidence of a Huron settlement in the Great Lakes region has revealed more than one hundred large structures that probably housed a population of between four and six thousand people in the fifteenth century. The Huron settlement was larger than the average European village of that period and larger than all but a handful of European colonial towns in America even after one hundred fifty years of colonization. In the Southwest, large pueblo settlements such as that at Acoma (known as Sky City) in New Mexico had existed since at least the twelfth century, A.D. Spanish explorer Franscisco Coronado in 1560 described the Acoma village, with its hundreds of residents, as "one of the strongest ever seen."

Even more than the Indians, however, the Europeans who colonized North America were urban-minded people, seeking commercial markets as well as the resources that the land promised to yield. A whole continent of forests, plains, and deserts already inhabited by diverse Indian nations opened before the colonizers, but before they could plunge into that wilderness they needed central places for trade, defense, government, and worship. Thus they created cities—settlements that functioned to organize and protect populations and to accumulate and disseminate goods and communications.

Interaction with Indians significantly shaped European patterns of settlement. Throughout the sixteenth century, contact and trade, although sporadic, provided Indian communities and European explorers with exposure to each other's cultures—and to each other's diseases. By the time European colonizers planted permanent settlements, they were often drawn to sites previously occupied but now abandoned by Indians. As the Spanish, who colonized first, overthrew the powerful Indian empires of Central and South America, they rebuilt settlements on the ruins of what once had been lavish capitals. Cartagena, Mexico City, Lima, and Bogotá grew on these sites, some holding as many as fifty thousand inhabitants by 1700, a size that dwarfed all colonial cities to the north.

In North America, Spanish colonizers committed to securing territory and Christianizing Indians in what are now Florida and New Mexico found Indians living in villages. St. Augustine (1565) was founded near villages of Saturiba people. Sante Fe (1610) was positioned in the center of native Pueblo settlements, close enough for conversion efforts but not so close as to heighten conflict over land use. The survival of Spanish colonizers depended

The Native American City of Cahokia.   This photograph is based on a reconstruction of Cahokia printed by Valerie Waldorf. At the center of community life was the large earthenware temple that rose to a height of one hundred feet. Cahokia artisans mass-produced knives, salt, and stone hoe blades for local consumption and export. Note the outlying farms surrounding the more densely settled areas. Cahokia may have been a crossroads of trade and water travel in the heartland of North America.

on Indian food supplies and knowledge of local environments. For example, soldiers at St. Augustine who did not follow the Indians' advice to drink boiled sassafras tea rather than local water died. Once it was clear that the Spanish intended to settle permanently, those Indians not weakened by disease contracted from Europeans attempted to expel the colonizers. Where Indians lacked internal unity, they were unsuccessful, but in New Mexico, Pueblo bands were able to join together in 1680 to drive out the Spanish. Twenty-five hundred Indians surrounded Sante Fe, and after a number of days, the Spanish surrendered. In 1693, with the help of superior weapons, the Spanish were able to retake the Santa Fe settlement, though the land and people beyond its walls remained outside of Spanish control.

Spanish colonizers were committed to founding cities because the Spanish system of government consisted of city-states and because Spaniards identified not with a kingdom or a province but with a city. Cities served a critical function as local symbols of political authority. The boundaries of a Spanish city extended into the hinterlands until they ran into the sphere of influence of another Spanish city. Until the late eighteenth century, St. Augustine represented in a corporate fashion all Spanish interests east of Santa Fe.

The Spanish also developed a formal system of town planning that they applied to their colonies in both North and South America. This was the Laws of the Indies, an enactment of 1583 that synthesized earlier practices of settlement, some from Roman times. The Laws specified uniform requirements for town location, street layout, and land use, and they shaped urban beginnings in Florida and the American Southwest. Early maps of St. Augustine, San Antonio, and San Diego show how the Laws influenced a common design of rectangular blocks, straight streets, and right-angle intersections grouped around a large, central plaza. Spanish colonization intended to distinguish among types of settlements: *pueblos* were to be centers of commerce and colonization; *missions* were established to promote religious conversion, and *presidios* were military outposts. But such distinctions often faded once actual settlement occurred. For example, San Antonio was originally established at the headwaters of a river on the site of an Indian village. Called Yanaguana by the Indians, it was rechristened in 1691 as San Antonio. A band of seventy-two soldiers, settlers, and monks settled in San Antonio in 1718, and a quarrel between the chief military leader and the missionary priest led to separate settlements of a presidio and the mission later famous as the Alamo. Presidios were established at San Diego in 1769, San Francisco in 1776, Los Angeles in 1781, and Santa Barbara in 1782, but soon house and farm buildings sprang up beyond the presidio walls, and the military communities looked indistinguishable from the civil settlements of the pueblos.

In contrast to the Spanish, French explorers came not as colonizers but as individual traders seeking personal gain. Needing centers for the exchange of goods, they founded commercial ports along the waterways of

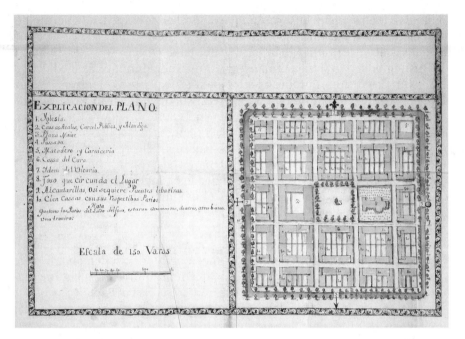

Plan of San Antonio, Texas. Spanish colonists built this town according to a 1573 ordinance that specified a layout that situated the church and government buildings around a central plaza. Countless settlements, especially in the American West, followed the same design.

colonial North America's perimeters. In the North and West, they built Quebec, Montreal, Detroit, and St. Louis, towns of varied design that usually conformed to the area's topography. These places acted as staging points for fur traders and missionaries who combed the Great Lakes and Mississippi River regions in the early 1700s. In 1718, Jean-Baptiste Le Moyne, sieur de Beinville, founded New Orleans near the mouth of the Mississippi, on a site previously used by Choctaw tribes, as the staging area for a project to expand the Bourbon empire by creating a colony based on slave-produced tobacco. By 1721, the population of New Orleans was half slave, and by 1731, slaves were four times as numerous as white settlers or French soldiers. In 1763, at the conclusion of the European colonial conflict known as the Seven Years' War, New Orleans was ceded to the Spanish. Designed as a large walled settlement with square blocks and an open field on the waterfront, New Orleans developed into an important commercial crossroads later in the century when settlers spilled across the Appalachian Mountains toward the western river valleys.

Dutch colonizers, like the Spanish, brought elaborate urban plans with them. In 1625, a group of colonists from the Dutch West India Company arrived on Manhattan Island with intentions to build a trading center called New Amsterdam, complete with a twenty-five-foot-wide main street and a

New Orleans, 1726. This French watercolor shows an infant port town carved out of the forest along what subsequently became known as the Mississippi River. For the French settlers as well as the English, water-born commerce was vital to urban survival.

central marketplace. The Dutch West India Company was a chief international supplier of slaves, and not surprisingly, slaveholding was extensive in New Amsterdam. Although the Dutch used New Amsterdam mainly as a fur trading center and made little effort to develop its harbor, the town soon would become one of the continent's great seaports.

These projects set important precedents for future American cities, but the English colonies along the North Atlantic coast were more numerous and ultimately more influential in shaping American urban life. It was especially in the several settlements along or near the Massachusetts coast that the urban frontier began. At first, these towns combined Puritan notions of social and religious harmony with the village orientation of agrarian peasant society. The town of Boston, however, recast the mold. According to the precepts of founder John Winthrop, the colony of Massachusetts Bay was to be "as a Citty upon a Hill," a place that bound people together in sanctification of God. But when, in 1630, the settlers relocated from Charlestown across the Charles River to Boston in order to take advantage of the better harbor there, they began a process that was to swell and diversify population and expand economic activity, thereby obliterating Winthrop's vision. For Boston was to become more than an agrarian-based town; its harbor and natural location as a commercial and administrative hub turned it into a prosperous, worldly city.

In subsequent decades, several other cities developed similarly along the Atlantic coast, all sustained by trade. In 1639, a group of religious dissenters founded Newport on the island of Rhode Island, ostensibly as a haven for the persecuted. The site they chose had the best harbor in southern New England, and it was this geographic advantage rather than religious tolerance that assured the town's future. When the British captured New Amsterdam from the Dutch in 1664, they inherited the finest natural port in

North America. They preserved the city's commercial functions and made it the capital of New York colony. In 1680, proprietors of Carolina colony moved their chief settlement from a marshy location to a peninsula jutting out between the Ashley and Cooper rivers in order to utilize its harbor and more healthful environs. The settlement, named Charles Town (later Charleston), soon became the largest and wealthiest town in the southern colonies. And in 1682, William Penn chose the site for Philadelphia one hundred miles up the Delaware River where it was joined by the Schuylkill. This was to be not only the capital of Pennsylvania colony and the most extensive experiment in city building that the colonies had yet witnessed, but also a place intended as "the most considerable for merchandize, trade, and fishery in these parts."

There were and would be others—Providence, Albany, New Haven, Baltimore, Williamsburg, Norfolk, Savannah—but throughout the British colonial period, the five cities of Boston, Newport, New York, Philadelphia, and Charleston were the largest and most powerful. Although their origins spanned a half century, these cities resembled each other in several important ways. Most fundamentally, all were ports. As depots for immigrants and as transfer points for resources and products going to and coming from other parts of the world, they all linked their fortunes to the sea. In addition, all had planned beginnings, and all were products of the same civilization. Except for Newport, all originated in intent and leadership in London and Amsterdam, both centers of societies that judged cities to be necessary and desirable. Thus it is not surprising that the Dutch and particularly the British established settlements that assumed characteristics of genuinely urban places: the concentration of people, resources, and ideas. These cities represented for their colonizers the transfer of civilization—meaning an urban environment and the activities associated with it—from the Old to the New World.

Because the major colonial cities were commercial and administrative centers, they grew rapidly, as the population figures below reveal. None of the American port towns could compare with even the secondary commercial

	Population		
	1690	1742	1775
Boston	7,000	16,382	16,000
Philadelphia	4,000	13,000	24,000
New York	3,900	11,000	25,000
Newport	2,600	6,200	11,000
Charleston	1,100	6,800	12,000

centers of western Europe, such as Lyons, which had reached forty-five thousand in the 1530s, or Norwich, which had grown to nineteen thousand by the 1570s. American port towns were small because they served regional populations that were still themselves small and because the risks of trade, the lack of agricultural hinterlands, and the low level of credit available to seaport entrepreneurs limited opportunities for growth of a market economy on a scale comparable to European commercial capitals. Still, this surge of urban population satisfied British mercantile objectives of centralization for the sake of control. Indeed, the Crown encouraged the growth of towns because such concentrations of population facilitated defense and government of the colonists.

But the size and economic opportunities of these cities also prompted activities that stretched the intended limits of colonial administration and eventually threatened the colonial system. As links in the mercantilist system, the colonial ports collected and dispatched raw materials such as grain, rice, fish, furs, and lumber that were needed by England, and they received the manufactured wares of British merchants for American consumption. Thus most lines of commerce initially extended from individual cities to the mother country rather than among the colonies themselves.

It was not long, however, before colonial towns bred merchants and tradesmen who began to look to the interior settlements in search of markets for locally produced as well as imported goods. Consequently, each city began to cultivate its own commercial hinterland, an activity that turned the colonial ports into small commercial powers themselves and enabled them to expand their economies beyond English goals of simple self-support. Just as the mercantile relationship to England drained the colonies of raw materials and what little silver currency circulated, the cities began to draw products and coin from the countryside. The fur trade depended on close relationships with natives, and had the effect of drawing Indians into commercial exchange. As early as the 1640s, Boston traders expanded commercial ties westward and southward to Springfield, Hartford, and along Long Island Sound. By the eve of the Revolution inland trade had become an important concern to all of urban America. In Rhode Island, for example, a Providence merchant, Welcome Arnold, shipped processed lime—a necessity for the production of mortar and plaster—not only to Boston, New York, Philadelphia, and Baltimore but also to smaller settlements in the New England interior. Arnold added retail consumer goods to his inland lime traffic, and he helped attach a broad hinterland to Providence that choked off any potential expansion by Newport, enabling Providence to surpass Newport's size and become New England's second city by 1800.

The importance of commerce partly explains why most major British colonial cities were located in the North. With the exceptions of Charleston and, to a lesser degree, Savannah and Norfolk, the South lacked the deep,

Colonial New Amsterdam. This extraordinary map is a redrawing by John Wolcott Adams and N. Phelps Stokes of the Castello Plan of New Amsterdam, first drawn in 1660. The street leading out from the fort and into the undeveloped area is Broadway. The road along the fortification separating the settled area from the unsettled land is Wall Street.

safe harbors that benefited northern ports. But unlike the North, the South had many rivers that were navigable far inland. Ports were therefore less important in the South because trading ships did not have to stop at the coast to transfer cargoes to wagons and smaller boats that could travel into the interior. Also, the southern economy, tied to staple-crop agriculture, tended to be more self-sufficient and less dependent on trade than that of the more diversified North. Southern plantations produced much of their own food and clothing, and the region's wealth was invested more in labor than in commerce and industry. Finally, because a large proportion of southern residents were slaves and indentured servants rather than wage laborers, there were relatively fewer people in the South with expendable incomes for commercial exchange.

Environmental factors gave the northern ports both advantages and disadvantages. Because Philadelphia was located on the Delaware River and thereby had a freshwater rather than saltwater harbor, boats could dock there for long periods without suffering damage from sea worms (barnacles) that lived in salt water and ate away at wooden bottoms. But the river also froze for several months in winter, stopping navigation. New York, with easy access to the ocean, had a harbor that never froze and was deep enough to accommodate the largest ships. Though barnacles endangered boats in New York harbor, its location near Long Island gave it protection from hurricanes and other storms that threatened the Atlantic Coast. Boston, another saltwater port, was protected from severe ocean storms by Cape Cod. Charleston, by contrast, was more vulnerable. In September of 1752, for example, a vicious hurricane blew all vessels in the harbor ashore, washed away all wharves and warehouses, destroyed 500 homes, and killed over 100 people.

Size and commercial activity, combined with benign neglect on the part of England, also forced colonial cities into the expansion of self-government. Most towns were created by charters of incorporation granted by the king or the provincial government. These charters defined the form and scope of local administration. Gradually, every colonial city except Charleston assumed self-management of local affairs, acquiring power either by piecemeal grant or by charter revision. Philadelphia and (after 1664) New York, capitals of proprietary colonies, resembled English municipal boroughs in that they were incorporated by royal charter and administered by a mayor and council. As in English cities, their local governments reflected their particular commercial quality. Political privileges (voting) rested in the hands of those who had skills or property, and the vast majority of local officials were chosen from merchants and artisans. In Philadelphia, many officers served for life, and in New York City the same officials were generally reelected year after year. Local ordinances were concerned with regulating and promoting trade. Most laws concerned such issues as limiting entry into certain skilled crafts, establishing standard weights and measures, fixing prices for locally produced goods, and controlling the quality of those goods. In New York and Philadelphia, the municipal corporation fixed a just price for bread and set the fees that carters could charge. Most city revenues were derived from license fees and rental of market stalls.

In contrast, the affairs of Boston and Newport were attended to in town meetings, an institution that resembled the assemblies of rural England yet also grew out of Puritan congregationalism. Several times a year all male residents (freemen) of the town met to conduct local business—to elect officials, pass laws, levy taxes, and settle disputes. Town meetings were thus symbols of order as well as agencies of government. However, like New York and Philadelphia, the governmental power in Boston and Newport rested in the hands of a few men. Town meetings took place only a few times a year. In between, selectmen—chosen as executive officials—assumed governmental duties. Their power over appointments, judicial decisions, and administration often diminished the democratic initiative of the town meeting. The same men, usually those of high standing in both marketplace and church, tended to monopolize councils of selectmen. Traditions of deference in Boston as well as in other colonial cities meant that a community's wealthiest and most well-established men stood for election and were regularly returned to office. Political factions or parties were considered dangerous, and municipal elections were not seen as forums for expressing differing political ideologies. Nor was political representation understood as expressing competing social, residential, or economic interests. Elections were a traditional means of confirming existing patterns of social order.

Throughout the colonial era the government of Charleston remained in the hands of the provincial assembly that appointed commissioners to manage the city's affairs. Assemblymen and commissioners often did not live in Charleston, and they represented interests that were seldom sympathetic to the city's welfare. The particular form of urban rule in Charlestown burdened the city with the least responsive government of the five ports.

Similar hierarchies were also the rule in non-British cities. During the French years in New Orleans, the city was governed by the superior council, the sole administrative and judicial body in the colony, run by a handful of planters appointed by the Crown. During Spanish sovereignty, the superior council was replaced by a Spanish council, *cabildo,* composed of the governor, six perpetual *regidors,* two judges, an attorney general, and a clerk. In reality, however, Spanish New Orleans was run by military officers and courts backed by a garrison of Spanish-speaking white or mestizo troops from Cuba. In Spanish Santa Fe in the seventeenth and eighteenth centuries, residents elected a four-member *cabildo,* which had responsibility for advising the Spanish-appointed governor and electing a magistrate, a bailiff, and a notary.

PROBLEMS OF GROWTH

The urban settlements of the British colonies did not seem much like cities in the early 1700s. Cattle grazed behind crudely built houses, and hogs wallowed in muddy streets. Urban dwellers of different classes, ethnic backgrounds, and occupations lived crowded together along streets near the harbor and wharves. No one could remain anonymous in a place whose boundaries extended no more than a mile in any direction. Paper money was scarce, so people often bought things by bartering with something they had grown or made. The church provided the principal social community beyond family and work lives; there were few newspapers, theaters, or other diversions. Oral discourse rather than written or printed words shaped communication, and a combination of superstition and belief in the Bible's prescriptions influenced people's behavior.

Yet, from their inception, local governments felt the pressures of urban growth. Many of the physical and social problems that vex modern urban society haunted every colonial city. Although the colonials lacked practical experience and technological tools to solve these problems, each town improvised, adjusted, and borrowed methods of response from Europe and from each other. Initially, individual citizens took steps to remove inconveniences, but quite early they combined and made collective efforts, often surrendering private initiative to government directive.

Urban organization requires efficient transportation and communication, so it is not surprising that town governments devoted much effort to determining where, how, and when new streets should be constructed. In every city—including Philadelphia, where gridiron street patterns had been established prior to settlement—individuals laid out new roadways where they were needed. As a result, narrow streets wound chaotically through some districts. In the 1700s, government intervened, and construction of new streets became accepted as a function of public policy, even though such roads were merely open stretches cleared of obstructions. In New York City, officers of the municipal corporation expected private citizens to assume the cost of laying out roads as well as filling in swamps, digging wells, erecting bridges, dredging harbors, and building wharves. The city's control of public property made it possible for the municipality to impose these responsibilities on individuals.

Altering the environment for the laying of streets, however, involved more than locating a route, removing stumps and rocks, and, occasionally, paving with gravel and cobblestones. Mud and stagnant water impeded traffic and threatened health, making drainage a pressing concern. Boston was most successful in meeting this problem: after 1713 the city began grading streets so that they slanted from the middle to side gutters. By the 1760s, other cities had initiated drainage projects. Cities dealt with related problems as well. The governments of Boston, New York, and Newport fined builders who erected structures in paths of traffic. Several towns constructed bridges over streams and marshes.

Once streets, sewers, and bridges were built, the difficulties were far from over, for as colonial cities grew, so did their traffic. Streets served not only as transportation routes but also as play areas for children and foraging grounds for hogs, dogs, and cattle. By the mid–seventeenth century, congestion and accidents had become common street nuisances. To protect pedestrians and playing children, several towns levied fines for riding at fast gaits and for failure to keep horses and other draft animals under tight rein.

Regulations could not lessen the volume of traffic, however. In an attempt to ease the pressure, cities built more streets, undertook grading and paving projects, and paid more attention to street cleaning. The best streets were those of Boston and Newport, whose governments could levy taxes for highway improvements. Other cities depended on private means or other sources of funds, such as fines, license fees, or lotteries. After the Spanish gained control of New Orleans in 1769, the *cabildo* raised revenue for levee repairs by an anchorage tax on every vessel. Where projects were elaborate, as in Boston, full-time laborers were hired at public expense. Most cities, however, followed the English custom of requiring each householder to devote a certain number of days each year to labor on public works or hire a substitute. In Charleston slaves did most of the public work, and in Boston each free African American was forced to work on the roads eight days a year instead of doing watch duty, from which blacks were prohibited.

Tossing refuse onto the streets had been one bad habit of European city dwellers, and colonial Americans were no more restrained. Their streets quickly became cluttered with human and animal waste, ashes, bones, shells, and other rubbish. Cities, beginning with Boston and New Amsterdam, responded by passing laws prohibiting the indiscriminate disposal of trash. A report from Boston in 1652 noted:

> At a meeting of all the Selckt men, it is ordered that no person inhabiting within said Town shall throw forth or lay any intralls of beasts or fowls or garbidg or Carion or dead dogs or Cattle or any other dead beast or stinkeing thing, in any hie way or dich or Common within this neck of Boston, but ar injoynened to bury all such things that soe they may prevent all anoyanc unto any person.

Such measures proved impossible to enforce and ineffective as deterrents. Nonetheless, American streets probably were cleaner, better constructed, and better lighted than most European counterparts. As early as the 1690s, Philadelphians were lighting lamps in front of their homes at night. Residents of other cities followed this example, and by the middle of the eighteenth century, local governments had begun to raise and allocate money for public street lighting.

Poor streets and traffic congestion caused only inconvenience; fire threatened existence. Indeed, fire was probably the most feared hazard of urban life and necessitated public regulations that were less imperative in the countryside. Most buildings in colonial American cities were made of wood and sat close together, so once started, a blaze was hard to confine. Lacking firefighting technology, local authorities could take only limited and precautionary measures, such as regulating storage of combustibles like gunpowder and establishing the first American building codes that included prohibitions on reed and straw roofing and on wood and plaster chimneys. Authorities also attempted to prevent fires by limiting places in which brush or rubbish could be burned and banning construction of wooden buildings in the center of town (brick structures were preferred). In 1649, Boston adopted the English curfew, requiring all house fires to be covered or extinguished between 9 P.M. and 4:30 A.M. Nearly all American towns adopted the European tradition of community responsibility for extinguishing fires. Each city contained at least one volunteer fire company composed of private citizens.

Unfortunately, towns usually did not react to such urban dangers as fires until after a disaster had occurred. This was to be a recurring pattern in American urban history. Destructive or disruptive events usually provoked

FIREFIGHTING SCENE. Fire posed the most serious danger to colonial cities, and putting one out was no easy task. Firefighting forces consisted of volunteers and firefighting equipment was primitive, consisting of ladders, hoses, and buckets of water passed along a line (bucket brigade).

some reform, but then concern would dwindle to apathy until another disaster struck and galvanized a new spurt of action. After the first of several major conflagrations struck Boston in 1653, public alarm prompted creation of the colonies' first urban fire code. The measure required every householder to keep a ladder to facilitate fire fighting. The town also bought ladders and hooks, and officials assumed the authority to order the leveling of any burning structure. Few other precautions were taken until 1676, when another conflagration threatened Boston. After it was extinguished, the town bought a fire engine from England and appointed a supervisor and twelve assistants to operate it. Even these measures were not enough, for in 1679 one of the worst fires in American history swept Boston, ravaging most of its commercial section. This disaster forced officials to organize the city into districts for more efficient fire control. Other towns acted similarly to meet the threat of fire, but Boston's destructive fires resulted in regulations and equipment that ranked among the most advanced in the world.

Protection posed another problem to the young cities. Seamen, transient laborers, and others attracted to the ports by the promise of jobs engendered by the market economy threatened the orderly world of family and communal governance, necessitating some type of agency to preserve the peace and protect property. At first, private citizens organized volunteer patrols. Later, colonial police forces copied the European system of daytime constables and night watches appointed daily and paid for by the public.

Although differing from town to town, the watch's duties consisted mainly of apprehending criminals, maintaining order by controlling brawlers and drunks, and watching for fires.

Constable and watch duty, required periodically of every male citizen, proved to be a thankless and dangerous job, and as time passed, increasing numbers of townsmen tried to evade service. The wealthy could hire a substitute or pay a fine for not serving. Thus, most early police were laborers and artisans—those who could least afford to contribute time from their daily livelihoods. Colonists' experiences while quartering the British army made them acutely aware of the abuses of power that could be taken by a standing army, and they were thus reluctant to create a permanent, professional police force. By the mid–eighteenth century, city dwellers faced rising danger to person and property from street riots, drunken brawls, and petty thievery. But they did not yet perceive this situation as a significant threat, and they remained uncommitted to the idea of a formal agency of law enforcement.

Notions of public health in the colonial era were probably more primitive than those of fire and police protection. The germ theory of disease had not yet been established; most people believed noxious vapors from stagnant water and decaying material caused sickness. Nevertheless, regulations that attempted to eliminate these vapors by controlling garbage disposal—a task at first left to hogs that roamed the streets—and prohibiting pollution of streams and ponds removed some breeding places of disease-carrying pests. Local laws prohibited citizens from dumping refuse in certain public places, and laborers were hired to carry away trash and human waste. Most cities eventually passed measures that regulated the location and depth of privies and graves and confined tanneries and slaughterhouses to the edge of town. Such measures were enacted with little, if any, objection to the use of governmental authority.

Town dwellers feared infectious diseases as much as fires, because once an epidemic began it was hard to stop. All the colonial cities except Charleston were located away from the climate and diseases of the tropics, but all were seaports and therefore vulnerable to epidemics brought in by infected seamen, vermin, and insects. Smallpox, the most frequent and dreaded danger, threatened every city. Boston and Charleston suffered smallpox epidemics that killed hundreds at a time. But as with fire, misfortune helped to create progressive policy, for by the 1760s, Americans were beginning to accept inoculation as the best preventive measure. Fevers, dysentery, and other diseases were also prevalent, and cities combated them by requiring inspections of entering ships and refusing landing to those on which sickness was found. By the early 1700s, most cities had followed Boston's lead in establishing quarantine regulations. In spite of limited medical knowledge, by 1770, city officials had succeeded in controlling some major scourges, though yellow fever and cholera continued to plague eastern and southern cities.

Another problem of urban growth was the large number of indigent residents, whose care became a major responsibility of each city. Poverty is not a problem peculiar to cities, but it took on new meaning in the urban context. In the early years of settlement, the incidence of poverty was low, especially relative to English towns. Generally, widows, orphans, and disabled people, impoverished by circumstances beyond their control, were the ones who required assistance. Colonists accepted the seventeenth-century English notion of public responsibility for the support of dependent classes. Poor relief accounted for much of local government expenditures. People in need remained with their families or in the homes of neighbors and were provided with clothes, firewood, and bread.

As towns grew, their involvement with unpredictable market forces brought increasing economic uncertainty—good times and bad times, high and low wages, periodic unemployment. The burden of providing manpower and resources for the European wars of 1689 to 1697, 1702 to 1713, and 1739 to 1747, and the inflation caused by emergency issuance of paper money, hurt a growing part of the urban population. Periodic unemployment, rising prices, and taxes that fell with unusual severity on the lower classes created poverty that was no longer the situational condition of the aged, widowed, or crippled but now a problem that touched the seasonally unemployed, war veterans, new immigrants, and migrants from inland areas seeking employment in the cities. Poverty was particularly visible in the cities, their being much more densely populated than the countryside. In Boston, expenditures on the poor rose from five hundred pounds in 1700 to four thousand pounds in 1736, and in New York from two hundred fifty pounds in 1698 to five thousand pounds in the 1770s. Boston, New York, and Philadelphia built almshouses in the 1730s in an attempt to reduce the cost of caring for the growing number of poor citizens by sheltering them under one roof. Some cities required the willing poor to support themselves by picking vegetables, weaving cloth, and making shoes. Almshouses also housed sick poor who could not work and the "Vagrant & Idle Persons" who would not work and were classed as criminals. Some cities stigmatized those on relief by requiring them to wear or carry badges designating their status as paupers. Another form of relief consisted of assigning (binding out) the needy to private businesses in a form of indentured servitude.

Many cities tried to minimize pauperism—as well as the money spent on the poor—by restricting immigration. Philadelphia, New York, and nearly all the New England towns had provisions requiring the registration, bonding, or inspection of all newcomers. Those who had no friends or relatives to vouch for them or who lacked visible means of support were ordered away. As the cities grew in size, however, so did the need for laborers and the opportunity for anonymity. By the early 1700s, the restrictions were breaking down, and many places were openly encouraging immigration.

Public relief efforts were increasingly supplemented by aid from private agencies. In the eighteenth century, organizations such as the Scots Charitable Society in Boston and New York, the Carpenters' Company in Philadelphia, and the Fellowship Society in Charleston, as well as churches and wealthy individuals, made substantial contributions for the alleviation of poverty. Still, as time passed, the numbers of urban poor grew ever larger. The proportion of a city's population assisted by public or private money at any one time is difficult to discern. But it seems that for every relief recipient several more lived at the subsistence level and received no aid and that poverty plagued American cities from the very beginning.

Attempts by colonial cities to solve their problems highlight an intertwining of private interest and public welfare. On the one hand, problems were common to all cities. They were predicaments of urban life, of many people living close together, and they required community regulation of formerly private activities. In a rural society, where a family built its house, dug its well, and threw away its trash seldom affected other humans. But in cities, these activities could become threats to other people's health and safety, and thereby necessitated surrender of individual rights to public control. Many problems of health, fire, water, and communications were insoluble at the time, and colonial city dwellers simply tried collectively to minimize them and then to adjust as technological and scientific developments offered solutions. Social problems such as disorder and poverty remained baffling. Nevertheless, a kind of public unity plus the inheritance of a European tradition of public endeavor enabled colonial cities to address their problems and to set precedents for future urban generations.

THE SOCIAL MOSAIC

Between 1690 and 1740, the small colonial seaports grew into commercial centers that rivaled British provincial ports such as Hull, Bristol, and Glasgow. Like their counterparts abroad, the American towns not only experienced similar problems but also developed similar social mosaics that set them apart from the surrounding countryside. Racial, cultural, and socioeconomic diversity jumbled urban society. Restrictions on immigration seldom worked; varied peoples quickly diluted the English composition of most cities. By the early 1700s, Africans and African Americans were almost as numerous as whites in Charleston, and there were substantial numbers of slaves in cities all the way up the coast to Boston. Scotch-Irish and Germans constituted important segments of the populations of Philadelphia and New York, where they met the growing need for laborers. The cities also housed more institutions for the entertainment, edification, and refreshment of their residents than did rural areas. The increasing population provided cities with human and economic resources for the creation of educational facilities and the dissemination of information from the outside world.

Most colonists migrated or descended from European society, where a distinct hierarchy of status prevailed, and they accepted the existence of social differences in America as being divinely sanctioned. Thus a Boston merchant asserted in 1700 that God "hath Ordained different degrees and orders of men, some to be High and Honourable, some to be Low and Despicable, some to be Monarchs, Kings, Princes, and Governours, Masters and Commanders, others to be subjects, and to be commanded." From the beginning an ordered social structure crystallized in colonial America, but it operated differently in the cities than in the country. In cities the market economy offered opportunity to accumulate wealth. But it also created growing inequalities between those whose extensive resources allowed them to take risks and make profits and those whose modest resources made them more vulnerable to economic fluctuation. Though geographical distance did not divide these groups very far from one another in the compact cities, social distances increasingly separated rich from poor, employers from workers.

Colonial urban society consisted of four socioeconomic groups, distinguished by male occupation and wealth. In the top rank were affluent merchants and investors, plus an occasional clergyman or government official. These generally were men who had become wealthy from overseas and inland commerce or had accumulated enough capital to use in lucrative moneylending or land-rental businesses. Merchants often did more than buy and sell goods. In a time when banks, law offices, and construction companies were rare, merchants used their money and influence to assume the role of banker, legal arbitrator, and land developer. As historian Gary Nash has argued, those who controlled mercantile endeavors gained a disproportionate share of economic power in colonial cities through their impact on shipbuilding, credit, real estate, and the flow of marketable goods.[1]

White males in the top status group controlled most of the local wealth (which consisted primarily of property) and filled the high positions in local government. As time passed, they procured proportionately more of the wealth than those in lower ranks. According to data compiled by Nash, in 1687 the wealthiest 10 percent of Boston's population controlled 46 percent of the taxable wealth; by 1771, the top 10 percent owned 63 percent. In Philadelphia, over a comparable period, the richest 10 percent of the population increased their holdings from 46 to 72 percent of that city's taxable wealth.[2] In Boston and Philadelphia, as well as in other cities, this upper order was not a closed aristocracy. Its membership was large and diverse, including men who had risen from a lower rank as well as those who had advantages of birth and position. Throughout the colonial period, wealth, more than birth, was the principal criterion for admission to this upper group.

Wives of wealthy merchants led lives that were very different from rural women. Wealthy urban women had the benefit of a pool of less-wealthy female workers who could be hired as servants. Supervision of domestic labor was an involved and time-consuming activity. But because wives could send servants to buy and prepare food and could hire seamstresses to create clothing, they had time to write letters and diaries and to engage in rounds of social visiting. Daughters in well-to-do eighteenth-century households were the only American women at the time who could accurately be described as leisured. They did not have to help with household work, so they were free to sleep late, study music and dancing, and read the latest novels. In cities, because goods were available for purchase, household production decreased as wealth and privilege rose. Once urban women were able to buy items such as tea, milk, butter, candles, linens, coats, and gowns, the seventeenth-century mode of housewifery symbolized by the spinning wheel became increasingly a badge of lower status.

Although wealthy capitalists wielded considerable power, the lower ranks better embodied typical colonial urban life. Beneath the merchants and their allies was a large, diverse, fluctuating population of craftsmen, retailers, minor jobbers, and innkeepers that constituted the middle class. Among the craftsmen and retailers were coopers, who provided barrels and kegs that were essential for shipping and storage; carpenters and woodworkers, who provided housing and furnishings; food dealers; metalsmiths; and printers. These individuals carried on local manufacturing and merchandising in the preindustrial city, running the shops that predominated in every town. Often they were aided by an apprentice, indentured servant, or wife. Individual shopkeepers and craftsmen generally lived and worked in the same house.

Within most of the crafts a wide range of wealth and status existed, reflecting the hierarchy within each craft from apprentice to journeyman to master craftsman. The range of wealth was thus related to age but also to the possibilities within each craft. Artisans working with precious metals were more likely to earn a comfortable living than were cobblers, and house carpenters were more likely to become property owners than were tailors and weavers. Artisans strived to earn a "competency," enough money to live in relative comfort, and in every city the average craftsman or shopkeeper usually owned enough property to vote, sometimes even holding a minor office. Shopkeepers' and artisans' wives probably did not have to spin or weave cloth, but occasionally they assisted in businesses and acted in place of their husbands in case of absence or death. They had responsibility for food preparation, which often included cultivating a garden and raising poultry. Daughters and wives also sewed extensively to keep their families clothed.

Economic expansion and the opportunity to rise in importance by acquiring wealth attuned colonial city dwellers to bourgeois standards. But such conditions also made "middling" classes vulnerable to economic dislocation: their position on the social scale rose and fell over time, depending on economic developments. The early years of urban growth offered lucrative opportunities for small-scale investors and entrepreneurs. As the cities grew, however, so did the size and specialization of their economic operations. By 1750 or so, larger businesses were squeezing small investors out of high-return areas such as commercial shipping. Between 1687 and 1771 the proportion of taxable wealth owned by Boston's and Philadelphia's middle classes declined while the percentage owned by the upper segments rose. Evidence indicates that economic opportunities of the urban middle class in most cities shrank until westward expansion and the dawn of industrialization in the early 1800s opened new avenues for advancement.

The third economic group consisted of a growing number of free unskilled laborers, mariners, and some artisans. These people owned little or no property. Many were transients, earning a living on the docks and at sea or moving from town to town in search of work. They loaded, unloaded, and served as crew on cargo ships that sailed between the seaports, Europe, and the West Indies. Other laborers dug wells, graded streets, and hauled goods. Their wives and daughters took in washing, kept boarders, spun cloth, and served as seamstresses and housekeepers for middle- and upper-class families. Many working-class families lived in crowded two- or three-room cottages at a bare level of subsistence, but in labor-scarce cities some could command high wages and acquire property. Geographic mobility and chances for improvement precluded the development of a permanent urban proletariat. The entrance to most crafts remained open, and local restrictions on newcomers failed to prevent working-class families from migrating. Still, cities housed much higher proportions of poor and propertyless people than did rural areas. By the close of the colonial period, the poor constituted between 20 and 30 percent of many a city's population—though the percentage was smaller in southern towns, where large numbers of slaves reduced the proportion of white laborers. The fortunes of the free urban working classes were especially sensitive to economic fluctuations. If the local economy was expanding, they could subsist and even improve their lot. But when economic uncertainty and decline brought sacrifice and deprivation to the middle and upper classes, the working classes struggled for survival.

Indentured servants were positioned below free labor and above slaves in the social structure. Indentured servitude was closely linked to immigration because most indentured servants traded four to seven years of labor for passage across the Atlantic and on arrival were sold at the docks to the highest bidder. They were an important part of the labor force in New York and Philadelphia. In the early years of urban settlement, many indentured servants were probably kin of emigrating Englishmen who paid their passage in return for their labor. By the 1730s, German and Scotch-Irish provided the majority of bound white laborers and were most numerous in

Philadelphia. There they worked not just in households but in ropewalks, shipyards, bakeries, and liveries; by the mid-1740s, they constituted more than one-fifth of the city's white male work force.

A rising standard of living and moderate mobility up the social scale were possible for about four-fifths of colonial city dwellers—a sizable majority—but the remainder, consisting of Africans, African Americans, and Indians, both slave and free, formed a permanent, inescapable lower class. In the Southwest the availability of exploitable Indian labor near the mission at San Gabriel was a main attractions prompting northern Mexican colonists to found the city of Los Angeles. Indian slaves could be found in several northern towns as well, though by 1715, the difficulties of dealing with Indian slaves prompted Massachusetts, Rhode Island, and Connecticut to pass laws forbidding importations from Charleston, the center of the Yamasee Indian slave trade.

African slaves were the most common form of bound labor everywhere. In 1690, about one in nine Boston households included at least one slave, and in 1698, more than one-third of New York households had slaves. Although the Quakers who dominated Philadelphia later repudiated slavery, earlier settlers freely bought and sold slaves. After 1714, sizable numbers of slaves were imported into all northern port towns. By 1750, about one-fifth of all Boston families owned slaves. By 1746, an estimated one-half of New York households owned slaves.

In most colonial cities, slaves did much of the heavy manual work and provided most of the domestic service. Slave ownership was almost universal among the urban elite; costumed slave coachmen and livery grooms were a common way of visibly displaying wealth. Newspaper advertisements in New York City for skilled male slaves suggest that some members of the artisan class prospered sufficiently to substitute bondsmen for apprentices. In all the ports, male slaves worked as seamen and in the ropewalks, shipyards, and sail manufactories. The importance of these slaves to the commercial growth of cities increased during the eighteenth century.

Northern slavery was characterized by particular patterns that distinguished it from slavery in the Chesapeake Bay area and low-country South. For one thing, northern slavery was disproportionately urban. During the eighteenth century, between one-fifth and one-fourth of the slaves in New York colony lived in New York City, one-third of the slaves in New Hampshire and Massachusetts lived in Portsmouth and Boston, and nearly half of Rhode Island's slave population lived in Newport. Crowded urban housing conditions forced slaves into back rooms, lofts, and makeshift alley shacks. Under these circumstances few masters held more than one or two slaves, and masters discouraged their slaves from establishing families. As a result there were more male slaves than females in the cities, especially in the early years, and slave women had fewer children than did white women. As historian Ira Berlin has argued, "The inability or unwillingness of urban masters to support large households of slaves put a severe strain on slave family life, but it also encouraged masters to allow their slaves to live out, hire their own time, and thereby gain a measure of independence and freedom."[3]

In the cities, slaves tended to live and work nearby to whites. This proximity gave slaves firsthand knowledge of their masters' world, as well as familiarity with the circumstances of working class whites, with whom they interacted in taverns and at fairs. This knowledge of white culture in combination with the job opportunities provided by the complex northern economy, the close ties between master and slave, and the social life of city streets helped urban slaves to make better lives for themselves. In the eighteenth century some urban slaves informally enjoyed the rights to hold property of their own, visit friends, live with their families, or hire out their own time, prerogatives that did not exist on plantations.

The cosmopolitan nature of the cities also sped the transformation of African to African American. In the early years of northern urban slavery, most slaves did not arrive directly from Africa but came through the West Indies or the mainland South. This seasoning in slavery had worked to destroy ties to African tribal culture but had also prepared slaves to turn urban opportunities to their own advantage. Between 1732 and 1754, slaves were imported into the cities directly from Africa. As Berlin has written, "Newly arrived Africans reawakened urban slaves to their African past by providing direct knowledge of West African society."[4] The result was the construction of separate communities, where blacks could find friendships, marriage partners, and other kinds of association based on racial commonalities. Northern slaves designated their churches "African" and called themselves "Sons of Africa." They displayed their new knowledge of African culture most clearly in the celebration of Negro Election Day, a West African ritual festival of role reversal celebrated commonly in New England and middle-colony towns in the mid-eighteenth century. Celebrations took different forms in different communities, but everywhere a day of merrymaking that drew in slaves from the surrounding countryside culminated in the selection of kings, governors, and judges. While the "governors" settled minor disputes, slaves dressed in their masters' clothing and rode their masters' horses. Negro Election Day ritualized a momentary release from bondage and also endorsed leadership within the African-American community. (Whites, confident of their control over the institution of slavery, supported Election Day, even sometimes joining in the festivities themselves.) In these interstices of urban life, slaves developed strong and cohesive African-American traditions that would sustain future urban black communities.

In southern cities like New Orleans, where Africans and African Americans outnumbered whites, the possibility of free blacks made whites nervous. Although a master very occasionally freed a slave, most slave owners abided by the laws discouraging emancipation. The only exception occurred in 1729, when the governor, concerned about threats from Natchez Indians who had allied with the French, freed two dozen slaves in exchange for their leading a bloody attack on a nearby Indian village. These freed slaves served as a regular company to fight with whites against the Natchez and Chickasaw in the 1730s. In 1751, however, the Louisiana superior council passed police regulations tightening the racial regime, prescribing regulations for the day-to-day governance of all blacks, not just slaves, by all whites.

After 1769, Spanish policy in New Orleans expanded opportunities for slaves to buy their freedom. The Spanish continued to regulate slaves and free blacks with extensive legislation, but they hoped that the system of freedom purchase would divide the slave majority by weakening its potential for united action and give a stake in the system to a small but growing number of slaves who might be able to garden, work at trades, hunt, or nurse the sick to gain money to buy their freedom. Taking advantage of this policy by industriously buying their freedom and often their homes as well, free blacks expanded their community in New Orleans slowly at first but at an increasing rate that would alarm French planters by the 1790s.

In southern port cities like Charleston and Savannah, urban slaves' extensive knowledge of white culture contrasted sharply with the survival of West African tribal traditions in the plantation areas. The coastal cities needed workers to transport and process plantation staples, to serve the hundreds of ships that docked at the wharves, and to run the planters' urban households. Slaves did most of this work. Throughout the eighteenth century, slaves constituted more than half of the population of Charleston and other low-country ports. Bondsmen handled virtually all goods arriving or leaving these cities' harbors. Slave artisans also played a large role in urban life, employed by master craftsmen in every variety of work. Slave artisans labored along the waterfront as shipwrights, coopers, and ropemakers and also in the higher trades as silversmiths and cabinetmakers. In addition, slave women controlled much of the marketing in the low-country ports, mediating between slave-grown produce from the countryside and urban consumption.

Mobile, often skilled, and occasionally literate, southern urban slaves understood the white world and, like their counterparts in northern cities, used their knowledge to enlarge their independence. They hired out their own time, earned wages, kept market stalls and shops, lived apart from their masters, and rented houses of their own, sometimes even keeping families intact. Some female slaves gained special positions as a result of intimate sexual relations with white masters, and the small free mulatto population of Charleston was the product of such relationships. In Charleston the considerable size of the slave population relative to the white population made slaveholders much less sanguine than their northern counterparts about the existence of an independent African-American community. But even though restrictions and regulations attempted to limit the autonomous space for communal institutions, the small communities that developed below the bluff in Savannah and along Charleston's Neck confirmed the growing independence of urban African-American culture.

Urban life, with its varied activities and social contacts, was less regimented for a slave than servitude in the country, but it remained restrictive. By the early 1700s most towns had passed ordinances, such as curfews, regulations of movement on city streets, and prohibitions on certain purchases, limiting the liberties of all nonwhites, slave and free. Actual slave insurrections in New York City in 1712 and at the Stono River in South Carolina (twenty miles from Charleston) in 1739, and rumors of slave conspiracy in New York City in 1741 inspired whites to react with terror and execution, exposing the violent coercion that lay just beneath the surface of white paternalism. After the 1712 revolt, thirteen slaves died on the gallows; one starved to death in chains; three were burned at the stake; one was broken on the wheel; and six committed suicide. Mounted whites who stopped rebels marching southward from Stono to Florida killed several slaves and set their heads on mileposts along the road. In New York in 1741, vengeful whites sentenced eighteen slaves and fourteen whites to be tortured and hanged; condemned thirteen slaves to burn to death at the stake; and deported another seventy to the West Indies.

White married women, like male and female slaves, were viewed as dependents whose status depended on their place within the household. Commonly accepted norms of paternal power, female submission, and mutual obligation dictated the nature of relations between wife and husband, just as they ordered those between man and God, slave and master, child and parent. The nuclear family was the central focus of colonial society, even more than in England, because migration had severed individuals and families from wider kin connections. As dependents, women generally were assumed to be incapable of expressing political or religious opinions. An adult woman's authority derived from her role as mistress of the household. Under her husband's supervision she directed the household's daily affairs, and should fate or circumstance prevent her husband from fulfilling his role as household head, the wife could appropriately stand in his place without changing the patriarchal order of society. Over time, however, colonial governments increasingly legalized the status of women as deputy husbands by passing statutes that allowed women some limited powers to run businesses when a husband was absent. The laws did not endorse women's economic independence; rather they were a means of preventing women whose men were dead or absent from relying on public relief. Nevertheless these laws facilitated women's economic activity, and they implicitly allowed a married woman to have a separate estate.

Unmarried women had somewhat broader independence, though that status often included greater poverty. In cities such as Philadelphia, single and widowed women comprised up to 20 percent of the adult female population, and in Boston 13 percent of the city's residents were widows. In both the seventeenth and eighteenth centuries, some working widows managed trades inherited from their husbands, at least until sons could replace them, and were therefore found in every type of occupation—including morticians, blacksmiths, and, among Quakers, ministers. Most employed women worked at trades connected to household production and in ventures such as midwifery and laundering that catered to female clients. But also, unmarried women operated commercial establishments. In Philadelphia, women ran an estimated half of the city's retail establishments and one-fourth of the taverns. In Baltimore, 8 percent of the city's households were headed by women in 1796; two-thirds of these were widows and the rest were unmarried. Although their number included publishers, mill owners, and speculators, positions they inherited when they became widows, most of Baltimore's working women, like those elsewhere, entered trades originating in domestic work: seamstresses, laundresses, soap and candle makers, and lacemakers. As shop proprietresses, they dealt in china, groceries, pastries, dry goods, and millinery. They also ran schools, inns, boardinghouses, and taverns. In every city, whether self-employed or working for others, women earned less than unskilled white men or hired-out male slaves, barely eking out a living for themselves and, if they had families, their children.

Ironically, by the late eighteenth century when colonial men were striving for independence from England, unmarried women were losing much of the economic independence they once had held. Whereas previously, property ownership had qualified women for limited political participation such as signing petitions and making speeches, by 1750 local politics had become masculinized. Moreover, women's access to poverty relief diminished. Previously, women, who everywhere dominated the poverty relief rolls, had received "outdoor relief"—food, clothing, and fuel to be used at home. But as almshouses began to replace outdoor relief, poor relief focused more on rehabilitating men into productive laborers and the needs of poor women, especially unmarried women, were frequently disregarded. Thus a new gender politics adversely affected colonial urban women.

The developing market economy in cities and the resultant economic specialization heightened distinctions between the world of men in the marketplace and the world of women in the home. In wealthy families in the North and South, use of servants for cooking and cleaning reoriented women's domestic activities to child rearing, and the importance of women's maternal responsitibilies began to be recognized. In the North, the special concerns of Quakers and Puritans with children's spiritual upbringing had the same effect of emphasizing the maternal role of women. Historian Mary Beth Norton has found that by the time of the Revolution, urban women's knowledge of family property was limited to the furnishings of the houses in which they lived, unless they were widows or had worked outside the home, while rural women's household tasks sometimes gave them access to information about family property in fields and livestock.[5] Men's knowledge of household accounts and household purchases was similarly limited. Norton's findings suggest that men and women did indeed inhabit different worlds and that the distinctive qualities of urban life sharpened the boundaries separating men's and women's daily lives.

The variety within colonial urban populations fostered new social institutions, modified old ones, and created new communities. An institution particularly affected by urbanization was the church. During the initial period of growth of American towns, religion pervaded every aspect of life. Whether in the Puritan North, the Anglican South, or the more divided middle colonies, the clergy were held in high esteem and exerted power over family life, education, and government. Religion defined and enforced social discipline and even influenced economic relations.

As time passed, two developments peculiar to urban growth threatened the supremacy of organized religion in the colonial cities. First, population growth and diversity spurred the multiplication of rival sects, which broke down religious unity. Baptists, Presbyterians, and Anglicans contested Quaker preeminence in Philadelphia and Congregational hegemony in New England cities. Particularly in New England, Puritan ministers

Inside a Colonial Tavern. Taverns, inns, and grog shops served as centers of male sociability, business, and politics in virtually every colonial city. This trade card, a form of advertisement by a Philadelphia tobacconist, shows the link between pipe smoking and drinking in a tavern.

could no longer command communal deference, because many families imitated the British aristocracy and joined the Church of England. The evangelical revivals known as the Great Awakening of the 1730s and 1740s had special force in the cities, where crowds massed by the thousands to hear the charismatic George Whitefield and other preachers assault traditional sources of authority and permanently shatter the monopolistic hold of the educated clergy on religious discourse. Second, cosmopolitanism and economic opportunity provided townspeople with tempting alternatives to church attendance. Secular activities and amusements increasingly lured some people away from worship, provoking Puritan minister Cotton Mather to lament with characteristic alarm that "the peculiar Spirit and Error of the Time [is] Indifference to Religion." Although church membership grew in nearly every city, it rose slowly, and as a result the gap between a town's total population and its total church membership continually widened.

As colonial towns grew, taverns began to intrude upon the churches' share of people's time. Men of all classes came to these public houses to drink, eat, talk, and hear news of the day. But taverns served more than mere social functions; they were centers for discussion of politics, transaction of business, distribution of broadsides and pamphlets, and delivery of mail from visiting ships. As the number of taverns multiplied and as members of various social groups began seeking out people of their own sort, many establishments acquired a reputation for catering to one class or another. But in most cities formal distinctions between taverns did not exist. Of course the services provided were for males only; it was highly improper for a respectable woman to be seen tipping a cup of grog.

By the early 1700s, taverns and groggeries had become flourishing centers of urban life. However, their informality and the profusion of rum and other alcoholic beverages also made them natural locations for disorder and vice. In response to rising complaints, most towns adopted the English policy of licensing establishments. This did not diminish the number of public houses—by the 1720s, there were more than a hundred licensed taverns in Boston, and in the peak year of 1752, New York authorities issued 334 licenses—but it did give governments some measure of control. Coffeehouses and inns also became important centers for social, political, and commercial activity. In New York, for example, the Tontine Coffeehouse served as the merchants' exchange, and the Exchange Coffeehouse was the clearinghouse for real estate transfers.

In addition to the activities of the public houses, cities housed the vast majority of educational and cultural opportunities in colonial America. Family and church had the primary responsibility for education, and most children still learned to read at home, but supplementary schooling was fairly widespread. Following the lead of Boston, many cities supported some type of public school by 1720, and they all could boast several private schools for the wealthy as well as religious and charity schools for the poor.

Even Indians and African Americans could obtain learning, however limited, from English missionary groups such as the Anglican-based Society for the Propagation of the Gospel in Foreign Parts. At the same time, scores of bookstores appeared in the larger cities, and the colonial bookseller became instrumental in the spread of literary culture. Cities, notably Boston and Philadelphia, also pioneered the establishment of public libraries.

Not only did cities house and distribute written works, but they also printed them. By 1700, printers in Boston, Philadelphia, and New York were producing books and pamphlets of secular and religious prose and poetry. More important, these printers supplied almanacs and newspapers, vital to urban life. In the eighteenth-century seaports the printing and distribution of political pamphlets, minutes of legislative proceedings and assembly votes, instructions to representatives, and special election pamphlets had the effect of broadening politics, giving all literate colonists access to the examination and discussion of controversial issues previously within the reach of only the political elite. In St. Augustine, under English control after 1763, there were still no local newspapers, but official notices were posted outside the stores of leading merchants, where broadsides critical of the government also could be read. Townspeople could hear news at taverns, at the town market, at the public slaughtering pen, and at other public places. And because the cities were the sites of almost all of the museums, scientific associations, concerts, and theaters, they dominated science and the arts. John Smibert, the noted eighteenth-century American portrait painter, worked in Newport and Boston; plays and dance exhibitions were increasingly popular in New York and Charleston; and writers from all colonial cities contributed scientific papers to the Philosophical Transactions of the Royal Society.

CITIES IN THE AMERICAN REVOLUTION

While colonial cities were generating common internal problems and complex social structures, they remained appendages of the British Empire, founded and governed as nodes in a larger administrative and economic network. For more than a century American city dwellers lived outwardly at peace with the mother country, but beneath the relatively calm surface three forces gnawed away at the foundations of British mercantile control. First, in order to meet immediate problems of local organization and services, the colonial towns had developed their own governments. These institutions exercised considerable authority over local ordinances, taxes, and finances because the Crown and Parliament either were uninterested in devoting attention to every detail of colony management or were unable to do so. This situation was particularly true in Boston, where the town meeting influenced so many local matters. By 1750, every one of the dozen or so other major colonial towns also had achieved some degree of governmental independence, and they jealously protected it.

Second, colonial merchants had managed to coexist with the restrictive Navigation Acts by arranging with sympathetic customs collectors to pay only a fraction of the required duties or by evading the law altogether and engaging in illicit trade. Thus much of the trading community acquired and expected profits outside of the mercantilist system. Such profits were not always assured, though. When British creditors demanded payments before American merchants were able to comply, or when local or foreign customers were unable to pay on time for goods delivered, a credit crunch staggered commerce. Such instances, however, prompted Americans to search even more avidly for new markets, outside the British colonies as well as inside. Third and perhaps most important, many colonial townspeople came to view their self-government and commercial independence as the most natural and just system for them, and any interference with it as illegal and tyrannical.

The Peace of Paris, which ended the French and Indian (Seven Years') War in 1763, signaled a new era during which new British policies agitated these forces and converted them into the sparks of American independence. At war's end Great Britain faced the tasks of organizing a newly enlarged empire abroad and relieving economic pressure at home caused by soaring costs of colonial defense and administration. Thus, in 1764, Parliament, under the leadership of George Grenville, passed the Molasses Act, attempting for the first time to collect meaningful revenue in America. This measure clamped down on smuggling and provided for stricter enforcement of a new, though reduced, molasses duty. Since 1733, the duty had been sixpence per gallon; now it was to be threepence. The Stamp Act followed in 1765, the first direct internal tax ever levied on the colonies. It required revenue stamps, costing from a halfpenny to upwards of twenty shillings, to be attached to all newspapers, almanacs, broadsides, pamphlets, advertisements, licenses, bonds, leases, and other legal documents and commercial papers. These acts hit cities the hardest, affecting merchants, lawyers, and printers directly and artisans, shopkeepers, and laborers indirectly. Repeal of the Stamp Act in 1766 did not lighten the burden, for in 1767 Parliament passed the Townshend Acts, adding import duties to glass, lead, paper, paint, and tea.

It is not surprising, then, that cities provided the arenas for much of the resistance to new British policies. The earliest and most organized activity came from merchants. For them the Peace of Paris brought not only restrictive taxes but also the demise of wartime prosperity, which had been derived largely from trade with England's enemies. The merchants' first reaction was to try to recapture evaporating profits by encouraging more inter- and intracolonial trade. In April 1764, some Boston merchants organized the Society for Encouraging Trade and Commerce Within the Province of Massachusetts Bay, and in the following months New York and Philadelphia merchants formed similar associations. That year, several prominent

New Yorkers revived the Society for the Promotion of Arts, Agriculture and Economy (which had existed briefly forty years earlier) to encourage more local manufacturing and ostensibly offset the Navigation Acts and the high prices of imported goods. Leaders of other cities followed this example. None of the efforts worked. They failed to change not only Parliament's policies but also the skewed balance of trade that drained the colonies of hard money, the only medium accepted by royal tax collectors and London creditors. Therefore, in 1765, merchants, particularly in the northern cities, adopted new tactics—boycotts and the nonimportation of British goods. They also formed associations to petition Parliament and the Crown for relief, to enforce nonimportation agreements, and to communicate with other colonies. It was this community of interests, activated in the 1760s but dating back to the seventeenth century, that coordinated resistance against the British and tied the first knots of American union.

Early protest activities included few notions of American independence. Merchants wished mainly to revive conditions that had existed before 1763 and that had brought prosperity to traders in every city except Boston. To be sure, the merchant community was not unified. Some, such as Thomas Hutchinson and his brother-in-law Andrew Oliver, were deeply enmeshed in British mercantile trading networks and obligated by profitable royal connections to support parliamentary policies. Men like Hutchinson and Oliver lived a lifestyle modeled on that of the British aristocracy and favored more, rather than less, British presence in America. Other merchants, however, had won wealth and status from smuggling as well as legitimate trade, without any help from the mother country, and cared little about the English social hierarchy. As their protests to economic restrictions mounted, they became increasingly antimonarchical and resentful that royal officials and restrictions blocked their exercise of political power. Still, until the 1770s, most merchants were concerned far more with profits than with independence.

While debate among the merchants was beginning to undermine the previously unquestioned consensus concerning the prerogatives of British government, conflict among merchants and artisans continued over who should rule at home. English norms of deferential politics had been profoundly challenged in periodic upheavals of divisive political partisanship. In Boston as early as 1689 a thousand townspeople resisted the usurpation of local prerogatives by Sir Edmund Andros, pouring into the streets, forming militia units, and surrounding the Town House. A committee of safety, consisting primarily of merchants and clergymen, assumed control and imprisoned Andros. This unusual mobilization of ordinary people prompted demands for a broadened suffrage and left in its wake continued questioning of the proper relationship between rulers and ruled.

Similarly in the late 1600s, tensions between elite and plebeian segments of New York's population surfaced during the few years in which

Jacob Leisler, a militia officer of German origin, established an interim government amidst the power vacuum created by the Protestant revolt going on in England. Shortly after they assumed power, the Leislerians freed imprisoned debtors. Then they called for the election of justices of the peace and militia officers and petitioned the Crown for a charter "in the like manner and with the same or more privileges as Boston," clearly aiming for a more participatory system. Leislerian mobs went so far as to attack the property of some of New York's wealthiest merchants. But when a newly appointed royal governor arrived in March 1691, Leisler surrendered the government. He was tried and found guilty of treason by an all-English jury, but the ethnic and class tensions that surfaced during his reign persisted. Also, in Philadelphia between 1684 and 1689 a religious schism split the Quaker community and expressed not only religiously-inspired but also widely felt political and economic grievances.

Throughout the eighteenth century, political and economic questions continued to divide the urban community. How much paper money should be issued, and would it be redeemed to benefit wealthy creditors or poor debtors? How best might Boston intervene in the provision of foodstuffs: to ensure a profit for provisioners or to make food available to citydwellers at the lowest costs? In New York, could the Morris faction of merchants successfully challenge the political hold of Governor Cosby? In Philadelphia, could Penn's proprietary party be dislodged from power? Even in a city like St. Augustine, where loyalty to the British seemed widespread and there were no organized groups of opposition, dissent within the governing elite opened questions about who should govern the city. A group of dissenters led by Chief Justice William Drayton challenged the authority of the British-appointed governor by calling for an elected house of assembly. The governor saw the opposition as fomented by revolutionary fervor, considering Drayton's principles as resembling "the seditions and rebellions in the other colonies." These issues aroused communities and transformed the character of urban politics from hierarchy and deference to contentiousness and participation.

The factional mobilization around these issues, the heightening of partisanship through the distribution of inflammatory political broadsides, pamphlets, and newspaper articles, the fluctuations between prosperity and hard times, war-inflated prices, and scarce money prompted artisans, shopkeepers, and small merchants to organize as political actors. These groups encountered the additional challenge of upper-class resistance to their economic and office-holding ambitions. Nevertheless most craftsmen qualified for the franchise, and by using leverage at the polls, they wedged their way into both legal and extralegal organizations. In Philadelphia, artisans filled half or more of local offices by the 1770s, and in Charleston in 1769, artisans assumed one-third of the positions on a committee to enforce a boycott against the Townshend Acts. Relations between merchants and artisans were often acrimonious, but many could agree on boycotts and nonimportation. In the end, both groups sought to advance their own interests, and increasingly their objectives were the same—relief from British oppression.

The grievances of the poor and propertyless classes also intensified in the two decades before the Revolution, but these groups could not vote, and none held office in colonial cities. High prices and unemployment were particularly severe in the 1760s, and thousands who lived at or near the subsistence level faced calamity. Jobs were even scarcer in cities where British troops were stationed, such as New York and later Boston, because many soldiers bolstered their meager pay by underbidding local laborers and artisans for employment. Moreover, the British navy continued to forcibly impress, or draft, American seamen and laborers for service on British ships, arbitrarily carrying off able-bodied breadwinners, angering and frightening whole communities. Historian Jesse Lemisch has estimated that on one night in 1757 a force of three thousand British soldiers operating in New York impressed some eight hundred men, about one-fourth of the city's adult male population.[6] Several hundred men were subsequently released, but the scope of the raid reveals the impact that mass impressment could have on a city.

Even without the vote the lower classes had a powerful way to express their political voice. When the rich would not act to relieve suffering in a period of economic decline, common people felt justified in taking collective action through rallies, petitions, club activity, and physical attack. In Boston there was a tradition of crowd action when working-class people felt that ideals of community well-being were being sacrificed to entrepreneurial greed. In 1710, because of Queen Anne's War, grain prices were higher in the West Indies than they were in Massachusetts, even though there was a bread shortage in Boston. When grain merchant Andrew Belcher decided to avail himself of the opportunity to sell at these higher prices, ordinary Bostonians descended on Belcher's loaded ship, sawed through the rudder, and tried to run it aground. Three years later the crowd again punished Belcher, who still insisted on his right to profit without regard to the cost to the community. This time, crowds attacked and emptied his warehouses, shooting the lieutenant governor when he tried to intervene. In 1727, a crowd of Bostonians destroyed a controversial public market that appeared to offer unfair competition to small retailers.

The lower classes used the same kinds of protest against what were viewed as unjust British interventions in American affairs and in doing so established themselves as a distinct political entity. A crowd battled against impressment by British naval officers for three days in Boston in 1747, attacking naval officers and their press gangs. Another crowd manhandled customs officials and destroyed customhouse property in Boston in 1768. Still another crowd battled British soldiers in New York's Liberty Hill riot in 1770. In many circumstances the crowds acted with the tacit approval of men of higher position. But the inclusiveness of the crowd, drawing women, children, servants, and black people into insurrectionary activity, and its empowering of otherwise dispossessed people always contained suspicion of wealth and the threat of wider social revolt.

In responding to the hated Stamp Act, crowds in many cities moved dangerously close to unsettling public order. In 1765, Boston crowds went beyond their goal of intimidating stamp distributor Andrew Oliver by burning and beheading his effigy, attacking Oliver's house, and exacting a public promise from him not to fulfill the duties of his office. Nine days later the crowd attacked the homes of several customs officials and then settled some old scores with Lieutenant Governor Thomas Hutchinson by demolishing his elaborately built house. Hutchinson had long been a supporter of British policies that fell with particular severity on the lower classes. In New York City, crowds pushed merchants beyond the more passive resistance of a boycott and nonimportation strategy into openly defying Parliament by continuing commerce without any stamps. In Charleston, in October 1765, an organized crowd forced the resignation of the South Carolina stamp distributor. By November 1, 1765, when the Stamp Act was to go into effect, not a single stamp distributor in the colonies was willing to carry out the duties of his office, due in large part to crowd activities in colonial ports. In most cities the merchant-gentry held the revolutionary initiative as the impending armed struggle with the British drew near, but crowd activism, an enduring legacy of eighteenth-century urban life, was having increasing effect.

New Hampshire Stamp Master in Effigy. This woodcut, produced fifty years later, shows a crowd parading the effigy of the New Hampshire stamp distributor through the streets of Portsmouth in 1765. The crowd carries a coffin to symbolize the death of the Stamp Act.

One city—Boston—epitomized all the elements that were pulling the American colonies away from the mother country. Boston, alone among American cities, did not experience population growth after 1740, and its economy had been floundering since the early 1700s. Not only did Philadelphia and New York undercut Boston's commercial dominance, but also nearby rivals such as Providence, Portland, Salem, Gloucester, and Lynn raided its regional hinterland, already too small to support the amount of interior trade that blessed cities to the south. Boston's early acceptance of public responsibility for social welfare became a liability as expenses and taxes soared in response to mounting numbers of poor and the city's heavy commitment to municipal improvements. As a result, the city lost its attractiveness; its population declined from 16,382 in 1743 to 15,631 in 1760. The economic maladies that brought discomfort to other cities in the 1760s aggravated existing sores in Boston.

During the Stamp Act crisis, mass protest had occurred in all cities, but after repeal of the Townshend Acts in 1768, crowd activities receded except in Boston. There, activities of the Sons of Liberty, particularly the harassment of customs officials, provoked the British into sending two regiments of troops. The presence of redcoats only deepened anxiety on both sides, and tensions burst on the night of March 5, 1770, when a line of soldiers fired into a jeering crowd in front of the customshouse, killing five and injuring six. Radicals such as Sam Adams were quick to capitalize on the "Boston Massacre," spreading word of all the (and some extra) gory details throughout the colony and down the Atlantic Coast. Although not the first clash between troops and colonists, the Boston Massacre deepened anger and resentment in Boston and raised fears in other cities that they would be the next recipient of British brutality.

Boston became the center of resistance three years later in a confrontation over the Tea Act, in which Parliament granted a virtual monopoly of the American tea trade to the British East India Company. When the first three ships carrying newly taxed tea arrived at Boston Harbor in December 1773, Sam Adams and his associates summoned an extralegal mass meeting whose results are well known—the Boston Tea Party. This gathering attracted five thousand people, nearly one-third of the city's population and the largest mass assembly in the city's history. As the meeting adjourned on the night of December 16, a number of men wearing Indian costumes boarded the ships and dumped their tea into the bay. The reaction of the British to this threat to imperial authority was an important catalyst in converting colonial resistance into rebellion. Parliament closed the Boston port and asserted its prerogatives in a series of four "coercive" acts, which limited town meetings and elections in all of Massachusetts, reasserted British prerogative to quarter troops in the colony's towns, removed the ability of the towns to try British officials accused of crimes in America, and organized a provincial government in Quebec without a representative legislature.

Only the Port Act punished Boston directly; the other measures reinforced the power of Parliament and the Crown along a broader spectrum. But they all struck at the two most cherished aspects of American urban life—self-government and commerce. By choking off the city's economic bloodstream and its organs of self-government, Parliament not only deepened desperation in Boston but also threatened the economies of other cities. Bostonians now faced certain ruin of the remainder of their commerce. Moreover, their town meetings and local elections had been reduced to meaningless exercises. All their attempts at reform and redress had failed. As G. B. Warden has observed, Sam Adams now "had little trouble in persuading his neighbors and countrymen that England was 'making war' against every colonial right, and destroying every traditional means of security and self-preservation."[7] It was not difficult for Adams to spread the fear that if the British could tether the freedoms of Massachusetts and Boston, they could do the same to other colonies and cities. When Adams and the Committee of Correspondence sent an appeal to Philadelphia and New York asking all Americans to join a boycott of trade with Great Britain, New York merchants responded by organizing the Continental Congress, which ultimately conceived American independence and nurtured American union. When British redcoats marched to Lexington and Concord in the spring of 1775 to arrest Adams and other radicals, it was clear that cities had played a major role in the timing of and justification for the American Revolution.

Once the Revolution began, women in cities were critical to its success, despite their formal status as dependents without political voice. They were central to the boycotts of imported products and later to the production of household manufactures. Their operation of businesses in their husbands' absences allowed cities to keep functioning during wartime. Women took part in revolutionary crowds and in New York countered wartime price inflation by forcing storekeepers to charge just prices. These activities did not expand the boundaries of women's sphere but rather took place in the areas where household and community interests overlapped and at a historical moment when household and community life were politicized. Neither interest in politics nor patriotic contribution enabled women to become full citizens, but the revolutionary years were shaped by women's as well as men's activities.

African Americans in cities did as much as they could to use revolutionary rhetoric and circumstances to challenge slavery. Slaves in Portsmouth, New Hampshire, pleaded with the legislature there that "the name of slave may not more be heard in a land gloriously contending for the sweets of freedom." Their efforts were critical to the northern states' gradual abolition of slavery in new constitutions and laws written after 1776.

The predicaments of cities did not alone cause the American Revolution; the final break with England resulted from a number of forces that had merged at various moments in history. Yet cities were deeply involved in the major events not only because they bore the weight of British policy but also because they possessed the facilities and human resources to implement resistance and then rebellion. Their meetinghouses provided forums for debate and protest, their printing shops spread news and propaganda, and their taverns and coffeehouses furnished workshops where logistics were planned.

The separation of the thirteen colonies from Great Britain mirrored a process that had been developing in the American cities for nearly one hundred years. Residents of each town ultimately cast off traditional notions of deference and replaced them with politics more contentious and more participatory, and these lay at the heart of new revolutionary understandings of representation. Urban citizens had developed a sense of community and an allegiance to a particular place where older visions of commonwealth mingled with newer visions of individual enrichment. Motivated by familiar ideals of public interest and newly developed conceptions of self-interest, merchants and mechanics could urge resistance to new British taxes and ultimately to the British Empire itself. In the process of freeing themselves, urban dwellers found that they had new thoughts of freedom, the perfectibility of humanity, and the desire to shape their own futures. By the 1770s, common interests and grievances, aided by increased intercolonial communication, had spread these concepts of community, individualism, and personal agency beyond particular cities to encompass all the colonies. Thus cities, with their experience of collectivism, opportunity, and diversity, not only kindled but fed the flames of American independence.

BIBLIOGRAPHY

Studies of colonial urban growth and government include Sylvia D. Fries, *The Urban Ideal in Colonial America* (1977); John W. Reps, *Town Planning in Frontier America* (1969); and Jon C. Teaford, *The Municipal Revolution in America: Origins of Modern Urban Government, 1650–1825* (1975). On Spanish colonial towns, see Dora P. Crouch, Daniel J. Garr, and Axel I. Mundigo, *Spanish City Planning in North America* (1982); Kathleen Deagan, *Spanish St. Augustine: The Archeology of a Colonial Creole Community* (1983); and Jean Parker Waterbury, ed., *The Oldest City: St. Augustine, Saga of Survival* (1983).

The cities of Boston, New York, and Philadelphia have received particular attention from colonial historians. Gary B. Nash's richly detailed study of the development of popular political consciousness in the century preceding the American Revolution focuses on these cities: *The Urban Crucible: Social Change, Political Consciousness, and the Origins of the American Revolution* (1979). See also Thomas J. Archdeacon, *New York City 1664–1710: Conquest and Change* (1976); Joyce Goodfriend, *Before the Melting Pot: Society and Culture in Colonial New York City, 1664–1730* (1991); Hendrik Hartog, *Public Property and Private Power: The Corporation of the City of New York in American Law, 1730–1870* (1983); Cathy Matson, *Merchants and Empire: Trading in Colonial New York* (1997); Simon P. Newman, *Embodied History: The Lives of the Poor in Early Philadelphia* (2003); and Sam Bass Warner, Jr., *The Private City: Philadelphia in Three Periods of Its Growth* (1968).

On urban slavery in this period, see Ira Berlin, "Time, Space, and the Evolution of Afro-American Society," *American Historical Review* 85 (February 1980): 44–78; Berlin, "The Revolution in Black Life," in *The American Revolution: Explorations in the History of American Radicalism,* ed. Alfred F. Young (1976): 349–82; Ira Berlin, *Many Thousands Gone: The First Two Centuries of Slavery in North America* (1998); Philip Morgan, *Slave Counterpoint: Black Culture in Eighteenth Century Chesapeake and Lowcountry* (1998); Thelma Foote, *Black and White Manhattan: Race Relations and Collective Identity in Colonial Society, 1626–1783* (1995); Kimberly S. Hanger, *Bounded Places, Bounded Lives: Free Black Society in Colonial New Orleans, 1769–1803* (1997); and Leslie M. Harris, *In the Shadow of Slavery: African Americans in New York City, 1626–1863* (2002).

On French and Spanish colonial urban policies with regard to slavery and free status, see Thomas N. Ingersoll, "Free Blacks in a Slave Society: New Orleans, 1718–1812," *William and Mary Quarterly* 48 (April 1991): 173–200; and Jane Landers, "Gracia Real de Santa Teresa de Mose: A Free Black Town in Spanish Colonial Florida," *American Historical Review* 95 (February 1990): 9–30.

The situation of women in colonial urban America is discussed in Kathleen Brown, *Good Wives, Nasty Wenches, and Anxious Patriarchs: Gender, Race, and Power in Colonial Virginia* (1996); Mary Beth Norton, *Founding Mothers and Fathers: Gendered Power and the Forming of American Society* (1996); Norton, *Liberty's Daughters: The Revolutionary Experience of American Women, 1750–1800* (1980); and Laurel Thatcher Ulrich, *Good Wives: Images and Reality in the Lives of Women in Northern New England, 1650–1750* (1982); and Karin Wulf, *Not All Wives: Women of Colonial Philadelphia* (2000).

Works elaborating the roles of city inhabitants and economies in the Revolutionary years include Paula S. Baker, "The Domestication of Politics: Women in American Political Society, 1780–1920," in *American Historical Review* 89 (June 1984): 620–47; Edward Countryman, *A People in Revolution: The American Revolution and Political Society in New York, 1760–1790* (1981); and Sylvia Frey, *Water from the Rock: Black Resistance in a Revolutionary Age* (1991); Paul Gilje, *The Road to Mobocracy: Popular Disorder in New York City, 1763–1834* (1987); and Charles G. Steffen, *The Mechanics of Baltimore: Workers and Politics in the Age of Revolution, 1763–1812* (1984).

NOTES

1. Gary B. Nash, *The Urban Crucible: Social Change, Political Consciousness, and the Origins of the American Revolution* (Cambridge, Mass.: Harvard University Press, 1979), 18.
2. Ibid., 395.
3. Ira Berlin, "Time, Space, and the Evolution of Afro-American Society on British Mainland North America," *American Historical Review* 85 (February 1980), 48.
4. Ibid., 53.
5. Mary Beth Norton, "Eighteenth-Century Women in Peace and War: The Case of the Loyalists," *William and Mary Quarterly,* 3d ser., 33 (July 1976), 386–409.
6. Jesse Lemisch, "Jack Tar in the Streets: Merchant Seamen in the Politics of Revolutionary America," *William and Mary Quarterly* 25 (July 1968), 371–407.
7. G. B. Warden, *Boston, 1689–1776* (Boston: Little, Brown, 1970), 293–94.

2

Commercialization and Urban Expansion in the New Nation, 1776–1860

THE COMMERCIAL REVOLUTION

After the thirteen colonies merged into the American Union, population migration, economic change, and technological advance broadened the scale of urban growth. Whereas only five major and about fifteen secondary cities constituted urban America in the colonial period, scores of new urban settlements sprouted and blossomed between the Revolution and the Civil War. When the federal government took its first census in 1790, only five cities could boast ten thousand or more inhabitants. By 1830, the number had risen to twenty-three, and it reached one hundred one by 1860. The number of people living in urban places swelled from two hundred thousand in 1790 to 6.2 million in 1860, approximately one-fifth of the total national population. New cities filled in the young country's urban network, stretching from Buffalo to Seattle, from Mobile to San Francisco. By pulling the line of settlement across the continent, by guiding the national economy, and by attracting talent and leadership, these cities, like their predecessors on the Atlantic Coast, steered the course of national development.

Eastern ports still dominated the urban scene as the young republic grappled with problems of independence, although Baltimore surpassed Newport among the top five. But in the 1780s, new difficulties compounded those that had nagged city dwellers since 1763. Merchants found themselves

This painting, from around 1797, illustrates the importance of commerce to early American cities. The Tontine Coffee House, shown here at the corner of Wall and Water Streets in New York, served as the location of the Stock Exchange and several insurance offices. In the background on the right are the masts of ships in the harbor, showing the vitality of water-borne trade and its proximity to the city's commercial nerve center.

deprived of the economic advantages and protection they once had taken for granted as members of the British mercantile system. The middle and lower classes faced shortages of housing and consumer goods, accompanied by rises in prices, unemployment, and rents. Between 1785 and 1787 a severe economic depression deepened distress among all classes. Because hard money and precious metals remained as scarce as before the Revolution, states issued paper money to serve as currency. Lack of uniform standards of this paper money tangled commercial exchange. In addition, uncertainty over the worth of money in circulation sparked conflicts between capitalists, who wanted a limited supply of stable currency, and debtors, who wanted more paper money that would reduce the cost of their debts. These tensions often involved geographic divisions, pitting commercial interests from urban and densely populated eastern regions against cash-poor farmers from the western frontier. The fiercest struggle occurred in 1786–87, when a band of two thousand debtor farmers from western Massachusetts, led by former Revolutionary War captain Daniel Shays, threatened a federal arsenal and halted the state from trying to seize property for nonpayment of taxes. The farmers dispersed only after merchants from the eastern part of the state hired a militia to hunt them down.

Shays' Rebellion strengthened the hands of citizens who were eager to replace the Articles of Confederation with a stronger central government.

Urban merchants involved in overseas trade were the first to agitate for a new governmental form that would facilitate commerce and create economic stability, and this group played a leading role in the formation and adoption of the Constitution. Though only 5 percent of all Americans lived in cities, twenty of fifty-five delegates to the Constitutional Convention in Philadelphia in May 1787 were city dwellers, and another twenty, mostly lawyers and merchants, had extensive urban contacts. The new Constitution that the delegates forged protected mercantile interests by granting Congress powers to tax, to borrow and coin money, and to regulate commerce and the economy by prohibiting states from levying their own tariffs, creating their own money, or issuing bills of credit.

When the Constitution was sent to state ratifying conventions, city interests lined up on the side of adoption. Not just merchants but also artisan organizations and the press came out in support of delegates to these conventions who favored a stronger national government. Out of a hundred or more urban newspapers printed in the 1780s, only a dozen opposed the

L'Enfant's Plan of Washington, D.C. Most of this plan was incorporated in the construction of the capital. Note the importance of wide, diagonal avenues on the gridiron layout. Although a few new towns copied this plan, most developers in the nineteenth century preferred a strict gridiron street system because it was easier to construct and made lot sizes more uniform.

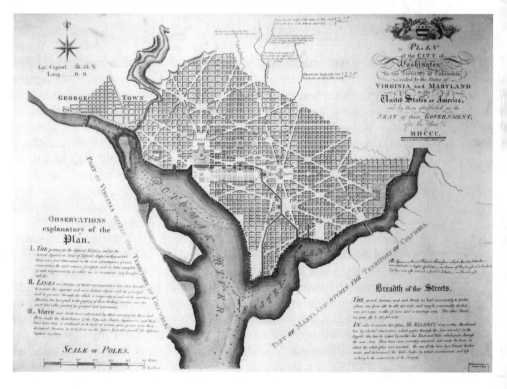

Constitution. Cities, towns, and their tributary regions in every state voted for delegates who supported the Constitution, while areas dominated by small farms chose delegates who opposed it. New Hampshire's coastal and river towns, commercially linked to Boston, helped swing the state in favor of ratification, and New Hampshire became the ninth and deciding state to accept the Constitution. New York City and its surrounding counties threatened to secede from New York state if it did not ratify. Virginia's eastern tidewater regions, including the city of Norfolk, were joined in support of ratification by western areas that were developing commercial outlets to the Ohio River.

Economic recovery for the new nation arrived by the end of the 1780s. Population increases and territorial expansion sparked economic growth in both trade and manufacturing, and increased numbers of participants entered the market economy. A remarkable spread of interstate and interregional trade generated demands for new roads and canals. At the same time, expanding commerce and improvements in inland transportation turned farmers into businessmen, at least in the North, as formerly self-sufficient farmers began to grow just one or two cash crops for market. Farmers sought out commercial markets, and inland cities sprang up to process and ship farm products, sometimes turning them into finished goods for sale back to the farmers.

WESTWARD EXPANSION

The path of western settlement illustrated this dynamic interaction between cities and countryside. Cities accompanied and even preceded the western frontier, acting as commercial outposts and depots from which settlement radiated. The growth of cities made western crops more marketable and boosted the value of western farmland. In turn, expansion of the farming frontier spurred the growth of cities as market and exchange points. Along the Ohio and Mississippi river valleys, the towns of Pittsburgh, Cincinnati, Louisville, Lexington, and St. Louis formed what historian Richard Wade termed an urban frontier, planted in the late 1790s before the surrounding soil was broken for cultivation.[1] Like their colonial predecessors, these cities were founded as commercial centers by commercial-minded people.

A generation later the city-building process repeated itself in the Great Lakes region. By 1840, Buffalo, Cleveland, Chicago, Milwaukee, and Detroit (though it had been founded by the French much earlier than the other lake cities) had emerged as important cities and had fostered settlement in the Old Northwest. In river and lake cities, commercial growth spurred manufacturing, and as demand for finished goods began to rise in interior America, these cities developed industrial bases to complement their commercial functions. Pittsburgh produced glass, Louisville textiles, Cleveland iron products, and Chicago agricultural implements.

Cincinnati from across the Ohio River, ca. 1855. One of the pioneer towns of the West, Cincinnati, like its East Coast predecessors, depended on water transportation for its commercial lifeblood. The towns of Covington and Newport, Kentucky, are depicted in the foreground of this lithograph.

In the Far West and Southwest, the 1834 Secularization Proclamation, which altered the status of vast tracts of mission lands, stimulated the commercialization of agriculture and the growth of cities. After the Civil War, railroad connections would enable southwestern cities like San Antonio, El Paso, San Diego, and Los Angeles to serve as commercial exchange centers that stimulated development of their surrounding countrysides.

The South had its own urban development, structured by the needs of staple-crop agriculture, particularly cotton and tobacco, and, after 1850, by a few industries. The cities of Baltimore, Charleston, Savannah, Mobile, New Orleans, Memphis, St. Louis, and Louisville encircled the South by 1840, each joined to its hinterlands by commercial connections stretching along the South's abundant navigable waterways. Southern urban economies revolved around the cultivation, marketing, and processing of a staple crop for its eventual delivery to a northern port. The dependence of southern merchants on New York City in particular for marketing, shipping, and credit inhibited the growth of parallel facilities in southern cities and drained capital from the region, thus limiting the extent of southern urbanization.

This pattern of commercial foundations and good transportation connections characterized city origins in the United States in the early nineteenth century. But expansion of the market economy prompted an additional source of urban growth: land speculation. Although historians have directed much attention to speculation in western farmland, they have often neglected the urban dimensions of this activity. The nineteenth century witnessed a mania of city building in the United States as energetic and sometimes shifty entrepreneurs bought and plotted land for new towns and then sold it for hefty profits to other eager speculators who hoped the property would appreciate even more. This kind of expectation produced spectacular land booms, such as one in Chicago during the 1830s. Here a choice eighty-by-one-hundred-foot lot that sold for one hundred dollars in 1832 brought three thousand dollars by 1834 and fifteen thousand dollars the following year. As one observer remarked, "Every man who owned a garden patch stood on his land and imagined himself a millionaire." But for every urban venture that succeeded, several did not. Some failed for lack of leadership, some for lack of money, some for excess of floodwaters. Many an optimistic urban speculator from the East came West holding a deed only to find his property located in a mosquito-infested swamp. Still, both the successes and the failures reveal that western speculation was as much urban as rural.

Economic and population growth strained established forms of urban government. The colonial model of the closed municipal corporation with its power to control labor costs and prices of commodities in the early nineteenth century impeded commercial growth. What had once seemed necessary to protect the community now appeared to limit free economic enterprise. Price regulations gradually collapsed, and municipally controlled markets disappeared. Local businessmen campaigned for new city charters that would give a city's government powers to raise revenue through taxes and to borrow money that could be spent on improvements that supported expansion of the market economy. Eighteenth-century ideas about municipal autonomy derived from a charter granted by the King withered under nineteenth-century ideas about sovereignty as granted by a legislature. Legal doctrines of eminent domain (the taking of private property for public use) and police power (government's prerogative to protect public health and safety) were summoned to assert public authority over rights of private property ownership in the name of economic development. Attention to social conditions that retarded or fostered economic development deemed beneficial to the community gradually replaced the old common-law emphasis on the sanctity of individual property and the need to keep one person's use of property from injuring another.

Although there was some popular opposition, most cities' charters of incorporation were revised between 1820 and 1860 to allow local governments to spend money on better water supplies, firefighting equipment, harbor improvements, canals, turnpikes, and eventually railroad connections. In some places, such as Chicago, however, local improvements of streets, sewers, and lighting were paid for by those property owners who would benefit from them rather than financed by taxes paid by all city residents. This privatized system of infrastructure improvement meant that those property owners who desired such improvements and who could pay for them controlled public policy, while lower-income residents who could not afford special assessments for upgraded facilities often were left without them.

Newer cities of the Ohio Valley and Great Lakes regions consciously emulated the institutional approach of older seaports. The government of Lexington, Kentucky, sent a leading citizen to Philadelphia to inspect the street lighting system, and Pittsburgh sent a delegation to Philadelphia, Baltimore, and New York on the same mission. The city council of Cincinnati ordered its board of health to consult officials in Boston, New York, Philadelphia, and Baltimore for recommendations on construction of a sewer system. Charters of western towns intentionally included the same regulatory and taxing powers as those in the East.

Imitation of these forms and functions coupled with commercial and cultural ties bound eastern and western cities into a national urban network that blurred sectional differences. Chicago, Baltimore, and Philadelphia resembled each other more closely than they resembled their surrounding countryside. But common interests and experience did not necessarily breed cooperation. Each successful urban center established an economic domain in its immediate vicinity, but commercial expansion was an ever-hungry process that required cities to search continually for more markets. Inevitably, such forays resulted in collisions between cities that laid claims to overlapping hinterlands. The ensuing rivalry, aptly dubbed "urban imperialism" by Wade, has been an important dimension of urban interaction from the early 1800s to the present.

The dual quest for growth and dominance made early nineteenth-century urbanization an aggressive, dynamic phenomenon. People believed that their city had to keep growing to prevent economic stagnation and to stay ahead of rival cities. Increased immigration, markets, and transportation connections fed upon one another to produce a multiplier effect, a spiraling process that spun off greater and greater profits. In the 1820s, for example, the young towns of Cleveland and Sandusky vied for the northern terminus of a canal between the Ohio River and Lake Erie. Although Sandusky had more natural advantages, the Ohio legislature chose Cleveland, primarily because that city's businessmen were able to exercise more political leverage, through bribery as well as through normal persuasion. This victory set in motion a chain reaction that accelerated Cleveland's growth. The canal enabled Cleveland to attract more businesses, consequently providing employment opportunities and spurring population growth. These factors in turn made Cleveland a natural transfer point when railroads began to cross the Midwest. New transportation links fostered more business, more population growth, more markets, and so on. Contests similar to that between Cleveland and Sandusky occurred scores of times in the West and South as upstart towns fought for such prizes as the site of a county seat, railroad or canal terminus, college, or land office.

Eventually larger cities clashed over hinterland markets. Here is where urban imperialism had national impact, for competing cities contributed to the construction of a national transportation network that rearranged axes of trade and politics. Construction of the Erie Canal (1817–25), which linked the Hudson River to the Great Lakes, not only bound growing western markets to New York City but also provoked Philadelphia, Baltimore, and Boston into constructing their own transportation lines westward. The results included a web of turnpikes, canals, and, ultimately, the Baltimore and Ohio and the Pennsylvania railroads. Competition between Charleston and Savannah and between New Orleans and Mobile spurred railroad construction in the South. When Chicago businessmen obtained railroad connections to the region beyond the Mississippi River while their rivals in St. Louis remained committed to river transportation, a shift in the direction of western trade resulted. Instead of following water routes southward to St. Louis and then to the port of New Orleans, by the 1850s many products from the West increasingly moved over rail to Chicago and from there as far east as New York. Although competition among larger cities did not leave any one contestant completely vanquished, feelings of urgency and fears for survival enveloped every rivalry. As one Philadelphia businessman remarked when Pennsylvania chose to construct a combination water and land transportation route between Philadelphia and Pittsburgh, the premium was on speed "before the commerce has acquired the correspondence and habitude that are so difficult to break."

Urban promoters attempted to create a loyalty to place that personified cities to their residents. A railroad or canal claimed to serve not only the interests of residents of Baltimore, Philadelphia, or Chicago but also Baltimore, Philadelphia, and Chicago as entities themselves. Private capital was scarce, so many projects were financed with state and local funds, making entrepreneurial interests the same as public interest. This urban chauvinism combined with the speculative nature of urban growth to produce "boosterism," the optimistic promotion of a city in grandiose language. Boosters used rhetorical metaphor to project continuity from the present into the future and spoke of dreams as reality. It was this spirit that prompted a St. Louis booster to predict that "we have but commenced to tell the wonders of a city destined in the future to equal London in its population, Athens in its philosophy, art, and culture, Rome in its hotels, cathedrals, and grandeur, and to be the central commercial metropolis of a continent."

The aggressiveness of this attitude sometimes had negative effects. In San Diego, boosterism entailed an effort to separate the Anglo community residentially and commercially from the old Mexican pueblo. Beginning in the 1850s, Richard Henry Dana, author of the popular novel, *Two Years Before the Mast*, led San Diego's Anglo merchants in a campaign to promote a

"New San Diego" by attracting Anglo settlers and investors and building new hotels and a wharf. Within a few years the town had taken on an Anglo character and the original Mexican settlers had been pushed aside.

Boosters were enthusiastic and enterprising entrepreneurs who hitched their private fortunes to their city's quick development; the more the city grew, the better for individual profit making. William B. Ogden's investments in land and railroads in Chicago made him a multimillionaire and helped simultaneously expand Chicago from a village when he arrived in 1835 to a metropolis of half a million people when he died in 1877. Dr. Daniel B. Drake, whose writing brought fame to Cincinnati, planned and invested in canals and railroads there. Boosterism had its drawbacks. The premium on growth contributed to unplanned expansion of American cities. Emphasis on speed also resulted in the hasty construction of railroads with little concern for safety. Booster rhetoric could be used by con artists interested more in getting rich quick than in city building. But boosters also helped to create institutions that were public resources as well as personal monuments; Ogden and Drake participated in most public enterprises undertaken by their respective cities—bridges, sewers, parks, hospitals, libraries, and medical colleges.

A lack of successful boosterism almost doomed the nation's new capital, Washington, D.C. As directed by Congress, President George Washington in 1791 selected the site for the city along the Potomac River next to Georgetown and appointed Pierre Charles L'Enfant, a French engineer and architect who had fought in the Revolutionary War, to prepare a design. L'Enfant envisioned a grand metropolis with broad avenues, public squares, fountains and statues. When the impetuous L'Enfant balked at selling public land quickly to raise money for the project, he was removed from his post. Meanwhile, real estate sales foundered, the syndicate responsible for sales went bankrupt, and the city acquired a reputation as a bad investment. Though the federal government moved there from Philadelphia in 1800, Washington grew slowly, hampered by unfinished buildings and muddy streets. Nevertheless, in 1900 a bill passed by Congress provided for completion of much of L'Enfant's plan, including a grandiose mall between the Capitol and the Potomac River.

BEGINNINGS OF URBAN INDUSTRIALISM

The commercialization of the countryside and growth of manufacturing in the cities proceeded in tandem. Farmers who raised cash crops needed to buy everyday necessities from urban craftsmen who manufactured shoes, cloth, furniture, wagons, and farm tools. Increased demand for such goods paved the way for changes in the organization of production. In the eighteenth century, master craftsmen and journeymen had produced goods directly for individual customers; thus a shoemaker made and sold shoes in the same room. In the nineteenth century, shoemakers began producing for a broader, more impersonal market. The business of selling shoes was separated from the process of making shoes, and the method of making shoes was subdivided into many steps, each requiring less skill than the formerly integrated process. Even before the development of mechanization and factories, control over production fell from shoemakers to merchant capitalists who had the cash and credit resources to purchase raw materials, organize large-scale production, market the finished product, and await delayed payment. Similar developments among metalworkers, tailors, hatters, clothiers, and boat builders diluted traditional skills, expanded the size of the work group, and enabled merchant capitalists to control profits and the work process.

Before the 1840s, most manufacturing in American cities was confined to two types of products: (1) consumer items, such as refined sugar, leather goods, and distilled products, that merchants could exchange for raw materials such as meat, grain, and cotton; and (2) commerce-serving items, such as ships, sails, paper, and barrels. However, along some New England rivers and streams, mechanized textile mills were beginning to establish genuine factory organization, and communities were emerging around them. Many of the mill towns in Connecticut, Massachusetts, and Rhode Island never grew beyond a few hundred people, most of them landless agrarians or families who split their time between millwork and farming. A few places grew larger, among them Chicopee and Holyoke, both founded by an organization of investors called the Boston Associates. The most famous project financed by the Boston Associates was Francis Cabot Lowell's industrial experiment at Lowell, Massachusetts, where recruited New England farm girls worked and lived in a tightly regulated mill community.

The factory system brought notable changes in work routines wherever it took hold. Use of mechanized devices instead of hand tools made ownership of the means of production almost impossible for wage earners, because only the wealthy could afford to invest in costly machines, especially those run by water or steam power. The use of machines to break down production into simple repetitive tasks meant that most workers no longer needed as full a range of craft skills or had responsibility for the quality of the item produced. The pace of machines regimented the workday in a way artisans had never experienced. Called to work by the bell, prohibited from talking to other workers, producing at the speed of the machines, and disciplined by foremen, factory workers could not slip off to go fishing, share a round of ale, or compete in foot races, as artisans' control over their workday had accustomed them to do.

Still, in many cities the factory system coexisted with traditional small-scale manufacture, because swelling urban populations continued to create demand for the products and services of many crafts. As a result, in these cities the number of workers in traditionally small-scale occupations increased along with the number of factory workers. Historian Bruce Laurie

An Early Factory. This factory in Waltham, Massachusetts, built by early textile manufacturer Francis Cabot Lowell, unified production under one roof. Using power-driven looms and machinery, such a building served as a prototype for textile mills built in other sites.

has identified five different types of production coexisting in antebellum Philadelphia: factories powered by steam or water, not-yet-mechanized central shops employing twenty-five or more workers, small sweatshops employing six to twenty-five workers, small neighborhood artisan shops where fewer than six toiled, and individual outworkers who did piecework in their homes. As evidence of fast economic growth, in 1850, nearly two-thirds of Philadelphia retailers had entered their business since 1845. In some places, particularly northeastern mill towns, an industrial working class constituted a large proportion of the population. But in larger, more diverse cities the occupational distribution retained a varied character.

SOCIETAL EFFECTS OF ECONOMIC CHANGE

Expansion of the urban economy meant that the rich were growing richer and the poor poorer. In Boston, where 5 percent of the population had owned 44 percent of all taxable property in 1771, the richest 4 percent owned 59 percent of the wealth in 1833 and 64 percent by 1848. In New

York, the upper 4 percent owned 49 percent of the wealth in 1828 and 66 percent in 1845. Similar concentrations of wealth could be found in Philadelphia, Brooklyn, Baltimore, St. Louis, and New Orleans. Every city had families with lofty fortunes who had maintained or increased the wealth accumulated by their forebears. Housed in mansions, transported in private carriages, clothed in the finest fabrics, fed the choicest delicacies, waited on by servants, entertained in exclusive clubs, the wealthiest urban residents could remove themselves from contact with the new urban masses. The middle and lower classes could advance by acquiring property or by moving into shopowner or skilled occupations. But such attainments were precarious. National economic panics and depressions, which occurred almost regularly—1819, 1837, 1857—and the growing scale of businesses stifled the chances of many a small investor. Thus even though upward occupational mobility seems to have remained fairly stable in places such as Boston and Philadelphia between 1830 and 1860, downward mobility increased.

At the lowest end of the social spectrum, pressures of city life weighed heavily. Wages rose slightly between 1820 and 1860 but remained meager in relation to prices. Daily pay for unskilled workers rose from eighty or ninety cents a day in the 1840s to slightly over a dollar a day in 1860. Factory workers earned even less. Spinners in textile mills, for example, received on average only $2.73 a week in 1842; by 1860 they were drawing only $2.85. Meanwhile prices for food, housing, and clothing rose more than 10 percent, offsetting wage increases. Some skilled workers, such as blacksmiths, machinists, and carpenters, earned $12 a week or more, but painters and wheelwrights received much less. Male factory workers could earn a dollar a day, but female factory workers, many of whom toiled fourteen or more hours a day, made barely $1 or $1.50 a week.

Few working-class families could manage on one income. According to the *New York Tribune*, the minimum budget for a family of five in 1851 came to $10.37 per week. This figure included $3 for rent, $2 for clothing, $1.40 for meat (two pounds a day at 10 cents a pound), 50 cents for a half-bushel of potatoes, 14 cents for milk, and 62.5 cents for one-eighth barrel of flour. The only nonessential item included was 12 cents for newspapers. When asked if such a budget was too high, its compiler replied, "Where is the money to pay for the amusements, for ice-creams . . . to pay the doctor or apothecary, to pay for pew rent in the church, to purchase books or musical instruments?" No wonder then, that thousands of families depended on women and children to supplement the earnings of the household head. Peddling, scavenging, theft, and prostitution joined casual laboring, sewing, and domestic employment as the means by which women and children helped their families make ends meet.

Literary accounts castigated the growth of urban inequality. Much that was written about the American city in these years in novels, stories, and sketches portrayed it as a font of evil and wickedness. Intellectuals such as

Ralph Waldo Emerson scorned the materialism and artificiality of urban life, and Nathaniel Hawthorne half seriously proposed that "all towns should be made capable of purification by fire, or of decay, within each half century." But popular nonfiction accounts of city life looked beyond sensationalism to attempt a comprehensive description of the new urban society. Their central revelation was the increasing wealth and pretentiousness of the very rich and simultaneous desperation of the very poor. It was not urbanization per se but the maldistribution of wealth and income that accounted for the disintegration of community; in New York City the geographic distance was minimal, but the economic divisions were enormous from Broadway's opulence and Wall Street's financial might to Five Points, the locus and symbol for the squalor and misery of the very poor.

The polarization between wealthy and poor was perhaps the most dramatic aspect of urban class structure, but the emergence of a middle class as a self-conscious group was an equally striking development in the antebellum city. The increase in retailers, investors, clerks, and managers placed a group of men and their families between the working classes and the controllers of capital. The separation of retailing from production and wholesaling, along with the development of far-flung markets, facilitated the emergence of small-scale, specialized retail merchants, managers of larger retail outlets, male office and store clerks, and contractors, who now helped to define the distinction between "commercial pursuits" and "mechanical trades," white and blue collars.

Given the era's economic instability, Americans could fall out of the middle class as rapidly as they rose into it. Nevertheless, recognizable characteristics came to define urban middle-class position. Americans with rising incomes, expectations, and living standards provided a demand for consumer goods—carpeting, pianos, clothing, books, and magazines. They also responded strongly to the evangelical religious renewal known as the Second Great Awakening, joined new voluntary associations, and supported codes of morality such as temperance, which they attempted to popularize among and ultimately to impose upon the working classes. The most distinguishing characteristic of the new middle class was its family life. Home came to be defined by its isolation from the public world. The urban middle classes were the most enthusiastic proponents of the work ethic, and family relationships were the template for new male and female personalities that expressed norms of respectability, hard work, and upwardly mobile striving for men and moral guardianship and sentimental nurturance for women.

Within middle-class urban families the everyday patterns of men's and women's lives were becoming more distinct. Male wage earning became tied to the routine of a clearly defined working day outside the home, while women continued to do home-bound and less clearly differentiated tasks of food preparation, child rearing, and washing. Increasingly the home became idealized as a bastion of what were defined as feminine virtues—piety, morality, affection, and self-sacrifice—qualities absent from the public world ruled by male values of competition and aggressiveness. Family incomes, even in middle-class homes, were so uncertain that women's maternal labors in keeping boarders, sewing, or opening schools in their homes were sometimes needed to provide income.

Nevertheless, the idealization of the home as spiritual refuge imbued household work and child care with new significance. Paternal authority in the urban household was beginning to weaken as maternal affection became the driving force in family life. According to historian Christine Stansell, middle-class men and women came increasingly to perceive the home as an institution where children and space were presided over by women.[2] Although middle-class status depended on male-earned income, the elusive quality of respectability derived from domesticity and sexual restraint provided by women's efforts. The smaller size and fewer children of the urban middle class was a critical factor by which respectable people measured their distance from farming and immigrant working-class families. Although national fertility rates fell almost everywhere after 1800, the most precipitous decline occurred among new urban middle-class families. Fewer children allowed families more resources to invest in education and allowed mothers to devote more time to instilling values that would enable their children to maintain a middle-class position.

There is some evidence that in the early nineteenth century elite women performed important political functions, especially in Washington, D.C., where leaders of the federal government were working to stabilize the new republic. Women such as Dolley Madison (wife of James Madison), Louisa Catherine Johnson Adams (wife of John Quincy Adams), and Hannah Nicholson Gallatin (wife of Pennsylvania financier and statesman Albert Gallatin) used their social roles as hostesses and conversationalists to build alliances between politicians, obtain jobs for their husbands' supporters, and even influence the passage of legislation.

Also, Evangelical Protestantism bolstered the ideology of women's sphere. Christian virtues of humility, piety, and charity coincided with new descriptions of female moral character. Although many men were converted in the evangelical revivals that swept the urbanizing Northeast and moved westward along the trail of settlement, women comprised the majority of converts and the bulk of congregations thereafter. By 1814, for example, women outnumbered men in religious societies of bustling Utica, New York, and the most zealous activists of the early revivals there were women of the new middle classes—wives and daughters of men with white-collar occupations. Forming voluntary associations with evangelical goals extended the realm of domesticity beyond the household. Middle-class women were excluded from business and politics, but, imbued with a positive sense of their responsibilities as women and supported by ministers, they created a community of their peers and an associational life that claimed space for women in between the poles of domesticity and male-dominated public life.

Even in the years of its greatest prevalence, the ideology of a separate women's sphere coexisted with exceptions to it. By midcentury, 10 percent of adult women, most of them in cities, worked for pay. Single women's alleged superior moral qualities made them prime candidates to fill the increasing number of teaching jobs, expanding with the spread of common schools. By 1860, in heavily urbanized Massachusetts, almost four-fifths of the teaching force was female, and one out of five women had taught at some point in their lives. For those largely unmarried women who produced textiles, clothing, and shoes in factories, constituting one-fourth of all laborers in manufacturing, the experience of living outside the family and earning wages appears to have altered their future domestic lives. They married at later ages than their mothers, married men who were more their equal in age, had fewer children, and settled disproportionately in cities rather than the countryside. The crowds of poor women in cities, competing for miserably paid garment piecework or peddling food or utensils for pennies on street corners to feed their families, were excluded by definition from the culture of domesticity. Not only in the East and Midwest, but also in frontier towns such as Santa Fe, San Antonio, Tucson, and Los Angeles the harshness of the urban environment mediated against female domesticity except in the wealthiest families.

Changes associated with commercialization extended into intimate corners of daily life. Until the expansion of the market economy and the emergence of merchant capitalism, most wage earners—apprentices and journeymen—in cities lived with their employers and shared their private lives. Work, leisure, and domestic life had been acted out in the same place and by the same people. Now the hallmark of the employer's home was its separation from production, its private social life, and its withdrawal from patterns of shared sociability. Apprentices were no longer thought to be members of the master's family; rather, they were considered trainees in a business that was now conducted outside the household. No longer members of a common household, masters and journeymen viewed themselves more as employers and employees. Their interests were more distinct and conflicting than they had been before, and they formed new class-conscious organizations to protect those interests. Between 1786 and 1816, at least twelve major strikes by various craftsmen occurred—the first major strikes by employees against employers in American history.

As commercialization drew farms and cities into greater economic dependence on each other, the resulting market expansion began to affect areas not usually identified as cities. On the western frontier, Mexican independence from Spain meant the end of trade restrictions with the United States. As a result, Missouri entrepreneurs developed a trade route known as the Santa Fe Trail that provided the pathway for commercial penetration of the Southwest, helping Anglo trade and traders to reshape the needs and wants of residents of Santa Fe.

The extension of improved transportation, post offices, and newspapers brought more people everywhere into contact with urban life. In eighteenth-century Massachusetts, Boston's print shops held a monopoly on the colony's news; by 1820, there were 120 print shops scattered throughout the state, publishing fifty-three daily and weekly newspapers for twenty-three different towns. Some 443 post offices blanketed the state, giving nearly every community access to a national communications system. A rich associational life in towns signified the social stratification and heterogeneity inherent in urban experience. Wherever population expanded and the number of men working as clerks, agents, and other nonmanual occupations increased, there was also a rise in the number of specialized voluntary associations such as charity organizations, libraries, firefighting societies, and Masonic lodges. Interest-group associations split the population into exclusive cells, sometimes overlapping and sometimes competing with prior loyalties to place, family, and church.

SERVICING THE CITY

All cities, whether upstart or established, needed a wide range of services to provide safety and health, water supplies, poverty relief, and education of their citizens. In meeting these needs, Americans contributed significant technological and organizational advances to the entire world. But the solutions to problems of urban life also brought unexpected and sometimes problematic consequences.

A vexing and threatening aspect of the phenomenal growth of American cities between 1830 and 1860 was the rise of what historian Roger Lane has termed "murderous disorder."[3] Though murders in cities were greatly outnumbered by murders in the rural South, where customs of racial violence and defending one's honor made for a perilous mix, city folk were beginning to kill each other to a frightening extent. Homicide figures for the era are hard to come by, and what numbers that do exist are difficult to interpret because the numbers of actual murders are always higher than the numbers of reported murders or arrests. Still, some comparisons are possible. For example, in Philadelphia there were 3.7 murder indictments per 100,000 population between 1839 and 1845. Between 1853 and 1859, the ratio rose to 4.0 per 100,000, an 8 percent rise. Much of the increase in the murder rate can be attributed to use of revolvers. Between 1839 and 1852, according to Lane, firearms accounted for 15 percent of murders; the proportion rose to 25 percent between 1853 and 1859. Although stories of love's passion and betrayal were the press's favorite murder themes, Lane has argued that competition for unskilled laborer jobs and for inexpensive housing in crowded urban neighborhoods provoked a recurrent real-life crisis that sometimes resulted in violence during this period.

Homicide, however, threatened urban order far less than did riots. Some of the dynamics driving specific urban violence are discussed in the next chapter, but whatever the provocation, nearly a thousand people died in antebellum urban riots. This happened partly because law enforcement agencies of constables, sheriffs, and night watchmen were unable to intervene effectively to stop violence, which was more likely to be aimed at specifically designated groups of victims and more likely to hurt or kill than eighteenth-century crowd actions, which had ordinarily been directed against property rather than persons. Young, white, unmarried, and usually unemployed or underemployed men were the most likely group to hurl bricks and wield clubs in street brawls and to commit the increasing number of murders that plagued city streets. Although he argued that urban homicide was less of a threat than urban riots, Lane found that in Philadelphia 90 percent of the homicide indictments named poor or working-class white males, whom he identified as part of a rough bachelor subculture organized around the pastimes of drinking and fighting. Although nearly one-fourth of the city's murders took place inside homes, nearly 40 percent occurred on the streets and another 10 percent in saloons.[4]

Though much serious crime could be found in poorer sections of cities, where both criminals and victims were part of the lower classes, the new mix of urban population, widening disparities of income, and decline of older patterns of household and neighborhood authority sparked anxiety over an increase in crime against property, especially burglary and arson. In St. Louis in the 1850s, only fifty daytime constables policed a population of one hundred thousand, and boosters were concerned that a reputation for lawlessness would hurt their city's attractiveness for commercial investment. A St. Louis newspaper editor spoke for local businessmen when he stressed that "the prosperity of our city, its increase in business, the enhancement in the value of its property . . . depend on the preservation of order."

By midcentury, fear of disorder had overcome longstanding reservations about salaried police in many cities. A sense that crime and disorder were on the increase prompted cities to establish permanent uniformed police forces, to be paid with revenues raised by taxes and by borrowing provisions in new city charters. In 1838 the Massachusetts General Assembly enabled Boston to appoint salaried police officers, stipulating that they be married taxpayers, presumably those with a stake in the community. New York City obtained similar authority in 1844, Philadelphia in 1850, and Baltimore in 1857.

Residents of these cities soon discovered, however, that creating a professional police force failed to solve old problems of law enforcement and even raised new ones. First, there seemed never to be enough policemen to do the job. Between 1845 and 1855, New York City's population grew from 250,000 to 630,000, while its police force was increased only from 800 to less than 1,200. Other cities suffered from similar shortages. In

Boston Policeman. Patrolling city streets without a uniform, early police officers had to battle not only criminals but also citizens distrust of military-like authority. Not until the 1850s did residents of big cities give in and allow policemen to wear uniforms and carry arms.

Lynn, Massachusetts, the largest number of police served on night duty, patrolling the streets on the lookout for burglaries and fires, but even this commitment did not satisfy some wealthy businessmen who complained about crowds of potentially disorderly strangers congregating in the streets before and after work and who hired specially deputized police to protect their buildings and machinery. Because there were too few officers to patrol an entire city, police protection was concentrated in commercial and affluent residential districts and was minimal in crowded, working-class neighborhoods. As a result, crime rates tended to rise in poorer districts; such neighborhoods were labeled as criminal by definition and their residents dismissed as "dangerous classes."

In addition, law enforcement could become embroiled in political conflict. Often, a police force was a highly visible body of men responsible not to the community as a whole but to the political party in office who hired them and funded their salaries. In an attempt to lift police appointments in New York City out of party politics, the New York General Assembly in 1857 created a state-controlled metropolitan police force. Mayor Fernando Wood resisted this imposition of state power over his regime and refused to disband the local police, with the result that the city temporarily was patrolled by two competing police forces. The U.S. Court of Appeals forced Wood to back down, and the metropolitan force remained in operation until the 1870s, even though it failed to improve law enforcement. Yet the New York example sparked the subsequent creation of state-controlled municipal police in more than a dozen large cities, including Baltimore, San Francisco, Detroit, and New Orleans.

More important, the police as agents of law enforcement were buffeted between conflicting urban groups who held different notions of what the law was and how it should be enforced. Some citizens, for example, demanded strict enforcement of vice, temperance, and fugitive slave laws. Yet police action in these areas could antagonize other citizens who saw no harm in a little gambling, whose cultural background included imbibing wine or beer, and whose moral values condoned the arrest and return of fugitive slaves to their owners. Roger Lane has pointed out that "depending on the political winds of the moment, [police] were alternately supposed to enforce or ignore a whole host of laws against drinking, gambling, and whoring that were widely unpopular in their own class and neighborhoods; there was more money in ignorance than in outrage. They could count on no automatic respect for The Law in cities full of clashing values and peoples."[5]

Reorganizations of fire departments duplicated some of the processes affecting police departments. Volunteer fire companies of artisans, who could leave their work to chase a fire and who enjoyed a battle with competing fire companies for access to water as much as the excitement of battling the fires themselves, were clearly inadequate to the task of protecting buildings, wharves, machines, and residences now found in commercial cities. By the 1860s, most cities had replaced hand pumps with steam engines and disbanded volunteer fire companies. In their place cities hired full-time firefighters on alert in specially constructed fire stations.

With or without the professional reorganization of firefighting, communities were not really safe from fire until they had efficient access to ample water. At an early date, fear of fire and disease induced urban officials to think more seriously about providing water for their citizens. In the 1790s, yellow fever ravaged the Northeast—particularly Philadelphia—convincing several cities that cleanliness was the only way to prevent or minimize disease. This need for sanitation meant more liberal use of water. Most urbanites had drawn their water from public or private wells, but the springs that fed these wells could not supply tens of thousands of people, and they were often polluted with seepage from privies and graves. Attention focused on nearby rivers and streams as sources of larger, purer water

supplies. Who should undertake projects to tap these sources, the municipality or private corporations?

Under pressures resulting from the yellow fever epidemics, Philadelphia constructed the country's first major public waterworks. In 1798, the
Philadelphia City Council hired engineer and architect Benjamin Latrobe.
He devised a system to pump water from the Schuylkill River to a high-
ground reservoir called Centre Square, from where it could be pumped
through wooden pipes to various parts of the city. Although it operated at a
deficit—largely because people could not readily accept the idea of paying
for water and because the steam pumps often broke down—the Centre
Square waterworks won national admiration. The system eventually accustomed Philadelphians to consider water as a public utility. When the city
outgrew the system, it constructed a larger waterworks in 1811, raising
water from the Schuylkill to reservoirs atop Fairmount Hill and distributing
it through iron pipes.

Philadelphia's public water company was the exception in these early
years. Other cities purchased water from private companies. The quality of
service ranged from adequate in Baltimore, where the Baltimore Water
Company was conscientious about its function, to intolerable in New York,
where the Manhattan Company devoted most of its attention and capital to
banking privileges granted by its charter. Private corporations wanted profits; few were willing to commit huge amounts of capital to the construction
and maintenance of an elaborate water system. In addition they catered to
paying customers and balked at extending service to low-income districts
that would furnish little revenue. Eventually, however, city leaders, looking
to the example set by Philadelphia, began to press for public waterworks. In
1835, New York voters solidly approved a project to bring water to the city
through an aqueduct from the Croton River. In 1845, an act passed by the
Massachusetts General Assembly enabled Boston to construct its own water
system. In 1857, Baltimore purchased its private waterworks and began
constructing an additional reservoir. In factory towns, industrialists pressured city officials to protect their property with municipal water systems.
By 1860, the country's sixteen largest cities had reasonably efficient water
systems, only four of which were still privately owned.

Yet leaders who congratulated themselves for providing their cities with
adequate water often became complacent. Abundance of water and higher
standards of public health created new habits of consumption. Though flush
toilets did not yet exist, private households, especially among the wealthy,
had more accessible water for personal use. More importantly, industrial use
of water for steam, cooling, and cleaning rose. But as population growth and
industrialization quickened, the ability of existing waterworks to meet local
demand faltered. The obstacle was one of leadership more than of technology. As Sam Bass Warner, Jr., has noted, Philadelphia's Fairmount works
made running water available for street pumps and homes of those who

could afford it, but public leaders were reluctant to provide running water where it was needed most—in the homes of the poor.[6] Industrialists in every city tapped water from public supplies because it was the cheapest and handiest coolant and waste-carrying agent; they had little concern for pollution or future shortages. This shortsightedness and the elevation of private needs over public welfare began to overload public water systems.

Professional police, fire, and water services relieved some problems of commercial cities, but poverty, delinquency, mental illness, disease, and moral decay defied easy solutions. Colonial practices of warning out debtors, fining and whipping criminals, and placing paupers and orphans with relatives and other townspeople were unfeasible in the nineteenth century. Cities grew too large for officials to keep track of all newcomers, and old forms of punishment and relief failed to stem increasing crime, sin, and poverty. Moreover, constant population migration churned the social structures of all cities, increasing anonymity and aggravating fears of anarchy and social breakdown.

To combat overcrowding, unemployment, and poverty, middle-class reformers created remedies that were shaped by their own gender, class, and ethnic prejudices. A characteristic response of antebellum reformers was to try to convert those whom they identified as poor and depraved, infuse them with Christian morality, and establish institutions that would inculcate values of diligence, order, and restraint. Housed together, away from their families and the temptations of city life, the poor could be rehabilitated in a controlled environment. Between 1820 and 1840, scores of communities opened almshouses and workhouses for the poor. These institutions won support as much because they removed the poor from the streets and were more economical than outdoor assistance as for their reforming functions. Nevertheless they signaled a new approach to welfare policy.

Penitentiaries, asylums, and houses of correction were constructed to serve the same functions for the criminal, the insane, and the delinquent that almshouses served for the poor—removing "deviants" from the city's temptations and restoring mental health and lawful behavior by exposure to a regimented institutional life. With the goal of returning inmates to a preurban social harmony, the institutions were located in rural settings, although the values of moderation, punctuality, and obedience that the institutions represented were more suited to life in the present than the past. Moreover, as David Rothman has shown, the ideal of confining deviants and dependents in order to reform them could easily harden into the objective of incarcerating these groups simply to isolate them from the rest of society.[7]

Almshouses, penitentiaries, and asylums could neither house nor reform all the poor, however. A more inclusive institution was needed to destroy the cycle of poverty, a process, according to some reformers, whereby succeeding generations of the same families failed to escape indigence and became perpetually dependent upon public support. Beginning in the

1820s, urban leaders rallied behind state-supported free education as the instrument that would break the chain of destitution while restoring social order in the same fashion as other institutional reform.

In the 1820s and 1830s, the most insistent voices for expanding public education were those of urban politicians, humanitarians, and educators who campaigned for school reform as insurance against social upheaval. Horace Mann, a Boston lawyer, Henry Barnard, a leading citizen of Hartford, Connecticut, and Calvin Stowe, professor of biblical literature at Cincinnati's Lane Theological Seminary, were among the most influential proponents of tax-supported public education. Schooling, they claimed, would instill virtue and patriotism in the lower classes and lift them from poverty into hardworking respectability. It would assimilate immigrants and teach all children to withstand temptations. As cities grew and social conflict became more threatening, the public education movement gained momentum. Boston established free elementary schools in 1818, New York followed in 1832, and Philadelphia in 1836.

By the 1850s, the majority of cities and states in the North and the West had some system of publicly funded education. Uniformly designed school buildings proliferated in diverse urban neighborhoods. Moreover, school organization had become more uniform. Pupils were placed in grades according to age and ability, procedures for advancement from grade to grade were standardized, decisions about curriculum and textbooks were centralized, and teachers were required to meet certain professional qualifications. Control was more firmly consolidated in the hands of city and state bureaucracies.

Public schooling in diverse communities was now shaped by the political, economic, and cultural agendas of native Protestant leaders, who intended schools to train students in punctuality, obedience, honesty, and persistence. McGuffey's series of readers, which after 1836 became the basic reading textbooks, taught schoolchildren to accept their position in the class hierarchy and strive for respectability rather than the trappings of wealth. The content of public education expressed values antagonistic to the cultures of Catholic, African-American, rural, southern, immigrant, and working-class peoples, the very groups who favored local community control of schools in opposition to the reformers' vision of centralized, homogenized education. When Catholics in New York City lost a challenge to the Protestant monopoly of public education in that city, the Roman Catholic church decided to establish its own school system, a costly program that took decades to complete. After Los Angeles was incorporated as a city in 1850, its Hispanic mayor, Antonio Franco Coronel, and the city council, the majority of whom were Mexican, supported the establishment of bilingual public schools. When the school board failed to find teachers who could teach in both English and Spanish, the first school opened with only English permitted for instruction, alienating many would-be attendees.

The expansion of urban schooling did not cause poverty to disappear. But reformers succeeded in winning public support for enormous expenditures on education because politics in antebellum cities called for a literate, informed electorate; because disorder and diversity in cities made bureaucratic standardization appealing; and because expanding commercial capitalism created demand for well-trained workers and managers. Despite its triumphs, however, the reach of public schooling was still limited. In many cities, population increased faster than schools could be built. As immigration accelerated in the 1840s, illiteracy rose instead of declined. More and more children were squeezed into existing classrooms. In 1850, Boston schools provided only one teacher for every fifty-five students. At the same time, school reformers, attempting to bring all children into schools, contended with officials and taxpayers determined to hold down public expenditures and with working-class and immigrant families who resisted educators' intervention in family decisions about children's upbringing.

In the 1850s, the attack on immigrant and working-class families implicit in calls for asylums and public schools became more explicit in a new reform strategy. The male and female reformers active in the New York Children's Aid Society and the Association for Improving the Condition of the Poor initiated an ambitious campaign to eradicate poverty by clearing children and women from the streets and transforming working-class family life. The new ways in which the middle class perceived the work ethic and ideology of domesticity made traditional working-class street life, particularly the visible activities of children, seem especially dangerous. Middle-class reformers were generally insensitive to working-class families' needs for incomes that women and children could earn in factories and street trades and thus believed that the enclosed, privatized, protected home and that the clearly differentiated roles for men, women, and children needed to be emphasized and protected.

From reformers' perspective, the active engagement of women and children in public wage work and social life rather than sheltered in a safe, moral home environment became in itself evidence of parental neglect, family disintegration, and the root cause of poverty. According to reformers, working-class households that sent women and children to find casual labor in the streets were not doing their civic duty. Some reformers viewed children on the streets as orphaned or abandoned, although in many cases they were neither. To "save" such children, New York reformer Charles Loring Brace established the Children's Aid Society (CAS) to remove poor children from their households, shipping boys off to farm labor in the countryside and teaching girls sewing, cooking, and housecleaning as preparation for a life of domesticity as wives or servants. Although the CAS solutions did not alleviate urban poverty, its attempts to control the streets and shape family life raised antagonisms among the poor that would remain long after the reform societies abandoned their mission.

Migration, industrialization, and social change charged the first half of the nineteenth century with extraordinary activity, for all these movements fused in the cities. Although the United States was far from an urbanized nation on the eve of the Civil War, the three decades before the war witnessed the most intense growth of cities this country would ever experience. Between 1830 and 1840, the number of urban residents grew by 64 percent; between 1840 and 1850, by 92 percent; between 1850 and 1860, by 75 percent. By 1860, twenty-one cities had more than forty thousand inhabitants (see Table 2–1). These places and the activities they supported helped bring the nation into a period of transition, suspended between preindustrial and industrial society, on the brink of still more major changes that lay ahead.

Until the Civil War, America's major cities remained primarily commercial in function, but by the 1840s, economic and technological changes were beginning to launch the cities and the nation into an age of industrialization. The Revolution loosened traditional restraints on incorporation, and the number of limited-liability corporations such as banks, insurance companies, and manufacturing concerns, plus bridge, road, and canal companies mushroomed. Expanded capital resources enabled regional railroad systems

TABLE 2–1 Populations of Major Cities, 1830–60

	1830	1840	1850	1860
New York	202,589	312,700	515,500	813,600
Philadelphia	161,271	220,400	340,000	565,529
Brooklyn	15,396	36,230	96,838	266,660
Baltimore	80,620	102,300	169,600	212,418
Boston	61,392	93,380	136,880	177,840
New Orleans	46,082	102,190	116,375	168,675
Cincinnati	24,831	46,338	115,435	161,044
St. Louis	5,852	14,470	77,860	160,773
Chicago		4,470	29,963	109,260
Buffalo	8,653	18,213	42,260	81,130
Newark	10,953	17,290	38,890	71,940
Louisville	10,340	21,210	43,194	68,033
Albany	24,209	33,721	50,763	62,367
Washington	18,826	23,364	40,001	61,122
San Francisco			34,776	56,802
Providence	16,833	23,171	41,573	50,666
Pittsburgh	15,369	21,115	46,601	49,221
Rochester	9,207	20,191	36,403	48,204
Detroit	2,222	9,102	21,019	45,619
Milwaukee		1,712	20,061	45,246
Cleveland	1,076	6,071	17,034	43,417
Total urban population	1,127,000	1,845,000	3,544,000	6,217,000
Percentage of U.S. population that was urban	8.8	10.8	15.3	19.8
Percentage of increase in urban population		63.7	92.1	75.4

Sources: U.S. censuses of 1850 and 1860; as appears in Blake McKelvey, *American Urbanization: A Comparative History* (Glenview, Ill.: Scott, Foresman and Company, 1973), Table 3, p. 37.

to grow big enough to deliver raw materials and finished products cheaply and speedily. The 2,800 miles of rail in America in 1840 grew to 30,600 miles by 1860, linking urban centers. Telegraph construction quickened the pace at which business was done; no longer did merchants and manufacturers have to depend on ships and stagecoaches to bring them news about markets. Expanded use of coal-powered steam engines allowed factories to locate inside larger cities and away from sources of waterpower. Production of interchangeable parts and development of the machine-tool industry aided the expansion of mechanized production. The exhaustion of New England farming soil and the mass exodus from harsh economic and social conditions in Europe provided factory owners with a growing labor supply. The development of the hinterlands and the new urban residents helped increase the size and number of domestic markets. The transportation revolution, with its steamboats and railroads; the commercial revolution, with its corporate enterprises and expanded marketing and credit techniques; and the beginnings of the Industrial Revolution, with its factories and mass-produced goods, had ushered in a new era in urban life.

BIBLIOGRAPHY

The growth of new cities in the West and South between 1780 and 1860 is examined by Jeffrey S. Adler, *Yankee Merchants and the Making of the Urban West: The Rise and Fall of Antebellum St. Louis* (1991); William Cronon, Nature's *Metropolis: Chicago and the Great West* (1991); David R. Goldfield, *Urban Growth in the Age of Sectionalism: Virginia, 1847–1861* (1977); Richard C. Wade, *The Urban Frontier: 1790–1830* (1957); and Kenneth W. Wheeler, *To Wear a City's Crown: The Beginnings of Urban Growth in Texas, 1832–1865* (1968). The changes in the law that facilitated urban growth are discussed in Stanley K. Schultz, *Constructing Urban Culture: American Cities and City Planning, 1800–1920* (1989).

Among the most notable works discussing urban rivalries are Wyatt W. Belcher, *The Economic Rivalry Between St. Louis and Chicago, 1850–1880* (1947); and Julius Rubin, *Canal or Railroad? Imitation and Innovation in the Response to the Erie Canal in Philadelphia, Baltimore, and Boston* (1961).

The development of city services has received attention in Susan Craddock, *City of Plagues: Disease, Poverty, and Deviance in San Francisco* (2002); Robin Einhorn, *Property Rules: Political Economy in Chicago, 1833–1872* (1991); Sarah S. Elkind, *Bay Cities and Water Politics: The Battle for Resources in Boston and Oakland* (1998); Joanne Abel Goldman, *Building New York's Sewers: Developing Mechanisms of Urban Management* (1997); David Johnson, *Policing the Urban Underworld: The Impact of Crime on the Development of the American Police, 1800–1887* (1979); Carl F. Kaestle, *The Evolution of an Urban School System: New York, 1750–1850* (1973); Gerard T. Koeppel, *Water for Gotham: A History* (2000); Roger Lane, *Policing the City: Boston, 1822–1885* (1967); Lane, *Murder in America: A History* (Columbus: Ohio State University Press, 1997); Martin V. Melosi, *The Sanitary City: Urban Infrastructure in America from Colonial Times to the Present* (2000); Charles E. Rosenberg, *The Cholera Years: The United States in 1832, 1849, and 1866* (1962); David J. Rothman, *The Discovery of the Asylum: Social Order and Disorder in the New Republic* (1971); Stanley K. Schultz, *The Culture Factory: Boston Public Schools, 1789–1860* (1968); and Joel A. Tarr, *The Search for the Ultimate Sink: Urban Pollution in Historical Perspective* (1996).

For the impact of change on the urban community, see Tyler Anbinder, *Five Points: The 19th Century New York City Neighborhood that Invented Tap Dance, Stole Elections and Became the World's Most Notorious Slum* (2001); Thomas Bender, *Toward an Urban Vision: Ideas and Institutions in Nineteenth-Century America* (1975); Stuart M. Blumin, *The Urban Threshold: Growth and Change in a Nineteenth-Century American Community* (1976); Paul Boyer, *Urban Masses and Moral Order in America, 1820–1920* (1978); Amy Bridges, *A City in the Republic: Antebellum New York and the Origins of Machine Politics* (1984); Michael Frisch, *Town into City: Springfield, Massachusetts, and the Meaning of Community, 1840–1880* (1972); Roger W. Lotchin, *San Francisco, 1846–1856: From Hamlet to City* (1974); Donald L. Miller, *City of the Century: The Epic of Chicago and the Making of America* (1996); and Sam Bass Warner, Jr., *The Private City: Philadelphia in Three Periods of Growth* (1968).

For a discussion of the transformation of the work process with the introduction of merchant capital, see Alan Dawley, *Class and Community: The Industrial Revolution in Lynn* (1977); Paul Faler, *Mechanics and Manufacturers in the Early Industrial Revolution: Lynn, Massachusetts, 1780–1860* (1981); Paul Johnson, *A Shopkeeper's Millennium: Society and Revivals in Rochester, New York, 1815–1837* (1978); Bruce Laurie, *The Working People of Philadelphia, 1800–1850* (1980); Sean Wilentz, *Chants Democratic: New York City and the Rise of the American Working Class* (1984); Billy Smith, *The "Lower Sort": Philadelphia's Laboring People, 1750–1800* (1990); and Richard Stott, *Workers in the Metropolis: Class, Ethnicity, and Youth in Antebellum New York City* (1990).

The rise of a self-conscious middle class is discussed in Stuart M. Blumin, *The Emergence of the Middle Class: Social Experience in the American City, 1760–1900* (1989) and Mary P. Ryan, *The Cradle of the Middle Class: The Family in Oneida County, New York, 1790–1865* (1981).

Some of the many works on early nineteenth-century social structure include Elizabeth Blackmar, *Manhattan for Rent, 1785–1850* (1989); Edward Pessen, "The Social Configuration of the Ante-Bellum City: An Historical and Theoretical Inquiry," *Journal of Urban History* 2 (May 1976): 267–306; and Stephan Thernstrom, *Poverty and Progress: Social Mobility in a Nineteenth-Century City* (1964).

On women in antebellum cities, see Alice Kessler-Harris, *Out to Work: A History of Wage-Earning Women in America* (1982); Suzanne Lebsock, *The Free Women of Petersburg: Status and Culture in a Southern Town, 1784–1860* (1984); Mary P. Ryan, *Women in Public: Between Banners and Ballots, 1825–1880* (1990); and Christine Stansell, *City of Women: The Female Laboring Poor in New York City, 1789–1860* (1986). For other materials on women and reform, see Lori D. Ginzberg, *Women and the Work of Benevolence: Morality, Politics and Class in the Nineteenth-Century United States* (1990); Nancy Hewitt, *Women's Activism and Social Change: Rochester, New York, 1822–1872* (1984); Michael McGerr, "Political Style and Women's Power," *Journal of American History* 77 (December 1990): 864–85; Teresa Anne Murphy, *Ten Hours' Labor: Religion Reform and Gender in Early New England* (1992); and Carroll Smith-Rosenberg, *Religion and the Rise of the City: The New York City Mission Movement, 1812–1870* (1971).

NOTES

1. Richard C. Wade, *The Urban Frontier, 1790–1830* (Cambridge, Mass.: Harvard University Press, 1959).
2. Christine Stansell, *City of Women: Sex and Class in New York, 1789–1860* (New York: Knopf, 1986)
3. Roger Lane, *Murder in America: A History* (Columbus, Ohio: Ohio State University Press, 1997), 92.
4. Ibid., 122–26.
5. Ibid., 107–8.
6. Sam Bass Warner, Jr., *The Private City: Philadelphia in Three Periods of Its Growth* (Philadelphia: University of Pennsylvania Press, 1968), 109.
7. David J. Rothman, *The Discovery of the Asylum: Social Order and Disorder in the New Republic* (Boston: Little, Brown, 1971).

Life in the Walking City, 1820–1860

THE WALKING CITY

Until the 1850s, almost all American cities could be characterized by their compactness. Located near harbors or river junctions, they focused their activities on the waterfront. Here, wharves, warehouses, mercantile offices, and small manufacturing establishments were located because access to water transportation was of principal importance. Public buildings, churches, hotels, and shops clustered nearby. Homes of prominent families often were interspersed among these structures or, as in Cincinnati, Providence, and St. Louis, sat on a hill overlooking the port. Around these cores and in the valleys between hills were the residential areas of craftsmen, storekeepers, and laborers. The two- and three-story structures in these districts contained shops and workshops on the lower floors and residential quarters in back or above. Businesses needing water supplies—mills, tanneries, slaughterhouses, breweries—grouped along nearby streams. As the nineteenth century progressed, some heavy industry, particularly base metals, grew in the outskirts near railroad connections. Most business establishments, however, remained dispersed throughout the settled areas of town.

Wagons, carriages, horses, and pedestrians jammed the central streets. Neither public officers nor mechanical signals regulated the speed and direction of traffic. People seldom observed any custom of keeping to one side of the street or the other; right of way at intersections went to the boldest or most reckless. Cobblestones or gravel paved only a fraction of urban thoroughfares; most retained their original dirt surfaces, which nature and traffic turned into choking dust or clogging mud. Though animal-drawn vehicles were common on the streets of the early American city, the vast majority of people walked to their destinations, and it was this form of transportation that determined a city's size and shape. Until the 1850s, the settled areas of even the largest cities, such as New York, Boston, and Philadelphia, rarely extended beyond two miles from the city center—the average distance a person can walk in half an hour. Thus historians have labeled this early urban configuration the "walking city" because of its size and major mode of conveyance. No policies or legislation limited the area of any city; it was simply more convenient for people to locate businesses and residences on available sites that had access by foot to most work, shopping, and social activities.

The limitations of walking largely contributed to the compactness of the premodern city, a compactness with several important features. First, land use was mixed; commercial, storage, residential, and industrial buildings mingled together. There were few distinct districts; even waterfront property had various uses. As cities grew, their business districts became more defined, but here, too, residences and primitive factories remained interspersed with stores, banks, and offices.

Hazards of Street-cleaning. Early nineteenth-century city streets became littered with debris and animal droppings, so that one of the earliest urban services was street cleaning. But as this drawing depicts, the service could be hazardous, as pedestrians who got into the way of spraying mechanisms could find themselves unwitting targets.

Second, mixed and intensive land use meant that city dwellers were relatively integrated. Short distances separated poor from rich, immigrant from native, African American from white—a proximity that may have sparked some of the conflicts over turf discussed in Chapter 2. Factory owners often built their residences next to their factories, within sight of workingmen's homes, and common laborers lived along alleyways inside blocks where the more well-to-do resided. Slaves in southern cities such as Charleston and New Orleans inhabited compounds behind their masters' houses. Row housing, the characteristic urban style in early nineteenth-century cities, accentuated the appearance of homogeneity, making inequalities of wealth less visible. Moreover, people lived not only nearby one another but also near, or at, their places of work. Those who worked away from their residences walked to and from their jobs.

As time passed and populations increased, enclaves did form. In Boston, newly arrived Irish filled the North End and neighborhood along the wharves. In Philadelphia, African Americans clustered in the southern wards. Residential districts of free blacks and living-out slaves grew on or outside the edges of Charleston and Richmond. Still, however, the relatively small areas of all cities left all groups of people physically close together.

Political leadership reflected circumstances of the integrated community. City councils were usually elected to represent the city as a whole rather than from distinct districts. Invariably urban governments were composed of members of the city's social and economical elite—bankers, merchants, lawyers. Rarely were those in the lower three-quarters of the social order elected. Without distinctive geographic enclaves that corresponded to social class, the capacity of the working classes to develop and effectively express a clear political view was limited.

Just as the necessity of walking confined the horizontal expansion of premodern cities, technological limitations prevented vertical expansion. Only after the 1850s did the invention of the elevator and the use of iron, rather than masonry, for structural support enable the construction of buildings more than a few stories in height. The skyscraper, with its steel frame and electric elevators, did not appear until the 1880s. Until then the built environment developed primarily when new structures covered remaining empty property within the walking city or when developers reclaimed land by leveling hills, draining marshes, or filling in coves and bays. As cities filled up and vacant lots disappeared, land values soared, especially in comparison with construction costs. Now more than just speculation and boosterism inflated urban land values (see Chapter 2); rising demand and diminishing supply became ever important. In Chicago, for example, total valuation for land within a one-mile radius of the central business district increased from $810,000 in 1842 to $50,750,000 in 1856, a 6,000 percent gain.

Meanwhile, many cities were practically bursting at their seams. It has been common for Americans to consider urban crowding a consequence of industrialization and mass immigration during the late nineteenth and early twentieth centuries. Yet at no time in the country's history were total urban densities as high as they were in the mid–nineteenth century. Chapter 2 noted that these years witnessed the greatest proportionate growth of urban populations this country has ever experienced. An almost annual excess of new arrivals over those departing doubled and tripled populations of most established cities between 1840 and 1850. Crowding in settled areas swelled. By 1850, there were 135.6 persons per acre in New York, 82.7 in Boston, 80.0 in Philadelphia, and 68.4 in Pittsburgh. In many cities at midcentury an average of two families occupied every dwelling, a much larger figure than in similar-sized European towns or even in fast-growing industrial cities of England. Inner-city wards in most large American cities would become even more densely packed in the latter half of the century, but because urban areas were smaller at midcentury, crowding spread to a larger proportion of their districts.

In the 1820s and 1830s, ferries and bridges opened up new areas for development. Smaller towns adjacent to and often dependent on a major city had existed since colonial days, but now many more neighboring regions became accessible. Areas of new settlement included the Jersey shore across the Hudson River from Manhattan; Roxbury, Cambridge, and Charlestown near Boston; and land across the Schuylkill River at Philadelphia, across the Allegheny and Monongahela at Pittsburgh, the Cuyahoga at Cleveland, and the New Buffalo Creek at Buffalo. Populations in these suburban places doubled and tripled in a single decade. Regular steamboat ferry service between Brooklyn Heights and New York City began in 1841, and by 1860, various East River ferries carried 33 million passengers per year. On the eve of the Civil War, Brooklyn contained more people than Boston and was the third most populous city in the country.

Many newly developed areas had their own economies and retained political independence, preferring only to purchase services such as water and gas from the nearby city. Settlements such as Boston's first suburbs were involved in a fringe economy that flourished between 1815 and 1840, housing those who raised and processed goods for city use, linking urban and rural economies by supplying milk and produce, and creating industries producing such urban necessities as bricks and glass. According to historian Henry Binford, these new functions would eventually crowd out the "scattered centers of craft and processing" that had characterized earlier settlements.[1] At the same time, the peripheral settlements gave big-city merchants opportunities to sell goods to new markets. Between 1845 and 1860, Boston's suburbs gained more than ten thousand commuters. These suburbanites would reshape the peripheral communities as domestic retreats for some of the wealthiest families to escape the crowded walking city, and to build homes, schools, and churches in more attractive surroundings.

SOCIAL COMPLEXITY AND CONTESTED TERRAIN

Migration, population increase, and economic transformation brought sweeping social changes to the walking city. Perhaps the most striking feature of the early nineteenth century was the heterogeneity of peoples and fragmentation of earlier communal institutions that had at least partially bridged social divisions and provided social cohesion. Now, a greater complexity arose as new groups competed for the employment and housing the city had to offer and contended for political inclusion and social recognition.

A free black community of institutional complexity was a particularly new feature of urban life. Before the Revolution, only a tiny fraction of the nation's African-American population had been free, consisting mainly of those who were either the product of mixed racial unions or former slaves who were too old to undertake productive work for their masters. But after the Revolution, considerable numbers of slaves obtained freedom, in the North through statewide emancipation, and in the South through individual manumissions or successful illegal flight from bondage. Free African Americans moved to cities in large numbers, making cities centers of free African-American life. While the total free black population of Virginia more than doubled between 1790 and 1810, that of Richmond increased

African-American Scrubwoman. In spite of their improved status over southern plantation slaves, urban slaves and free blacks normally held the lowest occupations. Domestic work was the most common form of job done by urban black women.

Mrs. Juliann Jane Tillman, Preacher. Free African Americans in northern cities were able to form their own institutions and assume leadership positions within them. This lithograph depicts a female preacher in a Philadelphia African Methodist Episcopal Church in 1844.

fourfold and that of Norfolk increased tenfold. By 1820, the nation's largest free African-American community lived in Baltimore, but Boston, New York, Philadelphia, Cincinnati, Charleston, New Orleans, and Mobile also had sizable free black populations. In New York City, freed slaves from the countryside and mulattoes fleeing Santo Domingo after the successful slave revolt there swelled the free population to 7,470 by 1810, more than 8 percent of the city's total. After 1810, slaves who were freed by the Gradual Manumission Act increased New York City's free African-American population even further.

Ex-slaves were drawn to cities because of opportunities for employment and because the concentration of free African Americans offered a greater chance to find an acceptable marriage partner, establish a family, and participate in activities of African churches, schools, fraternal societies, and benevolent organizations. In northern seaports, most free African-American men worked as laborers or mariners, but a few managed to work as artisans, particularly in trades identified with servile or dirty labor like barbering and butchering. In New York City, freed slaves were more than twice as likely to possess a skill than in Philadelphia, because white New York artisans had relied heavily on slave labor throughout the eighteenth century and because many of the city's mulatto émigrés from the South had skilled trades. A few freedmen were able to serve the urban black community as small proprietors, ministers, and teachers. In Charleston, free African-American men constituted 16 percent of the city's skilled male work force and 11 percent of the unskilled male laboring population. In Richmond and Lynchburg, Virginia, free African-American men comprised nearly 30 percent of the unskilled male work force.

In most cities, however, the majority of the free African-American population were women, who faced a much narrower range of occupational possibilities, working primarily as domestic servants, laundresses, produce sellers, and prostitutes. A few kept small shops and ran boardinghouses. In some places, such as Petersburg, Virginia, a few free black women worked as nurses, midwives, storekeepers, and bakers, and free women managed to accumulate half the property owned by African Americans in the city.

Although most free African Americans remained poor and propertyless, a group of black leaders emerged in Boston, Philadelphia, Baltimore, Richmond, Savannah, and Charleston. Wealthier and better educated than rural counterparts, urban African-American leaders petitioned Congress and state legislatures to abolish slavery and grant full political rights to black citizens. They also established community institutions where African Americans could pray, and educate their children. By 1800, African-American communities from Boston to Savannah supported their own churches, and in 1816, leading African-American churchmen from various parts of these regions joined to form the first independent black denomination, the African Methodist Episcopal Church.

From the beginning, African Americans gave their churches, schools, mutual assistance associations, and fraternal organizations names with African references, to signify their own group identity and to distinguish themselves from white society. In Philadelphia, the Angola Beneficial Society was established in 1808, the Africa Insurance Company in 1809, the Sons of Africa in 1810, and the African Female and Male Benevolent Societies in the following years. By the 1820s in Philadelphia, African Americans had created an institutional life that was richer and more stable than that of the lower-income whites with whom they shared neighborhoods. In a mixed uptown area in New York City, where small craft shops bordered on larger factories, a group of free blacks of modest means who had been able to purchase cheap house lots in the 1820s supported two black Methodist churches and a racially mixed Episcopal church, as well as a "Colored School," by the 1850s. In Boston, the African Society, founded in 1797, established the African School in 1798 and the African Meeting House in 1805. Although slaves living in white households were scattered throughout a city, free African Americans moved away from prior masters to cluster in particular neighborhoods, nearby African churches and schools. In New York City, many African Americans occupied the most inexpensive cellar housing, which offered easy access to the streets. Urban African-American self-expression and sociability could flourish in dancing halls and cellars where African-American residency was more concentrated.

As the free African-American urban population grew, so too did social conflict as white people used legislation to limit blacks' economic opportunities and to restrict their rights to vote and testify in court. But the dense network of urban black institutions and a rich community life made it more possible in cities than in the countryside for free African Americans to try to protect themselves and even sometimes to confront racism. This network provided a base for protest, supporting struggling black newspapers and sending delegates to black conventions to attack slavery and agitate for civil rights. Free blacks, particularly in cities, would play an active role during the Civil War and Reconstruction by asserting notions of black citizenship to include suffrage and by demanding that they themselves define the meaning of freedom.

Free blacks, however, remained a minority of the African American population, even in cities. In the antebellum years, slaves were an indispensable part of the work force in southern cities. In Charleston, Richmond, and Lynchburg, slaves constituted from 50 to 60 percent of all workingmen; in Mobile, Baton Rouge, and Nashville, they constituted 25 to 35 percent of the adult male workforce. Nearly all slaves did manual labor of some sort, ranging from domestic duties to artisan trades and industrial labor. Throughout the urban South, white merchants, professionals, factory owners, and some governments remained the largest employers of slave labor, and for the most part, these employers required unskilled rather than skilled laborers. During the colonial period, slaves had actively participated in most artisanal trades, but by the mid–nineteenth century there were a significant number of slave artisans only in Charleston.

Skilled and unskilled, urban slaves were a considerable social presence in southern cities. By the 1850s, slave "hiring out," whereby masters rented slaves to other employers, was commonplace and profitable to both masters and slaves. It provided slave owners, particularly widowed women, a steady income, and it gave slaves experience with wage labor and the marketplace, a possibility of accumulating cash, and an added measure of control over their lives. Because their work required them to travel on city streets, urban slaves enjoyed greater mobility and cultural autonomy than did their rural counterparts. Bondsmen on plantations lived in the slave quarters and saw only their masters' families and occasionally slaves from a nearby plantation. City slaves partook of a wider world. They had access (even when it was illegal) to food, drink, entertainment, and the common sociability of urban life. They sometimes ran their own churches, and they often sneaked away to talk and drink with fellow slaves, free African Americans, and even working-class whites in back-alley groceries and grogshops scattered throughout every southern city. Preferring to avoid costs of housing their slaves, some masters gave their bondsmen permission to live as well as work away. When slaves lived out, they often resided in rented rooms on the fringes of town where free blacks and poor whites also lived.

An underlying contradiction characterized urban slavery. The institution of slavery requires absolute control of bondsmen by masters, but the circumstances of work and, sometimes, residence, made it difficult for urban owners to supervise the activities of their bondsmen every minute of the day, and slaves who hired out and lived out challenged traditional patterns of control. In the fringe neighborhoods, a fugitive slave who had escaped from a plantation might hide and purchase forged freedom papers. A Richmond newspaper complained in 1860 that "not only free Negroes but low white people can be found who will secret a slave from his master." Cities responded to this challenge with stringent restrictions on the activities of all black people, slave and free. These codes, enforced with increasing vigor after 1830, resulted in formal segregation—the exclusion of black people from most public accommodations. A variety of laws required people of color to have licenses for certain occupations and barred them from others, forbade them to assemble without a license, and prohibited them from being taught to read and write and from testifying in court against white people.

In addition, white employers reacted by hiring more unskilled white laborers and by selling slaves to the plantations. As a result, between 1830 and 1860, the number of slaves in the work forces of southern cities decreased relative to the numbers of immigrant laborers. In 1840, the total slave population of the ten largest southern cities was 67,755; in 1860, it was 68,013. Meanwhile, the total white population of the same cities rose from 233,000 to 690,000. Only in Richmond, where slave manpower was essential to iron and tobacco processing, did a large proportion of slaves still persist in 1860. In New Orleans, on the other hand, the number of slaves dropped from 23,000 in 1840 to 13,000 in 1860. But in spite of the increase in restrictions and the decrease in slave populations, free African Americans and urban slaves continued to assert their claim to a place of their own in city life.

Crowds of transient white men and women looking for work were also a new sight in early nineteenth-century American cities. In manufacturing cities like Lowell and Lynn, farm sons and daughters worked in new textile mills and shoemaking workshops. In commercial boom towns like Rochester, New York, predominantly male migrants were drawn from the countryside to work on canals and railroads. By the 1820s and 1830s, a rising percentage of the urban population were propertyless wage earners. Many were new unskilled laborers and factory hands, unaccustomed to the particular patterns of impersonal employment or the discipline of manufacturing work.

As working-class neighborhoods became distinct from middle-class areas, separate patterns of sociability heightened the sense of distance between classes. Particularly, single employed men and women living outside of family households occupied rooms and lodging houses and participated in a working-class youth subculture that included new kinds of entertainment and relationships. As historian Christine Stansell has described New York City's Bowery, "At the end of the working day and on Saturday night, the dance halls, oyster houses, and the famed Bowery Theatre, built in 1827, came alive with workingwomen, journeymen, and laborers looking for marital prospects, sexual encounters, and general good times."[2] Variety shows offered skits, comedy, singing, and dancing; and theaters featured melodrama, burlesque, and blackface minstrelsy.

As unmarried men and women left the constraints of communities where they were known, they exchanged the haven of family and friends for new temptations and new dangers, including its vices and crimes. The lurid side of urban life was highlighted in 1836 when the reading public was transfixed by reports surrounding the shocking murder of Helen Jewett, a New England woman who had moved to New York City and become a highly-paid prostitute. Evidence for the murder pointed to a young clerk, Richard Robinson, who had been one of Jewett's steadiest customers and ardent lovers. When Robinson was acquitted after a dramatic trial, his fellow bachelor clerks cheered him, but the whole incident prompted observers to fret over the vulnerability of unattached young people in the impersonal city.

Immigrants, pushed out of Ireland, Germany, and England when their livelihoods were threatened by agricultural commercialization and competition from machine-made goods, added another new presence to nineteenth-century urban populations. By the 1850s, more than half the residents of Boston and New York City were foreign born, and in Philadelphia 30 percent of household heads were born in Europe. Major concentrations of Irish immigrants could be identified in New York, Boston, Philadelphia, and San Francisco, and strong German communities emerged in Cincinnati, Louisville, St. Louis, and Milwaukee. Southern cities in this era also received newcomers from abroad. By 1860, 40 percent of New Orleans's population was foreign born. Immigrant workers, mostly from Ireland and Germany, constituted more than half of Charleston's and Mobile's free adult workingmen's populations, and between 40 and 50 percent of free adult workingmen in Richmond, Nashville, and Baton Rouge.

Immigrants added new cultural qualities to American urban life. Irish and German immigrants brought their traditions of work and leisure, spirituality and sociability, which often came into conflict with those of native-born residents. Spanish and French traditions of carnival were celebrated in cities like St. Augustine and New Orleans, with maskers, Harlequins, and Punchinellos parading the streets with guitars, violins, and other instruments in the days before Lent. In St. Augustine, maskers on St. John's Eve marked the summer solstice with ritualized gender inversion, with paraders dressing up as highborn persons of the opposite sex. By the 1830s and 1840s, New Orleans revelers were throwing flour and pieces of brick as well as candies, cake, apples, and oranges to people along the parade route, and newspapers appealing to middle-class standards of civility were dismissing Mardi Gras celebrations as "vulgar and tasteless."

This diversification of urban population occurred within the context of broadened suffrage for male citizens, circumstances that reshaped political life. After the Revolution, open competition for office increased, and the number of contested elections multiplied and the turnover of legislative representatives accelerated. Still, until the 1820s, and later in some states, property restrictions continued to disenfranchise many men. Even among those granted the ballot, political interest and electoral turnout usually remained low. Many citizens appeared to have retreated from the extraordinary political demands of the revolutionary period, instead deferring once again to the political leadership of the community's most distinguished men.

After 1820, the gradual abandonment of restrictions on white male suffrage in state after state coincided with a reemergence of citizen interest

Election Day in Philadelphia, 1816. Viewing the consumption of alcoholic drink destructive to the family and the home, this temperance society offered a pledge, here taken by a husband and wife, certifying that the couple was banishing "demon rum" from their household.

in politics, including at the local level. But citizens, fearing loss of local control over economic decisions, were deeply divided on the direction the economy ought to take and the role government should play. Commercial transformation and ethnic, religious, and class tensions helped to spark a process by which community factions were institutionalized in the form of political parties with socioeconomic identities. Entrepreneurs, usually Whigs, relished the possibilities of using government to tie localities to new markets and hoped to use city politics as a vehicle for raising revenue to expand commercial facilities such as docks, warehouses, and transportation. The rise of workingmen's parties, either separate workers' organizations or affiliations of the Democratic party, in urban areas seemed to spring from a similar set of questions and unease about the direction of commercial capitalism. Political organization provided a set pattern of responses to divisive questions, and raising problems to a national level partly defused potential community divisions. First Federalists and Republicans, then Whigs and Democrats created formal organizations at the town level. As early as 1810, political sectarianism was a durable feature of local politics, although especially in older settled towns, politics sometimes returned to a search for consensual, nonpartisan solutions to community questions.

The growth of local parties meant that political leadership by the community's social and economic chieftains was sometimes challenged by a new breed of professional politicians who assiduously courted newly enfranchised workingmen. Men from low-income groups were still rarely elected to city councils; elections at large provided a structure for those dominant in the community's social and economic life to dominate in its formal political life as well. But political competition often set members of the business elite against each other, and the increasing numbers of working-class voters could sometimes check the ability of elites to exercise political influence commensurate with their economic and social power.

Urban politics often reflected new urban diversity. No issue was as politically divisive in early nineteenth-century cities as temperance. Drinking had previously been assumed to be an inevitable aspect of an artisans' working day. According to historian Paul Johnson, "liquor was embedded in the patterns of irregular work and easy sociability sustained by the household economy," and public drinking traditions persisted in the interstices of the expanding commercial economy where these older economic forms persisted.[3] But in the minds of employers, new standards of discipline within large workshops and factories required abstinence from alcohol. Indeed, in Massachusetts the manufacturers who were most technologically innovative were also those who most enthusiastically supported temperance. For the new middle classes, sobriety became the key to economic efficiency, individual success, happy homes, and quiet streets. The baser passions, including drunkenness, were considered inimical to the new, more private home life, under the guidance of pious housewives. Factory owners were among the first to banish liquor from their workshops and from their own homes, and as they did so, nonuse or use of whiskey marked the dividing line between middle-class respectability and working-class sociability. Drinking became a means of resistance and a common prerogative of an autonomous working-class social life, even before Irish and German immigrants brought distinctive ethnic drinking traditions to American cities.

The first temperance reformers were wealthy Federalists, whose organizations hoped to encourage drinkers to imitate their betters in abstaining from alcohol. In the 1820s, the success of evangelical revivals inspired formation of middle-class temperance organizations that were as hostile to wealthy drinkers as to the poor, denouncing liquor retailers as trafficking in vice. In Rochester, hotel proprietors and tavern keepers whose livelihoods depended on working-class drinking reacted by letting their church memberships lapse. But those manufacturers, merchants, lawyers, shopkeepers, master artisans, and skilled journeymen whose lives were changed for the better by the commercial revolution were the first and most enthusiastic supporters of the revivals and temperance. Progressing from tactics of moral suasion and conversion to firings, boycotts, and political campaigns to outlaw drink, the evangelical reformers by the 1830s converted thousands to new ideas about temperance and respectability.

It was not until the 1840s, after severe economic collapse following the Panic of 1837, that a genuine working-class temperance movement, the Washington Society, arose. In Cincinnati, the Washingtonians drew men who had formerly resisted temperance into an altogether different style of temperance organization than those organized by evangelical Protestants. Noisily public and male-oriented rather than under the moral guardianship of women, Washingtonian societies recruited in streets and grogshops, gathered together supporters in picnics and parades rather than in prayer meetings, and dramatized alcohol's depths of degradation rather than the righteous fruits of abstinence. In Philadelphia in the 1840s, waves of working-class revivalism sparked a working-class temperance movement, attracting master craftsmen, journeymen, shopkeepers, and the most ambitious unskilled laborers to its membership.

In all cities a decision to abstain from alcohol was the key symbol of a new morality and a commitment to self-improvement. But in the 1840s, native-born evangelical workingmen measured their own sobriety and discipline against the unreconstructed drinking habits of laborers from expanding Irish and German immigrant neighborhoods. While the Whig party drew churchgoing merchants, professionals, and master workmen into a campaign for coercive temperance, nonevangelical Protestants, immigrant Catholic workingmen, and the petty retailers who served them found refuge in the antitemperance, anti-coercion stand of the Democratic party. Native-born enthusiasm for temperance translated into passionate anti-Catholicism, sharply splitting the working class along ethnic lines and turning neighborhoods into

The Astor Place Riot.   On May 11, 1849, a serious riot and challenge to police authority occurred outside New York City's Astor Place Opera House when supporters of the popular American actor, Edwin Forrest stormed the theater where Forrest's rival British actor William Macready was performing. The violence, in which twenty-two people died and more than 150 were injured, reflected class and nationalistic conflict as well as the highly emotional following that entertainment "stars" collected.

battlegrounds. Incidents like the destruction of Irish weavers' looms and houses by native-born weavers in Philadelphia's Kensington in 1844, the fierce fighting between Philadelphia native-born and Irish fire companies in the 1830s and 1840s, the riot that ensued from a collision between a native-born fire company and an Irish funeral procession on Boston's Broad Street in 1837, and other anti-Catholic and anti-Irish riots in Baltimore, St. Louis, and Louisville that occurred in this period need to be understood in this context.

Abolition vied with temperance as an incendiary issue lying beneath the surface of political debate, fought out largely in extralegal battles in the 1830s. The political rhetoric of many northern workingmen increasingly featured claims to citizenship as free white men who stressed their distance from slavery as well as from free African Americans. Meanwhile, however, the campaign against slavery intensified. Between 1834 and 1835, the abolitionist organization, the American Anti-Slavery Society, became dramatically more visible. The number of local societies increased, and their constituency of women and free black people defied conventional notions of the exclusion of these groups from political participation. Using new penny postage and steam printing technology, abolitionists increased their distribution of antislavery propaganda, sending out millions of abolitionist tracts, newspapers, children's readers, even medals, emblems, bandannas, and chocolate wrappers. But in local communities, "gentlemen of property and standing"—prominent lawyers, bankers, merchants, doctors, and political leaders of both the Democratic and Whig parties—acted to defend the status quo by mobilizing disruption of antislavery conventions, attacks on abolitionist leaders, and destruction of abolitionist meeting places and printing presses. In Utica in 1835, a Democrat congressman led a crowd that drove the New York Anti-Slavery Society out of town. Abolitionist leader William Lloyd Garrison was nearly lynched by a crowd of respectable Bostonians in 1835, and abolitionist Elijah Lovejoy was killed while trying to defend a printing press from a crowd of prominent citizens in Alton, Illinois, in 1837. In 1834, leading New Yorkers cheered a crowd of butcher boys and day laborers who smashed and burned the home of Lewis Tappan, a prominent and wealthy local supporter of antislavery.

In other incidents, crowds turned on free African-American communities. Here, rioters were often white workingmen who expressed their economic and social grievances through racial violence. In the summer of 1835, in Washington, D.C., an angry crowd of striking ship carpenters searched the homes of free African-Americans for abolitionist literature, destroyed a black-owned restaurant, and burned or stoned other free black businesses, schools, churches, and homes. The mobs of mechanics and artisans who terrorized free African-American communities in Cincinnati, Providence, and New York City in the 1830s and 1840s were not directly competing with blacks for jobs but were fighting for urban turf, especially in neighborhoods that bordered African-American neighborhoods.

Other confrontations too explosive to be calmed through established political channels took place on the streets of antebellum cities. When the Pennsylvania state legislature gave permission in 1839 for a railroad to extend track down the main street of Philadelphia's Kensington section, residents voiced fears that burning coal embers and fast-moving trains would endanger their shops, homes, and children. When petitions to the legislature proved futile and railroad workmen began to tear up the street to build the railroad tracks, residents used the upturned paving stones as weapons to wage war on the proposed railroad. Two years of sporadic street battles and noisy public demonstrations finally resulted in the state legislature's acceding to neighborhood demands and revoking the railroad's right of way. Similarly, the limits of political action and legal recourse were tested in Baltimore in 1835, where citizens rioted when trustees and secret partners of the failed Bank of Maryland used various legal tricks for over a year to avoid settlement of the bank's affairs. The kinds of concerns that drew crowds into the streets could not be redressed through the ballot. The extraordinary pressures of diverse populations, new experience with heightened social and economic inequality, and fierce competition between groups contending for political power left the social and political terrain of antebellum cities deeply scarred and divided.

CITIES AND THE CIVIL WAR

The Civil War, like all wars, had a disruptive effect on American cities. Unlike the Revolution, when cities were relatively united in their support for independence from England, the Civil War evoked widely different agendas from urban dwellers. The issues of slavery and secession stirred local political debates, and the war itself pumped life into outfitting and manufacturing centers, particularly in the North. But the conflict also sparked social and economic conflicts that had been gathering long before the war began.

A characterization of a dichotomy between an urban-industrial North and a rural-plantation South before the war would exaggerate actual conditions. The North was still largely rural and only primitively industrialized in the antebellum years; the economies of northern cities from Boston to Chicago remained guided by commercial functions. The South was neither nonurban nor antiurban. Southern cities such as Louisville, New Orleans, Memphis, Mobile, and Savannah resembled northern counterparts in their commercial functions and social complexity. Southern businesspeople did, however, depend on northern capital and markets. New York City especially influenced southern affairs. By the 1850s, New York merchants bought and shipped much of the South's cotton and tobacco, and they imported many of the goods demanded by southern consumers. Investments from New York bankers helped finance the southern urban economy. In various northern cities, businesspeople valued southern customers and worked to keep them satisfied.

Although southerners expressed resentment over northern merchants' alleged high prices and profits, urban dwellers of both regions generally took conciliatory positions toward each other, even as the debates that would ultimately provoke war heated up. In this regard, they differed considerably from rural dwellers in each region who were more easily drawn to the extreme positions of the sectional conflict. Commenting on political divisions in its region in 1860, the *New Orleans Delta* noted that "three-fourths of the planters are of one party, and an equal proportion of merchants are the opposite." And the *New York Herald* similarly observed, "While merchants in the [southern] cities desire peace and Union, the planters desire protection in the Union, or independence under their own self reliance out of it."

The balloting in the presidential election of 1860 revealed a moderate stance of cities in contrast to the radicalism of rural districts in both South and North. Generally, urban dwellers from both sections favored

Richmond after the Civil War. Southern cities suffered extensive damage from Union troops during the Civil War. Richmond, Virginia, the Confederate capital, was particularly hard hit, along with those cities, such as Atlanta, that were burned by General William T. Sherman's destructive sweep through the South near the end of the war.

either the Democrat party candidate, Senator Stephen A. Douglas of Illinois, or the Constitutional Union party candidate, Senator John Bell of Tennessee, both of whom represented compromise, if not conciliation, in the sectional dispute over the extension of slavery. Meanwhile, southern rural voters strongly backed John C. Breckinridge of Kentucky, who had bolted from the Democratic party to run on a proslavery platform, and northern rural voters favored Abraham Lincoln, the Republican party candidate, who spoke out against slavery and for preservation of the Union. There were some notable exceptions to this pattern. A few northern cities, such as Pittsburgh and Chicago, strong centers of the fledgling Republican party, backed Lincoln. In the South, leaders in Charleston and Savannah backed Breckinridge and secession in hopes of finding in a separate southern confederacy independence from New York and the economic health they had lost to competition from Mobile and New Orleans. But generally, the votes cast by urban dwellers in the election implied a preference for moderation.

The war itself had varying effects on cities, depending on the social and economic climate of a particular place. In some cities, such as Philadelphia, relative unity prevailed. Industries there prospered by providing war matériel, and workers' wage increases enabled them to keep pace with inflation. Philadelphia residents responded relatively calmly to federal government quotas requiring that the city furnish a certain number of recruits for the Union army, and a strong police force deterred potential social upheaval.

Other cities experienced turmoil. In July 1863, a bloody riot erupted in New York City and lasted four days. At the time, officials estimated the death toll at well over 1,000, but recently historians have put the death count at slightly over 100 and have reduced the number of rioters from many thousands to about 3,000. Still, the riot was one of the bloodiest urban uprisings in U.S. history. It had several causes: labor unrest, an unfair draft law, class and ethnic tensions, and growing violence of street gangs. Most of all, it was a race riot, involving attacks on African Americans and wealthy Republicans by white laborers, many of them Irish immigrants, who feared that antislavery Republicans would encourage freed blacks to come North to fill the jobs vacated by men who had been drafted into the Union army.

New York City's rapid economic development in the 1850s had created conflicting socioeconomic interest groups—skilled workers seeking to preserve their independence, unskilled laborers buffeted by fluctuations in the economy and protective of their neighborhoods and jobs, middle classes who wanted to advance their morality of thrift and temperance, and elites who were divided internally between those who wished to control the working classes through persuasion and those who wished to use forceful agencies such as the police. Amid this volatile social complexity, racial animosity and resentment over the draft law, which conscripted low-income workers while enabling wealthier residents to pay three hundred dollars to avoid military service, erupted into violence. The upheaval even had an impact beyond the war, when the city's political machine was pressured to pay special attention to the economic demands posed by wage earners and elites during the war and used bribery and contract kickbacks to satisfy these needs (see Chapter 6).

The crises of the Civil War fell particularly heavily on southern cities. Preparing for and carrying out the military effort speeded southern urbanization. For example, the establishment and expansion of the Confederate government's bureaucracy helped to triple the population of Richmond. But the Union army's blockade of southern ports, the breakdown of the southern transportation system as a result of military activity, and wartime inflation exacerbated patterns of urban hardship, especially food shortages, which in some places reached starvation levels. In 1863, food riots broke out in cities across the South, including Atlanta and Richmond. In the latter city, crowds, mostly composed of women, broke into bakeries in search of bread. By the end of the war, both Atlanta and Richmond lay in smoldering ruins, victims of the Union army's invasions.

The war also had profound effect on western cities, where urban expansion not only affected the war's outcome but also reset commercial patterns after the war. In the 1840s and 1850s, St. Louis and Chicago were among the nation's fastest-growing cities, and merchants from both places eagerly sought to obtain profitable commercial ties with the newly settled regions around and beyond the upper Mississippi River valley. Located on the Mississippi near its junction with the Ohio and Missouri rivers, St. Louis lay at the heart of the great midwestern water network. Steamboats from distant corners of the nation's interior converged at St. Louis, profitably sustaining its economy. To the North, Chicago grew with the aid of railroads, and as a web of tracks extended in all directions outward from Chicago, the trains began cutting into St. Louis's commercial hinterland.

The economic rivalry between St. Louis and Chicago shifted the axes of trade in the West during the close of the antebellum period. While St. Louis businesspeople remained cautious about railroad investment and confident that the north-south flow of trade along the river through their city was a permanent and natural condition, the aggressive railroad construction to and from Chicago pulled the lines of commerce into an east-west orientation. More and more farmers in new western areas found it more convenient to send their grain and livestock to Chicago for processing and shipment eastward to New York for export rather than transporting these goods by water to St. Louis and southward to New Orleans. As early as 1851, New Orleans editor J. D. DeBow complained that northern canals and railroads had "rolled back the mighty tide of the Mississippi and its ten thousand tributary streams until its mouth, practically and commercially, is more at New York and Boston than at New Orleans."

The Civil War not only hastened the rearrangement of trade routes but also turned St. Louis's geographic advantage into a liability. When hostilities broke out, the Union army closed the lower Mississippi River to commercial traffic and imposed strict surveillance over all goods shipped out of St. Louis, even those headed northward. These conditions paralyzed the city's business and blessed commerce in Chicago by further diverting trade to an east-west flow. The results of Chicago's prewar expansion and the war's effects on St. Louis were that the West became the economic as well as the political ally of the North against the South. By the time St. Louis recovered, Chicago had surpassed it to become the principal commercial metropolis of the nation's heartland.

BIBLIOGRAPHY

The walking city is discussed in Samuel P. Hays, "The Changing Political Structure of the City in Industrial America," *Journal of Urban History* 1 (November 1974): 6–38; and Sam Bass Warner, Jr., *The Urban Wilderness: A History of the American City* (1972).

For a discussion of the form of early suburban communities, see Henry Binford, *The First Suburbs: Residential Communities on the Boston Periphery, 1815–1860* (1985); Kenneth T. Jackson, *Crabgrass Frontier: The Suburbanization of the United States* (1985); Sam Bass Warner, Jr., *Streetcar Suburb: The Process of Growth in Boston, 1870–1900* (1962); and Jon Teaford, *City and Suburb: The Political Fragmentation of Metropolitan America, 1850–1970* (1979).

On African Americans in cities before the Civil War, see Ira Berlin and Herbert Gutman, "Natives and Immigrants, Free Men and Slaves: Urban Workingmen in the Antebellum American South," *American Historical Review* 88 (December 1983): 1175–1200; Leonard P. Curry, *The Free Black in Urban America: The Shadow of a Dream* (1986); Leroy Graham, *Baltimore: The Nineteenth-Century Black Capital* (1982); Arnold R. Hirsch and Joseph Logsden, eds., *Creole New Orleans: Race and Americanization* (1992); James Oliver Horton and Lois E. Horton, *In Hope of Liberty: Culture, Community, and Protest among Northern Blacks, 1700–1860* (1997); Suzanne Lebsock, *Free Women of Petersburg: Status and Culture in a Southern Town, 1784–1860* (1984); Gary B. Nash, *Forging Freedom: The Formation of Philadelphia's Black Community, 1720–1840* (1988); and Shane White, *Somewhat More Independent: The End of Slavery in New York City, 1770–1810* (1991). See also Ira Berlin, *Slaves Without Masters: The Free Negro in the Antebellum South* (1974); Claudia Dale Goldin, *Urban Slavery in the American South, 1820–1860: A Quantitative History* (1976); and Richard C. Wade, *Slavery in the Cities: The South, 1820–1860* (1964).

On antebellum immigrants, see Kathleen Neils Conzen, *Immigrant Milwaukee: 1836–1860* (1976); Hasia Diner, *Erin's Daughters in America: Irish Immigrant Women in the Nineteenth Century* (1983); Jay P. Dolan, *The Immigrant Church: New York: Irish and German Catholics, 1815–1865* (1975); David Gerber, *The Making of American Pluralism: Buffalo, New York, 1825–1860* (1989); Oscar Handlin, *Boston's Immigrants: A Study in Acculturation*, rev. ed. (1959); and Earl F. Niehaus, *The Irish in New Orleans, 1800–1860* (1965).

On temperance movements, see Ruth M. Alexander, "We Are Engaged as a Band of Sisters: Class and Domesticity in the Washingtonian Temperance Movement, 1840–1850," *Journal of American History* 75 (December 1988): 763–85; Jed Dannenbaum, *Drink and Disorder: Temperance Reform in Cincinnati from the Washingtonian Revival to the WCTU* (1984); Robert C. Harpel, *Temperance and Prohibition in Massachusetts, 1813–1852* (1982); and Jama Lazarow, *Religion and the Working Class in Antebellum America* (1995).

On riots and vice in Jacksonian cities, see Jeffrey S. Adler, "Streetwalkers, Degraded Outcasts, and Good-for-Nothing Huzzies: Women and the Dangerous Class in Antebellum St. Louis," *Journal of Social History* 25 (Summer 1992), 373–55; Michael Feldberg, *The Turbulent Era: Riot and Disorder in Jacksonian America* (1980); Feldberg, *The Philadelphia Riots of 1844: A Study in Ethnic Conflict* (1975); Timothy J. Gilfoyle, *City of Eros: New York City, Prostitution, and the Commercialization of Sex, 1820–1920* (1992); and Paul Gilje, *The Road to Mobocracy: Popular Disorder in New York City, 1763–1834* (1987).

For works linking the development of egalitarian democracy and racialized white consciousness, see David R. Roediger, *The Wages of Whiteness: Race and Making of the American Working Class* (1991); and Alexander Saxton, *The Rise and Fall of the White Republic: Class Politics and Mass Culture in Nineteenth-Century America* (1990). To explore the popular culture interest in race, see Eric Lott, *Love and Theft: Blackface Minstrelsy and the American Working Class* (1993); and Robert C. Toll, *Blacking Up: The Minstrel Show in Nineteenth-Century America* (1974).

Political and cultural uses of public space are discussed in Susan G. Davis, *Parades and Power: Street Theater in Nineteenth-Century Philadelphia* (1986); David Henkin, *City Reading: Written Words and Public Spaces in Antebellum New York* (1998); Mary Ryan, *Civic Wars: Democracy and Public Life in the American City During the Nineteenth Century* (1997); and David Waldstreicher, *In the Midst of Perpetual Fetes: The Making of American Nationalism, 1776–1820* (1997).

For works on cities and the Civil War, see Iver Bernstein, *The New York City Draft Riots: Their Significance for American Society and Politics in the Age of the Civil War* (1990); J. Matthew Gallman, *Mastering Wartime: A Social History of Philadelphia During the Civil War* (1990); and Ernest A. McKay, *The Civil War in New York City* (1990).

NOTES

1. Henry Binford, *The First Suburbs: Residential Communities on the Boston Periphery, 1815–1860* (Chicago: University of Chicago Press, 1985).

2. Christine Stansell, *City of Women: The Female Laboring Poor in New York City, 1790–1860* (New York: Knopf, 1986), 89.

3. Paul Johnson, *A Shopkeeper's Millenium: Society and Revivals in Rochester, New York, 1815–1837* (New York: Hill and Wang, 1978), 56–57.

CHAPTER

4

Industrialization and the Transformation of Urban Space, 1850–1920

THE GROWTH OF MASS TRANSIT

Pedestrian traffic and animal power characterized movement and production in American cities for two centuries. But by the mid-nineteenth century three forces were breaking apart former urban patterns. The rise and spread of mass transportation, the application of technological and economic innovations to industrial production, and foreign and internal migration refashioned the contour and character of urban America and created the modern industrial city. The three developments are closely interrelated, but for the sake of simplicity, migration and immigration will be discussed in the next chapter. The remainder of this chapter will focus on mass transit and industrialization and their consequences.

According to Richard C. Wade, "No incendiary ever looked so poorly suited to the task of creating such far-reaching change as [the] awkward object moving down Broadway in 1829."[1] This object was an omnibus, a large, horse-drawn coach designed to transport urban riders over fixed routes for set fares. The omnibus combined the functions of two traditional types of public transportation: the hackney, an early version of the taxicab, which carried passengers where they wished; and the stagecoach, which operated over long-distance routes at scheduled times. The idea originated in France and first appeared in the United States in 1827 when Abraham

Brower ran a stagecoach up and down Broadway in downtown Manhattan, picking up and discharging passengers at their request for a fee of one shilling (twelve and a half cents) per ride. The scheme spread quickly as other entrepreneurs adopted it. By 1833, some eight omnibuses operated on the streets of New York, and by the middle of the decade transportation companies had appeared in Boston, Philadelphia, New Orleans, Washington, D.C., and Brooklyn.

An omnibus drawn by two horses normally seated twelve people, though at busy times, several more riders could be packed inside. In winter some operators replaced their wheels with runners for easier conveyance over the snow. Most omnibuses were owned by individuals whose objective was to make as much money as they could. Seldom, if at all, did they consider their operation a public service. Thus they ran their vehicles only on streets that promised the most riders. Almost all stretched their routes between two important centers of activity, usually a wharf, railroad depot, or suburb at one end and a focal point of the business district at the other.

Though there often was keen competition between operators for favorable routes, the rapid proliferation of omnibus companies and vehicles attests to their success. New York City alone granted licenses to 108 omnibuses in 1837, 260 in 1847, and 683 in 1853. One observer claimed that one coach coming from each direction crossed a particular intersection on lower Broadway every fifteen seconds. By midcentury the omnibus had become essential to travel in other cities as well. In busy areas coach traffic clogged thoroughfares and endangered human safety. Congestion and reckless driving provoked local governments to require the relocation of some omnibus routes and to fine drivers who failed to operate their vehicles safely. In spite of increasing regulations, the citizenry constantly complained that drivers intentionally ran down pedestrians and private carriages. Inside a crowded coach the situation was no better than outside. The seats were usually primitive benches, and construction was such that there was never enough ventilation in summer and always too much in winter. Such inconvenience did not discourage people from riding, however. An 1853 New York guidebook advertised that some 120,000 passengers rode the city's omnibuses daily.

In spite of its wide use, omnibus transportation remained a luxury. In the 1840s, 1850s, and 1860s, an ordinary wage earner received little more than a dollar a day and rarely more than two. Fares on most omnibus lines ranged from six to twelve and a half cents per ride. Few laborers could afford twelve to twenty-five cents a day for transportation.

Though a service mainly for the middle and upper classes, omnibuses altered urban life-styles in several important ways. It made wheeled transportation available to more people than did hackneys and carriages, and it carried riders on a reasonably predictable schedule. It facilitated intracity communications in an age when economic specialization was making such communications increasingly necessary. Probably most important, the omnibus created true commuters—enabling the affluent to escape the crowded walking city and live in outlying regions. And, the omnibus's rapid expansion and growing numbers of customers helped city dwellers develop what historian Glen Holt has called a "riding habit," a disposition few had ever had before.[2]

While omnibuses began rumbling down city streets, steam-powered trains had started to travel between cities. Although initially intended to carry freight and passengers over long distances, several early railroads also engaged in short-distance commuter services. By midcentury nearly all trains leaving Boston made stops within fifteen miles of the city, and railroads based in New York and Philadelphia ran several trains daily to and from nearby towns. Over the next decade such service spread into the Midwest. A person living outside the city could now take the train into town and then ride an omnibus, which stopped at the railroad depot, to his or her ultimate destination.

The commuter railroad, even more than the omnibus, was a convenience for the wealthy. A one-way ticket cost fifteen to twenty-five cents, too high for most working people. But, like the omnibus, the commuter railroad opened outlying areas for settlement. In 1854, for example, the Chicago and Milwaukee Railroad (later renamed the Chicago and Northwestern) built a depot in Evanston, Illinois, and helped populate—and popularize—that Chicago suburb. By 1859, forty trains ran daily between Philadelphia and nearby Germantown, and almost all their passengers were commuters.

The New York and Harlem Railroad pioneered the next major development in urban mass transportation when in 1832 it combined technologies of the omnibus and the railroad. By running horse-drawn coaches over rails instead of cobblestones, the company could offer faster, smoother rides and enable the horses to pull larger, heavier cars. Over the next two years the New York and Harlem laid four miles of track in Manhattan and thus began operating the first street, or horse, railway. By 1860, street-railway companies were operating in at least eight other major cities, and there were 142 miles of track in New York and 155 in Philadelphia. The cars held two or three times as many passengers as omnibuses and could travel faster, while utilizing the same number of horses. In addition, because horsecars moved on rails only down the middle of the street, they interfered less with other traffic than did omnibuses.

Horse railways created several social and political consequences. Rails made mass-transit routes completely fixed and predictable. This certainty combined with a new emphasis on the structuring of time, a product of incipient industrialization, to give people more regimented lives: personal travel routines came to be dictated by transit schedules and working hours. And because the equipment and construction of horse railways were so much more expensive than they were for omnibuses, company owners had to be even more concerned with laying track and running cars along profitable routes. Horse railways spread people into outlying areas, but because transit owners built track only where it appeared that settlement would be most dense and because builders located real estate projects near mass-transit lines, outward expansion proceeded unevenly. In St. Louis, for example, mass transit stretched the built-up area far to the northwest, but land to the southwest remained underdeveloped because it lacked transit service. In Boston early street railways extended real estate development in the same directions as omnibus lines; only slowly did vacant districts between existing fingers of settlement become built up.

The years in which streetcars became more affordable as means of urban transportation coincided with the renegotiation of racial boundaries. After the Civil War, streetcars were increasingly vital as a means of getting to and from employment in a city that had exceeded its walking boundaries, and they were symbolically important as a kind of contested public space. In several cities, African Americans campaigned for open access to streetcars. In New Orleans, African Americans rejected the all-black "star" cars the streetcar companies offered them in the 1860s, arguing that exclusion from "white" cars was inconvenient, a reminder of slavery, a public insult, and a mark of racial inferiority. They expressed their opposition by petitioning government officials, by boarding white cars and refusing to leave, and on occasion by stopping white cars and beating up the drivers. They were encouraged in their struggle by news of successful campaigns to integrate streetcars in San Francisco, Mobile, and Philadelphia. The widow of an African-American sergeant in the Union army was successful in her lawsuit to integrate streetcars in New York City in 1864.

When southern cities established Jim Crow laws that formally segregated African Americans at the end of the nineteenth century, protests over streetcar discrimination continued. In 1904, African Americans in Vicksburg, Jackson, and Natchez, Mississippi, launched a boycott of streetcars to protest a new law requiring segregated trolleys. Between 1900 and 1906, African Americans in twenty-five cities from former Confederate states engaged in various direct action campaigns against streetcar segregation. Although these campaigns were only intermittently successful, the demand for access to public transportation would continue to resurface whenever political and social change opened up new potential for success.

As transit companies expanded, the issue of control became more pressing. Early omnibuses had evoked few public regulations. Local governments established little more than licensing taxes, vehicle inspection, and speeding restrictions. But the laying of track and capitalization of horse-railway companies complicated relations between mass-transit companies and public authority. Incorporation of a company required a charter from the state, and construction of track on city streets necessitated permission from the local government. Beginning in the 1850s, such permission was usually obtained in the form of a franchise that enabled a company to operate over a specific route for a limited, though renewable period. Most early franchises granted monopolistic or semimonopolistic privileges, often for terms of fifty to one hundred years. Although contracts generally stipulated maximum fares, usually five cents, the privilege of an exclusive franchise, plus almost certain population growth—and therefore increasing numbers of passengers—assured high profits.

With several street-railway and omnibus companies contesting for such grants, mass transportation inevitably became involved in local politics. Besides mass transit, utilities such as street lighting and water were provided by private companies that also sought franchises. Some local officials were so intent upon securing these services for their community that they paid little heed to the consequences of generous franchises. In their anxiety they gave transit and utilities companies long-term, exclusive contracts that included low tax rates on their property and revenues, no responsibility to repair torn-up streets, and other advantages. Often these favors were obtained by political manipulation and corruption. The granting of public franchises in scores of cities in the latter half of the nineteenth century lured city officials and businessmen into collusions that included bribes, kickbacks, illegal stock transfers, and other influence-buying activities. These unsavory connections between business and politics would become objects of municipal reform in succeeding generations.

Perhaps the most important breakthrough in urban mass transportation occurred in the last quarter of the nineteenth century when innovators applied mechanical power to vehicles, beginning with the cable car. Cleaner and faster than horses, the cable car was introduced in San Francisco by Andrew Hallidie in 1873. Hallidie, a wire manufacturer, had witnessed English miners hauling coal cars along large cables, and he decided to try the idea on San Francisco's steep hills, where horsecars could not operate. His system utilized a continuously moving, underground wire rope driven by a steam engine. Each cable car ran along track and and moved by means of a clamp that extended through a slot in the pavement and attached to the cable. Brakes, similar to those on horsecars, could halt the vehicle after the operator released the grip from the cable. The scheme was so impressive that a company headed by California railroad magnates Leland Stanford, Mark Hopkins, and Collis P. Huntington applied for one of the first franchises.

Although the cable car has remained a historic relic of San Francisco, its widest use occurred in Chicago. Here cable-car lines spread rapidly in the 1880s, particularly to the city's South Side, and by 1894 Chicago had 86 miles of cable track and 1,500 grip and trailer cars. Initial costs of construction and equipment were very high, but cable cars were more economical to operate than horsecars, mainly because horses required higher maintenance costs. Cable cars had their drawbacks, however. A break in the cable halted all traffic, the intricate mechanical equipment suffered frequent break-downs, and operating a car required considerable skill. Nevertheless cable lines existed for varying periods of time in Washington, D.C., Baltimore, Philadel-phia, New York, Providence, Cleveland, St. Louis, Kansas City, Omaha, Den-ver, Oakland, and Seattle.

The cable-car era lasted less than two decades. By the beginning of the twentieth century, electric trolleys had almost completely replaced horse railways and cable cars as the major mode of urban transportation. Since the 1830s, inventors in Europe and America had been experimenting with elec-tricity to power vehicles, but it was not until 1886 that a major break-through occurred that revolutionized urban mass transit. The previous year James Gaboury, a leading promoter of mass transit in the South, had hired Charles J. Van Doeple, a Belgian engineer, to construct an electric railway in Montgomery, Alabama. Service began in the spring of 1886. The vehicles re-sembled those pulled by horses but contained a motor on the front platform. A chain running from the motor to the wheels powered the vehicle, and a cable from an overhead wire to the motor transmitted electrical energy. During the same time a young electrician, Frank Sprague, built a similar sys-tem in Richmond, Virginia. Its vehicles received electricity from a cable at-tached to a wheeled device that ran along the overhead wires. This device was called a troller due to the manner in which it was pulled, and according to John Anderson Miller, a corruption of the word produced "trolley," the term used for electric streetcars.[3] In 1888, Sprague demonstrated that his cars could conquer the steep grades of Richmond and that electrical genera-tors could provide enough power to operate several cars concentrated on a short stretch of track.

During the 1880s and 1890s, nearly every large American city granted franchises to trolley companies. In 1890, when the federal government first surveyed the nation's street railways, it found 5,700 miles of track for vehi-cles operated by animal power, 500 miles of track for cable cars, and 1,260 miles of electrified track. By 1902, the total of electrified track had swelled to 22,000 miles, while that of horse railways had dwindled to 250 miles.

At the turn of the century, companies in some of the largest, most con-gested cities raised part of their track onto stilts, giving vehicles unrestricted right of way and freeing them from the interference of pedestrians and animal-powered vehicles. These were the electric elevated railways—the els—and they became prominent in New York, Chicago, Boston, Philadel-phia, Brooklyn, and Kansas City. Although New York had had a successful steam-powered elevated since the 1870s, the noise, dirt, and danger to traf-fic below made other cities unwilling to risk an el. Thus it appeared in only a few places, even after Frank Sprague designed a mechanism that enabled els to be electrified.

Sprague's device, a master control that operated the motor and control on each car of the train, could be used for railways below, as well as above,

Trolley Cars in Chicago Suburb.   Trolley lines pulled residential outward from the city center to the periphery, giving women and men of the middle class new forms of commuting transportation and, as this photograph of suburban Chicago shows, a means to avoid muddy streets.

ground. The subway originated in London in the 1860s when coal-burning locomotives began pulling mass-transit cars through tunnels beneath the city. Promoters presented the idea to American cities, particularly New York, but fears of smoke and tunnel cave-ins, plus heavy opposition from street-railway companies, thwarted construction. Electrification and the success of the London experiment removed some of the objections, and in Boston Henry M. Whitney, who had consolidated most of the city's transit lines under his ownership, obtained permission to construct a subway one and two-thirds miles in length underneath Tremont Street. In 1897, its first year of operation, the service handled more than fifty million passengers, running as many as four hundred cars in each direction at peak periods and still reducing travel time through the downtown area. This success revived interest in building subways in New York, and in 1904 that city's first subway opened. The extraordinary costs of subway construction limited expansion, however, with the exception of a combined el-subway that appeared in Philadelphia in 1908, no additional underground projects occurred until the 1930s, when one began in Chicago.

Subways and elevateds were the only means of rapid transit that American city dwellers were to have, and in only a very few cities did schemes, which were many, materialize. Mass transportation was almost always considered a private business, not a public utility, so profitability was the chief criterion for construction of any system. At first omnibus and street-railway companies made huge profits from a population anxious to cut down travel time—or at least to travel farther in the same amount of time. There were other beneficiaries too. Land values along streetcar lines soared, and real estate developers scrambled to buy up property on projected routes. The screeching wheels and unnerving vibration of els eventually drove the wealthy classes away, but land adjacent to elevated track remained lucrative for tenement and commercial investment. Technological advances made mass transit more efficient and convenient, but they also raised costs of construction and maintenance. Because elevateds, subways, and street railways required heavy outlays of capital, mass transportation in many cities quickly became the domain of just one or two large-scale operations. As early as the 1880s shrewd businessmen consolidated independent companies under their aegis. Colorful personalities such as Henry M. Whitney of Boston and Charles Tyson Yerkes of Chicago deftly and ruthlessly established city-wide systems and huge personal fortunes.

Systems such as those of Whitney and Yerkes brought several benefits to their riders. The increased scale of operations enabled companies to preserve the five-cent fare, and the constant quest for new riders pushed track into new districts. Equally important, the merger of several lines produced free transfers from one route to another, enabling passengers to travel farther for a single fare. Yet also the combined functions of public service and private profit loaded transit companies with nagging predicaments. The limits of a five-cent fare, whether self-imposed or legislated by government, forced companies to seek higher revenues by increasing their ridership. But if they laid track into newer districts, they risked overextension and fewer riders than anticipated. If they restricted operations to densely settled areas, they faced public charges of inadequate and discriminatory service. In addition, the huge capitalization necessary for construction often invited stock watering and nonlocal investors. The result was that managers, intent on profits rather than service, directed company policies toward producing dividends for anxious stockholders.

The riding public understandably had little sympathy. According to Glen Holt, transit companies too often cited financial problems as an excuse for failure to improve service, and they used their indispensability to force local governments to grant additional privileges, such as renewed franchises or lighter taxes.[4] Moreover, when reformers sought to regulate public transportation, they encountered collusion between transit interests and local politicians, an alliance that included graft and fraud. Indignation at such activities often prompted reformers to seek municipal ownership of mass transit. New York in the early 1890s and Chicago in 1907 established municipal authority to build or buy public transit systems. As scores of companies went bankrupt during and after World War I, public ownership became the only way that many cities could sustain mass transit. But public assumption of transportation responsibilities occurred just when private automobiles began to replace streetcars as the major mode of conveyance. The American hunger for speed and convenience outgrew mass transit, but not until the omnibus and its descendants had made their mark on urban life.

SPATIAL SEGREGATION AND THE BEGINNING OF URBAN SPRAWL

Mass transportation altered the social and economic fabric of the American city in three fundamental ways. It catalyzed physical expansion, it sorted out people and land uses, and it accelerated the inherent instability of urban life. By opening vast areas of unoccupied land for residential expansion, the omnibuses, horsecars, commuter trains, and electric trolleys pulled settled regions outward much more distant from city centers than they were in the premodern era. In 1850, for example, Boston's outer borders lay scarcely two miles from the old business district; by 1900 the radius extended ten miles. Now those who could afford it could live far removed from the old walking city and still commute there for work, shopping, and entertainment. The new accessibility of peripheral land sparked real estate development and urban sprawl. Between 1890 and 1920, for example, real estate developers added 800,000 residential lots to the Chicago region—lots that could have housed five to six million people.

Of course, many lots were never occupied; there was always a surplus of subdivided, but vacant, land around Chicago and other cities. This excess underscores a feature of residential expansion related to the growth of mass transportation: urban sprawl was essentially unplanned. It was carried out by thousands of small investors who paid little heed to coordinated land use or to future land users. Those who purchased and prepared land for residential purposes, particularly land near or outside city borders where transit lines and middle-class inhabitants were anticipated, did so to create demand as much as, if not more than, to respond to it. Chicago is a prime example of this process. The new lots recorded on the city's outskirts reflected the booster spirit that had characterized the city's history, a spirit that represented the transformation of anticipation into reality. This belief led the *Chicago Times* to decree in 1888:

> Chicago, as most people are aware, is situated on an open prairie, skirted on the east by the lake. In the latter direction, therefore, the enterprising real estate developer meets with some difficulty in disposing of water lots, but westward there is an unlimited space, bounded only by the swamps of the Calumet, the Mississippi, the British Provinces, and the imagination. Some day the Queen's dominions will be annexed, and then there will be no limit to Chicago's enterprise.

A profound side effect of mass transit and constant expansion of city limits was heightened spatial specialization. Various urban districts became sharply differentiated. Downtown areas took on more distinct characteristics. Residential communities on the periphery reflected a new suburban lifestyle. Immigrants and working-class laborers settled in industrial districts adjacent to but separate from the city's older districts. New subcommunities generated more varied cultures, and cities became more fragmented and decentralized.

The downtown assumed a characteristic image as it developed to house a variety of mercantile endeavors, financial institutions, and cultural attractions. The new volume and complexities of trade required specialization in wholesale, retail, and credit functions. Retail activities were particularly transformed with the appearance of department stores. In New York, A. T. Stewart's magnificent Marble Palace, opened in 1846, was the prototype of grand downtown department stores to come, such as Macy's, Bloomingdale's, and Lord and Taylor in New York, Wanamaker's in Philadelphia, Marshall Field's and Carson Pirie Scott in Chicago, Jordan Marsh and Filene's in Boston, Rich's in Atlanta, Hutzler's in Baltimore, Bullock's in Los Angeles,

Consumerism in the Modern City. This busy Chicago street corner in the 1890s shows throngs of shoppers outside the famous Marshall Fields department store, an emporium of consumer goods now available to the public.

and I. Magnin in San Francisco. The department store's function was to display the abundance of mass production, its magnificence shining through large plate-glass windows, bestowing its aura on the surrounding sidewalks. Another quality of the emerging downtown was the gendered quality of its organization. Department stores needed to attract wealthy women customers by making downtown safe for the "lady" potentially endangered by the social and sexual mixing that seemed to be integral to downtown life. To counteract the threat, Macy's offered a ladies' lunchroom and ladies' parlor. Big-city hotels also demarcated women's space, offering ladies' parlors and drawing rooms. Libraries began to provide ladies' reading rooms, and even some post offices offered a ladies' window. By contrast, the banks, brokerage firms, and insurance companies, that serviced the concentration of capital, were downtown landmarks that were more clearly demarcated as male, increasingly likely to be housed in new multistory office buildings that shaped the city skyline.

By the mid-nineteenth century, residential sections characterized by single-family cottage homes—modest wooden structures of two to six rooms—were multiplying within growing cities, especially in the Midwest. Heavy demand joined with native inventiveness to produce a housing innovation called "balloon frame," consisting of simple box-frame construction that replaced the elaborate timber-frame style of previous housing and in the process eliminated much of the need for skilled carpentry. The balloon-frame cottage, which used nailed joints instead of complex fitted timers, could be erected speedily, and by around 1880, when factory-produced sashes, doors, and windows began to be produced, urban dwellers had access to the country's first inexpensive, mass housing.

Cottages were an appropriate home style for small, narrow lots in working-class neighborhoods in Chicago, Milwaukee, and other fast-growing cities where land prices were becoming increasingly high. Their low cost enabled many people of modest means to own their own homes. In some instances, a two-story cottage provided living space for two families, one on each floor, but most were occupied by a single family and consisted of a parlor and kitchen on one side and bedrooms on the other. Larger cottages, with more spacious rooms and a central hallway, became a common form of middle-class housing. For both middle and working classes, and especially for migrant and immigrant families, cottages provided a form of private, respectable housing, and became a visible part of the built environment.

As demand for urban real estate encroached on public open space, leaders began to argue for the preservation of green acres explicitly designated as parks. Historical precedents for parks included both formal hunting preserves and ornamental squares, and vernacular traditions of public open space, encompassing town commons and greens used for grazing, militia practice, public assembly, and festivals. In the antebellum period, the antecedents for parks were the rural cemeteries, such as Mount Auburn Cemetery (1831) in Cambridge, Massachusetts, and Laurel Hill Cemetery (1836) in Philadelphia, designed to inculcate morality by exposing the living to the contemplation of a constructed rural landscape.

The most important development in the American urban-park campaign occurred in New York City. According to historians Roy Rosenzweig and Elizabeth Blackmar, a complex political process prompted the state legislature to make unprecedented use of its eminent domain power to take possession of more than eight hundred acres for the construction of Central Park in Manhattan. Here, leading bankers and merchants campaigned for a park to demonstrate the city's claims to grand cosmopolitanism. Uptown landowners saw creation of the park as a means to enhance real estate values by clearing out the vast plot of land, which was the site of "a jumble of small craft shops, large factories, tiny garden patches, two-hundred-acre farms, plank shanties, country estates, and institutional homes for the poor, criminal, and insane."[5] Evicting the area's residents, 90 percent of whom were African Americans and immigrants, and clearing the land would facilitate more specialized reorganization of surrounding land for private homes for well-to-do residents. Public figures, such as landscape architect Andrew Jackson Downing and poet William Cullen Bryant, advocated that the park would have salutary social outcomes. As Downing wrote in 1848, "[Parks] will be better preachers of temperance than temperance societies, better refiners of national manners than dancing schools, and better promoters of general good-feeling than any lectures on the philosophy of happiness." A state-appointed commission sponsored a competition to determine the best design for the park. They awarded the prize to a young landscaper and journalist, Frederick Law Olmsted, destined to become one of the most influential figures in American urban and landscape design.

As superintendent of the Central Park project, Olmsted attempted to bring what he believed to be the physical and social enjoyment of rural beauty to city dwellers. Olmsted thought that quiet contemplation of a park's rural scenery would calm "the rough element of the city" and "divert men from unwholesome, vicious, destructive methods and habits of seeking recreation." Such goals implied gender assumptions about public space. Although the park would specify "retiring rooms for ladies" and "ladies' refreshment houses," the planners also hoped that if women accompanied men to the parks, they might be able to add their domestic influence to the impact of the scenery in calming the rough elements of male assertiveness. This objective involved Olmsted and his associate Calvert Vaux in two kinds of designing. First, they tried to create a pastoral effect by improving upon nature to suit different contemplative tastes. Their design included a series of distinct vistas, some rough in terrain, others more formal. They also built sunken roadways to conceal city traffic and planted trees strategically to screen out abutting buildings. Second, they inserted special facilities to meet different needs for human action. They laid 114 miles of pipe to feed and

Swan Pond in Central Park. New York City's Central Park, opened in 1863, provided city dwellers with space for leisure. The park's Swan Pond enabled park-goers to shut out the bustle of the city and promenade and boat in peaceful repose.

drain ponds for boating and skating, provided trails for riding and hiking, and designed a mall for social gatherings and concerts.

When the park opened for use between 1858 and 1860, its promoters deemed it an instant success, partly because wealthy and middle-class New Yorkers were the primary users of its drives and pathways. By 1879, Olmsted boasted that "no one who has closely observed the conduct of the people who visit Central Park can doubt that it exercises a distinctly harmonizing and refining influence upon the most unfortunate and lawless classes of the city—an influence favorable to courtesy, self-control, and temperance." However, Rosenzweig and Blackmar's research suggests that working-class New Yorkers were infrequent users of the park in the early years, their access restricted by long hours of work, low wages, relatively high costs of public transportation, and the park's distance from the downtown neighborhoods where they lived. In 1870, a new city charter shifted control of the park from a state appointed board of commissioners to politically connected municipal officials. Though maintenance of the park now suffered, over time the new commissioners lessened restrictions, such as prohibitions against walking on the grass and against Sunday activities, thereby facilitating the attraction of a broader cross section of the city's residents into the park. Olmsted remained as superintendent until 1878 and constantly studied the use and misuse of the park in order to preserve his vision of its purpose.

Central Park inspired similar projects throughout urban America, many of them undertaken by Olmsted and Vaux or by their influential contemporary

H. W. S. Cleveland. In eastern cities, where space was at a premium, park planners sometimes tried to exclude what they called the "boisterous fun and rough sports" of the working classes. Their parks were designed for individuals or small groups to quietly contemplate nature, not for a rowdy, collective style of play. The clash between conflicting definitions of a park's purpose— the upper-class definition with its emphasis on culture and refinement, and a lower-class definition emphasizing fun and games—characterized the history of park evolution in many communities. Several cities built multiple parks with varying functions. Boston park design consisted of an "emerald necklace" of interconnected parks and roadways, a multipart green corridor stretching out to the city's suburban reaches. Chicago and Kansas City also built metropolitan park systems; Chicago's ultimately covered almost sixty thousand acres. Some large parks contained ponds, pavilions, and picnic areas, and were located at excursion distance from the built-up parts of their cities, often at the end of a trolley line. Everywhere the establishment of recreational parks signified new specialization of urban space.

Commercial amusements demonstrated a similar pattern of specialization in the second half of the nineteenth century. Amusements in the walking city were part of an informal public life with little segregation by class or sex. In Richmond, Virginia, taverns near the capitol served all classes except blacks, and exhibitions, circuses, and theaters enjoyed the partronage of assorted groups. After 1850, however, this pattern began to change. Tavern patrons became more exclusively male, lower class, and foreign. As the middle and upper classes became preoccupied with ideals of restraint and decorum, "good" women were increasingly insulated from a rowdy public life. Men might still pursue informal pleasures in the semipublic milieu of the saloon or dance hall, but these were clearly separate from the institutions of respectable society. As well, early melodramatic theater had produced a variety of performances housed under one roof; mixed audiences in the 1830s might view drama, circus, opera, and dance on the same bill. In New York's Park Theatre, each class had its own section of seats, but all attended; mechanics in the pit, upper classes and women in the boxes, and prostitutes, lower-class men, and blacks in the gallery. After 1850, theaters were increasingly differentiated by class and function, and the legitimate theater and concert hall, appropriate for women and the genteel upper classes, distinguished themselves from popular performances of minstrelsy, variety, and burlesque. These popular entertainments were often located in the saloon, a lower-class and male preserve that offered liquor, sports talk, boxing, politics, and sometimes dancing and singing.

After 1900, the widespread use of electric power facilitated the association of major city downtowns with the allure and excitement of nightlife. According to historian David Nasaw, "Incandescent lighting transformed the city from a dark and treacherous netherworld into a glittering multicolored wonderland."[6] Streetlights flooded the shadows, making going out safer as well as more exciting. And the lowered mass-transit fares on electric trolleys helped to confirm downtown's specialization as a central shopping and entertainment district, easily accessible from outlying residential areas. Between 1900 and 1930, the expanding number of white-collar workers with more free time and discretionary income were the most avid consumers of an ever increasing number of popular theaters, vaudeville variety, dance halls, ballrooms, cabarets, and, eventually, motion pictures. These entertainments attempted to guarantee their respectability in order to attract a broad range of the public, including women and family audiences. One means of protecting their respectability was use of formal and informal means to exclude people of color. Racist representations of black culture continued to be a staple of popular entertainment, but even after talented black performers became featured attractions, African-American audiences could gain access to commercial amusement only in all-black venues or, occasionally, on separate days or in designated balconies.

The clear delineation of vice zones also stood as a hallmark of the new spatial specialization. In New York City, prostitution became more visible after 1820 as it moved from the docks to be more closely linked with the commercialized leisure in saloons, theaters, dance halls, hotels, and cheap lodging houses. Prostitution accompanied the city's explosive growth in the antebellum years, probably related to the rise in migration, the increasing misery of women as commercialization undermined skilled work, and the growth of transience in general. After 1850, prostitution in New York City was more clearly confined to "red-light" vice districts. In St. Louis, in the 1850s, the police tried to control brothels by raiding them when they became too connected with other criminal activity such as theft, if they became too publicly disruptive, or if they broke rules of social and sexual order by publicly displaying interracial sex. Red-light areas became more clearly demarcated when legal authorities used vagrancy laws to arrest streetwalkers (women working more informally or part-time as prostitutes), enabling madames to consolidate prostitution in brothels. The segregation of well-known red-light districts such as New York's Bowery, San Francisco's Barbary Coast, Chicago's South Side, and New Orleans's French Quarter, containing saloons, dance halls, and sporting houses, separated rough from respectable neighborhoods.

Of course, men of all classes continued to have access to red-light districts, and there were many small entrepreneurs and local political bosses with economic and political interests in resisting the "morals reformers." Existing outside the boundaries of polite society, these areas also constituted a meeting ground where racial borders were often crossed. In many cases they provided the only possible public interracial venue, given that interracial mixing was by definition antithetical to norms of public respectability. Vice districts in New Orleans, Memphis, and Kansas City as well as other cities of the South and Southwest provided the performance spaces for development of blues, jazz, and "hillbilly" music. These popular musical styles reflected the results of many cultural exchanges between white and black migrant musicians, railroad workers, coal miners, and sharecroppers, with additional traces of local and regional Italian, Polish, and Latin musical traditions.

Spatial specialization was considerably more effective in the new suburbs of the late nineteenth century, which institutionalized the division between work and home and recast the residential ideal. Prior to the development of mass transit, only the wealthiest merchants and professionals, who could afford leisurely trips to town in their own horse-drawn carriages or on expensive commuter railroad lines, had been able to buy a "box in the country," as Bostonian Harrison Gray Otis described his house in nearby Watertown. But after 1870, horsecars and trolleys opened up new residential areas that offered the opportunity for people with middle-class occupations and income to escape the central city's unappealing qualities. They could afford homes (if not to build or buy, then to rent) as well as the fares to commute to and from work every day. So they moved into the rings of residential areas that were forming outside the old urban cores.

Here they could fulfill a dream of a pastoral private life in a single-family dwelling, secure in an economically homogeneous community. When suburban builders advertised through brochures and newspapers, they promised an escape from the problems of poor health, social unrest, and immorality associated with urban life. A private dwelling in a safe residential neighborhood would protect especially women and children from the city's dangers. Greenery and fresh air supposedly would invigorate spirits deadened by urban drabness, and porches and yards would facilitate social contacts— while maintaining the boundaries of family privacy—to substitute for the uncontrollable sociability of urban streets. Promoters tried to identify their projects with the more exclusive picturesque retreats for the wealthy, but they were aiming for a different market. Subdivisions of small- or moderate-sized lots, near transit lines, were intended to attract families of salesmen, schoolteachers, clerks, and carpenters.

Suburban builders promised a combination of urban comfort and rustic simplicity, made possible by technological innovation. Availability of land, improvements in building techniques, and mass production of building materials enabled construction of houses with larger and more rooms than in homes of earlier eras. In the eighteenth century only the wealthy could afford houses with three or more bedrooms and separate living and dining areas. By the 1880s, however, such facilities were possible for a much larger segment of the urban population. The specialization of space inside the home, with formal social space, kitchen work space, and private upstairs bedrooms, paralleled the specialization of urban space the suburbs themselves helped to create. Initially, the suburban residential ideal had been promoted by men, with women apparently more reluctant, more interested in the social conveniences of urban living and more confident that they

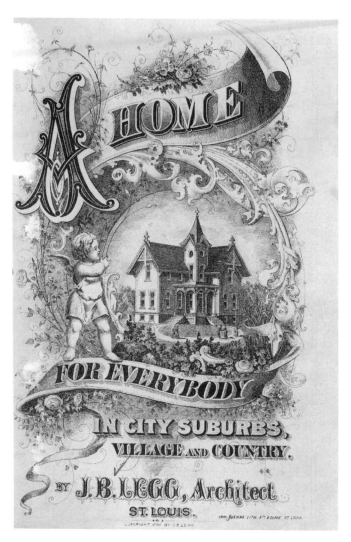

The Suburban Dream. This illustrated title page from an architecture book published in 1876 suggests the pastoral and romantic qualities of the suburban ideal.

could remake the city along the lines of the domestic ideal. By the eve of World War I, both men and women of the native-born middle and upper classes felt less confident of their ability to shape city life in the face of the cultural challenge from immigrant and nonwhite urban residents. And for different reasons, each felt more invested in a companionate ideal of marriage and family life, reflected in the increasing number of suburban houses in which sexually segregated parlors and libraries were replaced by multipurpose living rooms.

The Suburban Reality. Houses with balloon frame construction, shown in process on the far right of the photo, could be built quickly and efficiently, enabling suburban settlements, such as this neighborhood near Chicago, to sprout up almost overnight. Note how close the houses were to each other.

City outskirts became places of detached houses, private yards, and tree-lined streets, but suburban development was not uniform. The Chicago suburb Riverside, designed by Olmsted and Vaux, and Chestnut Hill, near Philadelphia, were luxurious communities inhabited by wealthy suburbanites. Chicago's Ravenswood and Normal Park, Boston's Roxbury and Dorchester, much of New York's Queens, and Milwaukee's Humboldt and Wauwatosa offered inexpensive lots to families of more modest means. Site plans of affluent suburbs, featuring curving paths and English garden landscaping, differed dramatically from the gridiron plots that facilitated subdivision of less expensive suburbs.

Still, within a given development, mass-production techniques in the building industry and an unspoken consensus encouraged builders to erect houses similar in style and size to those that surrounded them. At first, these homes tended to be elaborate versions of the cottages that were being built in the central city for families of modest means. But as the end of the nineteenth century approached, bungalow housing, which resembled cottages in floor plan but contained more amenities such as plumbing, electricity, and central heating, became the common suburban style. Like cottages, bungalows could be cheaply and easily constructed, and they enabled some working-class as well as middle-class families to have access to suburban residence in places such as Hammond, Indiana.

The growth of suburbs had a profound effect on urban centers. As early as 1873, nearly one hundred suburbs with a combined population of more than fifty thousand surrounded Chicago. Los Angeles, a city largely composed of discrete suburban developments, expanded from six thousand in 1870 to nearly one hundred thousand by 1887, adding new residents in sixty new communities spawned outside prior city boundaries. Smaller cities like Richmond, Memphis, and San Francisco were also surrounded by suburbs. Municipalities annexed new suburban areas as a way of holding on to the tax base and spreading the cost of city services. In 1854, Philadelphia's annexation of Philadelphia County allowed the city to expand from 2 to 130 square miles. In 1889, Chicago annexed 133 square miles of suburban territory, including the communities of Hyde Park, Woodlawn, South Chicago, and Pullman. In 1898, New York City grew from 44 to 299 square miles with the consolidation of Manhattan, Brooklyn, Queens, Staten Island, and the Bronx. Early Boston suburbanites were confident enough of their ability to exercise political clout to agree to annexation in exchange for the provision of services, and the annexation of streetcar suburbs Roxbury, West Roxbury, and Dorchester added 20 square miles to the city. But Brookline's refusal to be annexed in 1873 marked the beginning of a trend of suburban insistence on political independence, sparking a more antagonistic relationship between central cities and suburbs.

The new suburban developments changed common perceptions of urban space, particularly the use of streets. Older architectural styles placed housing close to the street, and street space served vital neighborhood and family social uses as routes for pushcart vendors, meeting place for adults, and play space for children. Historian Clay McShane has argued that late nineteenth-century urban residents expressed their commitment to this use of the streets by opposing pavement changes that would facilitate the high-speed

A Secondary Business Center. The intersection of Milwaukee Avenue and Chicago Avenue in Chicago became one of many nodes of retail activity that grew around crossroads of important arteries and streetcar routes.

movement of vehicles.[7] By controlling street paving, residents of older, more densely packed sections could prevent local government from turning their only open social and recreational spaces into transportation arteries whose sole function was to carry people and goods out of the city. By the 1890s, however, these low income groups had lost the battle; the consensus had swung in favor of smooth street paving that used new more easily drained surfaces and that reoriented city streets to high-speed travel. Supported as public works by socialists as well as machine politicians, lobbied for by municipal engineers and public health experts who argued that paved streets would be easier to clean, and demanded by residents in outlying districts whose concern was for fast travel, asphalt and concrete streets literally paved the way for the automobile. A suburban interpretation of street use for high-speed travel rather than as neighborhood social space was powerfully pervasive even before automobile use confirmed this reorientation of urban geography.

Another significant effect of residential sprawl was the decentralization of economic functions. The increased concentration of people living at the city periphery and traveling on mass-transit lines turned outlying transfer points, such as streetcar intersections and elevated railway stations, into natural business centers. The result was a multinuclear development of commercial districts. That is, as consumers moved outward, businesses followed them. Groceries, drugstores, specialty shops, and saloons developed at traffic centers in newly settled regions. There they were joined by chain stores, banks, and theaters that had branched out from the main business district. These secondary business centers quickly became important focuses for neighborhood life.

The same forces that fueled peripheral growth also altered the center of a city. What had once been the entire walking city now became the zone of work, crammed with offices, stores, and warehouses. As middle-class residents departed from inner residential districts, immigrants took their places, doubling and tripling up in old houses or filling tenements after single-family structures had been razed (this turnover is discussed in more detail in Chapter 5). Tenements and row houses encircled factories now outside downtown near rail and water outlets, creating vast and crowded working-class districts, such as the back-of-the-yards neighborhood in Chicago, which housed the meat-packing work force; and the eastern edge of Birmingham, Alabama, where steelworkers' housing clustered around the mills. Frequently, commercial buildings replaced residential structures, creating genuine business districts, such as the Loop in Chicago and lower Manhattan in New York. More than ever before, downtown districts contained an extraordinary concentration of economic and cultural functions. Chicago's Loop was the ultimate central business district. As one official described it in 1910:

> Within an area of less than a square mile there are found the railway terminals and business offices, the big retail stores, the wholesale and jobbing businesses,

the financial center, the main offices of the chief firms of the city, a considerable proportion of the medical and dental professions, the legal profession, the city and county governments, the post office, the courts, the leading social and political clubs, the hotels, theaters, Art Institute, principal libraries, labor headquarters, and a great number of lesser factors of city life.

Skyscrapers dwarfing NYC's older buildings.   The Woolworth Building on the left, completed in 1913 and 792 feet tall, was one of New York City's earliest skyscrapers and, along with other tall buildings helped to define the new downtown. This photograph captures the old and the new, as the skyscrapers dwarf the city's old post office and City Hall in the center.

A Typical City Traffic Jam. This jumble of people, animals, and vehicles of a Philadelphia cobblestone street in 1897 combines nearly all early forms of urban transport pedestrians, horse-drawn wagons and carriages, and an electric trolley car.

Thus, in pushing city borders outward and creating separate social and economic districts, mass transit was simultaneously a centripetal and centrifugal force. On the one hand, most of the city's important economic activities remained centralized within the old core, and commuters streamed inward each day on the trolleys and els to work and to shop. Downtown acquired a clear image: a place where tall buildings of stores and offices formed canyon walls surrounding streets clogged with human and vehicular traffic. On the other hand, the streetcars launched people (or those who could afford it) into the periphery, and the people dragged with them many economic institutions that began small-scale operations in the outskirts. Transportation also enabled new industrial plants, shut out from the crowded core, to build on vacant land outside the city. The growth of industry in these areas pumped life into many suburbs and created new boom towns, such as Cambridge and Somerville near Boston, and Cicero and Elgin near Chicago. Freight and commuter railroads shuttled between these places and the big city nearby. The expansion of transportation spread companies and people into regions far removed from the old walking city, while also drawing new areas into the city's orbit.

But social costs accompanied the outward sprawl and sorting out of people and districts. Nearly half the urban population could not afford the new way of living. Families whose breadwinners earned only a dollar or two a day and whose children worked in mills and sweatshops to help feed their brothers and sisters could dream of escaping their crowded quarters and filthy streets, but for many the goal was elusive. The exodus of the middle class intensified the problems that urban population growth had always bred. Those with resources fled and left the discomforts, disease, and decay to those least endowed to cope with them.

Eventually (often within the span of one generation) some lower-income families could and did escape, usually first to the zone of emergence—the ring between the slums and the areas of new houses—and then to the outer neighborhoods. But in many cases their outward migration destroyed the ideal that suburban development had sought to achieve. When lower-income groups sought homes in neighborhoods beyond the slums, they could afford only modest payments for mortgages or rents. Moreover, most were young families who needed four- or five-room cottages, not the six- or eight-room houses that had been built for larger, more affluent households. Thus some newcomers had to double up in dwellings originally built to house one family. Even a family that could afford to live alone in a house seldom had enough money to maintain the structure at the standards of repair that were originally intended. Those who moved from cramped flats and tenements into the single and divided houses of the outer neighborhoods undoubtedly improved their living conditions. But they also brought with them the consequences of more intensive land use—not just more people per acre, but more traffic, more garbage, more noise. The unplanned nature of outward growth, which had ignored future land uses and architectural needs, quickly began to haunt the modern city. Those who had enough money kept moving farther away, but the specter of decay was always close behind.

Besides physical expansion and land-use differentiation, a third consequence of mass transportation was its effect on population mobility. Trains and trolleys enabled people to travel farther and faster. Speed and punctuality became urban habits. The new urban sprawl reinforced the migratory tendency that had always marked American life. The numbers of people moving from one home to another throughout the nineteenth century and into the twentieth clearly reveal that residential mobility has been one of the most dynamic and pervasive features of American history. There are three kinds of population movement that affect cities: in-migration, out-migration, and intraurban migration. The first two are part of the process to be discussed in the next chapter. The third type, change of residence within the same city, was (and is) one of the most constant characteristics of city life. It affected practically every family, every neighborhood. It made the ideal of a stable community a fantasy, and it became an available means for those who sought a path to higher socioeconomic status.

Today analysts note with wonder that each year one in five Americans changes residence. Yet evidence suggests that decades ago residential mobility was as frequent as—if not more frequent than—it is presently. A study of Omaha, Nebraska, at the end of the nineteenth century and beginning of the twentieth revealed that less than 25 percent of the city's young and middle-aged family heads lived in one place for as long as five years; only 3 percent failed to move in twenty years. Of those who remained in the city for as long as fourteen years, over half had lived in three or more places over that time span; of those who remained for twenty years, one-third had occupied four or more dwellings. Not every group shifted with the same frequency: foreign-born moved less often than native-born, and white-collar workers moved less often than blue-collar.[8] However, differences between groups were slight; more important was the entire population's remarkable impermanence, an impermanence that characterized almost every city.

Certainly some of those who skipped from one home to another within a city never improved their condition; they were fleeing high rents or were seeking new quarters because their old residences were to be torn down. So they moved to a house or tenement down the street or around the corner. Yet it appears that many more people did better themselves by changing residence. In Boston, Atlanta, Omaha, and numerous other cities, thousands of families followed the streetcar lines into newer neighborhoods, where housing was roomier and yards were greener. A common residential pattern involved a series of moves, usually radiating outward from the central city toward the periphery or suburbs. The frequency of movement often frustrated reformers who sought to order society by creating stable communities. "I want to arouse neighborhood interest and neighborhood pride," pleaded

A Product of Geographical Mobility. Budding towns such as Helena, Montana, photographed here in 1870 sprouted all over the West as migrants sought their fortunes in urban as well as rural communities. Here a street of crude shops greets an arriving wagon train of settlers.

housing reformer Jacob Riis in 1901, "to link the neighborhood to one spot that will hold them [sic] long enough to take root and stop them from moving. Something of the kind must be done or we perish." Such a goal disregarded the dynamics of urban life. Quests for more space, more convenience, and better facilities uprooted families and overturned neighborhoods. In the half-century after the Civil War these urges were as strong as before the war. Only now new forces of urban growth and opportunity—outward sprawl, real estate booms, and mass-transit construction—spread people into new and more numerous directions.

THE QUICKENING PACE OF INDUSTRIALIZATION

Streetcars and els represent but one example of the interrelationship between urban growth and technological advance. While mass transit was changing the face, pace, and space of American cities, the larger force of industrialization was increasingly guiding the course of urbanization. If industrialization is defined as the coordinated development of economic specialization, mass mechanized production, mass consumption, and mass distribution of goods and services, it is important to emphasize that this phenomenon did not occur on a large scale in the United States until the last third of the nineteenth century. The construction of railroads and canals, the increased use of waterpower and steam engines, and the introduction of the factory system in the Northeast by 1850 laid the foundation for industrial growth. But the real burst came after the Civil War, when transcontinental transportation and the proliferation of urban sites created a national market for goods and services and when applications of science and new inventions radically altered production, business, employment, and living styles.

During the 1860s and 1870s, four transcontinental railroads pushed westward to the Pacific, triggering urban growth along their routes. Indeed the railroads helped to complete the national urban network, whose framework was laid in the first half of the century. Between 1860 and 1910, the number of cities with populations over 100,000 swelled from 9 to 50; the number with 25,000 to 100,000 grew from 26 to 178; and those with 10,000 to 25,000 increased from 58 to 369. A list of prominent new cities boosted by the railroads contains nearly the entire urban West: Albuquerque, Butte, Cheyenne, Dallas, El Paso, Fort Worth, Kansas City, Los Angeles, Minneapolis, Oklahoma City, Omaha, Portland, Reno, St. Paul, Salt Lake City, San Antonio, San Diego, San Francisco, Santa Fe, Seattle, Spokane, and Tacoma.

These western cities assumed particular regional characteristics. In places like Los Angeles, San Diego, and Santa Barbara the dramatic growth of the Anglo population began a process that shifted the local economy, lowering the status of Chicanos, residentially segregating them in barrios, and reconstituting them as an unskilled and semiskilled working class.

Desert cities like Albuquerque, El Paso, Phoenix, and Tucson stagnated until the coming of the railroad transformed them into focal points for surrounding farms, ranches, and mines. Extension of the railroad to Albuquerque created two towns: a boomtown of saloons and gambling halls that grew up around the railroad and the original part of Albuquerque, which became known as Old Town. The coming of four railroad connections to El Paso dramatically expanded its population from less than one thousand to more than ten thousand from 1880 to 1890. By 1887, El Paso was granting franchises for gas, electricity, and telephone companies, supporting streetcar systems, fire companies, police agencies, fraternal lodges, churches, and schools. Railroads brought a new kind of urban growth to the South as well, fostering growth of a more complex industrial base in cities such as Atlanta and Birmingham, and wider commercial and industrial possibilities in cities such as Memphis and Nashville.

Most of the towns that railroads helped boost to cities had been centers of commerce before any track had been laid. Omaha, for example, was an important outfitting center for settlers crossing the Missouri River, and Seattle served as a lumber port and intermediary transfer point between San Francisco and northwestern Canada. These places became natural locations for terminals once the railroads began construction. However, the iron horse could turn a regional trading post into a boom town, and competition for railroad connections amplified the urban imperialism that was so characteristic of American economic expansion. Omahans subscribed money to build a railroad bridge across the Missouri River; leaders of Kansas City offered railroads generous subsidies and land grants; and citizens of Seattle laid their own stretch of track—all to lure railroads to their front doors. Cities, therefore, built railroads as much as railroads built cities.

Meanwhile, the major components of industrialization were converging—new sources of raw materials and energy, new machines and modes of production, new supplies of labor and skills. During the 1860s, French and American inventors developed methods of producing high-quality steel from iron and carbon, thereby providing the basic staple of industry. Over the next generation technicians harnessed electrical energy to furnish power for operating huge machines or for lighting streets and buildings. At the same time, the refinement of petroleum, the production of high explosives, and the creation of alloys such as aluminum opened new possibilities for the application of physics and chemistry to industrial concerns. The development of successful new products and processes heartened would-be investors to deluge the U.S. Patent Office with ideas, prompted academic institutions to expand programs for training scientists and engineers, and inspired large businesses to establish their own laboratories or to subsidize research in universities. The demands for capital made by expanding industry encouraged widespread adoption of corporate organization with limited stockholder liability for company debts and bureaucratic management of operations. Increased scales of production, use of more mechanically powered devices, and adoption of interchangeable parts as a means of standardizing products paved the way for assembly-line manufacturing and created a huge demand for unskilled workers to run the machines, specialized and supervisory personnel to fix the machines and oversee the workers, and clerical and managerial employees to fill the business bureaucracy. These developments generated a pull factor of employment opportunities that attracted immigrants to America and prompted migration from one place to another inside the country's borders (see Chapter 5).

As places that centralized resources, labor, transportation, and communications, cities became the chief arenas of industrial growth. By the end of the nineteenth century, urban factories were responsible for nine-tenths of America's industrial output. The types of industrial cities responsible for this production were quite varied. Some utilized unskilled immigrant labor and new techniques of production to furnish goods for mass consumption. Thus the shoe industry became prominent in Rochester and Philadelphia, the clothing industry in New York, and textiles in Lawrence, Lowell, and Fall River. Other cities processed products of their agricultural hinterlands: flour in Minneapolis; cottonseed oil in Memphis; meat in Omaha; beer in Milwaukee. Others grew by extracting and utilizing other nearby resources: minerals in Denver; fish and lumber in Portland and Seattle; coal and iron in Cleveland, Pittsburgh, and Birmingham; oil in Dallas, Houston, Los Angeles, and Oklahoma City. And various cities specialized in products for the modern age: Detroit's automobiles, Akron's tires, and Dayton's cash registers. Much of this production came at a cost. Railroads and most factories were

Northern Industry. This photograph depicts silk warping and skein winding to spools at the Royal Weaving Company in Pawtucket, Rhode Island, about 1910. Machines and female operatives extend almost endlessly into the background, showing how an economy of scale permeated the textile industry.

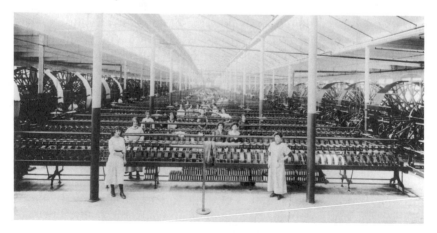

fueled from the burning of soft, bituminous coal that caused choking pollution. Skies over cities such as Pittsburgh and St. Louis were darkened by smoke that turned coated clothing, furniture, and statues with inky dust. By 1900, doctors reported a link between coal smoke and respiratory diseases such as bronchitis and pneumonia. Chicago and a few other cities passed antismoke legislation and hired smoke inspectors, but courts often declared such laws unconstitutional. San Francisco burned natural gas as a fuel, which was cleaner, and New York City tried to ban use of bituminous coal, but most cities could do little, especially since electric plants, as well as factories, burned coal to produce energy.

The relationship between urbanization and industrialization involved several common requisites. First, cities needed the traditional ingredients of economic growth: land, labor, entrepreneurship, transportation, market demand (a population of consumers), and specialization (some principal product or function that could be exported for profit). These elements had existed in American cities in one degree or another since colonial times. But by the late nineteenth century large amounts of available capital and increasing technological innovation appeared and mixed with the old factors to feed the process of industrial change. That is, industrialization proceeded most strongly in those cities where successful commercial activities produced capital for industrial investment. All the western cities and most of the eastern ones were founded on a speculative and commercial base. Their commercial functions—attracting and distributing raw materials, wholesaling and retailing goods and services—remained integral to their industrial development and their economic viability because they created capital for investment and because they generated a multiplier effect of spiraling growth. Only when their economies filled out with a complete range of business and consumer services could one-industry towns reach the stage of maturity that qualified them as genuine regional metropolises—nodes connecting and controlling a large surrounding area. To be sure, in the century's closing decades, manufacturing, rather than trade, provided the major impetus to urban growth, but still no city could exist without its commerce.

The growing importance of industrialization meant that factory owners' decisions to cut wages or lengthen workdays had decisive impact on city dwellers, both inside and outside the factories. Industrial workers often contested the political and social power of new industrialists, especially in smaller and medium-sized industrial cities. Immigrant and native-born poor as well as some craftsmen and artisans held values oppositional to managerial patterns of factory discipline. The concentration of working-class people in industrial districts helped different groups of workers develop sympathy for each other's causes. In 1877, factory workers, wives, and even local merchants aided railroad strikers in stopping traffic in cities along the railroad lines, from Baltimore to Philadelphia to Pittsburgh, eventually all the way to Chicago and St. Louis. Between 1885 and 1889, labor coalitions contended

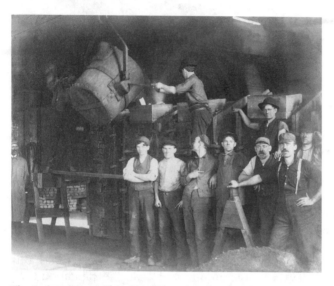

The Industrialized New South. In the closing decades of the nineteenth century, southern cities became the sites for important industrial development. One of the principal industries was steel making, and Birmingham, Alabama, became the southern center for the manufacture of this vital product.

for political power in cities diverse as Jacksonville, Boston, Baltimore, New Bedford, Detroit, Cincinnati, and Akron. They achieved electoral victories in cities like Milwaukee, Richmond, Harrisburg, Lynn, Chicago, and Dubuque. Thus industrialization sharpened divisions between urban residents at the same time that it generated new alliances among them.

Industrialization and labor conditions in southern cities reflected political, social, and economic divisions that arose after Reconstruction. Southern boosters of industrialization envisioned a "New South," with textile factories, steel mills, and tobacco and lumber processing plants that delineated new boundaries for racial separation by employing only white workers. The vision of New South proponents did not fully materialize; the fruits of industrialization flowed disproportionately to northern investors, and low wages barely provided subsistence to southern families dependent on factory work. But tensions related to the expansion of the factory system, the racial segregation of factory employment, and the new economic and social power of industrialists would only increase in years to come.

In summary, urbanization and industrialization were not the same process. Cities had grown long before modern manufacturing was possible, and factories could and did develop outside of urban areas. But by the onset of the Civil War, urban and industrial growth were bound tightly together. The commercial cities and transportation revolution of the early nineteenth century bred the manufacturing cities and industrial revolution of the late nineteenth century. The twin forces of urbanization and industrialization now fed upon each other: each reinforced and modified the course of the other. Together they sparked unprecedented economic change and freed the United States from reliance on European products and capital. Imports and foreign investments still flowed into the country, but increasingly cities and their factories transformed the United States from an agricultural, debtor nation into a manufacturing and financial power.

BIBLIOGRAPHY

Studies of the development and consequences of mass transportation include Charles W. Cheape, *Moving the Masses: Urban Public Transit in New York, Boston, and Philadelphia, 1880–1912* (1980); Clay McShane, *Technology and Reform: Street Railways and the Growth of Milwaukee, 1887–1900* (1974); and Joel Tarr, *Transportation Innovation and Changing Spatial Patterns: Pittsburgh, 1850–1910* (1972). On the expansion of city services related to transportation, see David E. Nye, *Electrifying America: Social Meanings of a New Technology, 1880–1940* (1990); Harold L. Platt, *The Electric City: Energy and the Growth of the Chicago Area, 1880–1930* (1991); Platt, *City Building in the New South: The Growth of Public Services in Houston, Texas, 1830–1910* (1983); Mark H. Rose, *Cities of Light and Heat: Domesticating Gas and Electricity in Urban America* (1995); Roger D. Simon, *The City-Building Process: Housing and Services in New Milwaukee Neighborhoods, 1880–1910* (1978); and John B. Stilgoe, *Metropolitan Corridor: Railroads and the American Scene* (1985).

On housing, see Joseph C. Bigott, *From Cottage to Bungalow: Houses and the Working Class in Metropolitan Chicago, 1869–1929* (2001); David P. Handlin, *The American Home: Architecture and Society, 1815–1915* (1979); and Gwendolyn Wright, *Building the Dream: A Social History of Housing in America* (1983).

On the reorientation of downtown, see Gunther Barth, *City People: The Rise of Modern City Culture in Nineteenth-Century America* (1980), 110–47. On the gendering of downtown space, see Mary P. Ryan, *Women in Public* (1990). On park building and the relationship to this reorientation, see Roy Rosenzweig and Elizabeth Blackmar, *The Park and the People: A History of Central Park* (1992). See also Galen Crantz, *The Politics of Park Design: A History of Urban Parks in America* (1982); and Cynthia Zaitzevsky, *Frederick Law Olmsted and the Boston Park System* (1982). For a discussion of parks as contested space, see Roy Rozenzweig, *Eight Hours for What We Will: Workers and Leisure in an Industrial City, 1880–1920* (1983); and Mona Domosh, *Invented Cities: The Creation of Landscape in Nineteenth-Century New York and Boston* (1996).

Works on the suburbanization process include Michael H. Ebner, *Creating Chicago's North Shore: A Suburban History* (1988); Matthew Edel, Elliot D. Sclar, and Daniel Luria, *Shaker Palaces: Home Ownership and Social Mobility in Boston's Suburbanization* (1984); Robert Fishman, *Bourgeois Utopias: The Rise and Fall of Suburbia* (1987); Kenneth T. Jackson, *Crabgrass Frontier: The Suburbanization of the United States* (1985); Ann Durkin Keating, *Building Chicago: Suburban Developers and the Creation of a Divided Metropolis* (1988); Margaret Marsh, *Suburban Lives* (1990); John Stilgoe, *Borderland: Origins of the American Suburb, 1820–1939* (1988); Jon C. Teaford, *City and Suburb: The Political Fragmentation of Metropolitan America, 1850–1970* (1979); and Sam Bass Warner, Jr., *Streetcar Suburbs: The Process of Growth in Boston, 1870–1900* (1962).

On popular amusements, see Robert C. Allen, *Horrible Prettiness: Burlesque and American Culture* (1991); Howard Chudacoff, *The Age of the Bachelor: Creating an American Subculture* (1999); Francis G. Couvares, *The Remaking of Pittsburgh: Class and Culture in an Industrializing City, 1877–1919* (1984); Perry Duis, *The Saloon: Public Drinking in Chicago and Boston, 1880–1920* (1983); Katrina Hazzard-Gordon, *Lookin': The Rise of Social Dance Formulation in African-American Culture* (1990); David Nasaw, *Going Out: The Rise and Fall of Public*

Amusements (1993); Thomas J. Noel, *The City and the Saloon: Denver, 1858–1916* (1982); Kathy Peiss, *Cheap Amusements: Working Girls and Leisure in Turn-of-the-Century New York* (1986); Madelon Powers, *Faces Along the Bar: Love and Order in the Workingmen's Saloon, 1870–1920* (1998); Steven Riess, *City Games: The Evolution of American Urban Society and the Rise of Sports* (1990); and Robert W. Snyder, *The Voice of the City: Vaudeville and Popular Culture in New York* (1989).

On the emergence of red-light districts, see Timothy J. Gilfoyle, *City of Eros: New York City, Prostitution and the Commercialization of Sex, 1790–1920* (1992); and Thomas C. Mackey, *Red Lights Out: A Legal History of Prostitution, Disorderly Houses, and Vice Districts, 1870–1917* (1987).

On the Southwest, see Philip J. Ethington, *The Public City: The Political Construction of Urban Life in San Francisco, 1850–1900* (1994); Rosales Francisco and Barry J. Kaplan, eds., *Houston: A Twentieth-Century Urban Frontier* (1983); William Issel and Robert W. Cherny, *San Francisco, 1865–1932: Politics, Power, and Urban Development* (1986); and Bradford Luckingham, *The Urban Southwest: A Profile History of Albuquerque, El Paso, Phoenix, and Tucson* (1982).

On industrial cities, see John T. Cumbler, *Working-Class Community in Industrial America: Work, Leisure, and Struggle in Two Industrial Cities, 1860–1930* (1979); Herbert Gutman, *Work, Culture, and Society in Industrializing America: Essays in American Working-Class and Social History* (1976); Steven J. Ross, *Workers on the Edge: Work, Leisure, and Politics in Industrializing Cincinnati* (1985); and Daniel J. Walkowitz, *Worker City, Company Town: Iron and Cotton Worker Protest in Troy and Cohoes, New York, 1855–1884* (1978).

Pertinent works on Chicago include William C. Cronon, *Nature's Metropolis: Chicago and the Great West* (1991); Carl Smith, *Urban Disorder and the Shape of Belief: The Great Chicago Fire, the Haymarket Bomb, and the Model Town at Pullman* (1995); and Karen Sawislak, *Smoldering City: Chicagoans and the Great Fire, 1871–1874* (1995).

On southern industrial cities, see Eric Arneson, *Waterfront Workers of New Orleans: Race, Class, and Politics, 1863–1923* (1991); Don Doyle, *New Men, New Cities, New South: Atlanta, Nashville, Charleston, and Mobile, 1860–1910* (1990); David Goldfield, *Cotton Fields and Skyscrapers: Southern City and Region, 1607–1980* (1982); and Thomas W. Hanchett, *Sorting Out the New South City: Race, Class, and Urban Development in Charlotte, 1875–1975* (1998).

NOTES

1. Richard C. Wade, "Urbanization," in *The Comparative Approach to American History*, ed. C. Van Woodward (New York: Basic Books, 1969), 191.
2. Glen E. Holt, "Changing Perceptions of Urban Pathology: An Essay on the Development of Mass Transit in the United States," in *Cities in American History*, eds. Kenneth T. Jackson and Stanley K. Schultz (New York: Knopf, 1972), 327.
3. John Anderson Miller, *Fares Please! From Horsecars to Streamliners* (New York: Appleton-Century-Crofts, 1941), 62.
4. Holt, op. cit., 335.
5. Roy Rosenzweig and Elizabeth Blackmar, *The Park and the People: A History of Central Park* (New York: Henry Holt, 1992), p. 62.
6. David Nasaw, *Going Out: The Rise and Fall of Public Amusement* (New York: Basic Books, 1993), 6.
7. Clay McShane, "Transforming the Use of Urban Space: A Look at the Revolution in Street Pavements, 1880–1924," *Journal of Urban History* 5 (May 1979): 279–307.
8. Howard P. Chudacoff, *Mobile Americans: Residential and Social Mobility in Omaha, 1880–1920* (New York: Oxford University Press, 1972).

5

Newcomers and the Urban Core, 1850–1920

MIGRATION, OLD AND NEW

Today the American metropolis is a population center separated into inner and outer parts. The division is a legacy from the social, economic, and technological changes that arose from the mid-nineteenth century onward, setting in motion centrifugal waves of settlement. While the middle classes accompanied the trolley lines into the periphery and suburbs, working-class migrants and immigrants squeezed into older districts and transformed the walking city into the urban core. To those on the outside, the residential rings that surrounded business and manufacturing districts embodied the worst of American urban life because of the problems they seemed to breed—poverty, crowding, crime, disease. Yet the inner city served necessary functions for those who lived there. It provided shelter and jobs. It eased newcomers into the urban-industrial world. And it created opportunities for mutual assistance within groups and social contact between groups.

Between 1860 and 1920, the number of people living in American cities of eight thousand or more inhabitants multiplied from 6.2 to 54.3 million (see Table 5–1). Although an excess of births over deaths accounted for some of this population growth, the bulk of the increase consisted of newcomers—people from American rural areas, foreign countries, or other American towns or cities. This migration resulted from both push and pull forces.

TABLE 5–1   Population Composition of Major Cities, 1910

	Total	Foreign-Born White		Native-Born of Foreign or Mixed Percentage		Black	
		Number	Percent	Number	Percent	Number	Percent
New York	4,766,883	1,927,703	40.4	1,820,141	38.2	91,709	1.9
Chicago	2,185,283	781,217	35.7	912,701	41.8	44,103	2.0
Philadelphia	1,549,008	382,578	24.7	496,785	32.1	84,459	5.5
St. Louis	687,029	125,706	18.3	246,946	40.0	43,960	6.4
Boston	670,535	240,722	35.9	257,104	38.3	13,564	2.0
Cleveland	560,663	195,703	34.9	223,908	39.9	8,448	1.5
Baltimore	558,485	77,043	13.8	134,870	24.1	84,749	15.2
Pittsburgh	533,905	140,436	26.3	191,483	35.9	25,623	4.8
Detroit	465,766	156,565	33.6	188,255	40.4	5,741	1.2
Buffalo	423,715	118,444	30.0	183,673	40.4	1,773	0.4
San Francisco	416,912	130,874	31.4	153,781	36.9	1,642	0.4
Milwaukee	373,857	111,456	29.8	182,530	48.8	980	0.3
Cincinnati	363,591	56,792	15.6	132,190	36.4	19,639	5.4
Newark	347,469	110,655	31.8	132,350	38.1	9,475	2.7
New Orleans	339,075	27,686	8.2	74,244	21.9	89,262	26.3
Washington	331,069	24,351	7.4	45,066	13.6	94,446	28.5

Source: 1910 U.S. Census.

A variety of pressures pushed individuals and whole families off their farms in the United States and Mexico and from their villages in Europe and Asia. In the United States and abroad, the impetus for migration derived from declining prices for crops, rising prices for provisions, high taxes and rents, eviction from farmlands, drought, hard winters, and insect plagues. Farm-to-city migration also was directly connected to the development of communications, markets, and capital—themselves signposts of economic change. Roads and railways, canals and steamships, post offices and telegraphs, banks, and travel agencies were the products of forces that were transforming American, Asian, and European countrysides.

Migrants left because there was somewhere else to go. In Europe, men (and some women) who were being displaced by tightening agricultural economies moved to nearby cities seasonally to take jobs in growing industries, then returning to the family farm when needed for planting and harvesting. But eventually, if not sooner, American cities, with their promise of money and more secure employment, beckoned. The country's rapid commercial and industrial expansion in the second half of the nineteenth century created jobs and opportunities that charged cities with magnetism. Moreover, cities themselves generated labor opportunities. Between 1850 and 1920, practically every major city constructed or enlarged its basic facilities, all with the help of unskilled immigrant labor and most with public funds. Streets, bridges, water and gas systems, sewers, schools, and government buildings were built by and for the new city dwellers.

Who were these newcomers? Many came from the American countryside. Although the number of American farms almost tripled between 1860 and 1900, and mechanization boosted productivity, national and worldwide supplies exceeded demand for agricultural products, so prices for staple crops dropped steadily. Meanwhile transportation, storage, and commission fees remained high, and costs of seed, fertilizer, manufactured goods, taxes, and mortgage interest drove many families deep into debt. Farmers were caught in a cycle in which the more they produced, the more prices fell because of oversupply. The future of farming belonged to large producers who could afford expensive machinery, crop specialization, and economies of scale. The impact of mechanization, the consolidation of landholdings, and the rise in farm tenantry pushed thousands of rural people toward the manufacturing cities of the Northeast and Midwest. Rural areas of several states, including New Hampshire, New York, Maryland, Ohio, and Illinois, suffered declines in population in the 1880s.

Movement off farms and into cities changed patterns of life in the countryside, particularly in the Old Northwest—Ohio, Indiana, Illinois, Michigan, and Wisconsin. In the last half of the nineteenth century, urban migration boosted growth not only in Detroit, Cleveland, Chicago, and Milwaukee but also in a host of secondary cities, which shortened distances between the rural markets and the nearest social centers. Dayton, Toledo, Indianapolis, Fort Wayne, Grand Rapids, Kalamazoo, Rockford, La Crosse, Oshkosh, and many more cities brought the amenities of urban life closer to farmer families. After 1896 rural free delivery gave easier access to letters, newspapers, advertisements, and catalogs, and after 1913 parcel post brought deliveries from big-city mail-order department stores such as Sears and Montgomery Ward. Still, rural emigrants streamed cityward; regional centers such as Atlanta, Los Angeles, San Francisco, and Seattle swelled, and upstart places such as Birmingham, Houston, Kansas City, and Albuquerque matched their growth rates. By 1900, 80 percent of Memphis's population came from the adjacent Mississippi or Tennessee countryside.

Trapped in debt and imperiled by the discrimination of Jim Crow laws, southern-born African Americans moved off tenant farms in wider and wider circles to earn supplemental wages. Many first went in search of work to southern cities. Between 1880 and 1900, the African-American population of Memphis tripled and that of Chattanooga grew by 600 percent. Others followed water and rail routes into expanding commercial and industrial centers in the North. Once they reached their destination, they encouraged relatives and friends to join them, supplying them with information about wage rates and access to employment. In 1900, there were thirty-two cities with more than ten thousand African-American inhabitants, and of all who lived in the North and West, 70 percent could be found in urban areas. In 1910, Washington, D.C. had the largest African-American population of any American city. New York was close behind, Philadelphia fifth, and Chicago eighth. By 1920, New York, Philadelphia, and Chicago ranked first, second, and fourth. Newer cities such as Denver, Oklahoma City, and Los Angeles also experienced notable increases in their African-American populations.

Some rural migrants were women who went alone to cities. Women who migrated to Chicago without families or relatives included native-born whites from the Northeast and Chicago's hinterlands; African-Americans who migrated from Kentucky, Tennessee, Missouri, and Deep South states; and some foreigners, especially Scandinavians, Poles, Canadians, and Irish. These women were drawn to cities by the possibilities for paid labor and by new attractions of urban consumer pleasure. They also moved to escape familial dependence or, sometimes, abuse. Although the wages women could earn were not enough to support independent households, they found and created settings in boardinghouses and women's clubs such as the Young Women's Christian Association (YWCA) where they could stretch their earnings and gain companionship and support with which to confront the dangers facing women alone in a strange place.

Immigration to the United States is usually split into two major waves: one beginning in the 1840s, peaking in the 1880s, and ebbing thereafter; and the other beginning in the 1880s, peaking between 1900 and 1910, and declining in the 1920s when federal legislation closed the doors to the unrestricted influx. The first wave consisted of five main groups: Irish Catholics, German Catholics, German Protestants, English Protestants, and Scandinavian Protestants. Also, before the Chinese Exclusion Act took effect in 1882, more than three hundred thousand Chinese entered the United States, settling mostly in the West. The newcomers built chains of migration, across which traveled relatives and friends to join them in the New World.

Many immigrants were too poor to go beyond their port of arrival, or they found ready use for whatever skills they had. Thousands of European immigrants remained in the eastern ports of Boston, New York, Philadelphia, and Baltimore, or they ventured only a short distance to growing secondary cities such as Providence, Paterson, Newark, and Reading. Others plunged into the hinterland. From the 1850s on, Germans, Swedes, and Norwegians took up farming in the Old Northwest and the Plains. English, Welsh, and Scottish immigrants traveled inland to work in coal mines of Pennsylvania, West Virginia, Ohio, and Illinois. Chinese railroad workers settled in towns along rail routes in California, Oregon, Utah, and Texas. A few migrated to the Midwest and the East, establishing nascent Chinatowns in metropolitan centers.

European newcomers also traveled on railroads into growing cities of the West, adding a foreign flavor not only to Great Lakes cities such as Cleveland and Chicago but to Minneapolis, Denver, and Los Angeles. By the

1860s, the Mexican influence, once predominant in western and southwestern cities such as Los Angeles, San Antonio, and Santa Barbara, faded as the large influx of Anglo and European-born migrants began to outnumber the native Mexican population. By 1879, the Irish were the largest foreign-born group in California. Often migrants settled in cities for no other reason than that their funds ran out, and they suffered the pangs of poverty as much in the West as their counterparts did in the East. But western towns offered opportunities for people with skills and resources, and many immigrants achieved nominal success—Scandinavians in construction trades, Germans in brewing, English and Irish in jobbing and retailing—and the commercial elite of western cities often included foreign-born members. Chinese entrepreneurs started cigar, shoe, and garment factories that competed with white-owned firms, and by the 1870s, these establishments were numerous enough to absorb many of the Chinese workers fired from factories as a result of anti-Chinese labor agitation.

These first-wave immigrants brought with them new and different traits that diversified American urban culture: dialects, dress, culinary and drinking habits (wine, ale, and beer now competed with traditional American rum and whiskey), and social institutions. One of the most consequential of the new features was religion. Between 1840 and 1890, 7.5 million Irish and German immigrants arrived in America; of these, 5.5 million were Catholics who transformed the United States from a Protestant to a Protestant-Catholic nation. By 1870, 40 percent of all churchgoers in the country were Catholics. Although American Catholicism lacked internal unity because of its ethnic diversity and the semiautonomous nature of local parishes, external forces imposed a kind of unity upon Catholics by emphasizing their difference from Protestants.

A latent fear of "popery," inherited from England in colonial times, surfaced and joined with growing nativist sentiment in the 1830s, 1840s, and 1850s to intensify criticism, discrimination, and violence. Occasionally, bloody clashes erupted, sparked by tense competition for employment and the threat of immigrant political mobilization. In 1834, a mob burned and sacked an Ursuline convent near Boston. In 1844, Protestants and Irish Catholics fought in Philadelphia, and thirteen were killed. In 1855, twenty died in a battle between Germans and nativists in Louisville. In other cities churches were burned and homes were looted.

Like their predecessors, most immigrants in the second wave were poor and of peasant origins. But they were much more numerous. During the first wave between 1840 and 1880, the average influx per decade numbered about 2.4 million, with a high of 2.8 million in the 1870s. When the second wave began in the 1880s, more than 5.2 million immigrants arrived; 8.8 million came between 1900 and 1910. Although large numbers of English, Irish, Germans, and Scandinavians continued to come, they were outnumbered by four new groups: Catholics from eastern Europe, Catholics

Trauma of Immigration.   The S.S. Patricia was one of many passenger ships that brought thousands of immigrants to American ports in the early 1900s. Arriving in New York City in 1906, this particular voyage brought more than 2,000 passengers who traveled in the horribly cramped under-deck steerage quarters.

from Italy, Jews from Russia and eastern Europe, and Catholics from Canada. Other sources included Greece, Syria, Mexico, and Japan. By 1910, arrivals from Mexico were beginning to outnumber arrivals from Ireland, and thousands of Japanese had moved to the west coast.

Even more so than earlier immigrants, later immigrants settled in cities. The Dillingham Commission of 1907–11, which in large part was responsible for perpetuating artificial and racialized distinctions between "new" immigrants and "old," reported that in 1920, 78.6 percent of those born in eastern and southern Europe lived in urban areas, compared with 68.3 percent of those born in northern Europe and the British Isles. Less skilled than the old immigrants, those arriving from new areas brought only their willingness to work. As one Italian immigrant woman explained, "I never have a lot of money, but I have my hands." These newcomers worked in the sweatshops and factories of larger cities and in the mills, slaughterhouses, construction gangs, and dock crews of most cities outside the South. Although many of these groups concentrated in eastern centers (particularly New York), they spread across the continent quite rapidly. By 1920, Poles were the largest foreign-born group in Detroit and Toledo, Czechs in

Omaha, Italians in Youngstown, and Hungarians in Akron. Indeed immigrants, together with their American-born children, dominated many cities. By 1890, three-fourths of St. Paul's population and four-fifths of Milwaukee's population were either foreign-born or native-born of foreign parents. Most southern cities in this period tended to attract native migrants rather than foreign immigrants. Although Memphis's population had been 37 percent foreign-born in 1860, the foreign-born part of the population dropped to 15 percent by 1900. Still, in Birmingham one out of four white industrial workers was of foreign stock.

The arrival of millions from Italy, Russia, Hungary, Rumania, and what later became Czechoslovakia and Poland completed the formation of America's white religiocultural mosaic. Newly arrived Catholics moved into industrial centers along the northeast coast and in many cities constituted at least half the population. As they traveled westward, they joined the Irish and Germans to raise Catholic proportions in Buffalo, Cleveland, Chicago, and Milwaukee to 40 or 50 percent. As before, the church lacked uniformity, primarily as a result of its very catholicism. Traditionally, geography determined parish boundaries. This system was derived from Europe, where most parishes contained only one nationality. But in American cities Catholics of different ethnic origins lived in close contact with one another, and in several cities Italian, Polish, and French-Canadian Catholics clashed with Irish and German bishops over demands for parish priests of the same nationality as themselves. Some of the newer immigrants struggled to retain familiar ethnic and religious rituals and to make them meaningful in their new environment. Others, including some of the descendants of earlier Catholic immigrants, embraced an Americanized church because they believed that as long as doubts existed about their own and their fellow Catholics' loyalties, Catholicism would never be accepted in America.

A group of Catholics led by Cardinal James Gibbons of Baltimore, Archbishop John Ireland of St. Paul, and Bishop John L. Spalding of Peoria worked to minimize points of conflict, such as language and parochial education, between Catholics and other Americans. Despite their efforts, hostility and distrust continued to confront Catholics, particularly during times when jobs and money were in short supply. Moreover, increasing Catholic immigration after the turn of the century only sharpened the dialogue between retentionists and accommodationists.

Jews also wrestled to retain their identity while adjusting to American urban life. They were probably the most urbanized of all immigrant groups— in 1910, close to 85 percent of Russian Jews lived in cities. New York City alone contained 1.5 million Jews, one of the largest Jewish populations in the world. Unlike their European ancestors, Jews in the United States no longer lived in forced isolation (ghettos); the law gave them religious freedom, civic equality, and political privileges. Children of earlier German Jewish immigrants had brought with them traditions of accommodation to

German culture that included public assimilation and private household ritual practice. Many of them adopted Reform Judaism, a movement originated in the 1840s by German intellectuals who wished to reconcile Jewish religious traditions with secular, middle-class culture. Leaders such as Rabbi Isaac Mayer Wise of Cincinnati reformed the prayer book, anglicized the service, and loosened the rigors of ritual.

At this time, however, disruption of the eastern European land system and brutal pogroms broke apart Jewish communities and sent waves of immigrants to America from Rumania and Russia. These Jews, poverty-stricken and often illiterate, crowded into the cities, where they soon outnumbered their coreligionists whose ancestors had arrived earlier. Newcomers from eastern Europe came from areas where traditional Jewish economic and cultural life had already been disrupted, and they carried with them a range of beliefs from religious orthodoxy to secularized progressive ideologies. Jewish institution building in this period reflected this variety of religious and cultural practices. Like Catholics, Jews faced hostility and distrust, which was expressed more publicly and frequently as their numbers increased.

Despite differences in origin, skills, and religion, most of the foreigners who entered American cities between 1840 and 1920 shared several characteristics. First, they were a long way from home. Their new surroundings confounded their lives with polyglot streets, new forms of labor, and the uncertainties of housing and employment. Their confrontations with many different cultures encouraged immigrants to assume new identities. Parochial and regional loyalties coexisted with newly constructed national self-definitions. People from County Galway and County Cork became Irishmen; those from Mecklenburg and Wurttemberg became Germans; and those from Calabria and Campania became Italians. Regional differences persisted in politics and associations, but all Germans could read the same foreign-language newspapers, and Italians from different villages could take communion together. Moreover, native-born Americans typed immigrants by nationality, usually on the basis of a hierarchical classification, drawing on widely accepted theories of biological and racial inferiority and superiority.

Second, nearly all who came to America during the years of mass immigration were lured by the promise of economic opportunity. The dream of land drove many, but more were attracted by the hope of jobs in the growing cities, for jobs meant money, and money meant security, something rare to the peasant. Many immigrants were advised by prior migrants as to specific employment opportunities in specific cities. For example, from the 1890s to the 1930s, a steady stream of Italians from the Ateleta in the Italian province of Abruzzi, came to the Bloomfield section of Pittsburgh to work in the Equitable Gas Company.

Many immigrants arrived with no intention of remaining. Once settled, however, the vast majority never realized their schemes of working for a while and returning home in affluence. "After six months," said an Italian who arrived in 1907, "I wanted to go back. What held me was that I didn't have enough money to go back." Still there was a substantial current of return migration. Although government statistics concerning this movement were not kept until after 1908, some evidence suggests that many foreigners remigrated, especially during hard times. Some even shuttled back and forth across the Atlantic and the Pacific to take advantage of seasonal wage differences. Return migration became especially feasible from the 1870s on, when steamships rendered ocean passage safer and faster and made more European and Asian ports accessible to America. It has been estimated that for every 100 aliens who entered the United States between 1820 and 1870, 10 to 20 left the country. The figures for 1870 to 1900 and 1900 to 1914 are 24 per 100 and 33 to 40 per 100, respectively.

A third characteristic common to both earlier and later immigrants was their experience of inhabiting, at least initially, the older, inner districts of a city. Especially after 1850 the concentration of urban employment in industrial districts strongly influenced residential choices of immigrants, most of whom sought low-cost housing close to their places of employment. Heavy concentrations of foreigners appeared in New York's Lower East Side, Boston's North End, Chicago's West Side, Los Angeles's East Side barrio, and the inner wards of Pittsburgh, Cincinnati, St. Louis, Buffalo, and San Francisco. In some neighborhoods, immigrant enclaves, composed of Italians from the same province, Japanese from the same island district, or Russian

Black Urban Laborers. After the Civil War, freed slaves migrated to southern cities to reconstitute families and communities. This photograph shows African-American dock workers in the busy harbor of Charleston with the nearby and growing downtown in the background.

Jews from the same *shtetl* dominated. These enclaves also supported ethnic businesses, churches, mutual aid societies, fraternal associations, and newspapers. Ethnic institutions and businesses, as well as friendship and kinship relationships in the crowded neighborhoods, reinforced identification with common origins. Elsewhere, in more mixed neighborhoods, immigrants found themselves learning from neighbors with different experiences and practices.

Although African Americans resembled foreign migrants in their peasant backgrounds, urban destinations, and economic motivations, several factors distinguished them. Because they were generally excluded from factory work and thus could not utilize kin to help them get industrial jobs, blacks in cities had to rely on their own resources if they wanted to improve their circumstances. Education provided what appeared to be the best path to such improvement, and African Americans expressed their self-reliance and hopes for their children through high school-attendance rates. By 1920, in Pennsylvania, 84.5 percent of black males ages fourteen and fifteen were enrolled in school compared to 72 percent of adolescent males of foreign-born parents. Black adolescent girls were more likely to be attending school than immigrant girls. In New York and New Jersey cities, black school attendance rates also exceeded those of immigrant children.

African Americans also had distinctive employment patterns and living arrangements. Whereas males tended to be overrepresented in foreign groups, black women outnumbered black men in most cities. As growing factory and clerical jobs attracted white women away from domestic service, African American women took their places. Thus, at least at this time, there was a greater demand for black female labor than for black male labor in cities. As a result a much larger proportion of black women than white held jobs. In 1900, although about one-fourth of all women in the eleven largest cities of the North were employed, 46.3 percent of African-American women were classified as wage earners. In New York the proportion reached 55 percent. Of all black males and females employed in the cities, two-thirds were engaged in domestic and personal service.

In northern and midwestern cities the institutional structures of racism, which excluded black workers from many avenues of employment, plus competition from immigrant labor concentrated black migrants in menial occupations. In Cleveland, 32 percent of the black labor force were engaged in skilled trades in 1870, but only 11 percent were so employed by 1910. Southern African-American males had a stronger grip on skilled trades than their northern counterparts, owing to the relative absence of immigrant competition. In New Orleans, blacks remained numerous in the building trades well into the twentieth century, and in Savannah they doubled their representation in several trades between 1870 and 1880. But in Boston, New York, Philadelphia, and Chicago, studies by social reformers identified the characteristics so common to African-American urban experience in northern and midwestern cities: higher infant mortality than for whites, higher rents for inferior quarters, and lower wages for the lowest jobs.

Sometimes by choice but usually from exclusion by white property owners, African-American migrants moved into all-black neighborhoods, which in nineteenth-century cities were characteristically scattered in several locations. In Washington, D.C., many migrants moved into houses facing on alleys that formed into self-sufficient neighborhoods interlaced with ties of kinship and friendship. Historian Howard Rabinowitz has argued that in Atlanta, Montgomery, Nashville, Raleigh, and Richmond, patterns of segregation emerged during Reconstruction as a means of protecting black institutions in the face of white racial animosity.[1] African-American community organizations honeycombed the neighborhoods, where churches provided vital services of Sunday schools, adult night schools, welfare, and social activities as well as religious sustenance.

As well, mutual-benefit societies arose within African-American communities to provide a cushion for sickness, death, or unemployment. Many of these societies evolved into small insurance companies, owned by and serving the African-American community. By the early 1870s, Richmond supported more than four hundred such societies. Richmond's Independent Order of St. Luke, begun in 1867 by Mary Prout as a sickness and death beneficial society for women that later admitted men, grew to a membership of one hundred thousand in twenty-eight states under the leadership of Maggie Lena Walker, who in 1903 also established the St. Luke Penny Savings Bank. Between 1870 and 1890 Boston blacks joined veterans' organizations, social clubs, music clubs, literary associations, churches, political clubs, and protest organizations. All-black women's clubs enabled women who had left their original communities to continue to associate with one another for individual and collective advancement. These associations proved to be critical in extending the resources of family and kin to protect migrants from the harsh racial discrimination of urban life and to provide a base from which to protest racial exclusion. For example, in Atlanta in 1881, African-American washerwomen organized a Washing Society, through which they articulated group demands for higher and uniform prices for washing, and eventually mobilized more than three thousand washerwomen to join them in a strike, inspiring similar efforts by hotel waiters and house servants. In this way, women's organizations proclaimed racial uplift as a collective strategy.

The white evacuation of the urban core between 1890 and 1920 prompted the consolidation of African-American enclaves into larger areas of black-only residence. These densely packed residential districts, with housing decaying from years of landlord neglect, became the womb of black urban culture. Within the neighborhoods, black Protestantism assumed its distinctive character. Each city had a few large black congregations of Methodists and Baptists, but numerous informal storefront churches, outgrowths of the southern experience, sprouted everywhere and became fixtures of neighborhood life. In several cities indigenous African-American leaders emerged, ranging from clergymen to small businessmen, educators, lower public officials, and doctors, proposing a variety of strategies for racial uplift in the face of widespread urban poverty and, in some cases, worsening practices of racial discrimination, exclusion, and injustice.

Beyond religious institutions, neighborhood associations, and community leadership, inner-city African-American districts served as critical cultural centers for the African-American community. Countless southern migrants to New York City described the thrill of finding themselves at the heart of a vibrant black culture in Harlem. But in all major cities, juke joints and honky-tonk dives nurtured musical expressions of the black experience. According to historian Tera Hunter, the music and dance that patrons found in these places met needs not satisfied by the church or other institutions because they countered "the debilitating impact of wage labor" and enabled African Americans to "reclaim their bodies from appropriations as instruments of physical toil."[2]

HOUSING AND HEALTH

Cities made no provisions for housing the millions of newcomers who arrived in the decades that followed the Civil War. As native and foreign migrants streamed into the inner regions of northern cities, they pressed private housing markets beyond their capacities. In the late nineteenth century three out of every four city dwellers lived in rented quarters; in working-class districts the proportion was much higher. Population increases and rising land values drove up rents and tempted landlords to squeeze every penny from their tenants. Thus inner-city rents became high, given the amount of services and space a family received for its money. The middle and upper classes could avoid this plight by moving to the outskirts, where costs were lower. Working-class families had to find a different solution. They frequently lacked resources to reduce costs per area. But they could reduce cost per capita by sharing their space—and their rents—with others. Countless families took in lodgers, and often two or three families occupied a single three- or four-room flat.

Builders and property owners developed several types of multiple-family structures, and the extent of crowding varied from city to city. But everywhere the private market fit supply to demand on a makeshift basis, with no assistance and little direction from public authority. Since the eighteenth century, row houses had been the most common form of housing in central Philadelphia, and after the Civil War, builders made them smaller and packed more people into them. The new-style row house was only 16 feet wide, but a two-story building held four to six families. The same pattern appeared in Baltimore. In New England the predominant style was the three-decker—a narrow frame building consisting of three floors and a loft. Pleasant-looking, substantial three-deckers housed one family to a floor and often appeared in middle-class neighborhoods. But because they were an inexpensive type of housing to construct, three-deckers more frequently were located in working-class districts of Boston, Providence, Worcester, and other industrial cities. Here they housed two and three families to a floor and one each in the loft and cellar. In Chicago and St. Louis, two- and three-story wooden buildings, and later brick tenements, squeezed against each other. In Detroit, Milwaukee, Memphis, and Seattle, immigrants crowded into converted warehouses and into single-family dwellings split up for multiple-family occupancy.

New York City was exceptional in its crowding and degenerate housing. But the development of mass housing there is important because it influenced construction patterns in other cities and prompted the first concerted effort for housing reform. The city plan of 1811 set a standard lot size of 25 by 100 feet over most of Manhattan. Thereafter, these measurements rigidly determined the exchange of land and the size of buildings. In the early 1800s one of these lots might have contained a single row house or cottage

Immigrant Neighborhood Life. This photograph of a group of immigrants gathered behind a tenement in the Italian section of Providence, Rhode Island, in 1912, was taken by documentary photographer and reformer Lewis Hine. Hines own caption for the photograph, "Housing Conditions. Rear of Republic Street," was probably intended to protest a back alley strewn with trash, festooned with laundry, and packed with people.

inhabited by one or two families. Because the lot was so narrow, the house may have abutted adjacent buildings, leaving no room for side windows. But there was access to light in front and behind, and enough space to accommodate four to six people. By the middle of the century, population growth, increased demand, and temptation for profit may have encouraged the house's owner to convert it into a four-family unit, with two or three families living on the ground floor and one each in the attic and cellar. Because the house occupied only 40 or 50 feet of the length of the lot, there would have been room to build another house in the back yard. This dwelling could hold four families in a fashion similar to the one in the front. By the 1860s the 25-by-100-foot lot, originally plotted to hold one family, now housed eight. As this process of transformation spread across the city, the growth of inner-city congestion accelerated.

But the crowding had only begun to approach its limits. New York property owners met housing pressure from immigration in the 1860s and 1870s by razing old houses and replacing them with four- and six-story tenements. These buildings were usually 80 feet long and contained four apartments to a floor. Each building could hold a minimum of 16 to 24 families. Usually, however, tenants shared an apartment or sublet rooms, so a single building would often contain nearly 150 people. A 200-by-1,000-foot block filled with these buildings might contain 2,500 families. The population density of such neighborhoods was rarely equaled in even the most crowded European cities. Inside the structures living conditions were abominable. Rooms were miniscule, some barely 8 feet wide. Only those few rooms facing the front or rear had direct light and ventilation. Indoor plumbing was almost nonexistent; privies were located in cellars or along the alleys. There were no kitchens, and a wood-burning stove was the only source of heat.

These conditions evoked the first concerted efforts at housing reform. Not all inner neighborhoods were so squalid, and New Yorkers had been concerned about poor housing well before the mid–nineteenth century. But the crowding, disease, and crime of the inner city that seemed to multiply as immigration increased upset middle-class notions of propriety and clouded visions of a well-ordered, conflict-free society. In 1876, for example, the *New York Times* reported, "Young girls are found sleeping on the floor in rooms where are crowded men, women, youths, and children. Delicacy is never known, purity is lost before its meaning is understood." Beginning in the 1850s, a mixed sense of alarm and optimism spurred reformers to seek ways of controlling the threat posed by these neighborhoods. Their alarm sparked investigations of inner-city life and support for measures that would regulate the practices of builders and landlords. Reformers' optimism convinced them that better conditions would result from heightened public consciousness and enlightened capitalism.

Housing reform originated in New York City. In 1864, the Council of Hygiene of the New York Citizens' Association undertook an investigation of housing and sanitary conditions to alert the public to the dangers of crowd-ing and filth. Directed by Dr. Stephen Smith, a leading figure in the nation's public health movement, the council's investigation produced an indict-ment of slum housing. The report raised enough publicity that when a cholera epidemic threatened in 1866, the state legislature created a Metro-politan Board of Health and gave it authority to regulate housing and sani-tary conditions through provisions of the Tenement House Law of 1867. This law required landlords to furnish minimum facilities for fire escape, ventilation to interior rooms, and indoor plumbing. The provisions were very weak (one privy per twenty inhabitants and one water tap per building satisfied the requirements), and enforcement was difficult. But the law had symbolic value because it imposed public regulation on a landlord's property rights, and it established a precedent for stronger codes in the future.

Meanwhile, other reformers were trying to reconcile housing im-provement with the aims of capitalism. Beginning in the 1850s, the New York Association for Improving the Conditions of the Poor (AICP) advanced the idea of a model tenement, a type of housing in which investors would accept lower profits for the sake of safer, healthier facilities and philan-thropic service to the poor. In 1882, a group of local businessmen invested $300,000 to construct the nation's first model tenement, and in 1901, the Tenement House Committee of the Charity Organization Societies of the City of New York sponsored a model tenement exhibit at the Pan American Exposition in Buffalo. Advocates wanted to limit profits from model tene-ments to five percent, but few investors were willing to commit to such a figure and the idea never came to widespread fruition.

The model-tenement idea was also responsible for the notorious dumbbell tenement that spread across New York after 1879. The dumbbell, named for its shape rather than its designer, was fashioned to meet provi-sions of the Tenement House Law of 1879, which required that every room in new tenements have a window. (The 1867 law required only that every room have access to a window.) An indentation on each side of the building gave a dumbbell its shape. The indentation, when combined with that of an adjacent dumbbell building, created an air shaft 5 feet wide. Each tenement was five or six stories high. Each floor contained fourteen rooms, in two three-room and two four-room apartments, and two water closets in the hallway. Ten of the fourteen rooms had windows bordering the air shafts.

That the dumbbell design was an example of housing reform—it was the winning entry in a contest to determine the best mass-housing plan to fit a 25-by-100-foot lot—dramatizes the tragic state of low-income housing in New York. The largest room in any dumbbell apartment measured only 10 by 11 feet. The narrow air shaft, designed to provide light and air, acted instead as a receptacle for garbage, a breeding place for vermin, and a duct for fire and noise. The dumbbell's major consequence was not comfort, but more crowding. Between 1880 and 1893, the density of New York's tenth ward, the heart of the immigrant-filled Lower East Side, increased from 432 to 702 persons per acre. By 1893, most of the ward's 75,000 inhabitants were packed into 1,200 tenements.

The dumbbell's rapid spread across New York and to other cities had two additional effects. One was the permanent association of the term tenement with working-class housing. Originally the word had applied to any multistory rental building housing more than three families. Now it became a term of discredit. Second, continuing deterioration of inner-city housing conditions ignited new reform crusades, not the least of which was a move to end abuses created by dumbbell tenements. Led by Lawrence Veiller, the nation's first full-time professional housing reformer, new investigations and outcries resulted in passage of the Tenement Housing Law of 1901, which revised existing regulations. The new code replaced the dumbbell's air shaft with a longer, more open court. It also required a separate water closet for each apartment, and it provided stronger fire-protection measures. Significantly, however, these regulations applied only to new buildings. The law included a few weak provisions to improve light, ventilation, plumbing, and fireproofing in existing tenements, but it could not effectively remedy the eighty thousand tenements that covered the five boroughs of New York City.

What happened in New York occurred in other cities. Multistory tenements, dumbbell or otherwise, did not appear to any great extent until the end of the century, but dilapidated shanties and cellar dwellings multiplied everywhere as swelling populations flooded housing markets. The situation was particularly severe in Chicago, where rear tenements blighted the inner city. These were flimsy shacks constructed in the space between an alley and the rear of the building that fronted the street. In southern cities such as New Orleans and Charleston, much of the housing available to African Americans consisted of converted slave quarters that remained in yards and alleyways behind white-owned homes.

The success of Veiller and New York journalists Jacob Riis and Richard W. Gilder in investigating inner-city crowding, in arousing public concern, and in prompting legislation generated similar movements in other cities. Civic organizations sponsored investigations and exhibits, and they lobbied successfully for the establishment of housing commissions and regulatory codes in cities such as Baltimore, St. Louis, Chicago, Kansas City, San Francisco, Philadelphia, New Orleans, Los Angeles, and Washington, D.C.

In some places reformers supported the removal of poor families from high-density central cities to less congested, more inexpensive land on the urban fringe. Assuming that their vision of the appropriate residential setting was inherently superior to what existed in the inner-city, reformers hoped that planned communities could grow up around industries that were locating outside city limits. Some applauded George Pullman's model factory town that opened in 1880 outside of Chicago. Located on Lake Calumet, Pullman, Illinois included rows of brick houses situated on tree-lined streets interspersed with churches, schools, and a hotel, all within walking distance of the sleeping-car factory, and, like the factory, owned by Pullman. However, worker dissatisfaction with Pullman's control over rents and politics as well as jobs provoked a strike in 1894. Sparked by Pullman's cutting wages in the shops while holding rents and prices steady, the strike, although eventually lost, contributed to the town's decline. Thereafter, large corporations generally shied away from building decentralized new towns, and housing remained the prerogative of private real estate speculators. Schemes to build towns on the model of Ebenezer Howard's English "garden cities" fizzled from lack of capital. Such small projects that were begun, such as the Russell Sage Foundation's Forest Hills Garden in Queens, New York, in 1911, could not reduce costs enough to attract working-class inhabitants. Decentralization, like housing codes and model tenements, never met the expectations of its proponents.

Efforts by reformers to improve housing conditions for low-income people often reflected middle-class values that raised opposition among urban dwellers who held different values. Many could not afford rents for rooms in improved buildings, and tighter housing codes only increased their economic pressures by raising costs. Because buildings were cheap to buy and provided high rates of return, some tenement dwellers saw themselves as potential tenement owners. Costly improvements required by reform codes discouraged investors from purchasing tenements and blocked an avenue of economic mobility for some individuals. Moreover, efforts to lessen crowding within buildings by limiting the number of people who could live in one apartment threatened the institution of boarding, one of the most pervasive and important forms of inner-city habitation.

The strongest restraint on housing reform was the privatism that governed prevailing attitudes toward property. Americans have always considered the freedom to purchase, manage, and sell land and buildings as a sacred civil right. Any interference with this right constituted a threat to a cultural inheritance. Thus not only did landlords resist and evade housing codes (which tended to be poorly enforced anyway), but also reformers avoided interference with the housing market. Public agencies could neither demolish dilapidated and dangerous buildings nor construct adequate housing for low-income citizens. Eventually, by expanding their police powers and their privileges of eminent domain, governments began to assume greater responsibilities for providing public housing. As later chapters will suggest, many of these efforts were clumsy, costly, and even detrimental. Nevertheless government initiative was a generally necessary, though late, improvement. During the nineteenth century private builders and speculators had assumed by default the responsibility for housing urban immigrants. Their profit motives dictated maximizing revenues and minimizing expenditures. The results were crowding and misery for that segment of the population least capable of improving its lot. Genuine concern, coupled with fear of disorder, spawned reform crusades. Although these efforts met with at best partial success, they at least established greater public responsibility for the health and safety of all a city's inhabitants.

Although housing reforms improved inner-city neighborhoods only slightly, public health professionals and municipal engineers made cities safer and healthier. Concern over housing and public health had much in common. Countless surveys revealed that death rates in slum areas were two to three times those in other urban districts. Congestion and poorly constructed housing amplified the problems of urban life: ventilation, fire prevention, sewage disposal, water purification, and control of disease. Advances in engineering and medicine reduced dangers in almost all these areas, and legislative bodies were willing to use public police power to prevent threats to public safety. Significantly, these advances occurred most readily in cities because only cities had the resources and institutions that could make their implementation feasible.

Discoveries by European scientists Koch, Lister, and Pasteur convinced most of the Western world that tiny organisms called bacteria caused specific diseases, such as cholera, typhoid, diptheria, and tuberculosis. This evidence strengthened the link between sanitation and public health. Since colonial times sanitarians and boards of health had emphasized the need for personal and public cleanliness. Support for sanitation intensified as inner-city areas spread in the 1860s and 1870s. Efforts of men such as Edwin Snow of Providence and George E. Waring, Jr., of New York, who crusaded for public hygiene and for improved sewer systems, succeeded in reducing mortality rates in American cities. As knowledge of the germ theory became more common in the 1880s and 1890s, state and municipal health boards (many of which had been established in the aftermath of cholera, typhoid, and yellow fever epidemics that had ravaged cities during the nineteenth century) could apply scientific certainty to the enforcement of cleanliness regulations.

Increasing knowledge about the origins of diseases also fostered public activities in the field of preventive medicine. Beginning in the 1890s, a number of cities established diagnostic laboratories to analyze the incidence of certain diseases and to try to avert their spread. Meat and milk inspections were established. Health departments sponsored education programs to alert the public to the causes and prevention of disease. Newspapers, pamphlets, and school programs explained contagion, personal hygiene, and proper diets. Around the turn of the century various clinics and dispensaries were opened. They provided information on baby care and dental hygiene, and they offered assistance to those suffering from tuberculosis, venereal disease, and minor injuries. Although they brought needed services to many neighborhoods, especially in New York, the clinics and dispensaries functioned mainly as charity institutions. Restoring the health of the poor would reduce relief expenditures and might keep the epidemic diseases of poor districts from spreading to well-to-do neighborhoods.

Improvements in fire protection and in other utilities increased public safety. The Great Chicago Fire, which consumed nearly 1,700 acres in 1871, and the huge conflagration that swept Boston in 1872 were evidence that fire remained the principal threat to urban safety. Building codes, architectural designs, and professional firefighting forces began to lessen this danger. New buildings (too expensive for poor people) increasingly included fire walls, fire barriers, and steel-frame, fire-resistant construction. Much of the drive for better fire protection was spearheaded by the National Board of Fire Underwriters, organized in 1866. The NBFU adopted a nationwide policy of drawing local maps, examining ordinances, and inspecting firefighting equipment as determinants of local insurance rates. This practice stirred cities to upgrade their building codes and fire departments. City governments purchased steam engines and pumping machinery and installed electric fire-alarm boxes, as well as expanded their fire-fighting personnel. In addition to fire protection, electricity (especially its use for lighting) and sewer construction promised new benefits in urban health and safety.

By the early twentieth century the United States had achieved the highest standards of mass urban living in the world. But neither the benefits nor the facilities reached all city dwellers evenly. By the 1870s, most municipalities had assumed responsibilities for constructing water and sewerage systems and for ensuring public health. But public responsibility virtually ended at the borders of private property. Landlords and builders who wanted water and sewers had to pay for connections between their buildings and the water main and trunk-line sewer. Owners of newly developed property were assessed for public improvements according to the amount of their land that abutted a street. Those who could afford such facilities, or whose tenants could absorb the costs in their rent, installed modern plumbing, heating, and lighting. But for those forced into high-density, low-quality dwellings, modern amenities were much scarcer. Inner-city landlords, eager to maximize profits, tried to avoid expensive improvements. And governments remained reluctant to enter the sanctum of housing construction and property management. Thus inner-city residents, most of them newcomers and most of them poor, were at the mercy of the housing market. Over time, some of the improvements in sanitation and housing construction trickled down to the poorest neighborhoods. For most people, however, the best solution was to escape, somehow to acquire a home beyond the inner core, or to pack up and take a chance that things would be better elsewhere.

COPING WITH INNER-CITY LIFE

People, crowded into too little space, created the problems in housing, health, and safety outlined above. But on the other hand, urban cores themselves transformed the everyday lives of their inhabitants. The congestion, the streets and neighborhoods, the housing and job markets—all necessitated some measure of coping, at personal, family, and community levels. Some forms of coping were easy and salutary. They were part of the process that enabled American cities to absorb a variety of people and cultures without too much trauma. Other adjustments left scars.

Unlike residents of the periphery or suburbs, whose environments consisted of detached single-family houses, inner-city residents seldom knew privacy. Blocks jammed with tenements, buildings housing a score of families, and apartments inhabited by a dozen people determined personal behavior and development. People had to endure the ways of others who lived close by. Toleration was not always easy; the strain from inadequate space and facilities tried tempers and created opportunities for misunderstandings. Domestic conflict and neighborhood fights were common. The shared spaces that helped generate sociability also created the conditions for violence. Observers from the middle class, accustomed to spacious surroundings and little public scrutiny, rarely understood how the circumstances of neighborhood life bred strong emotions that included shouting and fighting as a part of working-class coping mechanisms.

Crowding also complicated modes of living outside the tenements. In many areas each apartment building covered almost the entire lot on which it was built, leaving no room for recreational activity. Housing reformers urged that at least 35 percent of each residential lot be left open, but they could not undo the past and their guidelines were usually ignored. Unused space for yards and playgrounds remained scarce. Children were forced into the streets, where traffic interrupted their play and threatened their safety, or onto the roofs, where they found privacy but faced more danger. Adults who wished to escape the tenements frequented the neighborhood saloon, a custom that unnerved middle-class reformers. Yet by providing not only liquor but also newspapers, cards, free lunch, drinking water, and public toilets, saloons served inner-city men's needs. In working-class neighborhoods, bars were places where men relaxed, traded information, and organized activities from political campaigns to labor unions to funerals. Many workingmen used a saloon as a place to leave and pick up messages and meet friends, and as a bank, depositing money, cashing checks, or borrowing from the saloon keeper. In immigrant neighborhoods, men sometimes prevailed upon the saloon keeper to send money to their family back home. In spite of the drunkenness and occasional violence that it fostered, the neighborhood saloon proved to be one of the most durable features of the urban environment.

To afford minimal food and shelter, working-class families often pieced together an income from the labor of several family members. Women found that their household work had special economic value; the cost of feeding a family depended on women's skills in bargaining with grocers, fishmongers, and butchers. Women's skills at cajoling landlords could postpone when the rent was due. Women and children also exploited whatever opportunities presented themselves for generating income, such as cooking and cleaning for boarders and lodgers, washing laundry, peddling food, scavenging for fuel for the stove, and helping out in neighborhood shops.

In tenement sweatshops, whole families engaged in the production of clothing, cigars, artificial flowers, or foodstuffs, working long hours for low wages. Where it was available, women and children also did piecework manufacturing at home, finishing pants, linking jewelry chains, shelling nuts, or pulling lace threads for pennies an hour. One investigator found three- and four-year-olds aiding a cigar-making operation by straightening tobacco leaves and putting lids on boxes. Reformers were horrified to find women and children working at home because of the obvious exploitation and because such labor violated their norms of appropriate family life. Earning money while tending ongoing responsibilities for cooking and childcare exhausted homeworkers, but working together as a family at home was part of how working-class families taught their children to survive.

Residence in a single-family house rather than in quarters shared with others has been a deep-rooted American value. Historians who have investigated household patterns of past eras have discovered that this norm seldom occurred in urban cores. The great majority of families (kin groupings) were nuclear in structure, consisting only of the household head, spouse, and children all living in one place. But a large number of inner-city households (including all the people inhabiting one residential unit) contained lodgers and boarders. Evidence has revealed that at any point in time about one-fourth of all urban households contained nonfamily residents. Countless city dwellers boarded or lodged with others for at least a few years during their lives. The most common pattern was for young people, usually unmarried male migrants who had left their parents' household, to board with an older family whose children were grown. Sometimes, however, whole families boarded. Lodgers frequently stayed until they could obtain their own quarters.

Boarding houses and lodging houses also were common in cities. (Boarding houses served meals; lodging houses did not.) Though reformers and moralists decried the loneliness and degenerate behavior that they believed occurred in these settings, boarders and lodgers often made their own communities, including deep and lasting friendships that served as alternatives to family life for people who otherwise lacked family connections in the city. Inner-city neighborhoods containing clusters of boarding and lodging houses provided particular activities and institutions for the urban bachelor subculture that developed at the end of the nineteenth century. (In most cities, over 40 percent of all adult men were unmarried in 1890.) Unmarried men utilized the saloons, pool halls, cafe's, barbershops, clubhouses, and other venues to cultivate a social life for themselves and to indulge in behavior, such as gambling, rowdiness, and sexual freedom, that to some outsiders seemed to threaten social order but for the most part was relatively harmless. Unmarried women also formed peer group associations and, together with their bachelor counterparts, constituted a prime consuming group for new commercial entertainments such as amusement parks, dance halls, popular theater, and movies.

Middle-class and working-class families frequently took in boarders to help pay the rent. Immigrants and African-American migrants lodged newly arrived relatives and fellow villagers until they could establish themselves. Boarders were also often related to people in the households that lodged them, which meant that alleys and tenements that appeared to reformers as crowded horrors of social disorganization were more likely to be complex webs of kinship and friendship. Creating networks of mutual assistance by turning kin into neighbors was one of the ways that migrants shaped their residential space and enhanced their family resources. Housing reformers protested that boarding caused overcrowding and loss of privacy. Yet for those who boarded, the practice was highly useful. Boarding was a transitional stage of coping, providing boarders with a quasi-family environment until they set up their own households, easing migrants' struggle with anonymity in a strange city. And it gave the household flexibility, bringing in extra income to meet its needs.

In addition, approximately 15 or 20 percent of households included extended family members: parents, siblings, aunts, uncles, and cousins who lived as quasi-boarders. Often a family would take in a widow or unmarried sister or brother who would otherwise have had to live alone. Immigrants and migrants often doubled up with family who had preceded them to a city during the months or years while they were in the process of getting settled. Even when relatives did not share the same household, they often lived nearby. Tenements, triple-deckers, and duplexes were particularly well suited to the exchange of services such as shopping, child care, advice, and consolation. Women migrants particularly benefited from this exchange of assistance.

Obligations of kinship, however, were not always welcome or even helpful. Immigrant families often pressured last-born children to stay at home and care for aging parents, a practice that could stifle opportunities for education, marriage, and economic independence. As an aging Italian-American father confessed, "One of our daughters is an old maid [and] causes plenty of troubles. . . . It may be my fault because I always wished her to remain at home and not to marry for she was of great financial help." Tensions also developed when one relative felt that another was not helping out enough. One woman, for example, complained that her brother-in-law "resented the fact that I saved my money in a bank instead of handing it over to him." Nevertheless, kinship, for better or for worse, provided migrant families with an important set of resources for coping with the demands of urban life. Urbanization, industrialization, and migration did not crack the resilience of the family.

Although the city actually reinforced or augmented family life in several ways, the pressures of poverty and inner-city housing still threatened family solidarity. When they entered the urban job market, most migrant men and women took manual employment that was dangerous and physically wearing. Long hours of work in poor lighting and poor ventilation induced mental lapses that had harmful results. The incidence of industrial accidents was high, and there was no compensation to support families whose breadwinners or other members were killed or incapacitated. Moreover, men and women who worked eighty or ninety hours a week without proper rest and nourishment fell easy prey to tuberculosis, pneumonia, and other diseases. The death of the father of a working-class family at the age of thirty or thirty-five was a common occurrence. Widowhood among African-American and immigrant groups was more than a stereotype; it was a tragic reality.

Migration, city life, and poverty also touched children. The need for supplementary family income pressed many children into the labor market at early ages. Others, who did not have jobs but whose parents worked twelve to fourteen hours a day, roamed the streets away from adult supervision. Some of them became truants and petty thieves. Older youths joined gangs that cultivated peer-group solidarity but that also harassed merchants, antagonized police, and frightened neighborhoods with their defiant activities.

In spite of child labor, vagrant boys, and gang activity, by the end of the nineteenth century most inner-city children went to public schools. Yet here too problems arose, especially among immigrant generations. Children of foreign-born (or even of native-born rural) parents straddled two worlds. Although the public schools taught values of independence and self-made opportunity, parents often demanded that their children remain obedient and useful family members who would set aside self-fulfillment for the benefit of the entire family. Those who attended school assimilated more easily into the native middle-class cultural mainstream. Those who held on to their parents' values remained within their ethnic social structure and were generally less upwardly mobile.

Immigrant and African-American mothers had special roles in preserving ethnic and religious cultural traditions, maintaining family responsibilities in caring for kin, and contributing to a family economy. Mothers' rates of labor-force participation varied by race, ethnicity, husband's income, resources for caring for children at home, and urban occupational structure. In all cities black women mostly worked outside their homes as domestics. Italian wives worked with their children as family crews in vineyards and canning factories, and Mexican-American women joined with their families as farm laborers and in food-processing plants. Most unmarried daughters had opportunities for a wider range of jobs (as salesclerks, for example) than did their mothers, who were more constrained by maternal responsibilities and community norms. In some cities at least two-thirds of young women held paying jobs before marriage. Rates of labor-force participation after marriage varied, depending on class, ethnic group, and local economies.

Children lining up for work papers.   Child labor provided an important component of family income in working-class neighborhoods. Here a group of children have lined up to receive work permits in 1911.

Several demographic and social factors bonded family members close to each other. First, parents had more children—often four to six, compared with two or three today. Thus there were more siblings spread along the age continuum, which enabled older children to help raise younger brothers and sisters. Moreover, women's childbearing spans were much longer than they are currently: in the nineteenth century women began to bear children in their early or mid-twenties and often did not have their last child until they were in their late thirties or early forties. Thus childbearing lasted for twelve to fifteen years, compared with five or so more recently. This long span meant that at least some children were growing up and living at home when their parents were in their late fifties and early sixties, and thus parental responsibilities consumed almost all the adult lives of married men and women. When a parent died young, it was not unusual, particularly in an immigrant household, to find a thirty-five or forty-year-old unmarried son or daughter living at home with the widow or widower.

When they entered the inner city, immigrants brought their cultural baggage with them, but also the city altered long-held cultural patterns. Newcomers, particularly those from abroad, sought anchors of familiarity upon arriving in American cities. They often tried to live near friends and relatives. Whole villages were transferred from the Italian or east European countryside to New York, Philadelphia, and Chicago. Chinese migrants from the Panyu district dominated the Chinatown in Hanford, California, and much of the Teng (or Ong) clan from Kaiping settled in Phoenix, Arizona. The perpetuation of institutions, feasts, and pageants helped sustain memories of the homeland. Reformers, concerned with the poverty of immigrants, often overlooked the richness of group life that many immigrants sustained.

This group cohesiveness affected the larger urban society as well as daily life in the inner city. In factories immigrants often segregated themselves in individual departments, perpetuating their separation by recruiting fellow ethnics into similar jobs. In the steel mills of Steelton, Pennsylvania, in 1910, for example, native-born Americans plus Irish and Germans procured the most skilled, highest-paying jobs, while African Americans, Croats, and Serbs clustered in the lowest-paying and most dangerous departments. On the job, wage earners of all types had similar interests in opposing exploitation by owners and managers and in obtaining better wages and safer and more secure working conditions. Off the job, many immigrants withdrew into their own social organizations, neighborhood saloons, and churches. The American Federation of Labor, the main labor organization in the late nineteenth and early twentieth centuries, was not interested in organizing unskilled workers, which in practice meant that black and immigrant male and female laborers lacked representation. There were moments when groups of workers outside mainstream union organization crossed ethnic lines to work together in a strike. Steelworkers in McKees Rocks, Pennsylvania, in 1909; textile workers in Lawrence, Massachusetts, in 1912; copper miners in southeast Arizona in 1915—all built multiethnic coalitions that demanded recognition of workers' prerogatives. But in other circumstances, ethnic loyalties precluded cross-ethnic cooperation, and corporate use of Asian and African-American workers as strikebreakers further weakened protest efforts by unskilled laborers. Ethnic and racial disunity has been a legacy of the American labor movement that has distinguished it from its European counterparts.

Yet no group could live in isolation. Socially complex cities fostered contacts and exchanges between all people. Urban life altered old customs and spawned new institutions. The necessity of learning the English language, new patterns of employment, and the bustle of the streets all undermined attempts to re-create an unchanged Old World culture. Ethnic communities themselves were divided along class lines, between middle-class immigrants, who had arrived with greater educational and financial capital and thus were able to find employment and assume leadership, and working-class immigrants, who possessed fewer financial and educational resources. These divisions prompted debates within the ethnic community over Americanization versus cultural traditions and upward mobility versus labor solidarity.

A Market in an Immigrant Neighborhood. This view of Hester Street on New York Citys Lower East Side around 1900 scans a street lined with immigrant Jewish shops and peddlers. The photograph, showing confusion and clutter, also reveals the vitality of immigrant life in the city, an informality that is often viewed with nostalgia today.

Other forces aided a breakdown of ethnic consciousness. The voluntary nature of churchgoing in America tended to foster democratization and sectarianism among religious groups, diluting dogma and elevating personal rather than group religious experience. Public schools drew urban children together across ethnic boundaries. Commercial amusements such as sports, vaudeville, and movies gave disparate ethnic groups common exposure to American mass culture, although different audiences responded to the experience in ways that in part reflected their various cultural traditions. As they could afford them, immigrants filled their homes with mass-produced cabinets that substituted for traditional dowry chests, and with plush upholstered American furniture and voluminous draping that replaced handcrafted ornamentation. Chosen furnishings were part of immigrants' and their children's attempts to come to terms with American ways, to claim the good life that America promised, to assert that they were at home in urban America.

The ethnic neighborhood was one of the strongest institutions of inner-city life. The urge for familiarity and cultural identity drove many immigrants to seek out their own kind. Very quickly colonies of distinct nationalities formed, most noticeably in cities at or near ports of entry, but also in interior cities from Cleveland to Chicago to Denver. There were Little Italys, Bohemiantowns, Jewish sections, Greek districts, and other places identified with a particular ethnic group. Such communities softened the shock of migration and prepared immigrants for merger into American culture. Yet most of them were neither as stable nor as monolithic as people thought, because high incidences of residential mobility kept them in constant flux. Only rarely did one immigrant group constitute a majority of residents in an area. After living there for a few years, residents of these districts often scattered to other parts of the city or to other cities, so even the most homogeneous neighborhoods experienced rapid turnover. They appeared stable because people moving in were of the same nationality as those moving out. A 1915 survey of Italian and Polish districts in Chicago revealed that nearly half the residents moved each year. And a study of Omaha at the turn of the century has shown that members of all ethnic groups who remained in the city fanned out from the central city into many outlying districts within the span of one generation.

Thus for most immigrant families residence in a particular ethnic community was not a lasting experience. In some cities, principally New York and the congested industrial cities of the Northeast, pockets of single groups did form, and when the immigrants moved, they transferred their whole colony to another district. But generally, residential experiences of immigrants involved dispersion into a number of ethnically mixed neighborhoods. The ethnic community's major importance was commercial and cultural. In most places an area's institutions and enterprises, more than the people who actually lived there, identified it as an ethnic neighborhood. A certain part of town, familiar and accessible to a particular group, became the location of its churches, clubs, bakeries, meat markets, and other establishments. Some members of the group lived nearby, while others lived farther away but could travel there on streetcars or on foot. Thus some of the secondary business centers that formed at the intersection of mass-transit routes became locations of ethnic businesses and social activity. A Bohemiantown, for example, received its name because it was the location of Swoboda's Bakery, Cermak's Drug Store, Cecha's Jewelry, Knezacek's Meats, St. Wenceslaus Church, and the Bohemian Benevolent Association. Such institutions gave a district an ethnic identity even though the surrounding blocks were mixed and in flux.

If the term ghetto is defined as a place of enforced residence from which escape is at best difficult, only nonwhites and Latinos in this era had a true ghetto experience. Wherever Asians and Mexicans immigrated, they encountered discrimination in housing, employment, and public accommodations. Though these groups often preferred to remain separate in Chinatowns and barrios, white Americans made every effort to keep them confined. In the 1880s the city of San Francisco tried to prohibit Chinese laundries from locating in most neighborhoods, and in 1906 its school board tried to isolate Japanese children in special schools. A 1907 federal law prohibited Japanese laborers from entering the country. Restrictive covenants kept blacks, Asians, and Chicanos from buying property in various areas. Chinese were refused service in barber shops, hotels, and restaurants. Chicanos were restricted to certain schools and specially designated sections of theaters.

In southern cities, the practices of public segregation were elaborated at the end of the nineteenth century and beginning of the twentieth, in conjunction with successful campaigns to disenfranchise African-American voters. In northern cities, increasing pressure on limited housing resulting from the Great Migration of the 1910s and 1920s encouraged white realtors to organize protective associations that pledged not to sell homes in white neighborhoods to blacks and occasionally used violent harassment to scare away black families who did move in. Such efforts seldom worked. Whites who lived on the edges of African-American neighborhoods often fled, leaving their homes and apartments to be sold and rented to black occupants.

In almost every city, totally black residential districts expanded while native white and ethnic neighborhoods dissolved. By 1920, ten Chicago census tracts were more than three-fourths black. In Detroit, Cleveland, Los Angeles, and Washington, D.C., two-thirds or more of the African-American population lived in only two or three wards. Within these districts, African Americans nurtured distinct cultural institutions such as churches and organizations that reinforced racial unity. Some individuals and organizations sounded a new note of militance after 1890. Their activities ranged from boycotts against segregated streetcars in the South to support for black entrepreneurship and retaliation against white violence in the North. But the ghettos also bred frustration in the face of stunted opportunities and continuous confrontation with incidents of racial discrimination and exclusion.

PATTERNS OF SOCIAL MOBILITY

At the end of the nineteenth century, beliefs remained strong that there was an open road from the bottom of society to the top, or at least to the middle. The expanding urban-industrial economy spun off new jobs, new markets, new areas for investment. Although hard times punctured the booms with unprecedented frequency—there were serious, though temporary, economic declines in each of the four decades preceding World War I—the euphoria of expansion soothed harsh memories.

Yet dark clouds persisted. By the late nineteenth century the spread of slum decay, the power and impersonality of factories, and the ever-widening gulf between rich and poor withered the dreams of many. In addition, the social complexity, churning neighborhoods, and competition for space and jobs prompted fears that immigrants were displacing native workers, depressing wage rates, blighting residential districts, subverting traditional morality, and threatening political order. Newspapers and pseudo-scientific theories reinforced stereotypes of Italians as swarthy and stupid, Irish as lazy and drunkardly, Jews as greedy and cunning. After the turn of the century, lawyer and naturalist Madison Grant warned in *The Passing of the Great Race*, that among the new immigrants were

> a large and increasing number of the weak, the broken, and the mentally crippled of all races drawn from the lowest stratum of the Mediterranean basin of the Balkans, together with the hordes of the wretched, submerged populations of the Polish ghettos. Our jails, insane asylums, and almshouses are filled with this human flotsam, and the whole tone of American life, social, moral, and political, has been lowered and vulgarized by them.

These beliefs plus activities of nativist organizations, such as the American Protective Association and the American Patriotic League, impeded immigrants' (particularly Catholics') chances for betterment.

Basically there were three ways a person could get ahead: occupational advancement (and the higher income that accompanied it), property acquisition (and the potential for greater wealth it represented), and migration to an area of better conditions and greater opportunity. These options were open chiefly to white men. Although many women were employed, owned property, and migrated, their social standing was usually defined by the men in their lives—husbands, fathers, or other kin. Many women improved their economic status by marrying men with wealth or potential, but other avenues were mostly closed. Men and women who were African-American, American Indian, Hispanic-American, or Asian-American had even fewer opportunities. Disadvantaged by institutional racism, these groups were expected to accept their inherited station.

To a large number of people, however, urban and industrial expansion of the late nineteenth century offered broad opportunities for occupational mobility. Manifold businesses were needed to supply goods and services to burgeoning urban populations. As corporations grew larger and centralized their operations, they required more managerial personnel. Although capital for a large business was hard to obtain, a person could open a saloon or small store for only two hundred to three hundred dollars. Knowledge of accounting could qualify one for white-collar jobs that sometimes paid better

Commerce Comes to a Residential Street. A peddler displays his household goods for house-wives inspection and children's curiosity in Somerville, Massachusetts, near Boston in 1905.

and were more secure than manual labor. Thus nonmanual work and the higher social status that tended to accompany it were possible.

Such advancement occurred often. To be sure, only a few trod the rags-to-riches route that men like Andrew Carnegie and Henry Ford traveled. Studies of the era's wealthiest businessmen have shown that the vast majority started their careers with distinct advantages: American birth, Protestant religion, better-than-average education, and relatively affluent parents. Yet considerable movement occurred along the path from rags to moderate success as men climbed from manual to nonmanual jobs or saw their sons do so.

Rates of occupational mobility in late nineteenth- and early twentieth-century American cities were slow but steady. To be sure, mechanization and new products pushed some callings into obsolescence, but expansion in other areas more than compensated for the contraction. In new, fast-growing cities such as Atlanta, Los Angeles, and Omaha, approximately one in five manual workers rose to white-collar or owner's positions within ten years—provided they stayed in the city that long. In older northeastern cities like Boston and Newburyport, upward mobility averaged closer to one in six in ten years. Some people slipped from a higher to a lower rung of the occupational ladder, but rates of upward movement almost always doubled downward rates. Immigrants generally experienced lower rates of upward mobility and higher rates of downward mobility than natives did. Still, regardless of birthplace, the chances for a white male to rise occupationally over his career or to have a higher-status job than his father had were relatively good.

It must be remembered, however, that what constitutes a better job depends on culture and an individual's definition of improvement. Many an immigrant artisan, such as a German carpenter or Italian shoemaker, would have considered an office job demeaning and unproductive. People with traditions of pride in manual labor often encouraged their children to adopt their same trade. As one Italian tailor explained, "I learned the tailoring business in the old country. Over here, in America, I never have trouble finding a job because I know my business from the other side[Italy]. . . . I want that my oldest boy learn my trade because I tell him that you could always make at least enough for the family."

Moreover, business ownership entailed risks. Rates of failure were high among shopkeepers, saloon owners, and the like because business could be uncertain. Thus many manual workers sought security rather than mobility, preferring a steady job to the risks of ownership. A Sicilian who lived in Bridgeport, Connecticut, observed that "the people that come here they afraid to get in business because they don't know how that business goes. In Italy these people don't know much about these things because most of them work on farms or in [their] trade."

In addition to or instead of advancing occupationally, a person could achieve social mobility by acquiring property. But property was not easy to acquire in turn-of-the-century America. Banks and savings institutions were far stricter in their lending practices than they would become after the 1930s, when the federal government began to insure real estate financing. Mortgage loans carried high interest rates and short repayment periods. Nevertheless a general rise in wage rates enabled many families to build savings accounts, which could be used as down payments on property. In northeastern cities, small building and loan associations financed home ownership for working-class families. Moreover, the simplified process for constructing cottages (see Chapter 4) enabled many blue-collar families to build their own homes. Among working-class families who stayed in Newburyport for as long as ten years, a third to a half managed to accumulate some property; two-thirds did so within twenty years. In 1900, 36.3 percent of all urban families owned their homes.

Finally, each year millions of families tried to improve their living conditions by packing up and moving elsewhere. As early as 1847, a foreign visitor, amazed by American transiency, wrote, "If God were to suddenly call the world to judgement He would surprise two-thirds of the American population on the road like ants." The urge to move affected every region, every

TABLE 5–2   Percentage of Residents at Beginning of Decade Who Had Left by
End of Decade

Decade	City	Percentage Who Had Left
1870–80	Atlanta	56
	Poughkeepsie, N.Y.	50
	San Francisco	52
1880–90	Boston	36
	Mobile	62
	Omaha	60
	San Francisco	50
1900–10	Omaha	59
1910–20	Boston	59
	Norristown, Pa.	41

Source: Derived from Table 9.1 in Stephan Thernstrom, *The Other Bostonians: Poverty and Progress in the American Metropolis, 1880–1970* (Cambridge, Mass.: Harvard University Press, 1973), pp. 222–23.

city. From Boston to San Francisco, from Minneapolis to San Antonio, no more than half the families residing in a city at any one time could be found there ten years later (see Table 5–2).

Some evidence suggests that many people who left one place for another, particularly unskilled workers, did not improve their status. They probably moved in response to layoffs and unemployment, exchanging one low-paying job for another. Others, however, did find greener pastures. Studies of turn-of-the-century Boston, Omaha, Atlanta, and other cities reveal that most men who rose occupationally had migrated from somewhere else. Thus although cities frustrated the hopes of some, they offered opportunities to others.

In addition to population movement between cities, extraordinary numbers of people moved from one residence to another within the same city. In American communities today one in every five families moves in a given year. A hundred years ago the proportion was closer to one in four, or even one in three. In Omaha between 1880 and 1920, for example, nearly 60 percent of the families who remained in the city for as long as fourteen years had lived at three or more addresses during that span of time. Population turnover affected almost every neighborhood, every white ethnic and occupational group.

Social and geographical mobility did not eliminate poverty. Economic freedom and mobility produced greater distinctions between rich and poor, rather than more equality. Although few members of the middle class fell into the lower class, downward mobility did occur within the lower ranks, with somber results. Unemployment frequently ran high in industrial cities, and a breadwinner's loss of job or physical incapacitation could plunge a family into destitution. Additionally, myriad people entered urban society at the lowest levels and never rose. Thus absolute numbers of urban poor constantly expanded in spite of the opportunities that the urban economy promised.

As cases of dependency multiplied, public attitudes toward the poor hardened. Economy-minded officials and their middle-class supporters began to attack forms of outdoor relief. Believing direct grants of money and provisions encouraged pauperism, several city governments abolished outdoor relief by 1900, and others made such grants only in return for work. Poverty relief increasingly utilized institutions—poorhouses, almshouses, juvenile homes, and special homes for the blind, deaf, mentally ill, and physically handicapped. The trend was for states to assume management of these institutions, but efforts by state boards to change the poor into productive citizens usually fizzled. Increasing destitution exacerbated trends that had developed before the Civil War. The public was more anxious to remove "undesirables" from society than it was to help rehabilitate such people.

Reflecting the trend toward bureaucratic administration of all forms of organized activity at the end of the nineteenth century, private social welfare organizations emphasized coordinated, systematic efforts to relieve poverty. By the 1890s, many major cities contained a Charity Organization Society (COS) that organized communications among local charities, established agencies to find jobs for the unemployed, and sent agents to ascertain that every dependent was truly needy. These activities reflected the long-standing moralistic belief that individual weaknesses, such as drunkenness and laziness, caused poverty. Yet the investigations and close supervision of the poor stressed by the COS induced the conclusion that low incomes, low-quality housing, and inadequate sanitation, rather than individual failure, were responsible for dependence. The investigations led welfare agencies to support reforms to relieve the environmental problems afflicting the poor. These efforts slightly improved slum and factory conditions, but the public resisted large-scale change. The downwardly mobile and those immobilized at the bottom still had to fend for themselves.

The urban cores of industrial America were unusually volatile politically and socially in this time period. In the fifty years after the Civil War, urban areas suffered from increasing crime and civil discontent. Rising tensions between labor and capital generated violence in several cities in the 1870s and 1880s. More than fifty people were killed in Cincinnati in 1884 as the result of a three-day riot that burst out after an attempted lynching. New efforts to mobilize political support for immigration exclusion and racial disenfranchisement provided the context for an anti-Italian riot in New Orleans in 1891 and race riots in Wilmington in 1898, Atlanta in 1906, and Springfield, Illinois, in 1908, and flare-ups against Mexican immigrants in southwestern and Pacific Coast cities. As well, attacks on Chinese laborers united labor activists, small entrepreneurs and farmers, and opportunistic politicians in a full-fledged anti-Chinese movement, resulting in Chinese exclusion legislation and "anticoolie" associations that formed in various western cities. In 1871, a riot in Los Angeles ended with the murder of nineteen Chinese. And in 1885, mobs invaded Chinese sections of Seattle and Tacoma, burning down homes and destroying personal property. The violence prompted Washington's governor to request President Cleveland to send troops to restore order. Anti-immigrant and racist sentiments would continue to play a divisive role in labor and party politics for years to come.

But the extent of these incidents was much smaller than conditions might have warranted, because various "safety valves" relieved pressures of social unrest. First, geographic mobility left open a means of escape. America is not only a nation of immigrants, but a nation of migrants. If life was unsatisfactory in one place, the grass was always greener somewhere else. More important, nearly everyone could—and countless people did—seek greener grass in the cities. Migration patterns reversed Frederick Jackson Turner's theory that plentiful land in the West calmed urban tensions by drawing away the discontented. Instead, cities attracted those disappointed with farm life and those fed up with life in another city. To be sure, many dreams were wistful, and many migrants found only more of the same at their destination. But how was improvement to be measured? The worker who moved from the textile mills of Manchester, New Hampshire, to the grain mills of Minneapolis may not have increased his income, but he may have moved his family from a three-room dormitory apartment to a four-room rented house, and he may have paid a penny for a loaf of bread instead of two cents. Each city had its attractions, mythical and real. It took over a thousand dollars to start a farm but only a few dollars to buy a railroad ticket to Chicago or Kansas City. Why not go? Life there couldn't be worse.

Second, the existence and hope of upward mobility soothed the sores of urban dissatisfaction. As Stephan Thernstrom has written, "It is not equality of condition but equality of opportunity that Americans have celebrated."[3] In spite of the widening gap between rich and poor, the American economy left room for upward movement: if not at the top, then in the middle; if not for new entrepreneurs and industrialists, then for workers in new trades and services and for white-collar laborers in new commercial, industrial, and public bureaucracies. Even if there seemed to be no current hope of individual improvement, things might be better for the next generation. The big success story, the rise from bottom to top, was usually a myth. But improving one's status by taking a new job, acquiring some real estate, or buying a horse and wagon was altogether possible.

Thus mobility—whether geographic or socioeconomic—may have dampened class conflict in American cities. The ability of people to edge upward within or, occasionally, out of lower ranks meant that urban workers' expectations often were satisfied. For a poverty-stricken immigrant, a weekly wage and a home for the family represented genuine improvement over life in the old country. Such conditions gave many a feeling that they were part of the American dream, not outside of it.

The diversity of people, the intense social interactions, and the mobility along horizontal and vertical scales gave urban cores their dynamic quality. The migrant groups that peopled those cores each contributed from their cultural heritages: American folk music and literature, Italian and Mexican cuisine, Irish comedy, Yiddish theater, African-American jazz, and much more. Like their predecessors, newcomers in the nineteenth century changed the urban environment as much as they were changed by it. Ethnic, racial, and religious identity, key components of modern culture, derived from inner-city experiences. And in the half-century that followed the Civil War, the inner core provided not only the engine of social change but also the focus of most social and political issues.

BIBLIOGRAPHY

For an overview of urban immigration, see John Bodnar, *The Transplanted: A History of Immigration in Urban America* (1982); Ronald Takaki, *A Different Mirror: A History of Multicultural America* (1993); and Takaki, ed., *From Different Shores: Perspectives on Race and Ethnicity in America* (1987).

Studies of urban immigrant and African-American migrant groups include John Bodnar, Roger Simon, and Michael Weber, *Lives of Their Own: Blacks, Italians, and Poles in Pittsburgh, 1900–1960* (1982); Bradford Luckingham, *Minorities in Phoenix: A Profile of Mexican-American, Chinese-American, and African-American Communities, 1860–1992* (1994); and Iram Watkins-Owens, *Blood Relations: Caribbean Immigrants and the Harlem Community, 1900–1930* (1996).

Comparative studies of urban immigrants include Josef Barton, *Peasants and Strangers: Italians, Roumanians, and Slovaks in an American City, 1900–1950* (1975); Sucheng Chan, *Asian Americans: An Interpretive History* (1991); Roger Daniels, *Asian Americans: Chinese and Japanese in the United States Since 1850* (1990); Donna R. Gabaccia, *From the Other Side: Women, Gender, and Immigrant Life in the United States, 1820–1990* (1994); Gary Mormino and George E. Pozzetta, *The Immigrant World of Ybor City: Italians and Their Latin Neighbors, 1885–1985* (1987); and Judith E. Smith, *Family Connections: A History of Italian and Jewish Immigrant Lives in Providence, Rhode Island, 1900–1940* (1985)

Histories of specific immigrant groups include John Briggs, *An Italian Passage: Immigrants to Three American Cities, 1880–1920* (1978); Hasia Diner, *Erin's Daughters in America: Irish Immigrant Women in the Nineteenth Century* (1983); Steven Hertzberg, *Strangers Within the Gate City: The Jews of Atlanta, 1845–1915* (1978); Michael Leonardo, *Varieties of Ethnic Experience: Kinship, Class, and Gender Among California Italian-Americans* (1984); Timothy Meagher, *Inventing Irish America: Generation, Class, and Ethnic Identity in a New England City, 1880–1928* (2001); Robert Orsi, *The Madonna of 115th Street: Faith and Community in East Harlem, 1880–1950* (1986); George Sanchez, *Becoming Mexican-American: Ethnicity, Culture, and Identity in Chicano Los Angeles, 1900–1945* (1993); and Virginia Yans-McLaughlin, *Family and Community: Italian Immigrants in Buffalo, 1880–1920* (1978).

Other works relating to ethnicity and immigration include Albert Camarillo, *Chicanos in a Changing Society: From Mexican Pueblos to American Barrios in Santa Barbara and Southern California, 1848–1930* (1979); Richard Griswold del Castillo, *The Los Angeles Barrio, 1850–1890: A Social History* (1980); Mario T. Garcia, *Desert Immigrants: The Mexicans of El Paso, 1880–1920* (1981); Yuji Ichioka, *The Issei: The World of First Generation Japanese Immigrants,*

1885–1924 (1988); Ricardo Romo, *East Los Angeles: History of a Barrio* (1983); Virginia E. Sanchez, *From Colonia to Community: The History of Puerto Ricans in New York, 1917–1948* (1983); Robert A. Slayton, *Back of the Yards: The Making of a Local Democracy* (1986); and Judy Yung, *Unbound Feet: A Social History of Chinese Women in San Francisco* (1995).

On interconnections between immigration and race, see Noel Ignatiev, *How the Irish Became White* (1995); Matthew Frye Jacobson, *Whiteness of a Different Color: European Immigrants and the Alchemy of Race* (1998); and David Roediger, *The Wages of Whiteness: Race and the Making of the American Working Class* (1991). Racial exclusion has been explored by Thomas Almaguer, *Racial Fault Lines: The Historical Origins of White Supremacy in California* (1994); Virginia Dominguez, *White by Definition: Social Classification in Creole Louisiana* (1986); and Ian Haney Lopez, *White by Law: The Legal Constitution of Race* (1996). On nativism, see John Higham, *Strangers in the Land: Patterns of American Nativism, 1860–1920* (1955); Alan Kraut, *Silent Travelers: Germs, Genes, and the "Immigrant Menace"* (1994); and Stuart C. Miles, *The Unwelcome Immigrant: The American Image of the Chinese, 1785–1892* (1969). On the links between white egalitarian thought and racist exclusion, see Alexander Saxton, *The Rise and Fall of the White Republic: Class Politics and Mass Culture in Nineteenth-Century America* (1990).

Important studies of black migration, family, and residential patterns include James Borchert, *Alley Life in Washington: Family, Community, Religion, and Folklore in the City, 1850–1970* (1980); Lynne B. Feldman, *A Sense of Place: Birmingham's Black Middle-Class Community, 1890–1930* (1999); Peter Gottlieb, *Making Their Own Way: Southern Blacks' Migration to Pittsburgh* (1987); Robert Gregg, *Sparks from the Anvil of Oppression: Philadelphia's African Methodists and Southern Migration, 1890–1940* (1994); James Grossman, *Land of Hope: Chicago, Black Southerners, and the Great Migration* (Chicago: University of Chicago Press, 1989); David Katzman, *Before the Ghetto: Black Detroit in the Nineteenth Century* (1973); Kenneth Kusmer, *A Ghetto Takes Shape: Black Cleveland, 1870–1930* (1976); Gilbert Osofsky, *Harlem: The Making of a Ghetto* (1966); Elizabeth H. Pleck, *Migration and Poverty: Boston, 1865–1900* (1979); Howard Rabinowitz, *Race Relations in the Urban South, 1865–1890* (1978); Allan H. Spear, *Black Chicago: The Making of a Negro Ghetto* (1967); Richard W. Thomas, *Life for Us Is What We Make It: Building Black Community in Detroit, 1915–1945* (1992); Joe William Trotter, *Black Milwaukee: The Making of an Industrial Proletariat, 1915–1945* (1985); and George C. Wright, *Life Behind a Veil: Blacks in Louisville, Kentucky, 1865–1930* (1985).

On mutual aid associations, see José A. Hernandez, *Mutual Aid for Survival: The Case of Mexican Americans* (1983); Anne Meis Knupfer, *Toward A Tenderer Humanity and Nobler Womanhood: African American Women's Clubs in Turn-of-the-Century Chicago,* (1996); Ivan Light, *Ethnic Enterprise in America: Business and Welfare Among Chinese, Japanese, and Blacks* (1972); Daniel Soyre, *Jewish Immigrant Associations and American Identity in New York, 1880–1939* (1997); and Carlos Vélez-Iba-os, *Bonds of Mutual Trust: The Cultural Systems of Rotating Credit Associations Among Urban Mexicans and Chicanos* (1983).

Changing patterns of ethnic and religious identity are discussed in Harold J. Abramson, *Ethnic Diversity in Catholic America* (1973); Paula Hyman, *Gender and Assimilation in Modern Jewish History: The Roles and Representations of Women* (1995); and Randall M. Miller and Thomas D. Marzik, eds., *Immigrants and Religion in Urban America* (1977).

On housing reform, public health, and city services, see Robert B. Fairbanks, *Making Better Citizens: Housing Reform and the Community Development Strategy in Cincinnati, 1890–1960* (1988); Judith Walzer Leavitt, *The Healthiest City: Milwaukee and the Politics of Health Reform* (1982); Eric Monkkonen, *Police in Urban America, 1860–1920* (1981); Thomas J. Philpott, *The Slum and the Ghetto: Neighborhood Deterioration and Middle-Class Reform, Chicago, 1880–1930* (1978); Christine Rosen, *The Limits of Growth: Great Fires and the Process of City Growth in America* (1986); and Barbara G. Rosenkranz, *Public Health and the State: Changing Views in Massachusetts, 1842–1936* (Cambridge: Harvard University Press, 1972).

On urban women, see Ardis Cameron, *Radicals of the Worst Sort: Laboring Women in Lawrence, Massachusetts, 1860–1912* (1995); Sarah Deutsch, *Women and the City: Gender,*

Space, and Power in Boston, 1870–1940 (New York: Oxford University Press, 2000); Elizabeth Ewen, *Immigrant Women in the Land of Dollars: Life and Culture on the Lower East Side, 1890–1925* (New York: Monthly Review Press, 1985); Alice Kessler-Harris, *Out to Work: A History of Wage-Earning Women in America* (1982); and Joanne Meyerowitz, *Women Adrift: Independent Wage Earners in Chicago, 1880–1930* (1988). On urban men, see Howard P. Chudacoff, *The Age of the Bachelor: Creating an American Subculture* (1999).

Residential experiences and social mobility are examined in Howard P. Chudacoff, *Mobile Americans: Residential and Social Mobility in Omaha, 1880–1920* (1972); Peter Decker, *Fortunes and Failures: White-Collar Mobility in Nineteenth-Century San Francisco* (1978); Clyde Griffen and Sally Griffen, *Natives and Newcomers: The Ordering of Opportunity in Mid–Nineteenth-Century Poughkeepsie* (1977); Thomas Kessner, *The Golden Door: Italian and Jewish Immigrant Mobility in New York City, 1880–1915* (1977); Stephan Thernstrom, *The Other Bostonians: Poverty and Progress in an American Metropolis* (1973); and Olivier Zunz, *The Changing Face of Inequality: Urbanization, Industrialization, and Immigrants in Detroit, 1880–1920* (1982).

NOTES

1. Howard Rabinowitz, *Race Relations in the Old South, 1865–1980* (New York: Oxford University Press, 1978).
2. Tera W. Hunter, *To 'Joy My Freedom: Southern Black Women's Lives and Labors After the Civil War* (Cambridge, Mass.: Harvard University Press, 1997), 178–79.
3. Stephan Thernstrom, *The Other Bostonians: Poverty and Progress in an American Metropolis, 1880–1970* (Cambridge, Mass.: Harvard University Press, 1973), 256.

6

City Politics in the Era of Transformation

ORIGINS OF THE MACHINE

Several critical conditions generated unprecedented challenges for urban governments between 1870 and 1900. Huge increases in migration and immigration created an ethnically and racially stratified urban population. Acceleration of industrialization, commercial expansion, and technological change recast social structure and reshaped economic relationships. Tensions between workers and corporate employers exploded in violent strikes in the 1870s, 1880s, and 1890s. Overcrowding, ill health, poverty, substandard housing, and crime in poor neighborhoods fomented what some have termed a crisis of public order. Between 1870 and 1900, many cities enlarged their boundaries by thousands of acres, and myriad new businesses, industries, and households strained existing services and created an urgent need for water, gas, street lighting, sewer systems, police officers, firefighters, teachers, streets, schools, and government buildings. How would these improvements be financed? Who among contending groups would determine public priorities?

The governmental forms that had evolved during the urbanization of the early nineteenth century seemed to generate political chaos rather than effective governing strategies. After 1820, most city governments had copied the federal form: two legislative councils elected from districts (wards) and an executive (mayor) elected at large (citywide). Before 1850, most mayors could exert only limited control over municipal policy. Many mayors had ceremonial powers that entitled them to hand out keys to the city and cut ribbons, but they took only a minor role in administration. Many lacked power to veto council ordinances and were often unable to overcome the particular interests of councilmen. As the creators of cities, states jealously guarded their prerogatives to determine their cities' needs and to control finances by limiting local taxing and bonding powers. Consequently, most cities had to expand their functions in piecemeal fashion by petitioning the statehouse for charter amendments. Also, as new needs called for new officials, a confusing array of boards and commissions piled on top of each other. Some were appointed by the governor, some by the mayor, some by the city council, and some were popularly elected. Jersey City's charter was amended ninety-one times in forty years, and at one time thirty separate boards administered public functions in Philadelphia.

Governmental confusion and economic change tended to fragment political leadership. By the mid–nineteenth century local entrepreneurs—merchants, manufacturers, contractors, and real estate operators—vied for political control in order to steer public policy in directions suited to their own interests. At the same time, businessmen whose concerns focused on interurban and interregional networks of transportation, banking, and communications withdrew from active involvement with local affairs. Expansion of the franchise after 1820 created a new electorate with their own political goals and leadership. Independent political parties—the Free Soil, Know-Nothing, and numerous workingmen's parties—emerging out of divisions over labor, temperance, and land use confounded heads of the major parties. New kinds of political leaders, frequently self-made men who paid close attention to the concerns of their constituents, emerged from the newly enfranchised electorate. Political power, once based on general social deference, came to be based on party organization and mass partisan loyalty.

The emergence of career politicians and partisan loyalties deriving from ward and neighborhood organization became common features of local political activity. The less affluent career politicians who replaced the wealthy in office boasted of the benefits they brought to their constituents. As the ward became the basic unit of political life, both career politicians and patrician leaders depended on these benefits to justify their claim to office. Career politicians, however, lacked the personal resources of patricians; as a consequence, when politicians provided for constituents, they did so from the city coffers. To succeed, however, they had to associate themselves with others who shared their goals. By the 1860s and 1870s, what insiders called "the organization" and what outsiders disparaged as "the machine" shaped politics in many large cities.

As political associations distinct from established government agencies, machines flourished because they were able to satisfy diverse groups by centralizing political power and material resources. Machines offered utility franchises, contracts, tax adjustments, and favorable legislation to selected members of the business community, and provided jobs and favors to their constituency. Machine politicians used these resources to build a personal political following. By resourcefully distributing patronage and material benefits, machine politicians also built centralized party organizations that overcame the fragmentation of authority characteristic of the formal governmental structure. The machines acted as brokers among contending economic and political interests; they supplied material and symbolic rewards to immigrant and working-class residents who otherwise lacked resources; and by centralizing political authority, they brought some semblance of social and political order to the cities.

STRUCTURE AND FUNCTIONS OF THE MACHINE

Critics depicted political machines as monolithic mobs and bosses as despots who dictated every act, every crime. The images were seldom true. Like other political organizations, machines were coalitions. They appeared homogeneous because their leaders kept the parts well oiled, preventing friction and disintegration. Most big-city machines were federations, consisting of smaller machines organized at the levels of ward, precinct, and even block. The bosses who became the subjects of exposés were not insensitive autocrats; rather, they were executives, chairmen of boards, and brokers who coordinated whole hierarchies of smaller bosses.

Ward and precinct bosses utilized votes as a marketable commodity. To offer their constituents more, smaller bosses allied into a large organization under the aegis of a city-wide boss. It was the city boss's job to keep order within this organization, but often unity proved elusive. For example, throughout much of its early history Chicago changed so rapidly and spawned so many diverse power bases that a single city-wide machine could not be formed until well into the twentieth century. On the other hand, the establishment of Tammany Hall in New York in the early 1800s provided a foundation upon which political interests could combine. In most instances, an agent who could weld various local organizations into a more powerful machine could promise unprecedented benefits to all. Such promises gave city bosses their power.

Yet bosses held their positions as leaders of coalitions only by the support and goodwill of others. Their power was not absolute; the lesser bosses who operated the machine's gears checked it. Moreover, the entire system depended on a combination of business and neighborhood support. Corruption and chicanery gave bosses influence and leverage, but bosses sustained their power because they provided services that people wanted and needed. The specific functions of boss politics flowed in two directions. In return for material gratuities, machines granted privileges to real estate interests and segments of the business community. In return for votes, machines personalized government for their constituents. Both sets of functions reinforced American traditions of competitive individualism, entrepreneurial success, and private property. Immigrants looked to politics not as the fulfillment of abstract ideals but as an extension of the family and communal economy. Supplying work, charity, and personal service, bosses met immigrants' daily needs, but in doing so they diminished the ability of immigrant voters to use politics as a tool for redressing economic grievances. In the 1880s, independent political initiatives by labor organizations directly challenged machine candidates. In 1886, in one of the most famous contests, Henry George, running on the United Labor party ticket, narrowly lost the New York City mayoralty to Tammany Democrat and iron manufacturer Abram Hewitt, coming in far ahead of the third place candidate, Republican Theodore Roosevelt. But the collapse of labor politics by the mid-1890s left workers with little alternative to the major parties. In many circumstances, machines were actively antagonistic to the collective orientation of the labor movement, which threatened both the machine's electoral base and its business constituency. The rise of the machine was connected with a growing tendency in American political agitation to separate workplace concerns, relegated to unions, from community issues, left to an electoral fate.

Many bosses were immigrants or sons of immigrants, and they knew the inner city and its needs firsthand. Building constituencies by providing jobs, bosses used control of governmental offices as a means of influencing employment. The enormous public and private construction within cities in the late nineteenth century meant that many jobs fell within the reach of public officials. Public works boards and inspectors could convince contractors and other employers to hire men faithful to the machine. Bosses could also provide constituents with jobs on the expanding public payroll. Men who received work as a result of machine influence were always reminded where their jobs came from. Some were required to express their appreciation by making a contribution to machine coffers. This was especially true for public employees—policemen, firefighters, teachers, clerks, and janitors. All were expected to remember the machine on election day.

Bosses also maintained popularity by offering forms of public benevolence. Through control of city officials, they appropriated funds for neighborhood improvements such as parks, playgrounds, and bathhouses. They took children on summer picnics and sponsored free days at the amusement park. They distributed turkeys and other food on Easter, Thanksgiving, and Christmas. Each boss had his own style. James Michael Curley, mayor and boss of Boston in the early twentieth century, wrote of how he would approach an elderly woman plodding down the street by saying to her, "A woman should have three attributes. She should have beauty, intelligence, and money." As he handed her a silver dollar he would add, "Now you have all three." Reformers protested these forms of what they called mass bribery. Yet no one else was interested in providing welfare in such a personal way.

Bosses mediated between inner-city residents and formal political and legal structures, convincing authorities to look the other way when a neighborhood saloon wanted to stay open after hours or on Sundays, or when gambling houses or other vice establishments needed relief from police harassment. Most important, the boss intervened when a constituent ran afoul of the law. If arrested for intoxication, vagrancy, or assault, a neighborhood resident could call upon the boss to provide counsel and, in many cases, bail. This kind of intervention gave constituents a feeling that they were getting a break in an otherwise oppressive system.

Bosses cultivated popular support by making their power visible and accessible. They joined ethnic and neighborhood associations. They set up their own clubs, holding open house in informal offices, often saloon backrooms. They appeared at wakes and weddings, and offered cash to defray funeral expenses or to start a pair of newlyweds on the right foot. No wonder a boss's achievements, including the appearance of his name in the newspapers, reflected the glory of the neighborhood. National political issues were unimportant; a boss who became too interested in the tariff, public land policy, or the amount of silver in national currency soon lost his neighborhood following. In the streets and tenements local and personal issues came first. Here people measured a politician's success by two canons: "He gets things done" and "He keeps his word."

The political machine required constant attention. As ward boss George Washington Plunkitt preached at the turn of the century, "[The boss] plays politics every day and night in the year, and his headquarters bear the inscription 'Never Closed.'" Help from charities and government agencies often required an assessment of the worthiness of welfare recipients, but for loyal constituents, bosses asked no questions. Martin Lomasney, boss of Boston's South End, once told reformer Lincoln Steffens, "There's got to be somebody in every ward that any bloke can come to—no matter what he's done—and get help. Help, you understand, none of your law and justice, but help."

Bosses helped to transform politics into a full-time professionalized service, and encouraged people served by bosses to expect government to attend to the problems of everyday life. Before social security, unemployment insurance, medicare, food stamps, and aid to families with dependent children, bosses and machines informally distributed relief and welfare. Many people even in the poorest circumstances never used these services, but many believed they could receive help if they needed it.

Not all immigrant groups were represented in machines. In most cities the Irish initially dominated machine politics, and they frequently attempted to defend their organizations from infiltration by outsiders, such as newer immigrant groups or African-American migrants. In Boston, New

Haven, and New York, the Irish took a disproportionate share of the patronage jobs, holding on with particular strength to the police force. In Chicago, New Orleans, and Detroit, Irish-dominated machines ignored Italians and Poles for many years, and only a few machines offered any favors or concessions to blacks. These outsiders were the truly disadvantaged, for they were excluded from whatever helpful services machines could render as well as from the larger society.

Machines did not depend on goodwill alone to ensure success at the polls. There were few legal constraints on the election process; most cities did not adopt voter registration laws or the secret ballot until the twentieth century. Repeat voting, false counting, stuffed ballot boxes, and other voting fraud were common occurrences. Politicians bought votes and used violent intimidation to insure election victories. Kansas City boss Tom Pendergast used a combination of fraud and bribery, backed by an organization and a police force employing local criminals, to produce a majority for a proposed railway franchise. Chicago ward boss Johnny Powers intimidated voters by threatening landlords and merchants with loss of licenses unless they supported him in his campaign for alderman. The use of various forms of coercion was the underside of machine politics.

Neighborhood constituents were one special-interest group served by political machines; the business community was the other. The urban boom that spread after the Civil War unleashed torrents of construction and commercial activity. The increased population and need for municipal services resulted in an expansion of public agencies to administer them. Machines in political power could control the letting of contracts for public works, such as streets, sewers, and government buildings. They could influence the granting of streetcar, gas, and electricity franchises. They could juggle tax assessments for favored property owners. They could select printers, banks, and other firms to receive city business. These privileges had their price: favored businessmen were expected to pay the machines for contracts and franchises. Outsiders called the practice bribery. Bosses called it gratitude. Often politicians padded public contracts so that chosen firms could kick back funds to the bosses and their treasuries. Outsiders called this graft. Bosses doctored the ledger to hide it.

There were two kinds of graft. Honest graft, or "boodle," was the kind of investment capitalism that maximized profits while eliminating risk. From their positions within government, machine politicians had an advantageous view of where lucrative investments in real estate and utility companies could be made. Moreover, they could set policies that would assure the success of such investments. George Washington Plunkitt illustrated this kind of graft.

> My party's in power in the city, and it's goin' to undertake a lot of public improvements. Well, I'm tipped off, say, that they're going to lay out a new park at a certain place. I see an opportunity and I take it. I go to that place and I buy up all the land I can in the neighborhood. Then the board of this or that

makes its plan public, and there is a rush to get my land, which nobody cared particular for before.

Ain't it perfectly honest to charge a good price and make a profit on my investment and foresight? Of course it is. Well, that's honest graft.

Dishonest graft involved criminal activity such as shakedowns and payoffs from vice operations in return for protection from police harassment. This was the most sordid activity of boss politics, but it was difficult to avoid. Bosses were specialists in gaining exemptions from the law, and the line between who was to receive such favors and who would not seldom was drawn. Payoffs from gambling, prostitution, and illegal liquor sales provided the most accessible revenues for machines. Many bosses operated vice establishments themselves, and some entered politics from backgrounds in illicit activities. Kansas City's Tom Pendergast profited handsomely from his liquor and concrete businesses, and miles of excessive concrete paving still mark the city's landscape, but shaking down insurance companies made him vulnerable to federal prosecution, sending him to jail in 1939.

In addition to functioning as service agencies and dispensaries of political favors, machines provided one potential avenue of social mobility. Participation in politics particularly attracted some sons of immigrants, a restless generation. Their lack of skills, education, and capital frustrated their desires to move ahead in a supposed land of opportunity. They often felt the lash of discrimination and the chains of poverty. Yet their schoolbooks told them that government existed for the people, and machines offered them the opportunity to serve and be rewarded for their service. So they entered politics because the machine promised that the organization's success would also mean personal achievement. The magnetic force was the prestige that the machine could bestow, not only to the individual but to his family and his neighborhood, providing some of the support that enabled the boss system to withstand attacks for so many years.

SOME NOTABLE CASES

The essence of boss politics is best described by example. Sometimes a boss exerted power from an elected office. More frequently he pulled strings from backstage, attaching public officials to him by bonds of loyalty and patronage. Bosses could operate within the Republican as well as the Democratic party, although most machines developed as Democratic because of that party's attraction for workingmen and immigrants. Democratic bosses felt no discomfort working out contracts and deals with Republican businessmen. All bosses pursued power and advantage; some showed more concern for their constituents, whereas others devoted more attention to dishonest graft and self-serving. Still, all bosses used politics as a vehicle for personalized service, and they dispensed political favors on a cash-and-carry basis.

"Who Stole the Peoples Money?". This drawing by the famous political cartoonist Thomas Nast shows New York Tammany boss William Marcy Tweed and his henchmen trying to shift blame for the corrupt and excessive expenditures given to contractors for construction of a local courthouse in 1871. The corrupt alliance between machine politicians and certain businesses often stood at the center of early boss politics.

Modern urban bossism was reared in New York's Tammany Hall. The Society of St. Tammany evolved from an Anti-Federalist social club in the 1790s into a political organization that courted the expanded working-class vote in the 1830s. During the depression that followed the Panic of 1837, the Tammany Club distributed food, fuel, and clothing to the city's poor. It continued its relief services into the 1840s, paying particular heed to the increasing numbers of Irish immigrants. By this time Tammany had become a powerful wing of the Democratic party, and it used its charitable activities to win votes for its candidates. As the club acquired power, it exercised increasing control over local patronage. Party leaders consulted Tammany in the choice of candidates, and elected officials followed Tammany dictates in the distribution of government jobs, rewarding loyal members who worked for the club and the party.

William Marcy Tweed was the first Tammany leader to exert city-wide power. Son of a middle-class craftsman, Tweed rose from neighborhood gang leader to member of the New York City Council at age twenty-eight. Tweed's district elected him to the U.S. House of Representatives when he was thirty, but the debates of Congress bored him and he did not seek re-election. Instead, he returned to the city where in the late 1860s he used the

Tammany machine to win control of the entire city administration and part of the state legislature. As chairman of Tammany, he boosted his associates into public office and created what became known as the Tweed Ring.

With his henchmen secured in office through various types of vote fraud, Tweed mounted an assault on the public treasury. In 1870, he used his influence over the state General Assembly to obtain a new charter for New York City. Among other things, the charter created a board of audit that would handle all bills paid by the city and county. With the mayor's office and board of audit in the hands of Tweed's allies, contracts could be padded and kickbacks demanded. Construction of a new county courthouse provided such an opportunity. Inflated appropriations totaled $12,500,000, including $7,500 for thermometers, $404,347 for safes, $41,190 for brooms, and $2 million for plastering. In contrast, a similar courthouse was built in Brooklyn at the same time for $800,000.

By 1871, at age forty-seven, Boss Tweed, bald and weighing three hundred pounds, reputedly was worth $12 million. He had a Fifth Avenue mansion, a Connecticut estate, and a steam yacht. But he always had enough money for others. In 1870, he spent $500,000 on the poor of the Seventh Ward and raised even more for the Catholic church. And he willingly opened his wallet for Tammany candidates in need of campaign funds. Tweed recognized that in industrial America power and money were inseparable. He did not set the standards of his day. He merely embellished those established by ambitious businessmen.

Tweed's career collapsed in 1871, when the *New York Times,* acting on information divulged by a disaffected sheriff, printed "reliable and incontrovertible evidence of numerous, gigantic frauds on the part of the rulers of the city." The exposés of boodling, bribery, and embezzlement prompted formation of an investigating committee consisting of seventy community leaders. Eventually several Tammany leaders were indicted, and Tweed was arrested and convicted on 104 counts of fraud and bribery. He died in prison in 1878.

The Tweed Ring left confusion and debt in its wake. Between 1867 and 1871, New York's debt tripled, and its account books were left in chaos. Yet whatever his motives, Tweed oversaw important accomplishments. New York was growing too fast for existing institutions to meet its needs. Tweed's regime bypassed outmoded forms of administration. In doing so it built streets, granted franchises to transit and utilities companies, and developed Central Park. It also secured revision of the city's antiquated government with charter reforms that, at least in theory, increased efficiency. All the while, however, the boss and his henchmen lined their pockets at public expense.

The Tweed Ring's power rested on personalities and bribery; it was not a machine that tightly controlled policymaking. Tweed was a personal boss, not an organizational leader like those who followed him. He used votes and intimidation to build power, and he played the role of broker between business and government with optimal skill. To the poverty-stricken workers who received a free meal and a couple of dollars on election day or whose family received a food basket on Christmas, Tweed played the hero.

The demise of William Marcy Tweed did not signal the end of Tammany Hall. "Honest John" Kelly succeeded him as head of the machine and molded Tammany into a more efficient organization by centralizing decision making and appointing a more party-oriented breed of henchmen. After a brief hiatus Tammany candidates moved back into positions of power. In some ways Tammany Hall and similar machines elsewhere changed after 1880. Their graft and corruption became less flagrant, and they used the expanding municipal bureaucracy and the ever-pressing need for services to cement their influence. But machines still based their existence on numbers, jobs, and favors.

Richard Croker exemplified the late nineteenth-century boss. Born in Ireland in 1843, he sailed to the United States with his parents at the age of three. He grew up in the slums of lower Manhattan, dropped out of school when he was thirteen, and joined the Fourth Avenue Tunnel Gang. Here he learned the lessons that prepared him for his political career: discipline through loyalty, reputation through results, and leadership through strength. Using his forceful personality and pugilistic skill, Croker became the gang's leader and was recruited into Tammany Hall in the 1860s. He became Tammany's—and the city's—boss in the late 1880s.

An able politician, Croker could win a point with affable charm or with vicious attack; he also knew when to compromise. The reverence that the city's populace paid him was enormous. When he took his annual European vacation, thousands saw him off. When he attended the opera, the orchestra played "Hail to the Chief" while he took his seat. Unlike Tweed, Croker did not steal outright from the public treasury. Rather, he perfected the use of honest graft. By using control over city purchases and contracts, Croker could convince favored businessmen to grant stock in their companies to the boss and his associates or to offer tips on promising investments. Honest graft could not sustain the whole machine, however. Croker welded his underlings to him by permitting them to participate in dirty graft. He generally overlooked the activities of his ninety thousand precinct workers—many of them policemen, firefighters, and other civil servants—as long as they carried their districts for Tammany candidates on election day.

Croker had many friends but also some enemies. In 1894, opponents managed to dent Tammany's power when a committee under the chairmanship of State Senator Clarence Lexow undertook an investigation of police corruption in New York City. The Lexow Committee's hearings—six thousand pages of testimony—detailed an extraordinary degree of police graft and accomplished just what Croker's enemies desired: disenchantment with the machine. But Croker stayed one step ahead. He sensed the public mood and resigned as Tammany's chairman so as not to be linked to an electoral defeat. In the mayoral election of 1894, the reformers' candidate,

Republican merchant William Strong, won by forty-five thousand votes. After the election Croker sailed to England for a three-year vacation.

Strong and his police commissioner Theodore Roosevelt managed a few reforms, but their strict enforcement of the law made many people long for the looser Tammany days. In September 1897, with the Lexow revelations buried, Croker returned to New York and reestablished his control over Tammany. He was just in time. The state legislature had given the city a new charter that on January 1, 1898, would consolidate Brooklyn, Queens, Staten Island, and the Bronx with Manhattan. The winner of the 1897 mayoral election would administer a Greater New York City of more than three million people. Reformers entered Seth Low, president of Columbia University and former mayor of Brooklyn, as their candidate. Croker and the Democrats selected a political unknown, Judge Robert Van Wyck, and frankly aimed their campaign at the tenement districts, where reform crackdowns had been heaviest. Their slogan was "To Hell with Reform!" The strategy worked. The close election was decided by a Democratic landslide in the inner wards. Croker and Tammany again ruled the city.

New Yorks "King Richard". Tammany boss Richard Croker, with top hat and boutonniere, ruled the city from the drivers seat of a well-oiled political machine. He had no reservations about his motives. When a reformer once asked Croker if was working for his own interests, "King Richard" replied, "All the time, the same as you."

Croker's triumphant return damaged his political savvy. First, he divorced his wife and moved into the Democratic Club on Fifth Avenue. Here he kept a court, forcing lieutenants to visit him in their best dress and to remain standing at dinner until the boss was seated. Then Croker tried unsuccessfully to lead his machine into state and national politics. He pressured his organization to run a Tammany candidate against Teddy Roosevelt for governor in 1898, and he backed William Jennings Bryan for president in 1900. In both instances Croker's ignorance of larger issues and his antagonistic speeches hurt him and his candidates. In addition, reformers revived public disaffection with the machine in New York City. An investigation exposed Croker's connections with a firm that furnished most of the city's ice and that was planning to double its prices to consumers. Croker's participation in the scheme was still honest graft, but it was the kind that directly drained the pockets of ordinary, working-class families. Moreover exposés revealed that dirty graft had again spread throughout the city. These occurrences loosened Croker's grip on his machine. When Seth Low defeated the Tammany candidate for mayor in 1901, Croker again sailed for England.

Croker had presided over some thirty-five district leaders. The career of one of these smaller bosses, Timothy D. Sullivan, illustrates an ethnic boss's political possibilities. "Big Tim" Sullivan was a second-generation immigrant, raised by his widowed Irish mother. Like Tweed and Croker, he left school and became the leader of a gang. His savvy and brawn gave him ready entry into Tammany Hall. He became a political prodigy and was elected to the state legislature in 1886 when he was twenty-three years old. He later served a term in the U.S. House of Representatives, but he could not stomach life in Washington and returned to New York after two years.

Back in New York, Sullivan secured control over the Lower East Side and Bowery districts by learning Yiddish and soliciting support from the Jewish immigrants who were replacing some of the Irish residents. He used political leverage to place his supporters on public payrolls and to open a string of profitable gambling halls. He also skillfully cultivated his personal appeal. He arranged bails, sent food and medicine to the sick, gave shoes to needy schoolchildren, and sponsored annual summer picnics. His Timothy D. Sullivan Association was a poor man's club that operated out of neighborhood saloons, distributing jobs, food, and other services. Sullivan built his machine on trust and loyalty. It was said that he was so well liked that his portrait hung in nearly every building in his district.

In his later years, Sullivan, who had become wealthy from investments in gambling enterprises and movie theaters, helped expand Tammany and the Democratic party from their base of personal politics into support for social reform legislation. Deeply committed to the welfare of working-class people, Sullivan used his influence in the New York General Assembly to promote bills for the benefit of labor. He acted as mentor for Frances Perkins, then a lobbyist for the National Consumers' League and

The Ward Machine in Action. This photograph depicts one of many gatherings of the Timothy D. Sullivan Association, the political club run by ward boss "Big Tim" Sullivan from New York. Note that a political outing was generally an all-male event.

shortly to become a leading Progressive Era and New Deal reformer, and helped her pass a bill limiting working hours for women. Sympathetic to the crusade for women's suffrage, he also worked with Harriot Stanton Blatch, daughter of suffragist Elizabeth Cady Stanton, in support of women's political and economic equality with men. Sullivan's reform career was cut short in 1912, however, when he became ill and was committed to an insane asylum. He escaped but was apparently struck by a freight train and was found dead in a railroad yard. His funeral attracted more than twenty-five thousand mourners.

New York City provides the most colorful showcase for machine politics, but bossism flourished in many other cities as well. Philadelphia had "King" James McManes, a Republican who controlled the city's fiscal policies and electoral politics from the late 1860s until 1881. McManes achieved and exercised power by becoming the leading figure on a municipal board that superintended the city's gas utility. Using his authority over the distribution of jobs and letting of contracts, McManes influenced other city departments. He required city employees to kick back a portion of their salaries to his organization, and he manipulated elections for his own benefit. During his reign McManes reputedly earned two and a half million dollars, mostly from payoffs from favored contractors. Like other bosses, McManes alarmed opponents by his lavish expenditures of public funds. Between 1860 and 1880, Philadelphia's municipal debt swelled by 350 percent. Although much of the money facilitated the city's physical expansion, a number of Republican businessmen became outraged. They formed a Committee of One Hundred and joined local Democrats to defeat machine candidates in the 1881 elections. McManes retired to enjoy his private fortune, but even more effective boss rule returned to Philadelphia later in the decade, exploiting the reform campaign to centralize political authority and consolidating support with the state party organization.

Chicago had its own brand of machine politics. Practically every ward boss was an independent entrepreneur, each courting his constituency in his own style. Johnny Powers of the Nineteenth Ward was known as "The Chief Mourner" because of his attendance record at funerals. Michael "Hinky Dink" Kenna of the First Ward served free lunches in his saloon. His partner, "Bathhouse John" Coughlin, received his nickname for the kind of services he sponsored. "Blond Boss" William Lorimer worked to remove prejudices against Jews and other immigrants on Chicago's West Side. Although all but Lorimer were Democrats, no individual was able to construct one city-wide machine. Carter Harrison and his son Carter II held the mayoralty off and on through three and a half decades and cultivated faithful support among immigrants by championing personal liberty—meaning toleration of drinking and gambling. But neither Harrison could overcome the independence of the ward bosses.

Still, machine politics in Chicago contained familiar features. Political power derived from voters and favors. City employees paid off the boss who got them jobs. Graft was common. Powers maintained a mutually profitable relationship with streetcar companies. Roger Sullivan, one of the most powerful bosses of early twentieth-century Chicago, specialized in granting favors to—and receiving gratuities from—banks and gas companies. The lack of a strong city boss, however, produced two extremes of instability. On one hand, it was somewhat easier for reformers to gain a foothold in Chicago politics because they did not have to battle a single, entrenched machine. On the other hand, because there were so many bosses, so many enemies, reformers found it difficult to mount a unified attack against every boss.

It is important to note that bossism was not confined to large cities. Small cities also needed leaders who could coordinate political power, mediate between immigrants and their new environment, and organize physical expansion. In Omaha, Tom Dennison built a Democratic machine that influenced local affairs for nearly three decades. Dennison used politics to protect his multimillion-dollar vice business. By appealing to immigrant voters of the inner wards (Dennison's saloons were often the only places where immigrant workers could cash their paychecks), Dennison could place his lieutenants in high offices and through them act as broker between the city government and the business community. As in other cities, the boss accumulated boodle from firms receiving city business. Dennison remained in power from the early 1900s to the late 1920s and retired to California a wealthy man.

Practically every major city experienced a period of boss rule. In Pittsburgh, Christopher Magee supervised a Republican machine that lasted for half a century. In San Francisco, Abe Ruef, whose Jewish ancestry and college training distinguished him from other city bosses, operated from within the Union Labor party in the early twentieth century. Martin Behrman of New Orleans directed local affairs between 1900 and 1920 from his posts as mayor and as leader of the Democratic Choctaw Club. The Pendergast brothers, Jim and Tom, rose from Kansas City's river wards to rule the entire city from the late 1880s to the late 1930s. Edward H. Crump acquired power in Memphis around 1910 and did not lose control until the 1940s. Although he was never mayor, William F. "Billy" Klair dominated politics in the city of Lexington and in the Kentucky state legislature from the early years of the century to 1937. In Jersey City, Frank Hague ruled from 1917 to 1947 under the brazen slogan "I am the law." Like other bosses these men were coordinators, not dictators. They presided over federations, not over autocracies. Through key alliances with wealthy citizens and business interests, they offered a full range of services, from Thanksgiving turkeys to business franchises to gambling dens.

CITY GOVERNANCE AND MUNICIPAL REFORM

As early as 1860, lines in many cities were drawn in what would become characteristic political contests in the late nineteenth century: boss politics and the machine opposed by an elite minority organized under the banner of municipal reform. This latter group, which can be called municipal, or civic, reformers battled bosses in cities across the country by attempting to mold their own version of urban government. Mostly middle and upper-class, native-born, and Protestant, these people opposed immigrant-dominated political machines and offered various proposals to undercut bosses' power. To do so, they launched a campaign to alter municipal governance.

Though machines were often fragile alliances torn by internal rivalries, much of their political influence derived from the ward-based organization of city councils and boards of aldermen. In the mid-nineteenth century, the ward system, which resembles the geography-based representation of the U.S. House of Representatives, had begun to replace city-wide representation, and most councilmen and aldermen were elected by voters of a certain ward. By 1900, the typical ward-elected representative was a modest saloonkeeper, retailer, artisan, or laborer who customarily lived and worked in the ward. Professionals and downtown businessmen were greatly outnumbered. Residential patterns guaranteed that some wards would be dominated by working-class Irish, others by Italians, and others by native-born Protestants. The ward system was also the vehicle through which workingmen's slates and later socialist tickets won representation on city councils. The council served as the neighborhoods' voice, the channel through which constituents obtained pavements, sewers, and water mains. By 1900, American cities included disparate neighborhoods with different social and ethnic orientations and diverse transportation, paving, and drainage needs, and city councils provided the forum for debate over urban expansion and its implications.

During the late nineteenth century, urban elites became alarmed as they observed immigrants and their representatives gaining ground in city councils and party organizations. To counter erosion of their authority, business and professional leaders organized themselves to intervene in the political process. Through chambers of commerce, boards of trade, and specially constituted good government and municipal reform leagues, these citizens sought to restore urban rule to the "better elements." Chambers of commerce were particularly active in promoting changes they felt would make the atmosphere of the city good for business, arguing that economic growth would eventually help the working classes. Political alliances of merchants, lawyers, and journalists, arguing that they were acting in the civic interest, constituted themselves into groups such as the Committee of Seventy in New York and the Committee of One Hundred in Philadelphia and offered reform candidates that succeeded in ousting the Tweed Ring in New York in 1871 and the McManes machine in Philadelphia in 1881, at least temporarily. These reformers blamed bosses for wasting taxpayers' money and polluting the American system. Eventually, these short-lived and temporary alliances were replaced by municipal leagues with paid executives that competed with ward-based partisan politicians and promoted what were considered to be better qualified candidates. These associations campaigned for cuts in expenditures and tax rates, drafted legislation, and endorsed charter revision.

An important means by which municipal reformers could undermine city councils and recapture power involved was to shift authority from elected to appointed officials. Before the 1860s and 1870s, the city council had directly supervised municipal functions, determining appointments, hiring city employees, fixing policy, and deciding administrative details. By the 1880s and 1890s, as a result of some successes by municipal reformers, the supervisory role of the council had declined sharply, particularly in appointments and finances. New municipal charters, lobbied for by members of chambers of commerce and reform leagues, shifted authority to expert commissions and executive departments either appointed or elected by a citywide constituency that favored downtown business or professional interests. This was often accomplished with the help of state legislatures, frequently dominated by rural and business interests. New York City's reform charter of 1873, Boston's charter of 1885, and Baltimore's charter of 1898 all sharply limited aldermanic authority over public works, budgets, and police expenditures by substituting appointed commissions composed of specialists.

In the same years in which councils lost authority to special independent commissions, many mayors gained power through broadened use of the veto and expanded powers of appointment. Mayors, especially those elected when the general public became fed up with bosses' corruption and when reformers could mobilize middle-class voters behind candidates to challenge the machine, became the ones to initiate policy and to implement programs. Elected on a city-wide basis, reform mayors were likely to be drawn from the ranks of bankers, manufacturers, wholesale merchants, large-scale real estate developers, and lawyers with old-stock social-register pedigrees. Such mayors were not likely to be among the city's wealthiest men, but they usually belonged to what Victorians called the better class of citizens. Downtown businessmen were also likely to hold the crucial post of city comptroller, where their fiscal orientation guided the auditing of city accounts and preparation of budgets. Independent commissions that governed municipal parks, libraries, and police departments tended to draw their membership from the same social strata. Most commissioners held long terms of office and were increasingly likely to be independent from elected officials.

Furthermore, the importance of elected officials as policymakers paled in the face of a new group of urban professionals: civil engineers, landscape architects, public health officials, and school administrators who supervised permanent urban bureaucracies that built and operated waterworks, designed and ran the parks, guarded public health and safety, and oversaw the education of millions of urban schoolchildren (see Chapter 7). Together the downtown businessmen and professionals, and the new municipal experts claimed that their vision of the city constituted the true public interest.

GOALS AND TACTICS OF MUNICIPAL REFORM

Municipal reform included a number of specific goals and tactics, most of which were touted as efforts to remove partisanship from politics and politics from government and to establish city-wide rather than ward-based representation. In their attempt to dismantle party machinery, some civic reformers believed that they needed to limit suffrage. The commission appointed to investigate the Tweed Ring scandals recommended in 1878 that the vote be restricted to those who owned property. A leader in a campaign for municipal reform in Newport, Rhode Island, made the case in 1907 that universal suffrage failed to give property owners political power commensurate with their economic power: "The present system," he charged, "has excluded in large degree the representation of those who have the city's well-being most at heart." Rather than a government by the least educated, who he claimed were also the "least interested class of citizens," he proposed a system that gave majority representation to the city's wealthy citizens. As he put it, "It stands to reason that a man paying $5,000 taxes in a town is more interested in the well-being and development of his town than the man who pays no taxes." Although northern and mdiwestern municipal reformers looked with keen interest at legislation that had disenfranchised black and poor white voters in southern states, regulations that actually revoked immigrant voting rights never seemed politically feasible in cities because universal white male suffrage was too deeply entrenched.

In many southern cities, urban politics and civic reform were shaped by new racial and economic alignments. In Memphis, ward-based politicians struggled to meet local needs caused by post-Civil War economic contractions, competition for jobs between Irish immigrants and African-American migrants, new demands for services like street paving and police protection, and severe yellow fever epidemics in 1878–79 that drove multitudes of people out of the city. Severe budgetary problems gave wealthy taxpayers the opportunity to enlist the state legislature to overturn Memphis's home rule and replace the unlikely coalition of Irish, German, Italian and African-American political leaders with a city commission dominated by a white commercial elite. The new government kept taxes low by providing services only in wealthy white neighborhoods. Even after Memphis regained home rule in 1893, the city maintained this form of municipal governance. In Charlotte, North Carolina, racial and class integration of city neighborhoods promoted broad participation in local government between 1865 and the 1890s. But then, a reform campaign of white supremacy and Democratic "redemption" successfully disenfranchised black and illiterate white voters, establishing upper-class political control and redrawing boundaries between different classes and races much more sharply.

Instead of limiting the franchise to property holders, municipal reformers in the North and West turned to strategies that would lessen the impact of immigrant and working-class voters without actually interfering with voting rights. Several of these strategies were designed to regulate elections and to make nominations and election procedures more uniform. By 1905, registration laws requiring residency and strict idenfication of a voter were on the books everywhere, and in the next fifteen years, localities set up election boards, tightened laws making it illegal to vote more than once, and tried to define legitimate use of campaign funds. Also, electoral reform strategies were designed to weaken party machines and to remove party politics from municipal administration. Because bosses thrived on ethnic neighborhoods and party loyalty, reformers tried to institute at-large (city-wide rather than neighborhood-based) elections and nonpartisan ballots (no candidate could run for office under a party label) as a way of attacking the machines. Having to appeal to a large city-wide electorate rather than one neighborhood or ethnic group would diminish the ability of candidates from ethnic and working-class districts to gain office. Large organizations such as civic leagues and business groups would have an advantage in influencing city-wide elections and electing business candidates because they had resources to reach a large and diverse electorate.

Nonpartisan ballots symbolized reformers' claim that there was only one urban public interest, which businessmen best understood. Parties were not needed for public services to be provided as cheaply and efficiently as possible. Civic reformers contended that a city did not need a Democrat or Republican to build a school or lay a sewer; responsible local government was no place for party politicians. Yet removing party labels from election ballots, supposedly to cultivate civic loyalties rather than bloc voting, also had the effect of depriving working-class and ethnic candidates of party resources for campaigning and party employment. Few machine politicians could have stayed in politics without the party's help. Nonpartisan elections favored those who did not need party organization, men of wealth and social standing who restored their claim to office holding. Municipal reformers also campaigned for civil service along with at-large elections and nonpartisan ballots. Intended to destroy the machine's ability to provide employment to its foot soldiers, civil service provided presumably objective standards for hiring municipal employees, using written and oral examinations rather than party affiliation as the qualifying basis for city jobs.

Between 1900 and 1920, nonpartisanship, at-large elections, and civil service were successfully implemented in many cities. Municipal reform was less likely to penetrate large cities with complex electorates, where middle- and upper-class voters did not constitute an electoral majority; but smaller and fast-growing cities, usually in the Midwest and West, usually adopted reform provisions in their charters. Urban scholar Amy Bridges has argued that southwestern cities with a shortage of capital were particularly fertile ground for municipal reform. By emphasizing economic growth, using public policy to fulfill needs of core business supporters, and excluding working-class ethnics from policymaking, reform politicians in cities such as Albuquerque, Phoenix, San Diego, and Dallas succeeded in getting themselves consistently reelected, and in installing commission and city manager governance, non-partisan elections, and civil service. Even in some big cities, reformers succeeded in getting nonpartisan at-large elections adopted: Los Angeles in 1908, Boston in 1909, Akron in 1915, and Detroit in 1918.

Municipal reform campaigns changed patterns of representation. The switch from ward to city-wide electoral districts made it more difficult for ethnic and working-class wards and African-American neighborhoods to gain representation. Socialists in Dayton, Ohio, won 25 percent of the vote in 1909 and elected two aldermen and three assessors, but after a change to city-wide elections, they failed to elect a single candidate even though their share of the total vote increased to 44 percent. The shift to city-wide representation in Los Angeles prevented black and Mexican-American citizens from electing a single city council representative until the most recent period. And city-wide elections in Pittsburgh in 1911 enabled upper-class businessmen and professionals to replace working- and middle-class representatives on the city council and school committee.

The orientation of most civic reformers was reflected in their commitment to applying principles of business management to cities. Trying to make the structure of urban governance match the model of the corporation, reformers proposed reorganizing cities to separate policymaking from administration either through a commission or city manager form of government. The first city to adopt the business model was Galveston, Texas, where business and professional leaders had already secured a charter amendment from the state legislature that replaced ward representation with city-wide elections. Businessmen on the council continued to be outvoted by a nonbusiness faction, but in 1900 emergency circumstances following a disastrous hurricane and flood enabled the state legislature to replace Galveston's city council with a commission of businessmen, each of whom administered a different branch of municipal affairs. The city adopted the commission form permanently and elected seven commissioners on a nonpartisan, at-large basis. In Nashville, Boss Hilary Howse's attempts to spend (overspend, according to some people) public funds to improve the health, education, and welfare of ethnic and racial minorities who supported him provoked conservative business and Democratic party leaders to try to take power away from the ward bosses who were the foundation of his political structure. Charter reforms, establishing a commission government in 1913, led to Howse's ouster two years later. With its aims to streamline government and facilitate the participation of businessmen in government service, the city commission provided an attractive structure around which reformers could rally. By 1915 456 cities operated under commission governance.

The city manager form of government grew out of business reverence for expertise. In 1908, Staunton, Virginia, hired a city manager to administer local affairs in the place of a politically elected mayor. The idea spread slowly at first. But in Dayton, Ohio, John M. Patterson, the president of National Cash Register, working with the Chamber of Commerce and the newly organized Bureau of Municipal Research, began a campaign for charter reform that was enacted as a aiding recovery from a disastrous flood of 1913. Eventually the city manager plan was tried in such larger cities as Cleveland, Cincinnati, and Kansas City. This plan created a new separation of power. It usually provided for a small city council elected on a nonpartisan ballot that would determine policy and pass ordinances. The council would then appoint or hire a city manager, chosen for his (and virtually all city managers were male) administrative and technical skills, who, like a corporate chief, would implement council policies and determine budgets. In some cases the mayor was retained and given mainly titular functions. By 1920, more than 150 cities had city managers. Business interests consistently campaigned for this reform. For example, the *Dallas News* promoted the plan in 1930 by asking, "Why not run Dallas itself on a business schedule by business methods under businessmen?. . . The city manager is the executive of a corporation under a board of directors. Dallas is the corporation. It is as simple as that. Vote for it."

The efficiency argument also produced a more controversial reform: municipal ownership of public utilities. Some reformers believed that regardless of the form of government, bribery and corruption would always fester as long as politicians could collude with big business at public expense. These reformers thought they could destroy bosses' financial resources and provide better services by replacing private franchises with publicly owned operations. City-owned water systems had been common since the mid–nineteenth century. Now, a number of reformers began to advocate public gas, electric, and transportation systems. Although by 1910 several hundred cities, including Cleveland, Detroit, and Chicago, had experimented with this reform, public ownership succeeded mainly in smaller cities. Also, public ownership, supported by socialists, frightened many municipal leaders, and private investors were not of one mind about it. Expenditures on public harbors, roads, and sewers won general acceptance because they stimulated economic growth. But when advocates of public utilities such as gas and electricity tried to supplant private operations, they frequently met strong opposition. Nevertheless, most city dwellers eventually accepted some form of public regulation of utility rates and services, even if public ownership proved unacceptable.

Some bosses were able to adjust to new structures of city governance and even use them for their own purposes. When a city commission government threatened to subvert Omaha boss Tom Dennison's control of the city in 1912, the boss did not fight public sentiment. He merely entered his own slate of candidates for the commission, who then dominated that body for the machine's benefit. Boss Ed Crump solidified his grip on Memphis in the same way when a new city charter established a commission form of government in 1909. James Michael Curley was able to use new city-wide elections in Boston as a way of undermining the ward-based rivals with whom he was contesting for power.

The lines between some bosses and reformers blurred in late nineteenth- and early twentieth-century cities when these bosses supported civic reforms they thought they could take advantage of and when these bosses were pushed by their constituents to support reform campaigns such as public ownership of utilities and laws that promised to help neighborhood residents. For example, New York City's Big Tim Sullivan dashed to the statehouse in Albany to cast a decisive vote in favor of a bill limiting working hours for women to fifty-four a week. (He explained, "I had seen me sister go out to work when she was only fourteen and I know we ought to help these gals by giving 'em a law which will prevent 'em from being broken down while they're still young.") Republican boss George B. Cox of Cincinnati was pressured by the suburban allies to whom he owed his initial election to support the secret ballot and voter registration, usually anathema to a boss. Similarly, municipal reformers who hoped to solve problems of urban decay and poverty found themselves acting like bosses by using the prerogatives of centralized executive power and building political organizations to help them stay in office. Several big-city reform mayors, labeled by historians as reform bosses, responded to ethnic and working-class constituencies and moved beyond their initial goals of eliminating corruption to support measures toward establishing social and economic equity. The mayoral careers of Hazen S. Pingree of Detroit, Samuel M. Jones of Toledo, and Thomas L. Johnson of Cleveland illustrate this pattern.

Pingree was the first reformer to build his own political organization and the first politician to work explicitly for social reform. A Detroit shoe manufacturer, Pingree was drafted into the 1889 mayoral election by a group of Republican businessmen who wanted to rid Detroit of corruption. Pingree won the election by appealing to the city's German, Polish, and Irish voters. He immediately began to apply business principles of prudence and efficiency to government operations, and his success won him reelection in 1891. His struggles to limit the rates and privileges of street-railway, gas, electric, and telephone companies, however, awakened him to the dangers of such monopolistic enterprises and sharpened his concern for the public who paid for these services. When the depression of 1893–94 brought suffering to thousands of Detroiters, Pingree focused his administration directly on the welfare of the working classes. He bolstered relief agencies, authorized public works for unemployment relief, and cajoled merchants to keep prices low and not to lay off workers. Pingree's passion for the poor influenced administrators in other cities to assume greater social responsibilities, and his battles with utilities companies furnished other reformers with strong arguments for municipal ownership.

Pingree was one of the few reform mayors to work for more than economy and efficiency in government. During four terms as mayor he not only ended corruption but also built parks and schools, instituted a more equitable tax structure, established work-relief for the poor, reduced utility rates, and spoke out for a graduated income tax and municipal ownership. Moreover, he ignored efforts to impose middle-class Yankee norms on others. He refused to enforce Sunday closing laws applying to saloons, and he tolerated gambling and prostitution. His administration became a model for reform mayors in other cities.

Samuel "Golden Rule" Jones served as mayor of Toledo from 1897 until his death in 1904, and Tom Johnson was mayor of Cleveland from 1901 until a narrow election defeat in 1909. Like Pingree, Jones and Johnson were successful businessmen who became social reformers. Both actively supported municipal ownership of utilities, and both stressed the need for social justice and equality. Johnson was influenced by the ideas of Henry George, whose book *Progress and Poverty* (1879) made considerable impact on reform thought around the turn of the century. George's proposal to eliminate social inequality by taxing profits that property owners unfairly received from the unearned increase of land values inspired Johnson and others like him to work for social and economic reform. Many of the programs supported by Jones and Johnson bordered on socialism and alienated their business allies. Yet, like Pingree, both mayors sought only to preserve what they believed to be the American tradition, not to change it. Their popular appeal and social welfare projects extended well beyond ordinary economy and efficiency, yet they envisioned their goals as the fulfillment of the American dream.

Pingree, Jones, and Johnson were the exceptions. Most municipal reformers aimed only to "throw the rascals out," and when successful, their "clean governments" often could not match the functions performed by political machines. Although reformers called for honesty and efficiency in government, they rarely mentioned social welfare. Behind their proposals was the notion that city government should provide a climate for economic growth through the provision of efficient administration. The city-as-a-business orientation provided a sharp contrast with socialist, social reform, and working-class ethnic demands to establish social programs aimed at improving the health, welfare, and living conditions of inner-city residents.

Civic reformers' self-righteousness moralism and obsessive budget cutting seldom addressed urban demands for jobs, housing, and better public health. Their attempts to apply business principles to politics commonly underplayed the complexities of business and political administration. A reformer, said Mr. Dooley, the fictional Irish commentator created by newspaper columnist Finley Peter Dunne in 1902,

> thinks business an' honesty is th' same thing. . . . He's got them mixed because they dhress alike. His idea is that all he has to do to make a business administhration is to keep honest men ar-round him. Wrong, I'm not sayin', mind ye, that a man can't do good work an' be honest at th' same time. But whin I hire a la-ad, I find out first whether he is onto his job, an' after a few years I begin to suspect he is honest too. . . . A man ought to be honest to start with an' afther that he ought to be crafty. A pollytician who's on'y honest is jus' th' same as bein' out in a winther storm without anny clothes on.

Thus municipal reformers may have succeeded in improving the general quality of government management by reducing corruption, lowering taxes, and shoring up local services. But their tendency to view urban society only in business and moralistic terms ignored long-term political and social policy and posed an incomplete substitute for the welfare functions of political machines.

BIBLIOGRAPHY

Recent analyses of the relationship between urban political organization and power, governance, and the provision of city services include Amy Bridges, *A City in the Republic: Antebellum New York and the Origins of Machine Politics* (1984); Robin Einhorn, *Property Rules:*

Political Economy in Chicago, 1833–1872 (1991); Terrence J. McDonald, *The Parameters of Urban Fiscal Policy: Socioeconomic Change and Political Culture in San Francisco, 1860–1906* (1986); Terrence J. McDonald and Sally Ward, eds., *The Politics of Urban Fiscal Policy* (1984); and Jon C. Teaford, *The Unheralded Triumph: City Government in America, 1870–1900* (1984). Anthologies and group studies include John M. Allswang, *Bosses, Machines, and Urban Voters: An American Symbiosis* (1977); Blaine A. Brownell and Warren E. Stickle, eds., *Bosses and Reformers: Urban Politics in America, 1880–1920* (1973); Alexander B. Callow, Jr., ed., *The City Boss in America: An Interpretive Reader* (1976); Melvin Holli, *The American Mayor: The Best and Worst Big City Leaders* (1999); and Bruce Stave and Sondra Stave, eds., *Urban Bosses, Machines, and Progressive Reformers*, 2nd rev. ed. (1984).

On independent labor politics in this period, see Leon Fink, *Workingmen's Democracy: The Knights of Labor and American Politics* (1983); Steven J. Ross, *Workers on the Edge: Work, Leisure, and Politics in Industrializing Cincinnati, 1788–1890* (1985); and David Scobey, "Boycotting the Politics Factory: Labor Radicalism and the New York City Mayoral Election of 1884," *Radical History Review* 28–30 (September 1984): 280–325.

Among individual machines, Tammany Hall has received the most attention from historians, most notably from Daniel Czitrom, "Underworlds and Underdogs: Big Tim Sullivan and Metropolitan Politics in New York, 1889–1913," *Journal of American History* 78 (September 1991): 536–58; David C. Hammack, *Power and Society: Greater New York at the Turn of the Century* (1982); Leo Hershkowitz, *Tweed's New York: Another Look* (1977); Chris McNickle, *To Be Mayor of New York: Ethnic Politics in the City, 1898–1930* (1993); and Jerome Mushkat, *Tammany: The Evolution of a Political Machine, 1789–1865* (1971. William L. Riordon, *Plunkett of Tammany Hall* (1995) is a memoir of a boss and includes a perceptive introduction by Peter Quinn.

Other important studies are Steven P. Erie, *Rainbow's End: Irish-Americans and the Dilemma of Urban Machine Politics, 1840–1985* (1988); Philip. J. Ethington, *The Public City: The Political Construction of Urban Life In San Francisco, 1850–1900* (1994); Thomas W. Hanchett, *Sorting Out the New South: Race, Class, and Urban Development in Charlotte, 1875–1975* (1998); Carl V. Harris, *Political Power in Birmingham, 1871–1921* (1977); Joy J. Jackson, *New Orleans in the Gilded Age: Politics and Urban Progress, 1860–1896* (1969); Lawrence Larsen and Nancy J. Hulston, *Pendergast!* (1997); Peter McCaffery, *When Bosses Ruled Philadelphia: The Emergence of the Republican Machine, 1867–1933* (1993); Zane L. Miller, *Boss Cox's Cincinnati: Urban Politics in the Progressive Era* (1968); and Eugene J. Watts, *The Social Basis of City Politics: Atlanta, 1865–1903* (1978). On Chicago, see William J. Grimshaw, *Bitter Fruit: Black Politics and the Chicago Machine, 1931–1991* (1992); Edward R. Kantowicz, *Polish-American Politics in Chicago, 1888–1914* (1975); and Joel A. Tarr, *A Study in Boss Politics: William Lorimer of Chicago* (1971).

For perspectives on municipal reform, see Amy Bridges, *Morning Glories: Municipal Reform in the Southwest* (1997); James D. Bolin, *Bossism and Reform in a Southern City: Lexington, Kentucky, 1880–1940* (2000); Michael Ebner and Eugene Tobin, eds., *The Age of Urban Reform: New Perspectives on the Progressive Era* (1977); Kenneth Finegold, *Experts and Politicians: Reform Challenges to Machine Politics in New York, Cleveland, and Chicago* (1995); Maureen Flanagan, *Seeing with their Hearts: Chicago Women and the Vision of the Good City, 1871–1933* (2002); Melvin G. Holli, *Reform in Detroit: Hazen S. Pingree and Urban Politics* (1969); Bradley R. Rice, *Progressive Cities: The Commission Government Movement in America, 1901–1920* (1977); Martin J. Schiesl, *The Politics of Efficiency: Municipal Administration and Reform in America, 1880–1920* (1977); and Lynette B. Wrenn, *Crisis and Commission Government in Memphis* (1998).

7

Refashioning the Social and Physical Environment

IMPULSES OF SOCIAL REFORM

Urban bosses and municipal (civic) reformers contested within the same arenas: the electoral system and the established institutions of government. But in the closing years of the nineteenth century and dawning years of the twentieth, new efforts to address problems of urban life arose both within and outside normal political paths. This agitation emerged during a period of changing political contexts. Party loyalties began to erode as antiboss legislation tightened voter registration laws and instituted secret ballots and direct primaries. The political arena began to open to pressure groups, such as manufacturers' organizations, labor lobbies, civic leagues, women's clubs, and professional associations, making politics more fragmented, political combinations more fluid, and campaigns more issue oriented. Lobbying and coalition building supplanted older party channels, and reformers used new methods of trying to create and mobilize public opinion, such as sensationalistic journalism, celebrity picket lines, witness-calling investigations, referendum campaigns, and social science surveys.

Occasionally, maverick candidates such as socialists could win political office and reform coalitions could reorient the direction of urban politics. American socialists vigorously denounced urban inequality, poverty, and lack of welfare services, proposing their own remedies, which ranged from expanded public responsibility to hire the unemployed to municipal ownership of utilities and transportation. Municipal socialists were particularly visible in cities like Milwaukee, Reading, Schenectady, and Bridgeport, where socialist mayors were elected to office. In 1912 socialists held more than twelve hundred public offices in 340 cities and towns across the country.

Nationally, however, men's allegiance to political parties waned, and the male political culture, which had been the most striking characteristic of nineteenth-century political life, lost its vitality. As upper- and middle-class men abandoned partisan politics to working-class and ethnic machines and turned their interest to single-issue reform tactics, they found themselves in territory that women's voluntary reform associations had long occupied. As reformers tried to secure legislation to redress social problems by increasing the government's role in social welfare and economic life, men and women found themselves joining to achieve common goals. New ideas about government's broader social responsibility resonated with women's social concerns. Not surprisingly, then, female social activists played a major role in the articulation of urban reform, prior to their own direct participation as voters.

The liberal creed of the early nineteenth century had been laissez-faire, the belief that the natural order of things ensured equilibrium and that government ought not interfere with that natural order. But by century's end that faith had begun to dissolve. A broad phalanx of social reformers, ranging from wide-eyed humanitarians to calculating special interests, marched under a banner of public and private intervention to remove injustices from society. Their response to greed and individualism was community responsibility to promote the welfare of all. Historian Daniel Rodgers has described a shared language of social reform, influenced by goals and issues prevalent in Europe. The new thinking in America included a conception of social bonds that challenged older notions that success depended on strengths of individual character, that the economy was the product of individual calculations, and that governance was a matter of empowering the best men. This emphasis on public responsibility was expressed in a new interest in the social and physical environment, the discovery of what Rodgers termed "new forms of social sinning and corresponding new measures of social control," and an intense concern with community cohesion.[1] Social reformers also focused on protecting those whom they saw as victims of industrialization, such as women and child laborers, those injured by industrial accidents, the elderly, and unemployed people, and they pursued goals of industrial peace and cooperation.

Like civic reform, social reform grew out of changing economic and social conditions. Indeed, some social reformers were also civic reformers. It was based largely in the new middle class. Its membership consisted basically of men and women who were becoming specialists in expanding areas of law, medicine, education, social work, and other professions, as well as new-breed professionals in fields of business, labor, and agriculture. Their awakening professional consciousness encouraged them to apply their expertise to their environments. More important, it led them to support and to undertake scientific investigations of urban problems. From the 1870s onward, a number of different groups, mostly private and voluntary, sponsored formal examinations of aspects of urban life. These included surveys of public health and housing, studies of the incidence and location of poverty, and investigations of local corruption. One of the most striking qualities of early social science was the way in which the field tied scholarly methods to women's traditional community concerns. Agencies and organizations that were committed to social science methods provided women reformers with quasi-professional positions as investigators from which they carried domestic and social concerns into far corners of the city. By the turn of the century the methods and language of social science and women's role as social investigators had become institutionalized components of reform strategy.

The emphasis on investigation had two objectives. First, middle-class reformers were an inquiring generation: they felt a strong urge to know the facts. Many of them believed they had temporarily lost their ability to understand fast-growing, ever-changing urban society. Only by restoring that understanding could they soothe their sense of crisis and begin to formulate plans to improve present conditions. Second, reformers from new middle-class ranks had a strong faith in knowledge and conscience as reforming agents. Many believed that if the general public could be kept informed and if the major problems could be identified and exposed, an enlightened citizenry would rally behind programs to destroy injustice.

A new kind of journalism of exposure became a principal weapon in the campaign for reform. For nearly a century after the Revolution, few city newspapers gave more than a passing glance to local affairs. Most newspapers had limited circulation and acted as mouthpieces for a political party, focusing mainly on state, national, and international issues. But the decades following the Civil War witnessed an extraordinary popularization and proliferation of newspapers and magazines. The invention of the steam press, which could print copies much faster than the old hand presses, and increasing use of paper made of wood pulp instead of rags and linen enabled printers to produce copy much more cheaply and voluminously. The telegraph and telephone quickened the pace of communications and made information more accessible than ever before. To sell more newspapers, publishers began to replace political rhetoric with news and features. Journalists now created news as well as reported it. Circulation-hungry publishers such as Joseph Pulitzer, who bought the *New York World* in 1883, and William Randolph Hearst, who acquired the *San Francisco Call* in 1887 and the *New York Journal* in 1896, filled their pages with screaming headlines, sensational stories, and dramatic photographs. At the same time, literary magazines began to give way to more popular, cheaper periodicals, such as *Cosmopolitan*, *McClure's*, and *Everybody's*, whose circulations grew to hundreds of thousands.

Newspapers and magazines tried to attract readers by exposing the scandals and injustices of contemporary society. Some articles were lurid and ill informed, but many others were based on careful investigation—a major standard of social science—and were designed to alert the middle-class public to the need for reform. A leading spokesman for this journalism was Jacob Riis, a Danish immigrant who worked for twenty years as a police reporter for the *New York Tribune* and later the *Evening Sun.* Riis rose to national prominence in 1890 with publication of *How the Other Half Lives,* an intimate, shocking portrayal of the lives and housing of poor people in New York. In a tone that was alternately sympathetic and indignant, Riis tried to alarm readers by describing "what the tenements are and how they grew to what they are." Using the camera as an instrument of reform and propaganda, the book included numerous photographs, many taken by Riis himself, which graphically illustrated the misery of "the other half." But, also, Riis posed and framed his photographs in a particular way to convey his personal, middle-class values of order and morality.

Other journalists stirred public attention with investigations of political abuses. Probably the most well-known reporter was Lincoln Steffens, whose seven articles on urban corruption in *McClure's* in 1902–3 were combined in a book titled *The Shame of the Cities,* published in 1904. Steffens was incensed by the unfair privileges that he saw pervading American society. Through exposure of the misrule that he observed in St. Louis, Pittsburgh, Minneapolis, and Philadelphia and through his review of the partial success of reform in Chicago and New York, Steffens appealed to mass sentiments of responsibility, indignation, and guilt. Steffens and other journalists meant their exposés to arouse the popular will and to revive democracy. As Steffens wrote in his introduction to *The Shame of the Cities,* "These articles, if they have proved nothing else, have demonstrated beyond doubt that we can stand the truth; that there is pride in the character of American citizenship; and that this pride may be a power in the land."

Attempts at reform also pervaded fictional writing. Novelists probed the impact of urban life on human character. The quest for power and wealth was depicted by Theodore Dreiser in *The Financier,* and by Frank Norris in *The Pit,* Stephen Crane's *Maggie, A Girl of the Streets,* and Upton Sinclair's *The Jungle* protested what they identified as the degradations of urban poverty. Sinclair's novel also exposed loathsome practices of Chicago's meatpacking industry and shocked Congress into passing a federal meat-inspection law in 1906. New opportunities, pleasures, and vulnerabilty for women in the city shaped the narrative frameworks of David Graham Phillips's *Susan Lenox, Her Fall and Rise* and Dreiser's *Sister Carrie* and *Jenny Gerhardt.*

African-American intellectuals also contributed to the literature of social reform. Memphis newspaper editor Ida B. Wells wrote editorialss, essays, and pamphlets attacking the lynching of black men and exposing the use of dubious sexual accusations to serve as a cover for the real motivations of economic and political racism. W. E. B. Du Bois's book *The Philadelphia Negro* (1899) was a pioneering work of social science research that identified structural causes of poverty and identified important black political and economic contributions to the city. His eloquent book of essays, *The Souls of Black Folk,* (1903) used examples from African-American history, culture, and politics to educate readers on the "problem of the color line" and the black experience of "double consciousness."

In 1907–8, investigative social science and journalism combined to produce the most extensive catalog of modern urban life yet collected. Under the direction of Paul U. Kellogg, a professional social worker, and sponsored by the Russell Sage Foundation, the six-volume *Pittsburgh Survey* detailed the city's economic development and the social costs of industrialization. It particularly showed how political corruption and irresponsible business practices had contributed to Pittsburgh's problems of poverty, pollution, and inequitable tax structure. Kellogg and many like him in other cities strongly believed in the potential of reason and information as reforming instruments, investing their faith in the outrage of an informed public, but perhaps underestimating the strength of opposing forces.

REMEDIES OF SOCIAL REFORMERS

The activities of social reformers included a multitude of causes, ranging from religious humanizing of the Social Gospel movement to breadbasket issues of labor organizations. Such a variety of concerns does not fit a generalized interpretation that can categorize every program and personality. From an urban point of view, however, the most salient aspect of the reform movement was the attempt by middle-class individuals and groups to control and mitigate the problems of inner cities, where conditions seemed most menacing. In addition to the concerns with housing and health discussed in Chapter 5, and concerns with political process discussed in Chapter 6, social reformers' efforts in the inner city were concentrated in three major areas: moral and religious responsibility for social betterment, epitomized by the Social Gospel; the civic and cultural enlightenment of inner-city dwellers sponsored by educational reformers; and the settlement-house movement's drive to bridge cultural gaps and improve neighborhood life. Each of these areas opened new opportunities for women to participate in and influence public affairs, and activists in each area increasingly advocated government responsibility in refashioning a better urban society.

Religious and Moral Reform

During the 1870s and 1880s, a few clergymen of older Protestant sects reacted to social crises and labor struggles resulting from urbanization and industrialization by espousing a new interpretation of their religious mission. The Social Gospel, as this ethic came to be called, emphasized the humane aspects of Christianity. According to the Social Gospel the salvation of society replaced the salvation of an individual soul as the principal religious goal. Before the Civil War, Unitarian ministers such as Boston's William Ellery Channing and Theodore Parker had stressed the duty of Christians to attend to the needs of the poor. As problems of urbanization heightened after the war, this attitude spread and leaders of other Protestants sects tried to make their churches instruments of reform.

The leading figure of the Social Gospel movement was Washington Gladden, a Congregationalist minister in Columbus, Ohio. Gladden preached that modern Christians should seek salvation by attempting to realize the Kingdom of God on earth rather than worrying about the afterlife of their individual souls. Gladden, Walter Rauschenbusch, a Baptist minister and professor at the Rochester (New York) Theological Seminary, Josiah Strong, pastor of the Cincinnati's Central Congregational Church, Shaler Mathews of the University of Chicago Divinity School, and R. Heber Newton, a New York Episcopalian, stressed the social responsibilities of Christianity through good works and social betterment. Gladden supported arbitration as a means of achieving industrial peace between labor unions and employers. Rauschenbusch worked with Jacob Riis to obtain better living conditions for the poor. Other clergymen sponsored investigations and worked to improve conditions in slum districts.

Several socially conscious congregations, with help from wealthy members, established institutional churches in low-income neighborhoods. These churches offered nurseries, kindergartens, medical clinics, employment agencies, recreation centers, and adult education classes. The goal of all activities was service. As Josiah Strong wrote in *The Challenge of the City* (1898), "Inasmuch as Christ came not to be ministered unto but to minister, the open and institutional church, filled and moved by his spirit of ministering love, seeks to become the center and source of all beneficent and philanthropic effort, and to take the leading part in every movement which has for its end the alleviation of human suffering, the elevation of man, and the betterment of the world."

The Social Gospel was particularly influential in advancing an environmental explanation of urban social ills. Gladden and Rauschenbusch believed that people were not intrinsically bad; rather, the conditions in which people lived corrupted them. Social Gospelers believed that by reforming the environment they could create a moral society. Dismayed by the greed of industrial capitalism, they poured their energies into the inner city, and through investigations, missions, and institutional churches they awakened a host of sensitive men and women to the needs and methods of social reform. A few Social Gospelers took radical approaches to the solution of urban problems. Boston's W. D. P. Bliss, for example, helped found the Society

of Christian Socialists in 1889. The majority, however, were moderates, clergymen who felt guilty about their own and their churches' neglect of social
problems and who reacted by trying to reorient the gospel into a more secular direction. The Social Gospel influenced some Catholics and Jews as well,
and it also reached rural areas. But for the most part it evolved from the impact of urban problems on modern Protestantism.

Many Social Gospelers joined the drive to close down saloons. The temperance movement was not new to late–nineteenth-century urban America.
But after the Civil War the movement gathered fresh momentum, spurred by
activists who believed they could improve conditions of the laboring classes
by destroying the centers of immorality and political corruption. Temperance reformers were convinced that inner-city neighborhoods contained too
many saloons. (They may have been right; by the 1890s, many districts had
one saloon for every fifteen to twenty adult men.) Because competition was
keen, reformers theorized, a drinking establishment could survive only by
staying open after hours or by offering extra services such as gambling and
prostitution. Such temptations, plus the addictive effect of liquor, caused
men to squander their wages and weakened family life. Moreover, saloons
were the bunkers of boss politics. Destroy the saloon and you remove the
boss's base of operations.

The post-Civil War temperance movement was particularly fueled by
the energies of native-born Protestant women. They joined the temperance
crusade because it addressed the real problems of women victimized by alcoholic fathers and husbands and because as a social problem the issue of drink
fell within women's traditional domestic concerns. Women's first activities
were to stage marches, rallies, and prayer vigils to try to close saloons. Then
temperance activism took organizational shape in the Women's Christian
Temperance Union (WCTU), the largest women's organization, founded in
1874 and with 245,000 members by 1911. Under Frances Willard's leadership, local chapters organized departments in areas such as labor, health, social purity, education, and eventually, suffrage, all under the banner of "home
protection." The WCTU taught women how to translate domestic imperatives
into political action, and local chapters were directly involved in electoral politics. The pressure group tactics of organizations like the Anti-Saloon League
(founded in 1893), which ultimately resulted in state and national prohibition
laws, shared a great deal with the reform strategies engineered by the WCTU.

Although temperance and prohibition attracted large numbers of rural
enthusiasts who feared the city's evil ways, much of the leadership and financial support of these crusades came from city dwellers, largely native
white Protestants who inhabited the outer wards. Some temperance advocates were willing to abandon total prohibition in favor of more pragmatic
goals. They worked for enforcement of licensing and closing laws, and they
used pamphlets and public school programs to emphasize the dangers of
liquor and the virtues of abstinence. In a few cities temperance reformers

The Campaign for Prohibition. This postcard appeal circulated by the Anti-Saloon League to "defend the home" by shutting down saloons utilizes the Womens Christian Temperance Union's domestic rhetoric of "home protection," draping its native-born credentials (and stoking anti-immigrant feeling) in multiple American flags.

helped to establish local-option rules that permitted individual wards or precincts to vote themselves dry. The greatest successes occurred in Chicago, where, by 1908, almost half of the city was dry—mostly in the outer districts.

In the minds of many moral reformers it was a short step from the bottle to other temptations. Thus crusades against saloons often spread to gambling and prostitution. Most big cities tolerated unofficial segregation of gambling dens and brothels in red-light districts. Chicago's levee district, New York's Tenderloin, San Francisco's Barbary Coast, and New Orleans's Bourbon Street were well-known centers of vice and were generally safe from police raids. But what Victorians had regarded as a "necessary evil," reformers regarded as the "social evil," a moral problem and a national menace. Cleveland, St. Louis, and a few other cities experimented with police registration and medical inspection of prostitutes rather than trying to abolish their profession. But most of the outcry about the "white slave trade" (the kidnapping of young women for sale into brothels) triggered efforts to eliminate prostitution altogether.

Reformers' writings about prostitution reflected anxieties over unrestricted immigration, the anonymity of the city, the evils of liquor, the growth of what seemed to be an urban working-class culture far outside their control, and the changing role of women in society. The presence of women in public life had blurred the nineteenth-century distinction between "public" women, almost always synonymous with fallen women, and respectable wives and mothers. Female reformers saw prostitution somewhat differently, focusing on it as the symbol of sexual and economic exploitation. They condemned the pitifully low wages paid for women' work and identified prostitutes as the most victimized female labor. They hoped that eradication of prostitution would elevate the status of all women.

In the early 1900s, reformers in several cities established vice commissions to investigate prostitution and gambling and to recommend legislation. Reformers recommended four measures as remedies: (1) labor legislation to improve working conditions for women so that they would not be lured by adversity into prostitution; (2) education campaigns to alert the public to the dangers of venereal disease; (3) neighborhood recreational facilities to replace vice centers; and (4) nuisance and abatement laws by which citizens could obtain court orders to close down offensive establishments.

By the 1920s, however, technology enabled vice operators to circumvent most restrictive legislation. The automobile enabled gambling and prostitution to flourish in roadhouses outside city borders away from the law, and the telephone created the bookie and the call girl. In addition, the effect of legal crackdowns on prostitution was not to destroy it but to force prostitutes from the relative security of public brothels to the riskier act of streetwalking. Control of prostitution shifted from madams and prostitutes themselves to pimps and organized crime syndicates. Such changes meant that prostitutes faced new kinds of brutality from the police and from their new employers.

Educational Reform

Reformers had high hopes for using public schools as an agent of social reform. Education could be the key to instilling urban masses with reformers' standards of citizenship and democracy. However, late nineteenth-century critics of urban school systems charged that schools were disorganized, over-crowded, too vulnerable to political pressures from neighborhood interests, not effective enough in reaching immigrant children, and not relevant to the needs of modern industrial life. Before 1900, seldom more than two-thirds of school-age urban children attended classes—often because working-class families could not afford to withhold their children from the labor market.

An initial response to the problem of school attendance was the enactment of compulsory attendance laws, with truant officers mandated to enforce them. Such laws, passed in the 1870s and 1880s, along with increasing populations, caused enrollments to swell. Between 1870 and 1910, public school enrollments rose from 6.9 million to 17.8 million, and the number of public high schools increased from five hundred to ten thousand. These numbers confronted cities with problems of teacher shortages and inadequate buildings. New schools accounted for a large upsurge in bonded indebtedness in many cities during the last decades of the nineteenth century. Between 1860 and 1890, the number of normal (teacher-training) schools quadrupled, but they still could not meet the demand for teachers. Significantly, the increased demand opened up the profession to women, who now outnumbered men in the common schools. By paying women only half what they paid men (salaries of $600 to $700 per year for female teachers, $900 to $1,200 for males), school committees could increase teaching staffs without straining budgets.

A Progressive Schoolroom. By placing children, rather than subject matter, at the center of the learning process, school reformers helped make education more relevant to modern city life. This new approach also gave students freedom to participate in classroom activities, rather than forcing them to sit at rigid attention.

The pressures on public school facilities and personnel would have been worse had it not been for the expansion of parochial education. Responding to the needs of growing numbers of Catholic immigrants, the Third Plenary Council, meeting in Baltimore in 1884, urged that each parish provide schools for its children. By the end of the century, nearly a million children were enrolled in Catholic elementary schools and several dioceses had established parochial high schools. By 1920, parochial schools enrolled between 20 and 40 percent of school-age children in cities with large immigrant Catholic populations like New York, Boston, Philadelphia, Chicago, and St. Louis.

Social reformers saw school problems as extending beyond enrollment to more basic questions of school organization and curriculum. Reformers' commitment to scientific efficiency led them, like the municipal reformers discussed in Chapter 6, to advocate centralized rather than ward-based school districts and professional rather than politically based administrators. A pioneer in administrative innovation was William T. Harris, superintendent of St. Louis public schools from 1867 to 1880. Harris believed that urban education should conform to new patterns of economic organization—meaning the factory—and he stressed the need for rigorous school administration and pupil discipline. He supported reforms such as graded schools, centralized policymaking, standardized curricula, and even uniform architecture.

To expand the reach of education into burgeoning immigrant neighborhoods, school systems experimented with kindergarten programs for very young children, modeled on the scheme of German educator F. W. A. Froebel, and with evening schools to teach English and civics to immigrant adults. Kindergartens stressed the importance of pleasant surroundings, self-activity, and physical training as a means of developing learning capacities. According to the editor of *Century Magazine,* they also provided "the earliest opportunity to catch the little Russian, the little Italian, the little German, Pole, Syrian and the rest and begin to make good American citizens of them." Proponents of evening schools claimed that their manual training programs would promote social mobility and economic efficiency and that their classes in English instruction would Americanize immigrants and shift their taste away from moving picture houses and vaudeville theatres to good literature. Some localities even attempted to make evening instruction compulsory for immigrants, so convinced were they of the necessity of extending the public school's outreach beyond the daytime classroom.

One of the most important educational innovations proposed by reformers was vocational training. By the early 1900s, scores of cities had established trade schools and vocational programs to train children in industrial skills. A 1910 survey located such programs in twenty-nine states, mostly in urban schools. Proponents of vocational education claimed that it would give students discipline and make schooling more relevant to everyday life. Philosopher John Dewey believed that vocational training would restore what industrial progress had eroded. "The invention of machinery, the institution of the factory system, and the division of labor have changed the home from a workshop into a simple dwelling place," he wrote. "While need of the more formal intellectual training in the school has decreased, there arises an urgent demand for the introduction of methods of manual and industrial discipline that shall give the child what he formerly obtained in his home and social life." But increasingly vocational education, soon accompanied by programs of vocational guidance, functioned to track working-class and immigrant children into manual work and to redefine the mission of education. Family, ethnic, and class background tended to determine the measures used to determine which program would best fit a child's future position in life.

By the 1910s, expectations for what urban education could accomplish were extraordinarily high. According to historian Robert Wiebe, educational reform reflected a belief that "the schools would facilitate the arrival of Social Rationality, preparing the nation for a higher civilization."[2] Even those reforms directed at the middle class—high schools, for example—revealed a strong belief in formal schooling as the best instrument for shaping American culture and for bringing order to heterogeneous urban society.

Settlements

The settlement-house movement became one of the most influential branches of urban reform. The idea originated in England, where a group of young intellectuals established themselves in a residence called Toynbee Hall in the London slums in 1884. There, these men and women sought to improve living conditions for working-class laborers by bringing them education and appreciation for the arts. At the same time, Toynbee Hall residents believed they could learn about life from the people they hoped to serve and thereby bridge the gap between classes. Toynbee Hall inspired a number of young Americans who were visiting or studying abroad, and several of them organized settlement houses when they returned to the United States. Stanton Coit started the Neighborhood Guild (renamed University Settlement) in a New York tenement apartment in 1886. Over the next few years Vida Scudder and Lillian Wald established other settlements in New York, Jane Addams and Ellen Gates Starr founded Hull House in Chicago, Graham Taylor opened Chicago Commons, and Robert A. Woods founded Andover House in Boston. By 1897, there were seventy-four settlements in the United States, and by 1910, more than four hundred.

Most participants in early settlements were young, middle-class, educated, religious-minded, and idealistic women and men disturbed by the social barriers between classes and frustrated by their own apparent uselessness in a society that cried for reform. Settlement workers had a strong desire to help, to apply their ideas of service (influenced by the Social Gospel) to the challenges of the city. They also had a strong investigative impulse, an urge to find out for themselves what urban society's problems were like.

Settlememt Houses as Urban Neighbors. Settlement house workers hoped that educating young people would help create better citizens, and that children would encourage their families to join settlement house reform activities. Chicago's Hull House's initiatives included kindergartens, an employment bureau, an art gallery, libraries, English and citizenship classes, and theater, music and art classes. The actress Martha Scott is shown here playing the piano at Hull House and teaching singing to neighborhood boys.

Women particularly found new opportunities in settlements. Settlement work offered solutions to those young, college-educated women who felt they had no purposeful way to participate in "life," no outlet to apply their training. Replacing family roles with larger, public responsibilities, settlements fused social activism with conventional female concerns for nurture and sacrifice, and some women chose participation in reform as an alternative to marriage. A 1911 survey found that 53 percent of settlements surveyed housed women only. Even in those settlements containing both sexes, strong-minded, energetic women tended to dominate. The female communities established in these places created social and political networks that propelled settlement workers into leadership roles in early twentieth-century social and political reform agitation.

As residents of the inner city, settlement workers viewed problems of poverty firsthand, and they actively sought to improve living conditions for immigrants and other poor people. The settlement house itself became an hub of reform, acting as an educational center, information clearinghouse, and forum for debate. Settlement workers organized English and civics classes, amateur concerts and theatrical productions, and kindergartens. Jane Addams,

Robert A. Woods, and Lillian Wald joined educational reformers in lobbying for public adoption of kindergartens, vocational training, school nurses, and playgrounds. Because one of their major goals was revitalization of inner-city neighborhoods, settlement workers strongly backed housing reforms and regulatory legislation. In the cause of labor reform, settlements offered rooms for union meetings, and settlement leaders Florence Kelley, Mary McDowell, Jane Addams, and Mary Simkhovitch spoke out in support of workers' rights.

These activities had a special meaning for the female participants, for they enabled women not only to take part in public affairs but also to develop new, paid professions for themselves. As settlement-house workers moved their efforts on behalf of child protection, neighborhood health care, poverty relief, and labor relations into the public arena, they prompted private humanitarians and government agencies to fund such paid positions as juvenile court and probation officers, school nurses and public health administrators, social workers, and factory inspectors. Often, because of their experiences, women settlement workers were hired for these positions, and they created a new professional culture that combined their desire to serve with a mission to make scientific knowledge about social problems understandable to the public. Lillian Wald, for example, was a school nurse who helped create the first independent public health nursing service and helped define nursing as a dignified profession independent from doctors. Florence Kelley used her background as an advocate for better factory conditions to become Illinois's first chief factory inspector.

The importance of the settlement movement lay in its flexibility and influence. Settlement workers were occasionally romantic and naïve; they could not always erase attitudes of condescension and paternalism toward immigrants, and they kept facilities for blacks separate from those for whites for fear of driving whites away. But they invested faith in urban social interaction, believing that immigrants did not have to shed their cultural backgrounds to become good Americans and that middle-class Americans could learn from immigrants as well as teach them. Settlements were based, remarked Jane Addams, "on the theory that the dependence of classes on each other is reciprocal."

An important contrast developed between white female reformers, who worked mainly in settlements of northern cities, and black female reformers, who operated independently in both the South and, increasingly, in northern cities. While middle-class white women worked for government-sponsored programs to help people in need—mainly immigrant and native-born working classes—African-American women, barred from white political institutions, raised funds from private donors and focused on aiding members of their own race. African-American female reformers engaged in such efforts as funding black schools, old-age homes, and hospitals, and they also worked for race uplift and the protection of black women from sexual exploitation. Their ranks included Jane Hunter, who founded a home for unmarried black women in Cleveland in 1911 and influenced the establishment of similar homes in other cities, and Nannie Burroughs, who established a school for black females in Washington, D.C.

Eventually the settlement movement succumbed to professionalization. After World War I, the houses lost their attractiveness and their functions were assumed by trained social workers, who brought more expertise to the slums but also more bureaucratic impersonality. As a result the poor came to be viewed as clients rather than as partners in the battle against poverty and decay. Yet for a full generation settlements provided hundreds of women and men with training and experience in social reform.

Experience in settlement houses, and especially the efforts in support of school nurses, building safety codes, health clinics, playgrounds, labor legislation, and other reform activities, prompted urban social reformers to believe in greater government responsibility to ensure social justice and welfare. But raising public consciousness and obtaining reform legislation were not enough. Because they served a clientele who often could not afford their professional services, settlement workers constantly searched for stable sources of funding. Relying on the voluntary beneficence of individual humanitarians was precarious; only government could provide constant funding. So reformers lobbied state governments for the establishment of publicly funded employment bureaus, county governments for probation officers and social workers to help juvenile legal offenders, and municipal governments for playground construction and staffing.

Urban middle-class social reformers embraced the city. They believed that within the city lay the potential for human progress. As reformer Frederick Howe wrote in 1905, "The ready responsiveness of democracy, under the close association which the city involves, forecasts a movement for the improvement of human society more hopeful than anything the world has ever known." Along with the responsibility to help the masses, many social reformers also wanted to restore what they believed were traditional values of social deference and cultural purity. In this way, their spirit of service and sacrifice could easily be refashioned into condescension and paternalism, in many cases translating into support for immigration restriction and racial segregation. Many service-minded middle-class reformers wrongly assumed their perspective to be universally shared. As the fictional saloonkeepr Mr. Dooley candidly observed,

> [T]is a gr-reat mistake to think that annywan ra-ally wants to rayform. Ye niver heerd of a man rayformin' himself. He'll rayform other people gladly. He likes to do it. But a healthy man'll niver rayform while he has th' strenth. . . . But a rayformer don't see it. . . . [He] spinds th' rest iv his life tellin' us where we are wrong. He's good at that. On'y he don't unherstand that people wud rather be wrong an' comfortable thin right in jail.

What was service to some was meddling to others. Yet in spite of its limitations, social reform brought many changes to urban America, broadly constructing the foundation for the Progressive Era.

PLANNING AND ENGINEERING THE CITY

While social reformers, largely female and increasingly professional, tried to restore neighborhoods and social relations, various groups of males, professionals of another sort, tried to beautify the whole city and attend to everyday service needs of all city dwellers. Land use, sewerage and sanitation, streetlights, bridge and street building, and other such issues posed problems that required technological and professional, not political or humanitarian, creativity. In addressing these issues, American urban dwellers, especially the engineering profession, developed systems and standards of worldwide significance.

During the middle and late nineteenth century, efforts to create large, landscaped city parks had awakened people to possibilities of determining the mode and direction of future urban growth. By 1890, landscaping had merged with the new professions of architecture and engineering to create the City Beautiful movement, an attempt to improve life within cities by enhancing civic design. The City Beautiful blossomed at the World's

The Brooklyn bridge, completed in 1883, was celebrated as an aesthetic and engineering marvel, its graceful arches and intricate steel cables a testimony to the glories of technological progress and urban ascendancy.

Columbian Exposition in Chicago in 1893–94. This was the largest of a score
of fairs held in American cities during the last quarter of the nineteenth century and early years of the twentieth. Heralded as commemorative exposi-
tions, these extravaganzas were usually organized to advertise a city's
progress and opportunities. The 1893 fair marked the tercentennial of
Columbus's voyage to the New World. Congress had chosen Chicago as the
site because the city had made a remarkable recovery from its devastating
fire of 1871. The fair's impressive exhibits of agricultural and industrial technology, plus its fantastic entertainments (the Midway offered everything
from a Cairo street to a Hawaiian volcano), offered spectators visions of an
idealized future and a romanticized past.

More important, the Chicago exposition showed what planners could do
if they had the chance. Daniel Burnham, a prominent architect and the fair's
supervisor, mustered a battery of notables—including landscaper Frederick
Law Olmsted and maverick architect Louis Sullivan—to plan a fully new city
on Chicago's southern lakefront. More than seven thousand workers built a
"White City," with neoclassical buildings, streets, sewers, a water system, and
other services, all coordinated to a master design. The spacious, orderly, mon-
umental character of the exposition in no way resembled the gray, smoky,
teeming streets of most inner cities. Yet the White City captured the imagina-
tions of civic leaders and inspired them to beautify their own communities.
Most commonly the City Beautiful was translated into the construction of new
public buildings and civic centers. Burnham, Olmsted's son Frederick Jr.,
Charles M. Robinson (an architect from Rochester whose many publications
made him spokesman of the City Beautiful), and other planners were hired by
cities to draw plans for new courthouses, libraries, and government centers.

In a few instances the City Beautiful movement generated projects
that addressed the city as a whole, not just one part. In 1900, several planners who had been active in the Chicago fair were commissioned to prepare
a plan for the beautification of Washington, D.C. Their efforts left the city
with a mall between the Capitol and the Potomac River, a number of new
monuments, and Rock Creek Park, much of which had been envisioned by
Pierre Charles L'Enfant a century earlier. In 1906, the Commercial Club of
Chicago engaged Burnham and his associates to devise a comprehensive
plan for the city. Their scheme, submitted in 1909 and accepted by the city
council in 1910, shaped Chicago's development for the next five decades
and became one of the most influential documents in the history of city
planning. The Burnham Plan sought to create a "well-ordered, convenient,
and unified city." In practical terms this meant improved transportation, accessible areas for public recreation, and provisions to control subsequent
growth. The plan specified a new railroad terminal, an east-west boulevard,
a civic center, lakefront parks and beaches, and large forest preserves
around the city's borders. The project was expensive, and several of its more
elaborate schemes had to be abandoned. Yet most of it was eventually realized, and its scope and innovation aroused nationwide fascination.

"The Close of a Career." Around the turn of the century, thousands of horses trod city streets and often were abandoned when they died from old age or overuse. Their carcasses created health hazards as well as disgusting sights, though, as the photographer of this scene is trying to emphasize, children playing on the streets and adults going about their business apparently became so used to the problem that they ignored it.

Burnham's motto was "Make no little plans. . . . Make big plans; aim high in hope and work." Yet few other cities could reproduce Chicago's accomplishments. In most places City Beautiful projects consisted of attempts to make commercial districts more attractive and profitable for business. Problems of poverty and social inequality were not their primary concerns. Burnham, Robinson, and others were not oblivious to social problems, but they claimed that improvements such as parks and sanitation would correct imbalances. Their uncritical optimism—plus a faithfulness to the needs of private investment—limited the accomplishments of early planning. By the time of the St. Louis Exposition of 1904, the City Beautiful movement began to split, with some planners continuing to advocate aesthetics as the answer to urban problems and others involving themselves in planning that froze the divisions between uptown and downtown, center and suburbs, through the institutionalization of zoning and metropolitan and regional plans (see Chapter 8).

Even more relevant to the practical needs of urban dwellers than planning were issues of sanitation and health. In 1900, experts estimated that on average every resident of New York City annually produced 160 pounds of garbage (unused food and bones), 1,200 pounds of ashes (from stoves and furnaces), and 100 pounds of rubbish (discarded shoes, furniture, and other items). Europeans of that era generated only about half as much trash. At the same time, there were some three and a half million horses in American cities; each one produced about twenty pounds of manure and a gallon of urine daily. Moreover, each city had to dispose of thousands of carcasses of broken-down horses every year. When the huge amount of human body wastes are added, the total of waste needing disposal was reaching astronomical heights. In previous generations, most families and communities disposed of their waste by depositing it on the ground (simply throwing it away) or underground (in privy vaults). By the late nineteenth century, these methods threatened health and safety, and citizens were raising loud protests against inadequate refuse collection and disposal.

By 1880, most cities were switching to the use of water rather than land as a means of disposing of waste. A network of sewers used water from drains and runoff (such as from rain) to carry waste to a nearby river or lake. Depending on the proven theory that running water purifies itself, communities felt more secure in water-carrying methods, but at the same time their wastes were being passed on to become an increased problem for communities downstream. Thus it was not long before public health boards were advocating the new technology of filtration to enhance water purity. In addition, as bacteriology developed and identified the true causes of most diseases, some physicians and health officials urged cities to treat water supplies with chlorine that would destroy disease-causing germs.

By 1909, sewers served 85 percent of the population of cities with populations above 300,000 and 71 percent of those with populations between 100,000 and 300,000. Virtually all construction and control of these systems were under public auspices. Treatment through filtration and chemicals before water went into homes greatly lessened the threat of diseases such as typhoid fever and dysentery. Between 1890 and 1900 alone, the mortality rate for all diseases in the nation's twenty-eight largest cities fell by 19 percent. But physicians and engineers differed on what should happen to waste when it was discharged into waterways. To protect downstream communities, boards of health wanted state and federal governments to require treatment before discharge, but engineers, adhering to the theory that running water is self-purifying, argued that sewage treatment was unnecessary and too expensive. They said that each community could sufficiently protect itself by filtering its water at the place of intake. Between 1905 and 1914, cities such as Pittsburgh were successful in obtaining sewage treatment plants in instances where industrial and other solid wastes presented extreme nuisances, but for the most part the argument by engineers prevailed until well into the twentieth century. Today, most communities dispose of solid and hazardous materials in landfills and deep underground holes, but waste disposal remains as a growing and ominous problem.

By the early twentieth century, urban dwellers had become more receptive to the possibility of technological solutions to their practical problems, and municipal engineers had acquired reputations as problem solvers that gave them authority in the realm of city administration. Industrialization, with its daunting mechanical wonders and its obsession with efficiency, gave the public faith that technologically expert engineers not only could facilitate a city's expansion but also do so in a neutral way, above the petty frays of partisan politics. For their part, engineers, by creating professional bureaucracies, national organizations replete with conferences and professional journals, bolstered their reputations as trustworthy, impartial experts who could be hired by problem-plagued cities. By the early 1900s, engineers had become powerful figures in municipal administration, and it was no coincidence that the first city managers, in Staunton, Virginia, and Dayton, Ohio, were engineers.

In spite of these successses, however, the challenge of dealing with industrial pollution would fray the confidence in teachnological solutions and expert neutrality. Regulatory strategies in matters of smoke divided the interests of corporate employers, industrial workers, and homeowners. In Cincinnati, for example, the impetus for controlling smoke emissions from coal-burning locomotives came from middle class women intent on protecting homes and children from the intrusion of industrial dirt. But the budren of enforcing regulations once they were created fell on railroad employees, forcing the battle over smoke and soot to be fought out between the railroad company, the union, the civic elite, municipal officials, middle class women, and working class men. Throughout the twentieth century industrial pollution posed a singularly intractable urban problem.

REFORM BECOMES PROGRESSIVISM

The period between 1895 and 1920, when reform activism spread through almost all facets of American life, is known as the Progressive Era. Progressivism was not a single movement; it involved shifting coalitions of reformers operating on a number of fronts. Some progressive reforms, particularly those involving government reorganization and railroad regulation, were adopted from the Populist movement of the 1890s. Most progressive issues, however, were national and derived from urban problems. The Progressive Era culminated three decades of urban reform; its issues had been the concerns of civic and social reformers for some time. Progressivism in the cities distinguished itself from earlier urban reform by the strategic contribution of national organizations, led by like-minded reformers from different cities; the importance of female urban reformers; and the increased focus on government as provider and guarantor of justice and welfare.

Nationwide reform activism was the product of several ingredients. In large part it grew from reformers' basic optimism in their causes. No problem seemed too complex; no geographic area too large. Failure and frustration on the local level had not dampened reform ardor; these only made national programs more imperative. National organization was driven by the impulse for standardization and professionalization characteristic of new middle class confident expertise. And certainly faster and easier communications by mail, rail, telegraph, and telephone aided intercity contacts, just as they facilitated the growth of economic links that stretched between regions. Whatever the origins, large numbers of urban reformers now carried their particular causes to the national level and provided progressive movements with their intellectual and organizational bases.

One of the earliest of these organizations was the National Municipal League, organized in Philadelphia in 1894 by the First Annual Conference for Good City Government. The league attracted a number of civic reformers, and it included 180 affiliated societies by 1895. At first members favored the types of elitist reforms that business and professional groups had supported in the 1870s and 1880s—civil service, stronger vice laws, tighter fiscal policies. But the depression of the 1890s catalyzed broader concerns about urban society and prompted organizations such as the National Municipal League to consider more comprehensive reform programs. In 1899, the league consolidated its various governmental proposals into a model city charter that provided for home rule, a strong mayor, civil service, and ceilings on taxing and bonding powers. In 1916, members drew a revised model charter that included a combined commission-manager plan, nonpartisan elections, and shorter ballots. Also some, though not all, league members became advocates of municipally owned city services.

The model charters, support for municipal ownership, and other programs signaled the league's recognition that electing the best men and passing regulatory legislation were no longer adequate to remake the city. Civic reform needed a plan that could be formulated and supported nationally. Although no city adopted a model charter verbatim, the league's recommendations had considerable influence on local charter committees for the next several decades. To aid the planning process, bureaus of municipal research, often supported by self-interested corporate donors, provided important information and lobbying services to public officials and municipal reformers.

The desire for coordinated programs also characterized other national reform organizations. The National Civic Federation, founded by business liberals in 1900, organized local branches and enlisted prominent leaders to mediate in labor disputes. The federation also campaigned nationally for a moderate version of workmen's compensation and other forms of social insurance. In 1904, Florence Kelley and other social reformers launched the National Child Labor Committee, which campaigned for passage and enforcement of laws restricting child labor. Such restrictions had long been the goal of female reformers concerned about the welfare of working-class children and the conditions of tenement sweatshops. The Child Labor Committee also drafted a bill prohibiting child labor, which passed Congress in 1916, only to be overturned by the Supreme Court. The formation of the Federal Council of Churches of Christ in 1905 climaxed the Social Gospel movement. At its first annual conference in 1908, the council adopted a platform calling for improved housing, educational reform, government-sponsored poverty relief, better working conditions in factories, unemployment insurance, minimum wages for manual workers, and equal rights for all.

In 1910, Lawrence Veiller succeeded in combining various housing reform groups when he convinced the Russell Sage Foundation to sponsor the National Housing Association. Settlement workers helped to found the National Child Labor Committee and the National Playground Association of America, and in 1911 they organized their own National Association of Settlements. In 1909, architects, engineers, and reformers concerned with urban congestion and city planning formed the National Association of City Planning, forerunner of the American City Planning Institute (today called the American Planning Association). In 1906, proponents of vocational training organized the National Society for the Progress of Industrial Education, whose board of managers included efficiency expert Frederick W. Taylor, settlement-house leaders Jane Addams and Robert A. Woods, the president of American Telephone and Telegraph Company, and the head of the Union of Electrical Workers. After 1900, municipal employees formed specialized associations of the National Associations of Port Authorities, the Municipal Finance Officers Association, the American Association of Park Superintendents, the National Conference of Mayors, and the Conference of City Managers. This complex network of specialized organizations helped to develop reform agendas and a communications and lobbying network that financed and organized reform on a national scale.

Virtually all urban progressives urged the intervention of government into social and economic life, whether it involved ensuring the quality of food, providing aid for the unemployed and disabled, making factories safe, or infusing ideals of Christian service into human relations. Such expanded government responsibilities gave women, particularly educated, middle-class women, opportunities to fulfill traditional social expectations of nurture and sacrifice in new ways. As historian Robyn Muncy has concluded, women such as those involved in settlement houses had aspirations for service that they could transform into professional approaches—investigation, organization, lobbying of government, and creation of new bureaucratic positions— to the solution of the problems of urban-industrial society. Their efforts on the local level not only gave them strength of numbers but also helped develop strategies that could move social reform to the national level.[3]

By the early twentieth century national progressive reformers revealed a distinctive approach to social and political problems. Their tone was less indignant and less moralistic than that of reformers of the 1870s and 1880s. At the same time, the character of reform shifted from elitist paternalism—the idea that the best men should govern—to bureaucratic control—the belief that experts and specialized agencies should determine policies. Most urban progressives believed that trained professionals could best define the public interest, but their faith in scientific methods blinded reformers to the contradictions between disinterested (nonpolitical and uncorruptible) social engineering and democratic self-determinism. Thus they could advocate more trust in the people and more popular involvement on the one hand while they worked for centralized power and impersonal bureaucratic administration on the other. Moreover, they confused the independence of experts and bureaucrats with neutrality, when in fact government bureaucracies became as self-serving as the boss-led machines that reformers wished to replace. Attempts by progressive reformers to transfer their own values to all of urban society ran aground against entrenched economic interests and competing working class cultures and institutions. The impersonality of bureaucratic management of social problems and the inability to accept the complexities of urban society with its multiplicity of groups and overlapping interests limited the accomplishments of urban reform movements; the impassioned commitment both to social reform and scientific expertise constituted a lasting progressive legacy to the modern era.

THE RISE OF URBAN LIBERALISM

The Progressive era reforms relying on an ideology of government intervention to ensure the safety and promote the welafre of its citizens—involving labor and welfare issues, regulation of big business, and electoral reform—have been labeled as urban liberalism. The proponents of urban liberal reforms emerged directly from the cities, produced by the sometimes blurred boundaries between boss politics and urban reform noted in Chapter 6. During the progressive era, politicians from immigrant and working class districts, often aided by the resources of political machines, won seats in state legislatures and in Congress. Although their numbers remained too small for them to wield legislative power alone, these urban lawmakers frequently were able to coalesce with reform-minded colleagues to produce some of the era's most important measures.

Urban workingmen had long been at the forefront of campaigns for legislation promising safer conditions in factories and sweatshops, collecting labor statistics, and creating workmen's compensation. By the end of the century, laboring classes, often led by immigrant-based machine politicians, were pressing for housing and health reforms as well as for breadbasket issues such as higher wages, shorter hours, and better working conditions. During the Progressive Era, representatives of the ethnic working classes helped to sponsor reform measures such as widows' pensions, wages and hours legislation, workmen's compensation, factory-safety legislation, and tenement regulation.

In New York City, many of these laws grew out of the Factory Investigation Commission hearings instituted after the tragic Triangle Shirtwaist Company fire in New York City in 1911 in which 145 women workers were killed. Robert F. Wagner and Alfred E. Smith, graduates of Tammany Hall politics, chaired this commission, and they and their fellow Democrats introduced nearly all of the fifty-six welfare laws passed as a result of the commission's recommendations. In New Jersey, Irish-American Democrats from Jersey City and Newark gave strong support to workmen's compensation and factory-safety bills in the state legislature. Cleveland's immigrant-based Democrats pushed for welfare legislation in the Ohio legislature. And politicians with urban ethnic constituents supported similar issues in other northern and midwestern states. Their efforts were not always fruitful, and they achieved legislative success only when they worked in cooperation with other groups sympathetic to workers' concerns. But in each instance urban ethnic representatives exerted considerable force in guiding the course of reform legislation.

These same lawmakers also backed, though less successfully, measures to strengthen unions, regulate big business, and equalize tax burdens. Urban Democratic leaders often rose out of the ranks of organized labor and

Philadelphia Streetcar Strike. In 1909 and 1910, a series of bloody riots occurred as a result of a strike against the monopolistic Philadelphia Rapid Transit company. The public, incensed by muckraking articles exposing the company's arrogance, joined in sympathy with the workers, with men and boys attacking trolley cars and ripping up track while women and girls cheered them on. Such labor action prompted many reformers to advocate arbitration as a means of settling disputes and avoiding violence.

became strong advocates for the rights of unions to organize, bargain, and strike. In 1911, for example, Boston representatives to the Massachusetts Senate supported a bill permitting strikers to picket. Urban lawmakers generally favored government regulation of big business rather than breaking up trusts, because workers believed regulation was the surest means of stabilizing economic conditions and ensuring job protection. These Democrats particularly favored government control over the rates and services of public utilities, upon which working classes depended. Many of them supported municipal ownership of utilities and streetcar companies. For example, Edward F. Dunne, Democratic mayor of Chicago and governor of Illinois in the early twentieth century, backed measures to provide for municipal ownership of several utilities in Chicago. Though these measures were defeated, Dunne was able to create a public utilities regulatory commission in 1913. Urban legislators also worked to shift tax burdens to those best able to pay by supporting inheritance taxes, stronger enforcement of intangible property taxes, and, most of all, a graduated federal income tax. In New York, Massachusetts, New Jersey, Ohio, and other states, urban Democrats backed the Sixteenth Amendment to the Constitution, which established congressional power to levy an income tax, because they viewed it, in Robert Wagner's words, as "a tax on plenty instead of necessity. It will lighten the burdens of the poor."

Lawmakers with working-class and immigrant constituencies also promoted political changes that promised to bolster popular control of government. They opposed the kind of electoral reforms promoted by civic reformers, such as nonpartisan elections, civil service, short ballots, and at-large candidates, because such issues did not aid working people in need. But working-class ethnic interests often did favor broadening participation in government by establishing initiatives and referendums, recalls of appointed officials and judges, women's suffrage, and direct election of U.S. senators. Although urban machines initially opposed giving women the right to vote ("You can't trust these women," asserted Boston's Martin Lomasney. "They are apt to blab everything they know."), by the 1910s many inner-city leaders, including those of Tammany Hall, were backing women's suffrage in hopes of luring women into the Democratic party. And urban ethnic working classes also could lend support to measures such as city commissions and direct primaries when it proved politically profitable to do so.

Immigrant-stock lawmakers associated with urban liberalism did not support Progressive-era moral reform. In fact they actively fought key aspects of the middle-class moral reforms such as prohibition, Sunday closing laws, and other attempts to control personal liberty. Their opposition insisted on cultural pluralism, expressing the idea that in a heterogeneous society differing groups have a right to maintain their own customs and values as long as they did not harm anyone. The types of measures that new-stock urban lawmakers did favor—those establishing government responsibility for ensuring social welfare and those directed toward opening up political and economic opportunities—have become principal components of national reform from the Progressive Era to the present.

BIBLIOGRAPHY

For selected works on Progressivism, see Alan Dawley, *Struggles for Justice: Social Responsibility and the Liberal State* (1991); Noralee Frankel and Nancy S. Dye, *Gender, Class, Race, and Reform in the Progressive Era* (1991); Daniel T. Rodgers, *Atlantic Crossings: Social Politics in a Progressive Age* (1999); and Robert Wiebe, *The Search For Order, 1877–1920* (1967).

For local studies, see Edward Shannon LaMont, *Politics and Welfare in Birmingham, 1900–1975* (1995); Carl V. Harris, *Political Power in Birmingham, 1871–1921* (1977); Don Doyle, *Nashville in the New South, 1880–1930* (1985); William Issel and Robert W. Cherny, *San Francisco, 1865–1932: Politics, Power and Urban Development* (1986).

Studies discussing urban socialism include Mari Jo Buhle, *Women and American Socialism, 1870–1920* (1981); and Sally M. Miller, *Victor Berger and the Promise of Constructive Socialism, 1910–1920* (1973); and Bruce Stave, ed., *Socialism in the Cities* (1975).

On women's centrality to Progressive reform, see Maureen Flanagan, *Seeing with their Hearts: Chicago Women and the Vision of the Good City, 1871–1933* (2002); Glenda Elizabeth Gilmore, *Gender and Jim Crow: Women and the Politics of White Supremacy in North Carolina, 1896–1920* (1996); Linda Gordon, ed., *Women, the State, and Welfare* (1990); Robyn Muncy, *Creating a Female Dominion in American Reform, 1890–1935* (1991); Elizabeth Israels Perry, *Belle Moskowitz: Feminine Politics and the Exercise of Power in the Age of Alfred E. Smith* (1987); Dorothy Salem, *To Better Our World: Black Women in Organized Reform, 1890–1920* (1990); and Kathryn Kish Sklar, *Florence Kelley and the Nation's Work* (1995).

On settlements, see Allen F. Davis, *Spearheads for Reform: The Social Settlements and the Progressive Movement, 1890–1914* (1967); Jean Bethke Elshtain, *Jane Addams and the Dream of American Democracy* (2002); John H. Ehrenreich, *The Altruistic Imagination: A History of Social Work and Social Policy in the United States* (1985); Elizabeth Lasch-Quinn, *Black Neighbors: Race and the Limits of Reform in the American Settlement Movement, 1890–1945* (1993); Rivka Shpak Lissak, *Pluralism and Progressives: Hull House and the New Immigrants, 1890–1919* (1989); Eleanor J. Stebner, *The Women of Hull House: A Study of Spirituality, Vocation, and Friendship* (1997); and Judith A. Trolander, *Professionalism and Social Change: From the Settlement House Movement to Neighborhood Centers, 1886 to the Present* (1987).

On moral reform and reformers, see Paul S. Boyer, *Urban Masses and Moral Order in America, 1820–1920* (1978); Dominick Cavallo, *Muscles and Morals: Organized Playgrounds and Urban Reform, 1880–1920* (1981); Perry Duis, *The Saloon: Public Drinking in Chicago and Boston, 1880–1920* (1983); Mark Thomas Connelly, *The Response to Prostitution in the Progressive Era* (1980); Regina Kunzel, *Fallen Women, Problem Girls: Unmarried Mothers and the Professionalization of Social Work, 1890–1945* (1993); David Nasaw, *Children of the City: At Work and at Play* (1985); Thomas J. Noel, *The City and the Saloon: Denver, 1858–1916* (1982); and Ruth Rosen, *The Lost Sisterhood: Prostitution in America, 1900–1918* (1982).

For educational reform, see Ronald Cohen and Raymond Mohl, *The Paradox of Progressive Education: The Gary Plan and Urban Schooling* (1979); David Hogan, *Class and Reform: Schools and Society in Chicago, 1880–1930* (1985); Marvin Lazerson, *Origins of the Urban School: Public Education in Massachusetts, 1870–1915* (1971); James W. Sanders, *The Education of an Urban Minority: Catholics in Chicago, 1833–1965* (1977); and David B. Tyack, *The One Best System: A History of American Urban Education* (1974).

On planning, see M. Christine Boyer, *Dreaming the Rational City: The Myth of American City Planning* (1983); Howard Gillette, Jr., *Between Justice and Beauty: Race, Planning, and the Failure of Urban Policy in Washington, D.C.* (1993); Thomas S. Hines, *Burnham of Chicago: Architect and Planner* (1974); Judd Kahn, *Imperial San Francisco: Politics and Planning in an American City, 1897–1906* (1980); Stanley K. Schultz, *Constructing Urban America: American Cities and City Planning, 1800–1920* (1989); Christopher Silver, *Twentieth-Century Richmond: Planning, Politics, and Race* (1984); William H. Wilson, *The City Beautiful Movement* (1989).

For important works on the influence of technology and engineers on the urban infrastructure and environment, see Andrew Hurley, *Environmental Inequality: Class, Race, and Industrial Pollution in Gary Indiana, 1945–1980* (1997); Martin V. Melosi, *Garbage in the Cities: Refuse, Reform, and the Environment, 1880–1980* (1981), and Melosi, ed., *Pollution and Reform in American Cities, 1870–1930* (1980); Harold L. Platt, *City Building in the New South: The Growth of Public Services in Houston, Texas, 1830–1920* (1983); Platt, *The Electric City: Energy and the Growth of the Chicago Area, 1880–1930* (1991); Mark H. Rose, *Cities of Light and Heat: Domesticating Gas and Electricity in Urban America* (1995); David Stradling, *Smokestacks and Progressives: Environmentalists, Engineers, and Air Quality in America, 1881–1951* (1999); and Joel Tarr, *The Search for the Ultimate Sink: Urban Pollution in Historical Perspective* (1996).

On the rise of urban liberalism, see John D. Buenker, *Urban Liberalism and Progressive Reform* (1973); James J. Connolly, *The Triumph of Ethnic Progressivism: Urban Political Culture in Boston, 1900–1925* (1998); Michael Ebner and Eugene Tobin, eds., *The Age of Urban Reform: New Perspectives on the Progressive Era* (1977); Raymond R. Fragnoli, *The Transformation of Reform: Progressivism in Detroit and After, 1912–1923* (1982); and Thomas Kessner, *Fiorello H. La Guardia and the Making of Modern New York* (1989).

NOTES

1. Daniel Rodgers, "In Search of Progressivism," *Reviews in American History* 10 (December 1982): 125.
2. Robert Wiebe, *The Search for Order, 1877–1920* (New York: Hill and Wang, 1967), 157.
3. Robyn Muncy, *Creating a Female Dominion in American Reform, 1890–1935* (New York: Oxford University Press, 1991), 35–37.

8

Cities in an Age of Metropolitanism: The 1920s and 1930s

NEW URBAN GROWTH

The 1920 federal census marked a milestone in American history: its figures revealed that for the first time a majority of the nation's people (51.4 percent) lived in cities. This revelation, though, can be misleading: Massachusetts and Rhode Island—even California—had been predominantly urban long before 1920. Moreover, the bureau defined a city as a place inhabited by at least twenty-five hundred people—hardly a rigorous criterion. Nevertheless, the 1920 tallies had symbolic importance. In 1890, the Census Bureau had announced that the frontier no longer existed. Now, thirty years later, the figures confirmed that the nation had evolved into an urban society. The city, not the farm, had become the locus of national experience.

The agrarian way of life, with its slow pace, moral sobriety, and self-help ethic, had been waning ever since urbanization accelerated early in the nineteenth century. To be sure, by the 1920s the demise was far from complete. Several social reform movements and much political rhetoric looked nostalgically backward to the simple virtues of an imagined past. But everywhere signs pointed to an urban ascendance. A precipitous drop in commodity prices after 1920 spun small farmers into distress. Convinced that there was a better life elsewhere, an estimated six million Americans gave up the land and poured into cities like Pittsburgh, Detroit, Chicago, Denver, and Los Angeles.

After lagging behind the rest of the nation for nearly a century, the South now became the most rapidly urbanizing region in terms of proportionate population growth. Memphis, Atlanta, and Chattanooga experienced extraordinary expansion. The epitome of southern urbanization was Birmingham, Alabama. A burgeoning steelmaking center in the late nineteenth century, Birmingham developed a diverse industrial, commercial, and service economy in the 1920s. This expansion attracted workers and their families from all over the South, who boosted the population of Birmingham's metropolitan area from 310,000 to 431,000 during the decade (the population of the city proper was 260,000 by 1930). Smaller cities, many of them created by textile companies that had left New England to take advantage of low-wage southern labor and readily available hydroelectric power, also helped boost the urban population of the South to thirteen million by 1930.

The most visible contingents of native migrants from World War I onward were the millions of African Americans who moved into northern and southern cities. Pushed off tenant farms by failures in the cotton fields and attracted by jobs in labor-scarce cities, African-American families packed up and boarded the trains for Memphis, New Orleans, Chicago, Detroit, Cleveland, and New York. African Americans comprised already 90 percent of Birmingham's unskilled work force by 1910, half of the iron- and steelworkers, and 70 percent of the ore miners by the 1910s and 1920s. When the war cut off the influx of cheap foreign labor, some northern companies began to hire black labor. Short-term migration in search of wages in turpentine camps, sawmills, cottonseed oil mills, and other industries tied to agriculture began to acculturate young African-American men to industrial labor. Young black women similarly ventured into nearby cities and towns to find work as domestics.

By the time that World War I created increasing demand for labor in northern cities, thousands of African-American men and women were ready to mobilize family and personal networks, giving up the dream of autonomy based on landownership in exchange for the promise of full citizenship emanating from northern urban life and industrial employment. By 1920, four-fifths of the country's African Americans residing outside the South lived in cities. As migrations continued during the 1920s, New York's African-American population increased from 152,000 to 328,000, Chicago's from 109,000 to 234,000, Philadelphia's from 134,000 to 220,000, Detroit's from 41,000 to 120,000, and Cleveland's from 34,000 to 72,000. African Americans constituted between 5 and 10 percent of the population of each of these places. This migration continued into the 1930s as New Deal crop subsidies paid to landowners prevented tenant farmers from making their customary living.

Agrarian depression was only part of a broader phenomenon. Mining and other extractive industries as well as agriculture were receiving a diminishing share of national wealth, while retail and service establishments were mushrooming. An ever-larger white-collar, urban middle class became increasingly influential in local and national affairs. At the same time, some critics added a disdain for rural society to a general cynicism toward social conventions. Edgar Lee Masters' *Spoon River Anthology* (1915), Sherwood Anderson's *Winesburg, Ohio* (1919), Sinclair Lewis's *Main Street* (1920), and Thomas Wolfe's *Look Homeward, Angel* (1929) assaulted the drabness of village and small-town life. The term "hick" became a widely used derogatory adjective, equating something clumsy or stupid with the farm. Much of the contempt for rural life represented a larger revolt against what writers called Puritan moralism—a revolt reflected in the popularization of the writings of Austrian psychoanalyst Sigmund Freud. But the debunking of the sturdy yeoman and small-town folkways also underscored a cultural shift that accompanied the city's rise to numerical superiority.

During the 1920s, urbanization took place on a wider front than ever before. Maturing industrial economies boosted the populations of many areas, particularly steel, oil, and automobile centers such as Pittsburgh, Cleveland, Detroit, Akron, Youngstown, Houston, Tulsa, and Los Angeles. New commercial and service activities primed expansion in regional centers such as Atlanta, Cincinnati, Nashville, Indianapolis, Kansas City, Minneapolis, Portland, and Seattle. The most exceptional growth, however, occurred in warm-climate resort cities. As the prime beneficiary of the Florida real estate explosion of the twenties, Miami attracted thousands of land speculators

The Age of the Skyscraper. A workman sits on the end of a beam and bolts together the framework of the Empire State Building. Completed in 1930, this skyscraper operated with huge financial losses during the first six years of the Depression.

and home builders. Between 1920 and 1930, the population of Miami ballooned from 29,571 to 110,637. Tampa and San Diego doubled their populations during the twenties.

Urban populations in this period revealed a decline in foreign-born residents. After World War I, nativist arguments for restricting immigration gained broader support. By 1919, reformers who had formerly opposed restriction were convinced that the melting pot had not worked and that many immigrants—particularly those from southern and eastern Europe—stubbornly resisted assimilation. Labor leaders, fearful that a new flood of unskilled aliens would depress wages, looked at the high postwar unemployment rates and increased their longstanding support for restriction. At first businessmen opposed the rising clamor out of self-interest: they hoped that a new surge of foreign workers would not only aid industrial expansion but also cut wage rates and curb unionization. But by 1924, when Congress was debating whether to close the doors more tightly, many industrialists were willing to support restriction because they discovered that mechanization and native migration from farm to city enabled them to prosper without foreign-born labor.

Congressional acts of 1921, 1924, and 1929 successively reduced the numbers of immigrants who could be admitted annually. A racially motivated system of quotas, ultimately based on the number of descendants from each nationality living in the United States in 1890, severely limited immigrants from southern and eastern Europe, the very groups who had dominated urban cores since 1880.

The laws left the doors open only to those coming from Western Hemisphere countries. Mexicans now became the largest foreign group entering the country. Many came to work in the fields and vineyards of the Southwest, but others streamed into the region's booming cities. By the end of the 1920s, Chicanos made up more than half the population of El Paso, slightly less than half that of San Antonio, and one-fifth that of Los Angeles. Other Mexicans found employment in the automobile factories of Detroit and the steel mills, tanneries, and meat-packing plants of Gary and Chicago. By 1930, more than 15 percent of Mexican immigrants lived outside the Southwest. Chicano women took work in cities as domestics and in textile and food processing factories. Crowding into old barrios or forming new ones, Chicano migrants often lacked decent city services such as sanitation, schools, and police protection. But the barrio community provided an environment where immigrants could sustain customs and values of the homeland and develop institutions to protect them from the uncertainties of urban life. In the same period, Puerto Ricans began to arrive on the American mainland in significant numbers, primarily settling in neighborhoods in Brooklyn and Manhattan, identified by their bodegas (grocery stores), restaurants, and boardinghouses. Social and cultural diversity continued to be a distinctive quality of urban life that distinguished cities most sharply from the relative homogeneity of rural and small-town social relations.

Historian Alberto Camarillo has suggested that urban neighborhoods of ethnic and racial concentration in the 1920s and 1930s served as borderlands, geographical areas marking the margin between the dominant society and the newer groups that were always in flux. Many of these borderlands were typically multiethnic in their early years, although patterns of institutional and racial discrimination helped to turn many of them over time into what Camarillo termed "color-line" borderlands.[1] Barrio neighborhoods of southwestern cities such as El Paso and Los Angeles became increasingly distinct in these years as Mexican and Mexican-American migration to cities increased, although their exclusion from areas outside the barrios was never complete. An increasing reliance by realtors on the use of real estate covenants, by which white property owners pledged not to sell homes to members of racial and/or ethnic minorities, helped sharpen lines of racial segregation from the 1920s onward, more tightly confining Mexicans, Asians, African Americans, and Jews to certain neighborhoods.

Urban America's coming of age was proclaimed by the establishment of its own academic discipline. The study of city life was formalized at the University of Chicago's school of sociology, where Robert E. Park and Ernest W. Burgess trained scholars to draw relationships between city people and their environment in much the same way that biologists examined interactions between plants and animals and their surroundings. The Chicago school's approach to the city was known as human ecology. According to this theory, the cultural dimension of human life and the forms of communication it facilitated were what held communities together. Migration to cities, said the Chicago sociologists, severed traditional forms of communication and community and created a disorganized society that isolated individuals amid rapid change.

The Chicago sociologists believed that they could understand the chaos of the city by studying its various "natural areas"—types of communities they identified as downtowns, slums, ethnic neighborhoods, suburbs, and artists' colonies, that formed as people adapted to the urban environment. Thus sociologists set out to collect data—numbers, characteristics, maps, ratios, interviews, and the like. The data then reinforced the general theory that neighborhood communities had become the cores of individual and group life in the city and that these communities held the keys to people's adjustment to urban society.

These ideas were central to such studies as Burgess's concentric-ring thesis, which depicted urban growth in terms of a series of concentric zones radiating outward from the urban core; Harvey W. Zorbaugh's *The Gold Coast and the Slum* (1929), which outlined the life patterns of contrasting neighborhoods; Louis Wirth's *The Ghetto* (1928), which probed the development of a single residential type; Frederick Thrasher's *The Gang* (1927); and Roderick D. McKenzie's *The Metropolitan Community* (1933). These scholars often failed to identify relationships within families and among neighbors that inner-city residents preferred to keep invisible to outsiders, and critics have charged that their emphasis on neighborhood looked nostalgically backward toward an imagined preurban village. Still, the Chicago school's commitment to urbanism as a legitimate field of inquiry, like the census milestone, unmistakably marked the city's importance in twentieth-century culture.

SUBURBANIZATION AND METROPOLITANISM

Ironically, at the moment that urban life had achieved ascendancy in the United States, important patterns of suburban development challenged the city's economic viability and political centrality. For one thing, industry began to decentralize. Electric power gave factories flexibility in location and made possible the assembly line, which required sprawling one- and two-story plants, not compact multistory ones like those in the city. Corporations began to locate beyond city limits, where land was cheaper and tax burdens less onerous. Industrial satellite suburbs such as East Chicago and Hammond outside of Chicago, Lackawanna outside of Buffalo, East St. Louis and Wellston near St. Louis, Norwood and Oakley beyond the Cincinnati city limits, and Chester and Norristown near Philadelphia became the location of factory employment. As the proportion of factory employment located within city limits declined, city tax bases suffered a corresponding loss.

As industry decentralized, suburban areas were increasingly likely to reject municipal expansion through annexation and consolidation. Upper-class residential suburbs had been resisting central-city annexation since the late nineteenth century, but now corporate leaders exerted economic and political influence in local governments and in state legislatures to assure that the political independence of suburbs would be maintained. As one suburban editor explained, "Under local government we can absolutely control every objectionable thing that may try to enter our limits, but once annexed we are at the mercy of City Hall." As sharp racial, ethnic, and class divisions separated city and suburbs, new laws made incorporation easier and annexation more difficult, and suburbs were able to gain access to improved services without annexation. Newer southern, midwestern, and southwestern cities were able to continue to annex suburban areas, ensuring that urban growth and economic vitality would continue. But older cities came to be ringed by incorporated suburbs that emphasized their distinctiveness from cities rather than their ties to them.

When industry moved out of the central city, many white workers followed to be near their jobs. The availability of inexpensive automobiles (by 1908, twenty-four American companies produced cars at relatively low prices) allowed even more workers to reside beyond and between the reaches of urban mass transit. In 1910, Henry Ford moved his own auto production factory outside of Detroit to Highland Park. Less expensive suburban house lots afforded white workers an opportunity to build their own modest bungalows, and engage in domestic production, raising vegetables and animals to supplement wages. Suburban home ownership by African Americans partially served to buffer against aspects of racial discrimination. Black residents created suburban enclaves in Lincoln Heights and Chagrin Falls, Ohio; LeDroit Park outside of Washington, D.C.; New Bern, Raleigh, and Durham, North Carolina; Evanston, Illinois; Mt Vernon, New York; and East Orange, New Jersey. Suburbs such as these contained space for black families to provision their own tables by raising vegetables and chickens and to continue reliance on extended kin for childcare and emotional as well as financial support.

Suburban expansion in the 1920s owed much to the automobile and its related industries. Real estate interests, the construction industry, the auto, rubber, and oil industries joined automobile owners in pressing for new roads to facilitate high-speed travel. Automobile wheels destroyed whatever was left of older, lower-speed gravel surfaces. But smoother pavements and wider streets encouraged even more urban residents to invest in automobiles, generating more traffic and demands for additional roads. The building of expressways and parkways encouraged still further suburban migration.

In 1920, the growth rate of suburbs exceeded that of the cities for the first time. Among the most rapidly growing suburbs in the 1920s were Elmwood Park, Berwyn, and Wilmette near Chicago; Beverly Hills and Inglewood near Los Angeles; Grosse Point and Ferndale near Detroit; and Cleveland Heights and Shaker Heights near Cleveland. Of seventy-one new towns incorporated in Illinois, Missouri, and Michigan in the 1920s, two-thirds were suburbs of Chicago, St. Louis, or Detroit. Many were residential communities for the upper and the middle classes, and others were industrial and mixed-use suburbs where factory workers constituted a fifth or more of the population. Both commercial agriculture and industrial suburban belt settlements sprung up south and east of Los Angeles. In the 1920s, the Los Angeles community of Watts, initially a labor camp for the Pacific Electric Railroad, was home to blacks, Mexicans, European immigrant and native born whites, settled in different sections of town. Although other early working-class suburbs housed diverse groups, suburban populations were overwhelmingly likely to be racially homogenous.

As more people moved to the suburbs, retailing followed. Older secondary business centers at streetcar transfer points were replicated by those springing up at major highway intersections. Neighborhood banks, movie theaters, office buildings, branches of major department stores, and chain stores such as Woolworth's, Kresge's, and Walgreen's brought the amenities of downtown to the periphery. The twenties also witnessed the birth of the country's first suburban shopping center. In 1922, Jesse C. Nichols, a Kansan versed in land economics, built the Country Club Shopping Center as the commercial hub of his huge real estate development in Kansas City. A few years later Sears Roebuck and Company began to build stores in outlying districts to reap sales from growing suburban populations. The major proliferation of shopping centers would occur following World War II (see Chapter 9), but throughout the twenties and thirties, doctors, saloon keepers, restauranteurs, and independent merchants followed clients and customers out to expanding residential areas until business districts speckled every quadrant of a city's metropolitan area. By the time of the economic collapse in 1929, the population of the suburbs was growing twice as fast as that of central cities. The more that industry and retailing decentralized, the more roads were built; the more roads that were built, the more automobiles became a social and economic necessity for suburban residents.

Streetcars, once the marvels of progress, declined as automobile suburbanization proceeded. After World War I, the cumulative effect of publicized abuses by streetcar franchises, strikes by streetcar employees, and accidents was that streetcars lost public support during precisely the period when companies were seriously strained by postwar inflation, overextended lines, and competition from automobiles. Millions of Americans continued to depend on mass transit to get to work, but by the end of the decade the number of white mass-transit riders began to decline, leaving public transportation in some cities increasingly dependent on African-American riders. As automobile use made central-city streets more congested, streetcars and the buses that began to replace them could no longer provide a convenient ride to work, and the farther away a commuter lived from downtown, the more benefits accrued from car travel. In the 1920s, cars counted for between 20 and 30 percent of daily traffic into central business districts even in congested cities such as Boston, New York, and Chicago, and as much as 50 to 66 percent in smaller cities like Kansas City, Milwaukee, and Washington, D.C. Streetcar revenues began to fade, and even with rate increases, the companies could no longer earn enough to meet operating expenses.

Instead of mass transit, city and state governments invested heavily in street improvement, traffic regulation, and new road construction. Highway building has been subsidized by government in a way that mass transit, considered a private investment, has never been. By the 1920s, street and highway construction constituted the second largest item in municipal and state budgets. Between 1915 and 1930, the city of Chicago widened and opened 112 miles of streets at a cost of $114 million. New York City parkways built between 1923 and 1937 opened up for development seventeen thousand acres around the city. Urban roadbuilding failed to relieve congestion in the central business district or even keep pace with the spread of auto use, but it did encourage car travel, overloading streets and thoroughfares as soon as they were built and ultimately stimulating travel that avoided the central business district altogether.

Although cities were unable to secure much direct assistance from state capitals or from Washington in meeting local traffic needs during the twenties, urban interests were successful in influencing the evolution of national highway policy. Early in the twentieth century, urban merchants and industrialists had organized the Good Roads Association because they believed that more and better highways would aid business. But among the most influential advocates of federal assistance were agrarian interests, such as the National Grange Association, which wanted to improve transportation between farm and market. The first attempt to initiate federal aid to highway construction reflected this rural base. In 1902, Congress considered, but did not pass, a bill that would have created a Bureau of Public Roads within the Department of Agriculture and would have provided $20 million in matching funds to states wishing to construct rural roads. The bill prohibited cities from receiving any appropriations.

It was not long, however, before metropolitan interests helped to swing federal highway policy to an urban axis. By 1915, increasing truck traffic gave urban businessmen stronger arguments for the construction of arteries to aid freight transportation between cities rather than to help farmers bring their crops to market. The Roads Aid Act of 1916, the first legislation to create federal responsibility for highway improvement, revealed an ambivalence between support for arterial commerce between cities and aid for farm-to-market routes. The act authorized the secretary of agriculture to make matching grants to state highway departments for the improvement of post roads. World War I demonstrated the nation's need for trunk highways, especially after the Council for National Defense was forced to use trucks to relieve rail congestion. As a result, Congress passed the Highway Act of 1921, which provided federal aid to primary state roads that would contribute to a system of connecting interstate highways. More important, the act created the Bureau of Public Roads, which by 1923 was planning a national highway system that would connect all cities of fifty thousand or more inhabitants. The new highway complex reflected the emerging dominance of metropolitan interests in national affairs.

At the same time that manufacturing was relocating outside the city, the proportion of communications, finance, management, clerical and professional services situated in downtown increased. The spreading out of factories on the periphery and the proliferation of skyscraper office buildings downtown represented a new stage in corporate organization: the separation of the production process from administrative functions. The massive corporations expanded by vertical and horizontal integration made such a separation advantageous, and transportation between offices and factories via streetcars and highways plus communication over the telephone made separation possible. By 1929, the editors of *The American City* could count 377 buildings at least twenty stories tall. Although New York claimed nearly half of the nation's skyscrapers, Syracuse, Memphis, and Tulsa also boasted of their own. Just as factories and railroad stations symbolized prosperity and growth in nineteenth-century cities, skyscrapers offered visual proof of progress in twentieth-century cities. Corporate offices, along with the banks, law offices, and advertising agencies that serviced them, now towered over downtown streets. Cleveland's 52-story Terminal Tower, Chicago's 36-story Tribune Tower, and New York's 102-story Empire State Building represented the reorientation of downtown space in the transition from industrial to corporate city.

Competition from suburban shopping districts and the reorganization of downtown threatened major department stores, which found sales slipping by the 1920s. To recoup revenues, stores went to great lengths to entice customers to shop downtown. According to historian William Leach, "The department store became a zoo (Bloomingdale's and Wanamaker's in New York had enormous pet stores), a botanical garden (floral shops, miniature conservatories, roof gardens), a restaurant (some of the major stores had lavish restaurants bigger than any other in their cities), a barber shop, a butcher shop, a museum (gift and art shops, art exhibits), a world's fair, a library, a post office, a beauty parlor."[2] Downtown nightclubs, movie palaces, cabarets, and restaurants could afford premium space only by charging high prices and cultivating a following among the wealthy and those aspiring to an expensive lifestyle. Older neighborhoods near high-rent sections continued to be characterized by a mix of commercial, industrial, and residential space. But as office towers replaced factories, small retail businesses, apartments, and tenements that had previously occupied the downtown, streamlined buildings and specialized land use defined what was valuable in the central city. Older, more varied neighborhoods came to be seen as slums.

Acceptance of the new spatial specialization and especially of a suburban mentality dominated the thinking of political, social, and physical reformers who planned cities and formulated policy from the 1920s until the 1960s. A commitment to decentralization implicit in its title characterized the Regional Planning Association of America (RPAA). Convened in 1923, the RPAA included among its members architect and former settlement-house worker Clarence Stein and fellow architect Henry B. Wright, plus intellectuals Lewis Mumford and Benton McKaye. Wright and Stein asserted that uncontrolled expansion was causing unnecessary congestion and that decentralization would relieve pressures of housing and traffic. Following the English model of Ebenezer Howard's Garden Cities—new, planned communities with limited populations and surrounded by open land—the RPAA tried to prove the merits of decentralization by planning two projects near New York City. In 1924, it sponsored Sunnyside, a limited-dividend housing corporation in Queens planned by Wright and Stein and intended for low-income residents. Radburn, New Jersey, a genuine garden city, was begun in 1928 on a large tract seventeen miles from New York. Although Sunnyside and Radburn won much publicity for their advanced design, both were too expensive to build to offer a feasible model for low-income housing or a solution to the problems of urban overcrowding.

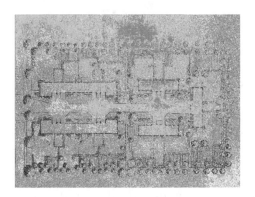

A Green-Belt Town. Left, a plan of Greendale, Wisconsin, prepared in 1936 by the Department of Suburban Resettlement of the U.S. Resettlement Administration. Right, a photograph of a Greendale neighborhood in 1939.

Impulses toward decentralization did not halt with Sunnyside and Radburn, however. In the 1930s, New Deal faith in the beneficial effects of modern suburbanization prompted Rexford Tugwell, head of the U.S. Resettlement Agency, to plan a network of garden suburbs that he visualized as Green-Belt cities. These were to be of limited size (about ten thousand people), located on the outskirts of metropolitan centers, surrounded by farms and open lands, built with federal funds, and leased to cooperatives of local residents. Tugwell hoped that his Green-Belt cities would relieve slum congestion, provide low-cost housing, and rebuild community cohesion. Tugwell planned twenty-five Green-Belt cities, but only three were actually built: Greenbelt, Maryland, north of Washington, D.C.; Greenhills, near Cincinnati; and Greendale, southwest of Milwaukee. Private developers' opposition to plans to house low-income people in Green-Belt communities, and to government-sponsored planned communities in general, squelched the program. For example, building and loan associations in Milwaukee sued to prevent Greendale from being built. In 1938, the Resettlement Administration was abolished, and after World War II the government sold the communities to nonprofit corporations.

Regional planning was popular among planners, but seldom implemented. The New York Regional Plan was presented in 1931, and surveys were also taken for the metropolitan areas of Philadelphia, Chicago, Boston, San Francisco, Los Angeles, and Cleveland. Civic leaders held conferences and appointed commissions to discuss regional problems of highways, land use, and water supplies, but political and economic rivalries and suburban insistence on political independence prevented substantive reforms such as consolidation of cities with their surrounding territories. Schemes to combine city and county governments by Cleveland, St. Louis, and Seattle were defeated, and efforts to integrate planning in Cook County, Illinois (the Chicago region), were tabled. Whenever it was implemented, regional planning had the impact of certifying growth as inevitable and celebrating the automobile as the best possible means of transportation, undervaluing possibilities for controlled growth and giving highways precedence over mass transit.

More narrowly defined planning strategies such as zoning and traffic control, popularized in the 1920s and 1930s, rigidified the divisions between urban and suburban space. Originally intended as a means of achieving stability, zoning became a tool of exclusion that still governs land-use patterns today. Copied from Germany and elsewhere abroad, zoning is a type of local police power that restricts certain types of buildings or land use to certain districts of the city. The earliest comprehensive zoning ordinance was passed by New York in 1916 to prevent skyscrapers and garment-industry lofts from encroaching on the fashionable Fifth Avenue retail district. By 1924, every major city, plus hundreds of smaller cities, had established zoning regulations. Although loopholes left room for circumvention, the laws generally controlled heights of buildings, determined boundaries of commercial and residential zones, and fixed density limitations.

The U.S. Supreme Court upheld zoning in *Village of Euclid, Ohio v. Ambler Realty Co.* (1926), a landmark case that had consequences for future urban land-use policies. The court ruled valid a local law that zoned a parcel of land as residential and that prevented a property owner—in this case, the Ambler Realty Company—from using residentially zoned land for industrial purposes. According to the Court, zoning was a legitimate use of police power under which local government had the authority to abate a nuisance. This decision gave local governments much stronger prerogatives against formerly sacred rights of property owners, but zoning proved to be no panacea for urban ailments. Zoning laws aimed to establish stability in existing districts and orderly growth in newer regions, but they primarily protected the interests of real estate developers and owners of commercial property by ensuring that residential or commercial zones would not be invaded by unwanted features such as multiple-family dwellings and factories. Later, zoning would commonly be used to exclude "undesirable" people from the suburbs, and it therefore became a means of using spatial and economic definitions to tighten racial segregation.

In the 1920s, zoning became the principal activity of the scores of planning commissions established in cities across the country. By decade's end, three-fifths of the nation's urban population lived under some kind of zoning controls. Planning staffs spent much of their time drawing maps that identified patterns of land use, traffic, health, lighting, utilities, and other aspects of the urban environment. Such projects proved helpful in systematizing policy planning, but they mainly ratified the status quo. Zoning maps could not renovate dilapidated housing, abolish want and crime, or improve the quality of life for all city dwellers.

Unplanned urban sprawl, new suburban expansion, and "automobility" drew country and the city closer together. Automobiles quickened travel, extended distances that could be traversed easily, and gave tourists access to rural areas as a recreational playground. On weekends, thousands of cars pierced the countryside, carrying picnicking and sightseeing families, many of whom thought that farmers' fields were appropriate places for pitching tents and disposing of tin cans. Service stations, motor camps, and tourist restaurants sprouted along highways, and as farmers relied more heavily on automobiles for travel to purchase necessary supplies, small crossroads market centers lost their general trade and service functions to larger towns. With access to urban stores, goods, and services, farm families became less culturally isolated from urban life.

These regional networks formed metropolitan districts—regions that included a city and its suburbs. In 1910, the Census Bureau gave the concept official recognition by identifying twenty-five areas with central-city populations of over 200,000 as metropolitan districts. By 1920, the total of metropolitan and near-metropolitan districts had grown to fifty-eight, and together they contained two-thirds of the nation's urban population. By 1930, there were ninety-three cities with populations of over 100,000. In 1933, a member of a government-sponsored study on modern social trends described the decentralization of urban space and centralization of rural space as the national paradigm:

> The large center has been able to extend the radius of its influence. . . . Moreover, formerly independent towns and villages and also rural territory have become part of the enlarged city complex. . . . Nor is this new type of metropolitan community confined to great cities. It has become the communal unit of local relations throughout the entire nation.

The rise of urban America had been eclipsed by the metropolitan age.

CITIES AND CONSUMER CULTURE

The mass-consumer culture that characterized the nation in the 1920s concentrated in cities. City dwellers, now a majority of the country's population, more than ever provided workers and consumers for expanding industry and related services. American industrialists utilized new mass-production techniques to market a dazzling array of goods that many white-collar and skilled workers' families could afford. Installment buying made acquisition of automobiles, radios, washing machines, vacuum cleaners, refrigerators, and phonographs possible. Advertising helped to make acquisition desirable by celebrating consumerism in newspapers, magazines, radio, billboards, and motion pictures. Advertising strategies shifted from merely developing the brand-name loyalty of particular products to associating the possession of these products with states of well-being and the absence of them with anxiety and inadequacy.

This crowd lined up outside of Chicago's Comiskey Park to cheer for White Sox symbolizes how higher productivity and shorter work hours gave people spendable income and more time for leisure activities. The park's original capacity to accommodate 32,000 fans was expanded in 1927 to seat 52,000.

Advertisers aimed their campaigns at urban consumers, particularly at the middle class, because these were the people who had money to buy new products—or at least to make a down payment. Between 1920 and 1929, farmers' share of the national income dropped from 16 percent to 9 percent, while incomes of urban skilled industrial and white-collar workers expanded. Moreover, the proportion of urban dwellings wired for electricity rose from 10 percent in 1920 to over 50 percent by 1930, whereas even at the later date few farmhouses had electricity. Thus most household appliances, vanguards of the new materialism, could be sold initially mainly to urban and suburban families.

Advertisers claimed that refrigerators, washing machines, stoves, canned goods, and ready-made clothing would transform housework and liberate wives from constant drudgery. Though running water and gas or electric stoves lightened housewives' burdens by freeing them from the necessity of hauling water and stoking fires, in reality other new household conveniences and appliances actually failed to cut labor time spent in housework because rising standards of cleanliness kept women just as busy.

Washing machines enabled housewives to wash their family's clothes frequently rather than sending them out to commercial laundries; vacuum cleaners changed rug cleaning from a once-a-year to a weekly or daily task. The decentralization of retailing made marketing more time-consuming because goods previously available downtown now had to be purchased at stores scattered throughout the suburbs. Whether working as domestic producers or as domestic consumers, urban women with children at home found household responsibilities continuing to weigh heavily on them.

Another type of consumption basically supported by city dwellers was the expanding range of leisure activities. A mania for sports, movies, and music gripped every city. Passionate interest in sports had been building since the late nineteenth century. In 1923, 300,000 fans attended the six-game World Series of baseball between the New York Yankees and the New York Giants. In 1926, the attendance of 130,000 at the first Jack Dempsey–Gene Tunney heavyweight championship prizefight in Philadelphia broke all records. Each week millions of sports enthusiasts practiced baseball in sandlots and filled tennis courts, golf links, and beaches.

The rise of show business paralleled the rise of sports, maturing with the growth of cities. Shrewd promoters turned vaudeville into big business, presenting magic and animal acts, juggling stunts, comedy (especially ethnic humor), and song and dance. Playing continuously for hours, vaudeville's variety made it attractive to mass audiences, including families. Music halls, cabarets, and nightclubs brought performers and audiences closer together, dancing to new kinds of ragtime and jazz band music in an informal setting that celebrated pleasure and a more explicit sexuality.

Motion pictures also attracted enormous crowds in the 1920s. During the banner years from 1927 to 1929, weekly movie attendance reached an estimated 110 million people—at a time when the nation's total population was just over 120 million and total weekly church attendance was under 60 million. Many moviegoers were country folk who streamed into the Bijou on Main Street in a thousand towns and villages. But many more were city dwellers who stood in line for one of the six thousand seats in Roxy's in New York or in one of the ornate Balaban and Katz movie palaces in Chicago. Silent movies could attract a linguistically diverse urban audience, although by 1927 familiarity with English was widespread enough for the introduction of sound in *The Jazz Singer* to make movies even more appealing. Mass spectacles such as Cecil B. de Mille's *The Ten Commandments* (1923), sexually charged romances such as *The Four Horsemen of the Apocalypse* (1920) and *The Sheik* (1920), and slapstick comedies, which often poked fun at authority, were widely popular to a variety of different class and ethnic audiences. African-American audiences in big cities also viewed Hollywood films, sometimes from separate balconies reserved for people of color. They actively supported films depicting familiar cultural dilemmas such as those made by the popular African-American filmmaker Oscar Michaux, shown on a circuit of

The Palatial Urban Movie Theater.   Movie fans crowd the sidewalk in front of the opulent Warners Theater in New York, August 6, 1926, for the opening of Don Juan, starring John Barrymore. Note the lavish use of electricity for air conditioning as well as for lighting.

independently and sometimes black-owned "race" theaters (for black audiences only) from New York to Texas, which also showcased African-American musical and vaudeville performers. Movies helped to popularize urban culture as national culture by presenting scenes involving diverse city people such as wise-cracking and worldy working-class characters, including a range of ethnic and racial types.

Radio brought the new world of entertainment and advertising directly into urban homes in the 1920s. By 1930, radios were a fixture in approximately 40 percent of all American households, and radio production had become a billion-dollar industry. Stations sprouted in hundreds of cities. In Nashville a local insurance company pioneered new marketing techniques by operating its own radio station to sell its product through advertising and by creating a new entertainment institution, the Grand Ole Opry, as the station's chief listener attraction. In 1926, a network of stations was formed by the National Broadcasting Corporation, and in 1927, the federal government created the Federal Radio Commission, which distributed broadcasting licenses and frequencies among 412 cities. National radio broadcasting linked people living distant from one another in new ways, enabling listeners to share a common experience with a national audience, and radio advertising brought the message of consumption into every listening household.

A new emphasis on spending, consuming, and playing replaced older values of frugality, hard work, and self-denial; external characteristics of

Los Angeles Suburbanization. This photograph of Whittier Boulevard in Los Angeles, California, illustrates the interconnections among automobiles, electrification, and suburbanization in the 1920s.

personality substituted for internal strength of character. The glitter and glamour of city life beckoned from the urban settings that radio and films projected. Cars, new goods and services, and nightlife infused cities with an expansionist spirit. But by mid-decade, dark clouds were gathering. Speculation in securities was draining private capital from mortgage markets and pushing the costs of home ownership beyond the reach of many families. Housing construction ebbed in both the inner cities and the outskirts. As prices for land and buildings soared, real estate operators used inflated paper profits as security on loans obtained for stock market speculation. Moreover, advertising and consumer credit had created huge demands for products, but demands themselves could not raise buying power. To be sure, the new prosperity had lifted the wages and living standards of urban workers, but a rising proportion of private incomes was spent on interest payments for installment purchases, instead of on goods and services. The economy of the urban nation was teetering on a weakening base—a base that crumbled in 1929.

CITIES AS A CULTURAL BATTLEGROUND

Commercial amusements drew on diverse cultural traditions for their popular appeal. African-American music, dance, and minstrelsy humor were utilized in the creation of "respectable" forms of entertainiment in white-supported urban commercial amusements such as vaudeville theaters, dancehalls, and movie theaters. White suburbanites trekked to Harlem nightspots to hear the hottest African-American jazz bands, and New Orleans–born Italian-American Louis Prima played jazz trumpet and performed with his orchestra for African-American audiences at the Apollo Theater in New York and the Howard Theater in Washington, D.C. Much of American popular music emerged out of a process of cultural exchange and mixing. For example, the first published blues to reach a wide audience, "Memphis Blues," was originally written by the African-American W. C. Handy, classically trained as a composer and also a veteran of the black minstrel tent show circuit, as a campaign song for Memphis's political boss Ed Crump. As well, immigrant Jewish singers Fannie Brice and Sophie Tucker and African-American dancer and comedian Burt Williams won loyal followings on the vaudeville circuit, although often their humorous appeal depended on perpetuating demeaning stereotypes of their own group experience. In less respectable bars and brothels in the South and Southwest and in vice districts in cities such as New Orleans, Kansas City, and Memphis, the lines of formal racial segregation blurred, and musical traditions from white and black southern culture mixed with local Italian, Polish, and Latin ethnic traditions to produce popular jazz, blues, and "hillbilly" music.

Urban commercial culture's potential for undermining older patterns of separation and for mixing ethnic groups and races was a source of great concern to some urban residents. The disruptive potential of commercial culture seemed to converge with new possibilities of independence and vulnerability for the thousands of country-born young men and women moving to cities. Issues like prohibition, union organizing, and immigration restriction sharply divided urban populations, and lynchings and race riots bared deeper tensions lying beneath surface accommodations. The city in the 1920s was often a battleground as various groups within the population struggled for social and cultural authority.

The triumph of national prohibition in 1919 and rebirth of the Ku Klux Klan after 1915 seemed to be last gasps of fading rural resistance to urban civilization. However, important segments of city populations contributed to the initial successes of these campaigns, while other urban groups brought about their ultimate failure. Although rural groups, particularly small-town Methodists and Baptists, had been in the vanguard of the crusade against alcohol, a number of urban interests also supported the Great Cause. Middle-class Protestants in the cities (with the exception of Episcopalians and Lutherans), mostly residents of peripheral and suburban districts, supported prohibition as a reform instrument. They linked liquor to poverty, vice, and corruption. And they believed that enforced abstinence would improve worker efficiency, fortify family life, and blunt the power of political machines.

It is probable that national prohibition, established by the Eighteenth Amendment to the Constitution in 1919, would not have passed without support from urban groups. On the other hand, city dwellers were also instrumental in crippling the crusade. Although enforcement of the law worked well at first, smuggling and illegal distilling were increasing rapidly by the mid-twenties. The Volstead Act, which provided for enforcement of the prohibition amendment, forged new links between local police and federal agents in the attack against bootlegging. But it was impossible to dry up the cities. Not only were local efforts less than energetic, but federal enforcement was sporadic, undermanned, and inept.

The results are well known. Large numbers of people refused to renounce the bottle, speakeasies blossomed in cities across the country, and crime became a big business. By the early twentieth century organized crime had adopted business techniques that utilized payrolls, modern communications, and coordinated management. But the public desire to evade prohibition gave crime syndicates new opportunities to consolidate and centralize in the twenties. Like other twentieth-century businesses, crime had been rationalized. In New York, Chicago, Detroit, Cleveland, Kansas City, Buffalo, New Orleans, San Francisco, and other cities, big-time criminals expanded from illegal activities into labor racketeering and control of small businesses, such as restaurants, barbershops, and dry cleaners.

The most notorious feature of organized crime in the 1920s was the use of extortion and murder to win customers and eliminate competition. Merchants who refused to accept gang-controlled business, such as slot machines or bootleg beer, or who refused to pay protection money, were beaten and their property was destroyed. Between 1925 and 1928, over four hundred gang-related bombings of business establishments occurred in Chicago alone. Rivals who contested a gang leader's will were assassinated, and their bodies, feet encased in cement slippers, were dumped into nearby rivers and harbors. In Chicago a dispute over the bulk of illegal liquor traffic burst into violent war when henchmen of crime boss Johnny Torrio murdered archrival Dion O'Banion in O'Banion's florist shop in 1924. Torrio and his lieutenant, Al Capone, were considerate enough to send a basket of flowers to O'Banion's lavish funeral, but the gesture failed to console the florist's gang, now led by Hymie eWeiss. The gang went on a bullet-filled rampage, driving Torrio into retirement, and Capone assumed full control of Torrio's legions. Combat raged for more than four years, climaxing on St. Valentine's Day, 1929, when Capone's agents, posing as policemen, trapped seven members of the O'Banion gang in a North Side garage and executed them with submachine guns. By this time Capone ruled the Chicago suburb of Cicero and had spread his influence from bootlegging into a huge network of rackets that included ninety-one trade unions. He was earning over $100 million a year, and his flamboyant habits made him as famous as Charles Lindbergh and Babe Ruth. He was not yet thirty-two years old.

During the twenties, Chicago, New York, Kansas City, and Detroit witnessed hundreds of gangland killings, almost all of which went unsolved.

These were only the most grisly features of what had become a big business. Other factors besides prohibition contributed to the rise of big-time crime. Trucks and automobiles gave criminals and illegal commerce new mobility. Submachine guns and other weapons inherited from World War I made crime more threatening. And the times themselves had given birth to an indiscriminate worship of swagger. Organized crime provided a ladder of social mobility, a means of making it for immigrants and other groups forced to live on the margins of society. A 1930 report of 108 crime leaders in Chicago revealed that 32 were Italian, 31 Irish, 22 Jewish, and 13 African-American. By supplying liquor, gambling facilities, and prostitutes, organized crime served a consuming public. Thus Al Capone defended himself as an ordinary businessman. "All I do is to supply a public demand," he once remarked. "I do it in the best and least harmful way I can."

By 1933, Capone was in jail and prohibition was repealed by the Twenty-First Amendment. The return of legal liquor swept away most of the bootlegging but left behind more sinister underworld activities that had accompanied the growth of organized crime in the twenties—extortion, racketeering, and narcotics (activities in which gangsters created demand far more than they served existing needs). These areas gave the underworld its future.

Race relations became explosive when the unprecedented Great Migration of African-American migrants from 1915 onward unsettled prior patterns of racial accommodation. Tensions over housing shortages, inflation, black voting strength, the labor movement's unsuccessful initiatives amid postwar labor surpluses, and new antiunion offensives inflamed racial hostilities along the shifting boundaries separating black from white residential areas. An increase in lynchings during and immediately after World War I was one way that white racists tried to reestablish racial boundaries and enforce submission in black communities, and it sparked increasing resistance by African-American organizations, especially by women's associations. A race riot in East St. Louis in 1917 erupted when some African Americans, having been beaten repeatedly by white gangs, shot into a police car. In the dusk they mistook it for another Ford automobile containing white joyriders who had shot up black homes earlier in the evening. In 1919, a race riot in Longview, Texas, occurred after some African Americans shot whites who entered their neighborhood seeking a teacher who had reported a recent lynching to the African-American newspaper, the *Chicago Defender*. A riot ensued in Elaine, Arkansas, when blacks returned fire after two white law enforcement officials shot into an African-American church.

In the summer of 1919, race riots broke out in twenty-six cities. The worst violence occurred in Chicago, where vicious violence erupted after whites stoned to death a black youth swimming off a Lake Michigan beach after he had drifted into water unofficially reserved for whites. When the city was finally quieted, 38 people had been killed (23 blacks and 15 whites), 520 were injured (342 black and 172 white), and 1,000 black families were left homeless by arsonists and vandals. Riots erupted in cities as diverse as Omaha, Knoxville, Charleston, and Washington, D.C. The 1921 riot in Tulsa, Oklahoma, one of the deadliest outbreaks in the nation's history, originated when a crowd of armed African Americans assembled before the courthouse to prevent the lynching of a black arrested for allegedly attacking a white girl. Some African Americans shot at the white police and civilians who attempted to disperse them. Whites then destroyed a 34-block area of black residences and killed almost 300 people.

Unlike previous race riots in which African Americans had been relatively passive victims of white mob action, the typical pattern in all these blowups was retaliation against white acts of persecution and violence. Whites perceived this retaliation as an organized, premeditated conspiracy, which then unleashed the armed power of white mobs and police. In the face of overwhelming numerical superiority, African-American resistance collapsed fairly early during the riots, especially in the South. Still, the riots left deep scars and divided communities.

Partly in response to race riots and threats, thousands of African Americans in northern cities joined movements that called for black independence. The most influential of these black nationalist groups was the Universal Negro Improvement Association (UNIA), headed by Marcus Garvey, a fiery and flamboyant Jamaican immigrant who believed that blacks should separate themselves from a corrupt white society. Proclaiming, "I am the equal of any white man," Garvey cultivated racial pride through mass meetings and parades. His newspaper, the *Negro World,* refused to publish advertisements for hair straighteners and skin-lightening cosmetics, and his Black Star Shipping Line intended to help blacks emigrate to Africa. The UNIA declined in the mid-1920s when the Black Star Line went bankrupt (unscrupulous dealers had sold it dilapidated ships) and when antiradical fears prompted government prosecution (ten of the organization's leaders were arrested on charges of anarchism, and Garvey was deported for mail fraud). Nevertheless, the organization had attracted a huge following in New York, Chicago, Detroit, and other cities, and Garveyites would resurface in later years as civil rights leaders.

White fears of African-American urban migration were one of the forces underlying the reemergence of the Ku Klux Klan in this period. Urbanization and industrialization in the South seemed to feed a new expression of what historian Nancy MacLean has identified as reactionary populism. This sentiment included extreme racism and nativism, militant sexual conservatism, and hostility toward both big capital and working-class radicalism.[3] These were the sentiments of the crowd in Atlanta that in 1915 lynched Leo Frank, a Jewish northern-born factory supervisor, accused of murdering Mary Phagan, a thirteen-year-old white girl who worked in his factory. They were also the defining elements of the revived KKK unveiled two months later by William J. Simmons, an Atlanta evangelist and insurance salesman, at a ceremony attended by many purportedly involved in the Frank lynching. Simmons extended the racist mission of the Klan to include the purification of southern culture, and he revived the hoods, mystical rituals, and tactics of terror and intimidation of its forerunner.

The Klan grew slowly until 1920, when Simmons hired two public relations experts, Edward Clarke and Elizabeth Tyler, to recruit members. By sending agents into Masonic Lodges and other organizations, Clarke and Tyler built membership to a figure between two and four million by 1924. Using threatening assemblies, violence, and political pressure, the Klan for a time wielded frightening power in Arkansas, California, Indiana, Ohio, Oklahoma, Oregon, and Texas. Although, like its predecessor in the 1860s and 1870s, the new Klan vowed to maintain forever white supremacy, its constitution also pledged Klansmen "to conserve, protect, and maintain the distinctive institutions, rights, privileges, principles, traditions, and ideals of pure Americanism," and added antiimmigrant, anti-Catholic, anti-Jewish, and antifeminist venom to its racist poison. From 1921 onward, Klansmen paraded, harangued, and assaulted in the name of Protestant morality and Anglo-Saxon purity, meting out vigilante justice to bootleggers, wife beaters,

Ku Klux Klan on Parade. For a brief period of time, the revived Ku Klux Klan attracted large numbers of disaffected urban dwellers in the Midwest and Northwest as well as in the South. Note the phalanx of women at the head of this parade held in Washington, D.C.

and adulterers; forcing schools to adopt Bible readings and stop teaching the theory of evolution; and campaigning against Catholic and Jewish political candidates.

Although the Klan flourished in rural districts and small towns of the West and South—areas where people feared and distrusted the city—it also enjoyed success in metropolitan areas. Historian Kenneth T. Jackson has estimated that half the Klan's membership lived in cities of over fifty thousand people. Detroit, Atlanta, Indianapolis, Memphis, Philadelphia, Portland, and Denver had sizable contingents. Chicago, with an estimated fifty thousand Klansmen, contained the largest operation in the country. The urban Klan thrived in the zone of emergence, the belt of modest neighborhoods that separated the inner core from the periphery. Here, working-class and lower middle-class white Protestants, one step removed from the slums, grew increasingly apprehensive when blacks, Catholics, and Jews began to press upon housing markets in nearby neighborhoods. Many white families, still on the lower rungs of the socioeconomic ladder, grasped for some means of soothing their anxieties and reinforcing their identification with "100 percent Americanism."

In cities Klansmen often turned to politics rather than relying on parades, cross burnings, and lynchings to achieve their goals. Usually operating within one of the two major parties rather than independently, the KKK was partially successful in influencing local elections: it helped to elect a Republican mayor of Indianapolis and Democratic mayors in Denver and Atlanta. But after 1924, racked by scandals and dissidence, the Invisible Empire swiftly declined. The Klan waned locally because its political machinations failed to bring substantive results. Politics provided the only avenue by which nativists could translate 100 percent Americanism into policy, but even the election victories produced only short-term effects. Moreover, by the mid-twenties Catholics and Jews, along with liberal Protestants, could outvote the Klan. By 1930, the Klan had resubmerged into the current of intolerance that has flowed beneath the stream of American history, but racism and nativism in the twenties opened new sores that still have not healed today.

Besides joining movements for moral purity such as prohibition and the Ku Klux Klan, perplexed, native-born city residents also provided a base of support for religious fundamentalism. A literal interpretation of the Bible and unquestioning faith provided not only a means to salvation but also a comforting defense against the skepticism and irreverence of what these individuals saw as materialistic and hedonistic urban society. The most famous religious clash of the decade occurred in Dayton, Tennessee, in July 1925. Here, at the trial of John Thomas Scopes, a high school biology instructor arrested for teaching the theory of evolution, city leaders encouraged a showdown between fundamentalists and modernists, the unquestioning religion of the country against the scientific higher criticism of the city. The prosecution enlisted the counsel of William Jennings Bryan, self-proclaimed defender of the faith, and the defense obtained assistance from big-city lawyers Clarence Darrow, Arthur Garfield Hays, and Dudley Field Malone. Although the jury found Scopes guilty of breaking a Tennessee law prohibiting instructors in state-supported schools from teaching that humans had descended from lower orders of animal, it was a Pyrrhic victory for the fundamentalists. Scores of newspaper reporters conveyed the circus-like event to a national audience and made the trial an object of ridicule, especially after Darrow cross-examined Bryan and bared all the ambiguities of literal interpretation of the Bible. Afterward, humorist Will Rogers remarked, "I see you can't say that man descended from the ape. At least that's the law in Tennessee. But do they have a law to keep a man from making a jackass of himself?"

It appeared, then, that cosmopolitan urban culture could shrug off the challenge of rural old-time religion. Yet at the same time, pietistic fundamentalism, with its holiness and pentecostal churches, was surging in cities across the country. In part this upswing accompanied the move of African Americans to cities. African Americans transplanted their churches from the rural countryside and looked to them for solace and affirmation. The majority of urban fundamentalists were white, however. Like the Ku Klux Klan, urban fundamentalist churches drew much of their membership from groups caught between the middle and lower classes. Many were rural migrants attracted by the friendliness, lack of dogma, and closeness to God that the various storefront churches and revivalist tabernacles promised.

Most leaders of these churches were professional evangelists, charismatic figures who operated outside of regular Protestant denominations. Using the pageantry of the new advertising age, they attracted huge followings and stirred up a revivalistic fervor. In Los Angeles, Aimee Semple MacPherson, the widow of a missionary, established the Four Square Gospel Temple, where she produced extravaganzas of religious vaudeville. Sister Aimee's lavish services, flowing gowns, and moving sermons captivated thousands of newly arrived midwesterners and southerners. Her Sunday evening "shows for the Lord" were broadcast by her own radio station, KFSG, throughout southern California each week. Similar cults, founded by evangelists and graduates of Bible institutes, appeared in other cities. They included Clinton H. Churchill's Evangelistic Tabernacle in Buffalo, Paul Rader's Chicago Gospel Tabernacle, Katherine Kuhlman's Denver Revival Tabernacle, E. J. Rolling's Detroit Metropolitan Tabernacle, T. H. Elsner's Philadelphia Gospel Tabernacle, Karl Wittman's Tabernacle in Toledo, and Luke Rader's River Lake Gospel Tabernacle in Minneapolis. Most of these churches had their own radio programs and newspapers, Bible camps, and foreign missionaries.

Yet fundamentalist churches, along with prohibition and the Klan, were not unique responses by native Protestants trying to infuse their urban experiences with ideals of a romanticized past. Rather, these institutions were part of a larger organizational impulse that pervaded all of urban society. City populations were too large and diverse to sustain a unified sense of community that many believed once existed in small towns and villages. In a fragmented society people turned to new forms of association that revolved around interest-group identities. Memberships in middle-class organizations such as Rotary, Kiwanis, Lions, Elks, and women's clubs swelled during the twenties. Football, baseball, and basketball games brought people together in new forms of community identification. Community chests, which were campaigns for support of local welfare projects, increased in number from twelve in 1919 to 363 in 1930. Each of these activities and associations reflected a type of social adjustment to the new urban society, where tight-knit communities no longer existed and where people tried to bring order to the complexities of group and personal loyalties. The impulses of group organization had always been characteristic of the city, but the tensions and self-consciousness of the years between World War I and the Depression heightened the search for identity.

URBAN POLITICS IN THE 1920S

Urban governance in the 1920s reflected a readjustment to these new allegiances and organizations. To be sure, bosses and reformers still contested for the reins of power, but now both had to be more sensitive to the electorate's changing patterns. For one thing the curtailment of European immigration, by World War I and later by legislated restriction, shut off one important source of urban population growth. Newcomers still poured into many cities, but these were poor rural southerners, African-American and white, and migrants from Mexico and the Caribbean. At the same time, the children of immigrants who had arrived during the early 1900s were growing up. In 1907, the year of the heaviest foreign influx, two-thirds of all school-age children in the nation's thirty-one largest cities had foreign-born fathers. During the twenties these children became voters, workers, and parents. Their impact upon urban politics and society now bore considerable weight.

In the 1910s and early 1920s, it was usually the Democratic party, already established as the party of ethnic voters, that recognized the potential of these trends. The first ethnic politician to enter the arena of national politics was New York's Alfred E. Smith — legislator, governor, and the nation's first Catholic presidential candidate. Smith's early career almost duplicated the backgrounds of the Tammany bosses who ruled the city during his youth. Born to Irish parents on New York's Lower East Side, Smith left school at an early age to support his widowed mother. Smith's toughness and ambition led him into Tammany Hall, where he rose rapidly within the organization and within the Democratic party. In 1903, he won a seat in the state legislature, where he managed to satisfy Tammany chieftains and at the same time ally with prominent progressive reformers such as Robert F. Wagner and Frances Perkins, supporting welfare and labor-reform legislation. Smith ran successfully for governor of New York in 1918 and served from 1919 to 1921 and again from 1923 to 1928.

Smith's political successes and broad appeal made him a logical presidential candidate. His attempt to win the Democratic nomination in 1924 failed, but in 1928 he could not be denied. His campaign against Republican Herbert Hoover was vigorous and boisterous, stressing labor reform and an end to prohibition. Although both candidates tried to avoid religious issues, bigots managed to hurl some malicious barbs at Smith's Catholicism. But prosperity was the major issue. Hoover and his party readily accepted credit for the good economic times, and Smith was badly beaten at the polls. Nevertheless the voting returns revealed some suggestive results. In almost every major city, Smith drew a significantly higher proportion of the total vote than had any other Democratic presidential candidate for the past generation. For the first time since 1892 the Democrats carried several large cities in the presidential election. Hoover and the Republicans managed to retain majorities in places like Indianapolis, Akron, Kansas City, and Portland where native white Protestants still predominated, but Smith carried immigrant cities such as Providence, Jersey City, New Orleans, Milwaukee, and St. Paul. Although successes of Democratic candidates for national office in off-year elections were not consistent enough in the cities to justify calling 1928 the year of the "Smith revolution," his candidacy nevertheless signaled the emergence of urban ethnic America as a strong factor in presidential politics, a factor that reinforced the census returns.

THE GREAT DEPRESSION

After nearly a decade of optimistic economic expansion, something uncharacteristic happened to the American nation in the autumn of 1929: a wildly plummeting stock market dissolved $30 billion of personal wealth and pushed the country into a decade of sacrifice and deprivation. In retrospect the signs of imminent decline seem clear. Farmers had been suffering long before 1929. The construction industry had weakened after 1926. Automobile manufacturers and related industries had overextended production relative to the general public's buying power. Unbridled speculation, encouraged by irresponsible banking practices, had created huge paper profits that masked the economy's shakiness. The stock market crash bared these weaknesses, and during the last weeks of October an era of expansion gave way to an era of depression. In spite of considerable trauma, American cities survived the ensuing decade. But economic collapse pulled them and the federal government into a new alliance, one in which Washington became the dominant partner. The American economic system depended heavily on a national network of

Hooverville, Seattle, 1933. Men and women who found themselves jobless and homeless as economic conditions worsened during the depression built squatter settlements such as this one on the outskirts

cities, and government could not ignore how vital that network had become. During the 1930s, urban problems became national problems.

Just as (or perhaps because) prosperity in the 1920s had been most visible in the cities, economic crisis struck city dwellers with particular severity. The effects came slowly, however. At first the depression seemed far away, a temporary setback that bankrupted a few New York investors. Workingmen in Minneapolis and Houston joked about frantic stockbrokers jumping out of hotel windows, and advertisers in Atlanta and Los Angeles continued to celebrate the virtues of credit and consumerism. But the crash generated a brutal recession that gradually deepened in every city. Factories and stores cut back payrolls. Families were forced to consume less. Private loans and IOUs circulated widely. In Chicago, Cleveland, Milwaukee, and Grand Rapids, teachers went without paychecks for months. In New York City, the International Apple Shippers Association sold crates of surplus apples to six thousand unemployed workers, who then peddled the fruit at five cents apiece. Relief rolls in Detroit swelled while automobile assembly lines slowed to a snail's pace. Everywhere savings accounts dwindled, insurance policies lapsed, and mortgage payments fell delinquent.

The major source of hardship was unemployment. The depression spun a vicious cycle: the more the business community contracted production in order to economize, the more people it threw out of work, and the more it diminished the nation's purchasing power. By 1932, about a quarter of Americans were jobless. The figures were astronomical in big cities: one million unemployed in New York, 600,000 in Chicago, 298,000 in Philadelphia, 178,000 in Pittsburgh, and 105,000 in Los Angeles. The weight of unemployment fell most heavily on the unskilled, the young, and people of color. Employers laid off those who were needed least, and many factory owners downgraded skilled workers so they could fill unskilled jobs. Local surveys revealed that joblessness among people in their late teens and early twenties ran twice as high as among other age groups. Much of the unemployment resulted from the fact that young people entering the job market for the first time simply could not find work. Although African Americans were able to retain jobs in some industries—meat packing, for example—the aphorism "last hired, first fired" rang true. A census of unemployment in 1931 found that in fourteen of sixteen northern and western cities the percentages of African Americans out of work were much higher than those of whites. In Chicago, Pittsburgh, and Philadelphia, rates of joblessness among employable African Americans reached 50 percent and higher.

The displacements of the depression saddled local governments with unprecedented responsibilities. President Herbert Hoover, believing that the crisis should be attacked at the local as well as the national level, in November 1929 called upon governors and mayors to initiate public works projects to provide jobs for the unemployed. In 1930, Hoover appointed the Emergency Committee for Employment, reorganized in 1931 as the Organization on Unemployment Relief, to encourage local communities to care for their jobless citizens. But at the same time, he emphasized the need for balanced budgets that he believed would stabilize all levels of the economy.

Municipal governments responded quickly. Even before the stock market crash, Cincinnati city manager, C. O. Sherrill, partly influenced by the local Citizens' party, a group of political independents, organized a committee to survey possibilities for public works, job training, and job placement. After the onset of the depression other cities copied the Cincinnati model. By the end of 1930 the seventy-five largest cities were spending $420 million annually on public works projects. Yet even the most generous efforts failed to keep people out of bread lines and off the relief rolls. In 1929, Detroit spent $2.4 million on relief; in 1931, it spent $14.9 million. Over those same two years relief expenditures rose from $620,000 to $2.9 million in Milwaukee, and from $582,000 to $3.5 million in Philadelphia.

The problem for cities was basically a financial one, but underlying that were serious political and ideological issues. The depression caught municipalities between two millstones. On one side the need for services hiked costs of government operations, while on the other side unemployment and falling business reduced municipal tax revenues. One of the most universal problems was property tax delinquency. In 1930, among the 145 cities with fifty thousand or more inhabitants, about 11 percent of local taxes went unpaid. By 1933 the rate had reached 25.2 percent. To collect more revenue some cities, such as Dayton and Des Moines, agreed to accept late payments without penalizing the delinquents. But business leaders charged that such breaks only encouraged irresponsibility among taxpayers. Other cities spent budgets based on anticipated full collection of tax revenues or borrowed against uncollected revenues, thereby falling deeper into debt.

On top of revenue problems lay financial burdens inherited from the past. During the expansion years of the early 1900s, and especially during the 1920s, cities had borrowed extravagantly through bond issues that came due in the 1930s. Unable to make payments on either principal or interest, many cities defaulted. Others were able to meet their obligations only by depleting their sinking funds — emergency monies to be used only in the last resort. As a result, the value of municipal bonds held by investors plunged. By 1933, bond issues of Detroit and of Greensboro, North Carolina, were worth forty cents on the dollar. In Los Angeles, debt charges (that is, interest payments and retirement of principal) accounted for 78 percent of the 1934–35 budget. Local officials were quick to point out that rates of default by municipal governments were much lower than those by private corporations. Nevertheless, the financial problems of cities affected a greater number of people. In 1932, during the depths of the depression, many people became distrustful of failing banks and hoarded so much currency that the amount in circulation declined precipitously. The shortage became so acute in the South that a few cities — Richmond, Knoxville, and Atlanta, for example — began to print their own scrip to pay public employees and relief recipients.

Cities' failures to meet their debt obligations raised cries for state control of local finances that echoed the charges of fiscal irresponsibility that reformers had leveled at boss-ridden city governments in the 1870s and 1880s. The real tug, however, was less between city and state than between those who advocated prudence and those who favored more debt and liberal public spending. Many civic leaders, such as Milwaukee's socialist mayor Daniel W. Hoan and the members of the International City Managers Association, believed that public funds should be conserved to protect the solvency of local governments. They adopted a pay-as-you-go policy toward relief projects, approving only those that would not drain the public till. Others, such as mayors Frank Murphy of Detroit and Fiorello La Guardia of New York, preferred to expend whatever money was available and borrow more for relief, even if it meant paring budgets of other municipal services. Both policies — economizing and spending for relief — severely limited the activities of those departments deemed nonessential. Planning boards, underfinanced even during the 1920s, shrank to skeletons in the early years of the depression. In 1933, 57 percent of the nation's 739 city planning boards received no appropriations, and 25 percent received less than $1,000. Between 1929 and 1933 total expenditures by parks and recreation departments in 795 cities and towns decreased by 50 percent. Public parks programs in Fall River, New Bedford, Providence, and San Antonio were completely eliminated; the parks were saved only by private donations.

The drive to economize produced some beneficial results. For example, to conserve funds Fresno, California, and New Haven, Connecticut, combined previously separate parks and recreation departments. More important, city and county departments were merged to create more centralized administration to meet metropolitan needs. The Chicago Park District, created by the Illinois state legislature in 1933, consolidated the nineteen independent park districts of the Chicago area under one board. Cincinnati's welfare responsibilities were absorbed by Hamilton County, and in New Jersey and New Hampshire state agencies assumed welfare functions formerly handled by their various cities. In other places city and county health departments were combined.

Whether or not public leaders favored belt tightening or more spending, the epidemic of hardship brought intense pressures for the relief of hunger and unemployment. Public and private agencies everywhere struggled through the depression's early years, groping for ways to help. During the fall of 1931 the National Association of Community Chests and Councils, following President Hoover's suggestion, raised $85 million for relief in cities and towns throughout the nation. That sum was hopelessly inadequate. In Milwaukee all municipal salaries were reduced by 10 percent, which freed a million dollars for temporary job relief in 1932. The next year, however, the city voted a drastic tax reduction, thereby eliminating a large portion of public revenues and forcing money saved by salary cuts to be used to support essential services. But as the depression continued to deepen, many families who had teetered on the margins of subsistence for two or three years succumbed and applied for relief. Faced with mounting hardship and shriveling revenues, even the most resourceful municipalities began to run out of funds. (Per capita government expenditures in cities with over 100,000 people dropped from $78 in 1929 to $67 in 1933, while per capita expenditures on relief rose from $0.90 to $2.94.)

Inevitably, cities looked to Washington for help. In May 1932, at the invitation of Mayor Murphy, twenty-six mayors met in Detroit and appealed to the federal government for $5 billion to finance public construction projects. This group became the nucleus of the United States Conference of Mayors (USCM), the first permanent organization formed to bring urban concerns before the president and Congress. By making Washington the focus for urban lobbying activities, the USCM opened a new era in American urban history. Frustrated by rural-dominated state governments and overcome by economic and social pressures, urban officials came to believe that the road to relief led to the federal government. In 1934, after a year of lobbying and resulting federal programs, Louis Brownlow, a New Deal adviser and former city manager, remarked that "it has been said that the Federal Government has discovered the cities; it is equally true that the cities have discovered the Federal Government."

In 1932, however, Washington approached urban problems gingerly. President Hoover rejected the mayors' request but did approve the Reconstruction Finance Corporation (RFC), an agency that loaned money to banks, railroads, and other big businesses in hopes that stabilizing these institutions would enable recovery to filter down to the rest of society. Later the RFC was authorized to make loans to local government agencies for self-liquidating projects. Money trickled into the cities at a very slow pace, however, and the bankers who increasingly assumed control as cities defaulted on debt payments could offer little help except to institute further retrenchment. Moreover, the RFC failed to bring relief to the unemployed, who needed it most. Hoover vehemently opposed direct assistance and squelched congressional proposals for public works projects designed as unemployment relief. Instead, he continued to push voluntaristic efforts.

Mayors, city managers, and other civic leaders did not uniformly favor greater assistance from the federal government. A number supported Hoover's policies, and they accepted the RFC as a meaningful reform. Yet, with their local economies and services continuing to collapse, by the fall of 1932 many leaders began to ponder the possibilities if the Democratic presidential candidate, New York's governor Franklin D. Roosevelt, should win and carry out his promise for a "new deal."

When Roosevelt did win, cities were quick to revive their pleas and the new government was quick to respond. In time *a* new deal became *the* New Deal: the legislative and administrative measures generated by Roosevelt and his advisers to bring about relief, recovery, and reform. Once in office Roosevelt galvanized his programs quickly. Within one hundred days he had instituted measures affecting banking, agriculture, industry, and conservation. These measures affected cities only indirectly, if at all. In fact, several New Deal measures revealed a bias against cities. For example, a back-to-the-land intent was clearly part of the Subsistence Homestead Division, a program inaugurated in 1933 to remove inner-city residents to some one hundred government-sponsored rural communities.

Yet New Deal policymakers did accept the fact that cities had become the principal centers of national life. To be sure, concern was directed not so much at urban life itself as toward the ways in which urban problems existed as part of the national economic crisis. Still many of the bills that were passed and the agencies that were created grew out of the urban experience, where thrift, self-help, and rugged individualism had always shared the stage with mutual benefit and public responsibility. The effect, if not the intent, of the New Deal was to meet traditional needs of city dwellers.

Relief and Welfare

Unemployment loomed as one of the most serious problems facing FDR when he assumed office. Its impact upon cities had been devastating. By 1933, unemployment rates approached 40 percent in Chicago, 30 percent in New York, and 26 percent in Cincinnati. Roosevelt responded first by proposing the Federal Emergency Relief Administration (FERA). Created by Congress in May 1933, the FERA distributed $500 million to the states for direct relief. Although the program was not explicitly designed to aid city dwellers, 42 percent of the 1933 appropriations were spent in five heavily urbanized northern states.

By the winter of 1933–34, almost eight million families, comprising twenty-eight million individuals, were receiving federal relief. The heads of nearly half of these households were enrolled in work-relief projects sponsored by the Civil Works Administration (CWA), an agency created in November 1933 to give jobs to the unemployed. Before it was dismantled and absorbed by the FERA in April 1934, the CWA pumped a billion dollars into the economy and carried millions of people through the winter, providing them with incomes to purchase needed goods and services. Many of the CWA's 400,000 projects were located in, and directly benefited, cities. CWA workers built five hundred airports and improved many more. Many of the fifty thousand teachers employed by the CWA offered adult education classes in city schools. Millions of construction workers developed city parks, dug city swimming pools, and laid city sewer lines. Moreover, wages paid for

Working for Uncle Sam. The many projects in which WPA workers participated included fixing roads and cleaning up after a flood. The agency not only supplied needed unemployment relief to the jobless during the depression but also aided thousands of communities with its public works projects.

City Streets as Playgrounds. Russell Lee's 1941 photograph shows how children in Chicago's South Side made do with whatever play space they could appropriate.

CWA jobs were spent in business-starved city establishments — barbershops, shoe stores, drugstores, and clothiers. The Public Works Administration (PWA), a similar work-relief agency, also proved beneficial to cities. It built a new water-supply system in Denver, a municipal auditorium in Kansas City, and thousands of schools and hospitals across the country.

In 1935, the Roosevelt administration responded more radically to continued cries for more jobs and security. Congress created the Works Progress Administration (WPA) to finance public projects, many of which were located in municipalities. Although it never employed as many as the CWA, the WPA included over two and a half million workers on its payrolls by 1936. Under the guidance of Harry Hopkins, the WPA filled needs that had been neglected or postponed by private enterprise and civic initiative. Between 1936 and 1941, almost one-fifth of the nation's work force was employed by the WPA at one time or another. WPA workers built almost 600 airports and landing fields, 500,000 miles of roads and streets, 100,000 bridges and viaducts, 500,000 sewerage connections, and 110,000 libraries, schools, auditoriums, stadiums, and other public structures. Like the FERA and CWA, many WPA projects pumped new life into civic improvement. Indeed, the U.S. Conference of Mayors, now headed by New York's Fiorello La Guardia, strongly influenced the size of WPA appropriations by pressing urban needs before the White House.

The Social Security Act, passed in August 1935, had a more permanent impact than did the relief agencies. The act created programs of old-age insurance, unemployment insurance, and federal assistance to the blind, the disabled, and dependent children. The consequences of these programs were not felt at the time, but the Social Security Act set a momentous precedent for the nation and its cities. Care of the aged and the distressed was now accepted as a national rather than a local concern, and the path had been broken for a long line of antipoverty programs that would follow. Collective responsibility for the relief and prevention of poverty, long a major issue of urban growth, had been nationalized.

Housing

Between 1929 and 1935, the volume of new housing construction shriveled to almost nothing. In 1932, the editors of *Fortune* magazine wrote, "At least half of America's 30,000,000 families are not even decently housed." As well, the specter of eviction threatened millions of home owners. Between 1926 and 1933 the number of annual mortgage failures quadrupled, and by the latter date home mortgages were being foreclosed at the rate of one thousand per day. In New York City alone, 186,000 families were served eviction notices during eight months ending in June 1932. By 1933, 70 percent of building trades workers were on relief.

These circumstances made housing an early concern of the New Deal. The Roosevelt administration adopted a two-pronged approach: an insurance program to stabilize financial conditions for homeowners and mortgage lenders, and publicly sponsored construction and slum clearance to improve housing conditions for the poor and boost employment in the building trades. Both programs influenced subsequent urban growth. Mortgage insurance made possible a massive wave of suburbanization after World War II. Public housing and slum clearance brought the federal government into the urban core. As well, however, the two-tiered housing policy had strong racial consequences. Mortgage insurance mostly aided white families eager to escape central cities for the suburbs, while housing assistance to the poor implied that poor people, especially people of color, belonged in areas separate from more privileged urban dwellers.

During its first one hundred days, the New Deal Congress created the Home Owners Loan Corporation (HOLC) to bail out endangered homeowners and stabilize mortgage markets. The HOLC almost exclusively served urban interests. (The Emergency Farm Mortgage Act, passed a month earlier, was designed to prevent rural foreclosures.) The HOLC was empowered to refinance private loans with government money carrying interest of 5 percent, giving borrowers fifteen years to repay. The loans were to enable homeowners to escape foreclosure, pay taxes, and make needed repairs. The HOLC did not reduce a person's debt, but it did save millions from defaulting. In three years of lending, the HOLC granted $3 billion in loans to one-fifth of the nation's nonfarm households and held about one-sixth of all urban home mortgage debt. In keeping with prevailing biases against inner-city ethnic and racial minorities, however, the HOLC established appraisal criteria that rejected financing in "redlined" neighborhoods that were dense, aging, or occupied by people of color.

Mortgage relief was only a stopgap measure; it did little to aid either the construction industry or housing markets. Thus at FDR's instigation, in June 1934 Congress passed the National Housing Act, which created the Federal Housing Authority (FHA), an agency to insure loans made by private lending institutions to families wishing to renovate or build homes. Over the next six years the agency underwrote $4.25 billion for the modernization of 3 million existing units and the construction of over 600,000 private homes. The FHA drastically revised the nature of mortgage lending and by doing so initiated a new housing trend in metropolitan areas. Because the FHA would guarantee a borrower's mortgage (the borrower had to pay only a small fee for the insurance), lending banks could reduce the interest rates to as low as 4 percent and could stretch out loans to twenty-five or thirty years. These new terms contrasted sharply with the loans of five to seven years and interest rates of 6 to 12 percent that had been common in the preceding half-century. Thus long-term, federally insured mortgages made home building and homeowning much easier than in the past. In effect, federal mortgage insurance created subsidies for low-density, detached, owner-occupied single-family housing, virtually excluding other types of dwelling units. FHA terms in effect denied benefits to black people and in general deflected investment money away from the central city and encouraged flight to the suburbs because families could finance a new home in a development springing up along a highway outside the city more inexpensively than they could repair or modernize an older building in an inner-city neighborhood.

Both the HOLC and FHA offered little to the one-third of the nation whom President Roosevelt described as ill-housed, ill-clad, ill-nourished. The plight of these groups raised to national dimensions the specter that had haunted urban reformers for a century: the slum. By amplifying local decay, the depression alerted even the most economy-minded leaders to the costs of physical deterioration. Studies of Cleveland and Boston early in 1930 revealed that maintenance of city services in slum areas was much more expensive than in other districts. Such studies galvanized new efforts to abolish blight and provide low-income groups with adequate housing. These had been longstanding reform goals, but the new component was the belief that projects should be financed with public funds. For decades most Americans had cast only a cursory glance at the impressive public renewal projects in European cities such as Paris, Glasgow, Vienna, and Berlin. By the 1930s, however, many civic leaders were able to view fiscal and physical decay as part of the same problem, and they paid more attention to European precedents.

In the summer of 1933, the Emergency Housing Division was attached to the PWA. This agency financed local projects for slum clearance and for construction of low-cost housing. Although the work was done by private contractors, the projects were intended to provide job relief for people on PWA rolls. In four years the PWA Housing Division financed about fifty projects. The first was in Atlanta, where workers leveled eleven slum blocks and replaced them with Techwood Homes, a group of low-rent apartments. Other slum-conversion projects included Lakeview Terrace in Cleveland, Jane Addams Houses in Chicago, and Williamsburg Houses in Brooklyn. PWA funds financed construction of some twenty-two thousand dwelling units. Yet most projects failed to help those in need. Rents averaged twenty-six dollars per month, still too high for the working-class families whose incomes were under a thousand dollars a year. Clearance programs only pushed these people deeper into the slums. The first wide-scale federal participation in housing reform resulted in the demolition of some of the worst urban eyesores and the construction of better facilities for some lower-middle-class groups. But because it placed its major emphasis on work-relief and self-liquidating projects, it failed to address the most acute problems.

The obstacles to housing programs were political. As in the past, public officials were reluctant to lead government, whether local or national, into the hallowed region of housing construction and maintenance. Even President Roosevelt preferred that Congress support private rather than public housing. Opposition to direct federal participation won the upper hand in 1935 when a U.S. district court, in the *Louisville Lands* case, ruled that the federal government could not condemn private property for low-cost housing. Although subsequent court action reversed the ruling, the original decision had the effect of steering federal programs away from direct involvement and toward indirect grants-in-aid or loans to municipalities, which could then use the funds at their own discretion.

This, in effect, was the strategy adopted by the U.S. Housing Authority (USHA), created by the Wagner-Steagall Housing Act of 1937. Passed by Congress only after Senator Robert F. Wagner of New York, long a champion of public housing, had secured the reluctant support of FDR, the bill authorized $500 million for loans and grants to state and local authorities for slum clearance and housing developments. The law stipulated that tenants in USHA units be in the lowest income third of the population, and it particularly benefited African Americans. Some 47,500 federally financed, low-cost dwelling units, nearly a third of those built in northern and southern cities, were occupied by black families in segregated projects. Critics charged that USHA-sponsored public housing was undermining the private market, but most of the accusations were false. Without the aid of public funds, private enterprise was unable and unwilling to construct modern, low-cost housing. Units built under the USHA averaged $2,720 in cost, about 25 percent less than privately erected housing but still too high for the poorest families. It razed more substandard housing than had any other program in the previous

African-American Housing During the 1930s. These shanties in a black neighborhood in Atlanta typified the quarters that the U.S. Housing Authority attempted to replace.

half-century, but it only dented the problem. Millions of families still lacked decent housing, and federal policies helped to enforce the color line even in the face of major population movement.

Public concern with housing during the New Deal era split into two points of view, each with its own constituency. On one side stood philanthropists, social workers, economic liberals, tenants, and unions who wanted government to take responsibility for removing slums and assuring a supply of decent housing. The U.S. Housing Act defined a slum as "any area where dwellings predominate which, by reason of dilapidation, overcrowding, faulty arrangements and design, lack of ventilation, light, or sanitation facilities, or any combination of these factors, are detrimental to health, safety, or morals." Slum-clearance reformers adopted this definition to reinforce their belief that government must assist people to achieve better health, safety, and morals by sponsoring slum clearance and construction of low-cost housing.

On the other side stood landowners and business owners who worried about falling property values and rising taxes. Their concern was with blight, the deterioration in an area that made it no longer profitable to maintain or improve. These people were concerned with profits rather than with social conditions. Their motives were not pure greed; they simply believed that if an area was economically viable, its effects would benefit all groups. Thus

Home Life in the 1930s. During the Depression, newspapers and radio broadcasts played important roles in providing home entertainment. Note the clothing styles and furniture of this middle-class household.

they sought government aid, in the form of loans and clearance projects, to protect their investments. They opposed public housing because it interfered with private enterprise. Passage of the Housing Act crystallized these two points of view and began a debate that influenced federal policies concerning urban renewal and redevelopment after World War II.

POLITICAL AND SOCIAL LIFE IN THE 1930S

The New Deal etched its mark on cities in other ways as well. The National Recovery Administration (NRA) mustered local producers and consumers behind industrial codes of fair trade and price limits, and it encouraged labor organization by guaranteeing collective bargaining. The Wagner National Labor Relations Act, passed in 1935 after the Supreme Court had dissolved the NRA, rescued and reiterated the NRA labor provisions, clearing the way for future unionization drives in many occupations, including municipal employees. The NRA, the Wagner labor bill, and the Fair Labor Standards Act of 1938 were not aimed at cities, but they did implement some of the goals of over half a century of urban reform: minimum wages, maximum hours, and an end to child labor and sweatshops. Still, many African Americans and women workers were excluded from social security coverage and minimum wage provisions because these did not extend benefits to waiters, cooks, hospital orderlies, janitors, farm workers, or domestics. Other NRA codes allowed pay differentials based on gender, so that women's minimum wages were frozen at a lower rate than those for men. An unprotected low-wage labor market for blacks and women in cities was the result.

The depression years also left a legacy of urban protest. As early as 1930 in Chicago, Los Angeles, and Philadelphia, the unemployed had marched on city hall, agitating for jobs and fighting evictions. In 1932 fifteen thousand black and white unemployed World War I veterans and their families made a historic journey to Washington, D.C., demanding immediate payment of veterans' bonuses due in 1945. Chicago schoolteachers protested budget cuts by pulling down the 1933 World's Fair flag and storming City Hall. The Congress of Industrial Organizations (CIO) used the sit-down strike to mobilize broad-based community support for unionization; unorganized groups as diverse as laundry workers in Chicago and dime-store clerks in Detroit also sat down to protest unfair working conditions. In northern cities, blacks protested the persistence of racial discrimination by boycotting stores as part of Don't-Buy-Where-You-Can't-Work campaigns and organizing tenants' unions to fight high rents. In 1939, in Chicago, social activist Saul Alinsky began to apply the principles of labor organizing to neighborhoods, setting up a model for community organizing with the Back of the Yards Neighborhood Council. Depression-era protest gave a generation of urban residents experience with organizing that would be a frequently utilized resource in the years to come.

New Deal progams had been committed to getting Americans spending again, and the decade of the 1930s shows the remarkable resilience and even expansion of consumer values despite economic collapse. For example, passage of the Rural Electrification Act brought electricity to isolated rural households and helped bring urban conveniences such as appliances and radios into the countryside, lessening the distinction between city and farm. Attendance at baseball and football games, which dropped between 1930 and 1935, revived later in the decade. Big-city tabloids tripled their circulation during the thirties, mostly by publicizing human interest stories such as the kidnapping of the son of Charles A. and Anne Morrow Lindbergh, the birth of the Dionne quintuplets, and the killing of bank robber John Dillinger.

Radio's importance increased in the 1930s, especially after FDR began to broadcast his "fireside chats," reaching out to many Americans with sets in their living rooms. After 1933, much daytime radio programming consisted of soap operas such as "Stella Dallas," "Guiding Light," and "Search for Tomorrow," which translated social distress into individual domestic tales of woe, making housewives feel less alone and that their problems were not unique. Movies also thrived in the 1930s. Although a third of the nation's movie houses closed in the early years of the depression, remaining movie theaters offered reduced prices, ladies' nights, sneak previews, and raffles to keep up attendance. Horror films like *Dracula* (1932), *Frankenstein* (1932), and *King Kong* (1933), adventure films such as *Mutiny on the Bounty* (1936), historical films evoking a bygone era such as *Gone With the Wind* (1939), and animated fantasies such as *Snow White and the Seven Dwarfs* (1937) attracted audiences of eighty-five million viewers per week. Urban settings became especially prominent in several of the film genres popular in the 1930s, and in turn, the films embedded images of urban life in the popular imagination. Screwball comedies often included scenes of sophisticated urban night life. Backstage musicals centered on the promise of bright lights and urban performance opportunities. Gangster films and related hard-boiled detective films familiarized an urban milieu of alleys, rain-soaked streets, and inner-city tenements.

Deprivation and fiscal collapse did not dim the appeal of mass culture; indeed they often encouraged the search for escape. The Parker Brothers' successful board game Monopoly enabled would-be entrepreneurs to make a killing in real estate when economic conditions all but prohibited such results in real life. Urban consumers continued to dictate popular tastes across the country. The focus on consumption heightened pressures on men to provide, making unemployment especially humiliating, and drew married women and daughters into the expanding clerical and service work force in order to raise their families' standards of living. Although consumption patterns in some ways sharpened distinctions between people, in other ways

Movies Dreams, 1939. The world Hollywood created in films was all the more compelling in the Depression. A photographer working for the Farm Security Administration captured this image of a young boy in Memphis, Tennessee, outside the entrance to a movie house on Beale Street.

they helped to create a shared culture that had the potential to cut across ethnic and racial lines, promising a better life, which gave new meaning to Americanism and new legitimacy to workers' demands for wage increases and unionization as the path to job security. The consumer culture's focus on leisure time instead of working time paralleled the division between home and work, between suburb and city, that was the hallmark of the metropolitan era.

Meanwhile, the New Deal shifted urban political loyalties. By the mid-thirties, two-thirds of the populations of the eleven cities with over a million inhabitants were first- or second-generation immigrants, most of whom had few loyalties to rugged individualism and few scruples about state interference in their lives. These were the same people who had come to expect assistance in times of need from their leaders and who had exerted strong influence on the development of an urban liberalism. Franklin Roosevelt responded to these ethnic city dwellers more than had any previous national leader. During Roosevelt's early career in New York politics, boss Big Tim Sullivan had told him, "The people who had come over in steerage . . . knew in their hearts and lives the difference between being despised and being accepted and liked." As president, FDR remembered this advice. He exuded warmheartedness, and his New Deal agencies offered direct relief with a minimum of questions. Thus political support flowed to FDR because the effects of many of his national programs resembled what bosses and machines traditionally had done on the local level. Important New Deal personalities such as Rexford Tugwell, Harry Hopkins, Frances Perkins, Robert F. Wagner, and Harold Ickes had backgrounds in urban reform, and they helped shape federal programs into a national urban policy during the thirties.

Urban voters voiced their reactions to the New Deal in the presidential election of 1936, and Roosevelt won a resounding victory by carrying every state but Maine and Vermont. Support for FDR was particularly strong in the cities. The nation's ten largest cities contributed one-third of Roosevelt's eleven-million-vote margin over Alfred M. Landon. Smaller places such as Duluth, Gary, Scranton, Canton, Youngstown, and other cities that had supported Hoover in 1932 gave nearly three-fourths of their votes to FDR. In 1936, six million more voters went to the polls than in 1932, and it has been estimated that Roosevelt attracted five million of them. Immigrants and their children, who had responded to Al Smith's candidacy in 1928, moved solidly behind FDR. A new segment of the electorate, urban black voters, joined the Democratic fold. Although the New Deal in many ways failed to remedy racial problems, it had at least dispensed relief with less discrimination than had any previous government effort. As a result, African Americans broke their ties with the party of Abraham Lincoln and joined FDR's camp. African Americans in Chicago, Cleveland, Detroit, and Philadelphia, who had supported Hoover in 1932, now swung to the Democrats and became important fixtures of the party's national base.

New Deal programs and political realignments created a changing environment for boss politics. The most powerful urban leaders survived and flourished during the New Deal: Crump of Memphis, Hague of Jersey City, Pendergast of Kansas City, and Kelly of Chicago. Although a number of bosses originally supported Al Smith for the Democratic nomination in 1932, almost all accepted Roosevelt by the time of the election. FDR maintained good relations with these men, and they often turned to the president for assistance.

Yet the New Deal did alter the nature of boss politics in important ways. The Christmas turkeys, burial money, summer outings, and free shoes for schoolchildren no longer made an impact in the widespread trauma of Depression conditions. The federal government's assumption of responsibilities for offering relief and insuring security had the potential to scale down the bosses' power. To be sure, many New Deal benefits were filtered to the needy through local politicians, but the recipients knew the jobs and cash were coming from Washington. Equally important, by fostering the growth of organized labor the New Deal indirectly chipped away several functions of bossism. Under the CIO and other unions, more laborers than ever before had access to jobs, protection on the job, and unemployment compensation. Moreover, union halls offered new social centers to workingmen, sometimes replacing saloons. Union leaders organized picnics, speeches, and other affairs that had previously been the prerogative of political machines. Because the labor vote became an increasingly important political force, craft and industrial unions commanded the attention of city halls, state capitals, and Washington.

On the other hand, the New Deal gave some bosses new opportunities. By directing CWA, WPA, and other money to local projects, the federal government created new sources of patronage jobs, paid with federal funds but controlled by local leaders. Particularly in cities such as Pittsburgh and Chicago, where ward and precinct representation had not been replaced by city councils or city commissions elected at-large, the reinvigorated Democratic party offered employment possibilities to many people. In Pittsburgh, the New Deal helped Democrats oust Republicans from power and install Democrat David Lawrence as a powerful boss. In Boston, Mayor James Michael Curley and his successors used New Deal programs to reward the party faithful, especially Irish-stock voters Although they supported Roosevelt and benefited from his policies, Boston politicians continued to be guided more by local conditions and ethnic rivalries than by national New Deal philosophy. Elsewhere, local political traditions, such as a commitment to states' rights, conservative Democratic leadership, and disdain for relief, moderated the impact of New Deal programs. In Baltimore, city officials provided only minimal unemployment assistance, conditional on means testing, low wages, and inferior working conditions to all workers but especially to white women and African-American men and women. Atlanta, Birmingham, Memphis, and New Orleans were reshaped by the ways that federal programs were used to resettle African Americans in downtown areas while home improvement loans facilitated white suburban flight.

As bosses adjusted to increased federal influence at the local level, their intermediary functions became more important. Only those bosses who recognized the need for new flexibility could survive after the New Deal. They could still control patronage, nominations for political office, and elections, but to do so meant acquiring a broader image. The best-known mayor of the New Deal era, and the one who epitomized the merger of machine politics and social reform, was Fiorello La Guardia of New York, a former insurgent congressman who could outduel any machine politician in popular appeal. Born in the Lower East Side of New York, La Guardia spent his youth in Arizona, where his Italian immigrant father was a bandmaster for the U.S. Army, and his young manhood in southeastern Europe, where he worked for a U.S. consulate. In 1906, he became an interpreter on Ellis Island, the famous entry station for immigrants coming to the New York port. Here young La Guardia acquired firsthand experience with the plight of newcomers to the American city. He attended New York University Law School at night and entered politics. Squeezing his way up through the Republican party, he won a seat in Congress in 1916, where he quickly gained notoriety as a people's advocate. He then made some frustrated attempts to unseat Tammany Hall from power in New York City and finally was elected mayor on a Fusion-Republican ticket in 1933, after Jimmy Walker, the scandal-tainted Democratic mayor, had been removed from office.

La Guardia immediately became a national spokesman for the urban cause. Along with Mayor Murphy of Detroit, he took a leading role in the newly formed U.S. Conference of Mayors. In New York, La Guardia's fiery, dynamic personality won him great affection, particularly from the city's many ethnic groups. As one news reporter wrote,

> "La Guardia is melting-pot America-first-generation Italian-American, with a Jewish great-great grandparent. . . . The Mayor is adept in all branches of political fanfaronade: he can lead the Fire Department Band, he can dress up in a sand-hog's helmet to inspect new tunnels, he can step into the pitcher's box on opening day at the Yankee Stadium and cut loose with a high hard one in the general direction of home plate."

As mayor, La Guardia not only succeeded in obtaining large shares of PWA and other federal relief funds but also started a local program of public works and slum clearance, restored the city's credit, improved public facilities, obtained a new city charter, and initiated low-rent public housing. He was reelected twice, serving until 1945.

By the end of the 1930s the rising prominence of cities in national affairs had prompted new initiative on the local and metropolitan levels. Planning commissions revived projects postponed by the depression. Responding to new pressures from automobile traffic, New York, Los Angeles, Detroit, Pittsburgh, and Cleveland planned or constructed belt highways and freeways, often with the aid of federal funds. Still, however, efforts of local planners, builders, and scholars paled beside the activity of the federal government. The

New Deal had tightened the federal-city knot, and local officials were reluctant to loosen the bonds. Skeptics like Harold Buttenheim, editor of *The American City,* warned that Uncle Sam was becoming Boss Sam, but most urban leaders accepted federal programs and appropriations without fear of interference by Washington in local affairs. It is significant that at this time the federal government sponsored the first national study of urban life. In 1937, the Committee on Urbanism within the National Resources Committee, a branch of the Department of the Interior, published a report entitled *Our Cities: Their Role in the National Economy.* This study, headed by Clarence Dykstra, former city manager of Cincinnati, was intended as a complement to the report of the Country Life Commission, which had examined rural society for President Theodore Roosevelt three decades earlier. In its foreword the National Resources Committee clearly recognized the central themes of the evolution of America as an urban nation:

> The city has seemed at times the despair of America but at others to be the Nation's hope, the battleground of democracy. Surely in the long run, the Nation's destiny will be profoundly affected by the cities which have two-thirds of its population and its wealth. . . . The failures of our cities are not those of decadence and impending decline, but of exuberant vitality crowding its way forward under tremendous pressure—the flood rather than the drought.

The report urged the federal government to pay more attention to the needs of city dwellers. After a brief history of American urbanization, it cataloged the nation's unsolved urban problems (no less than thirty-six of them) and presented a list of recommendations. The solutions proposed nothing new. They included public housing for low-income groups, more planning, increased and more equitable welfare services, slum removal, streamlined local governments, and more research. But the fact that these suggestions were being offered by the federal government presaged a new era in the country's urban history.

BIBLIOGRAPHY

Overviews which cover urban growth in this period include Janet Abu-Lughod, *New York, Chicago, Los Angeles: America's Global Cities* (1999); Rosalyn Baxandall and Elizabeth Ewen, *Picture Windows: How the Suburbs Happened* (2000); Blaine Brownell, *The Urban Ethos in the South, 1920–1930* (1975); Robert Fogelson, *Downtown: Its Rise and Fall, 1880–1950* (2001); David Goldfield, *Region, Race, and Cities: Interpreting the Urban South* (1997); Thomas W. Hanchett, *Sorting Out the New South City: Race, Class, and Urban Development in Charlotte, 1875–1975* (1998); Kenneth T. Jackson, *Crabgrass Frontier: The Suburbanization of the United States* (1985); and Jon C. Teaford, *City and Suburb: The Political Fragmentation of Metropolitan America, 1850–1970* (1979).

Local studies include Greg Hise, *Magnetic Los Angeles: Planning the Twentieth Century Metropolis* (1997); Patricia Everidge Hill, *Dallas: The Making of a Modern City* (1996); Char Miller, *On the Border: An Environmental History of San Antonio* (2001).

Recent studies of early working class suburbs include Margaret Crawford, *Building the Workingman's Paradise: The Design of American Company Towns* (1995); Matt Garcia, *A World of*

Its Own: Race, Labor, and Citrus in the Making of Greater Los Angeles, 1900–1970 (2001); Becky M. Nicolaides, *My Blue Heaven: Life and Politics in the Working Class Suburbs of Los Angeles, 1920–1965* (2002); and Andrew Wiese, *Places of Their Own: African-American Suburbanization in the Twentieth Century* (2004). On middle and upper class suburbs, see Michael Ebner, *Creating Chicago's North Shore: A Suburban History* (1988); Margaret Marsh, *Suburban Lives* (1990); Zane Miller, *Suburb: Neighborhood and Community in Forest Park, Ohio, 1935–1976* (1981); Carol O'Connor, *A Sort of Utopia: Scarsdale, 1891–1981* (1982); and William S. Worley, *J. C. Nichols and the Shaping of Kansas City* (1990). An attempt at a comparative assessment is Mary Corbin Sies, "North American Suburbs: Cultural and Social Reconsiderations" and "A Dialogue" in *Journal of Urban History* 27, no. 3 (March, 2001): 313–361.

On automobiles and their impact, see Paul Barrett, *The Automobile and Urban Transit: The Formation of Public Policy in Chicago, 1900–1930* (1983); Mark S. Foster, *From Streetcars to Superhighways: American City Planners and Urban Transportation, 1900–1940* (1981); Clay McShane, *Down the Asphalt Path: The Automobile and the American City* (1994); Howard L. Preston, *Automobile Age Atlanta: The Making of a Modern Metropolis* (1979); and Martin Wachs and Margaret Crawford, ed., *The Car and the City: The Automobile, The Built Environment, and Daily Urban Life* (1991).

On regionalism and decentralization, see Joseph C. Arnold, *The New Deal in the Suburbs: A History of the Greenbelt Town Program, 1935–1954* (1971); and Daniel Schaffer, *Garden Cities for America: The Radburn Experience* (1982).

On the spread of new patterns of consumption and leisure, see George Chauncey, *Gay New York: Gender, Urban Culture, and the Making of the Gay Male World, 1890–1940* (1994); Howard P. Chudacoff, *The Age of the Bachelor: Creating and American Subculture* (1999); Ann Douglas, *Terrible Honesty: Mongrel Manhattan in the 1920s* (1995); Ronald Edsforth, *Class Conflict and Cultural Consensus: The Making of a Mass Consumer Society in Flint, Michigan* (1987); Lewis A. Erenberg, *Steppin' Out: New York Nightlife and the Transformation of American Culture* (1981) and Erenberg, *Swingin' the Dream: Big Band Jazz and the Rebirth of American Culture* (1998); William Howland Kennedy, *Chicago Jazz: A Cultural History, 1904–1930* (1993); David Nasaw, *Going Out: The Rise and Fall of Public Amusements* (1993); Kathy Peiss, *Cheap Amusements: Working Women and Leisure in Turn-of-the-Century New York* (1986); Burton W. Peretti, *The Creation of Jazz: Music, Race, and Culture in Urban America* (1992); the essays on Tin Pan Alley, the blues, and jazz in Rachel Rubin and Jeffrey Melnick, ed., *American Popular Music* (2001); David Stowe, *Swing Changes: Big Band Jazz in New Deal America* (1994); and William R. Taylor, *In Pursuit of Gotham: Culture and Commerce in New York* (1992).

On the transformation of the urban household, see Susan Strasser, *Never Done: A History of American Housework* (1982). On sports, see Steven A. Reiss, *City Games: The Evolution of American Urban Society and the Rise of Sports* (1991). On early radio and movies, see Michele Hilmes, *Radio Voices: American Broadcasting, 1922–1952* (1997); Lary May, *The Big Tomorrow: Hollywood and the Politics of the American Way* (2000); and May, *Screening out the Past: The Birth of Mass Culture and the Motion Picture Industry* (1980); and Gregory A. Waller, *Main Street Amusements: Movies and Commercial Entertainment in a Southern City* (1995). For the development and effects of urban crime, see Humbert S. Nelli, *The Business of Crime: Italians and Syndicate Crime in the United States* (1976).

On nativism in this period, see John Higham, *Strangers in the Land: Patterns of American Nativism, 1860–1925* (1955). On the revival of the Ku Klux Klan, see Kathleen Blee, *Women of the Klan: Racism and Gender in the 1920s* (1991); Kenneth T. Jackson, *The Ku Klux Klan in the City, 1915–1930* (1967); Shawn Lay, *Hooded Knights on the Niagara: The Ku Klux Klan in Buffalo, New York* (1995); Shawn Lay, ed., *The Invisible Empire in the West: Toward a New Appraisal of the Ku Klux Klan in the 1920s* (1992); and Nancy MacLean, *Beyond the Mask of Chivalry: The Making of the Second Ku Klux Klan* (1994). On the Scopes, see Edward J. Larsen, *Summer for the Gods: The Scopes Trial and America's Continuing Debate Over Science and Religion* (1997).

Ethnic and racial boundaries are discussed in Ronald H. Bayor, *Neighbors in Conflict: The Irish, Germans, Jews, and Italians of New York City, 1929–1941* (1979); Bayor, *Race and the Shaping of Twentieth-Century Atlanta* (1996); Elizabeth Clark-Lewis, *Living In, Living Out:*

African-American Domestics and the Great Migration (1994); Juan R. Garcia, *Mexicans in the Midwest, 1900–1932* (1996); Cheryl Lynn Greenberg, *Or Does It Explode? Black Harlem in the Great Depression* (1991); Earl Lewis, *In Their Own Interests: Race, Class, and Power in Twentieth-Century Norfolk, Virginia* (1991); John T. McGreevy, *Parish Boundaries: The Catholic Encounter with Race in the Twentieth-Century Urban North* (1996); and George Sanchez, *Becoming Mexican-American: Ethnicity, Culture, and Identity in Chicano Los Angeles, 1900–1945* (1993). Race riots are discussed in David Allen Levine, *Internal Combustion: The Races in Detroit, 1915–1926* (1976); Tim Madigan, *The Burning: Massacre, Destruction and the Tulsa Race Riot of 1921* (2001); and William Tuttle, Jr., *Race Riot: Chicago in the Red Summer of 1919* (1970).

The depression in the cities is discussed in Jo Anne E. Argersinger, *Towards a New Deal in Baltimore: People and Government in the Great Depression* (1988); Richard O. Davies, *From Metropolis to Megalopolis: A History of Urban America Since 1930* (1980); William H. Mullins, *The Depression and the Urban West Coast, 1929–1933: Los Angeles, San Francisco, Seattle, and Portland* (1991); Harvard Sitkoff, *A New Deal for Blacks* (1978); Douglas L. Smith, *The New Deal in the Urban South* (1988); and Charles H. Trout, *Boston: The Great Depression and the New Deal* (1977).

On the history of public housing, see John F. Bauman, *Public Housing, Race, and Renewal: Urban Planning in Philadelphia, 1920–1974* (1987); John Bauman, Roger Biles, and Kristin Szylvian, *From Tenements to the Taylor Homes: In Search of an Urban Housing Policy in Twentieth Century America* (2000); Arnold Hirsch, "Containment on the Home Front: Race and Federal Housing Policy from the New Deal to the Cold War," *Journal of Urban History* 26, no. 2 (January, 2000): 158–189; and Gail Radford, *Modern Housing for America: Policy Struggles in the New Deal Era* (1996).

On politics in the depression years, see Roger Biles, *Big City Boss in Depression and War: Edward J. Kelly of Chicago* (1984); Lyle W. Dorsett, *Franklin D. Roosevelt and the City Bosses* (1977); and Bruce Stave, *The New Deal and the Last Hurrah: Pittsburgh's Machine Politics* (1970). For an engaging memoir of the period, see James Michael Curley, *I'd Do It Again* (1957).

On labor, civil rights, and neighborhood organizing in the 1930s, see Lizabeth Cohen, *Making the New Deal: Industrial Workers in Chicago, 1919–1939* (1990); Robert Fisher, *Let the People Decide: Neighborhood Organizing in America* (1984); Michael Honey, *Southern Labor and Black Civil Rights: Organizing Memphis Workers* (1993); Sanford D. Horwitt, *Let Them Call Me Rebel: Saul Alinsky, His Life and Legacy* (1989); Robin D. G. Kelley, *Hammer and Hoe: Alabama Communists during the Great Depression* (1990); Kelley, *Race Rebels: Culture, Politics, and the Black Working Class* (1994); and Patricia Sullivan, *Days of Hope: Race and Democracy in the New Deal Era* (1996).

Mark I. Gelfand's *A Nation of Cities: The Federal Government and Urban America, 1933–1965* (1975) provides indispensable perspectives on the development of federal urban policy during the New Deal. Other important works are Phillip J. Funigiello, *The Challenge to Urban Liberalism: Federal-City Relations During World War II* (1978); and the Urbanism Committee to the National Resources Committee, *Our Cities: Their Role in the National Economy* (1937).

NOTES

1. Albert Camarillo, *Not White, Not Black: Mexicans and Ethnic and Racial Borderlands in American Cities* (forthcoming: Oxford University Press).
2. William Leach, "Transformations in a Culture of Consumption: Women and Department Stores, 1890–1925," *Journal of American History* 71 (September 1984): 326.
3. Nancy MacLean, "The Leo Frank Case Reconsidered: Gender and Sexual Politics in the Making of Reactionary Populism," *Journal of American History* 78 (December 1991): 920–21.

CHAPTER

9

The Politics of Growth in the Era of Suburbanization, 1941–1974

THE IMPACT OF WORLD WAR II ON CITIES

During and after World War II, the American economy entered a long and steady period of growth and productivity that would last for some thirty years. This expansion had uneven effects on cities, which were buffeted by opposing forces of centralization, represented by the influx of new residents, and decentralization, in the form of suburbanization of people and businesses. Although war spending provided a temporary industrial boost and encouraged cityward migration, long-term political, economic and social forces contributed to a decline in central city tax bases, the isolation of urban dwellers from suburban residents, and powerful new mechanisms of racial segregation. Postwar capital restructuring encouraged industrial dispersion to low-wage nonunion areas in the South and West and eventually outside U. S. borders. Federal housing policies had the effect of hardening racial boundaries and creating new, larger racial ghettos. Federal involvement in urban affairs expanded and more than ever before, matters that affected cities affected the nation.

Military spending, rather than the New Deal, really ended the Depression and put people back to work. The unprecedented federal activity during the 1930s paled in comparison to the extraordinary federal mobilization from 1941 to 1945. This mobilization played a key role in propelling urban growth on the West Coast, where coalitions of politicians and business boosters, who even before World War II had made their cities the locations of naval bases and the aircraft industry, aggressively lobbied for more military bases and repair facilities. These efforts created what Roger Lotchin has called "metropolitan-military complexes" that included cities such as San Diego, Los Angeles, and San Francisco.

When Japan's surrender on August 14, 1945, brought an official end to the war and crowds surged into the streets to celebrate, no one knew whether the postwar economy would deliver depression or prosperity. Wartime emergency circumstances had effected enormous changes in American life. How would these changes shape and affect urban society?

The war's most notable phenomenon was full employment. In 1944, at the war's height, only 1.2 percent of the labor force was jobless. Washington funneled $175 billion in contracts to various corporations between 1941 and 1944. Corporate profits doubled between 1939 and 1943; wages and salaries rose more than 135 percent. The federal bureaucracy swelled from 1.1 million workers to 3.4 million. FDR's "soak the rich" tax policies in combination with full employment achieved some redistribution of income from the wealthiest downward, leading economists charting income inequality to label this period as "the Great Compression."

Little Tokyo, Los Angeles. During World War II, Japanese Americans were removed from their homes and detained in camps outside major urban centers, ostensibly for security reasons. As a result, communities such as this one lost their vitality but rebounded quickly after the war ended.

Wartime economic opportunities boosted urban populations. Industry had to recruit workers to supply the rapidly expanding need for military equipment, and African Americans, southern whites, teenagers, Mexicans and Mexican Americans, and women filled these jobs. Migration created new critical masses of black urban population. Some 1.6 million African Americans moved from the South to industrial cities of the North and West in the 1940s, more than the total migration of the previous thirty years. African-American men and women quit work as sharecroppers, domestic servants, and menial employees in restaurants, dime stores, laundries, and hospitals to seek the better working conditions, higher pay, and union benefits of industrial employment.

Other groups were on the move as well. Reversing its Depression policy of repatriation, the government began in 1942 to admit Mexicans to the United States as *braceros* on short-term work contracts for farm and industrial labor. Although the newcomers encountered discrimination, they seized new economic opportunities. More than fifteen thousand Mexican workers relocated to Chicago. In Los Angeles, thousands of Mexicans found shipyard jobs when before the war none had been available. Similarly, displaced white coal miners and marginal farmers from the hills of West Virginia and Kentucky left to work in booming war industries of Detroit, Cleveland, Columbus, and Cincinnati. Most of the six million women who entered the labor force during the war worked in cities, some in clerical jobs, others in manufacturing. Among women workers, 75 percent were married and two-thirds were mothers. And by 1944, three million children, one-third of those between ages fourteen and eighteen, were also employed.

Cities hummed with vitality during the war, with multiple work shifts keeping people on the streets day and night. Nightlife was active. Swing bands reached their height of popularity, blues and jazz musicians played in many venues, and dance halls, nightclubs, bars, and restaurants were filled with war workers and soldiers on leave and with spendable cash. Movie theaters were packed, attracting weekly audiences of 85 million by 1945. As places that sponsored war bond campaigns and served as collection points for scarce war goods, movie theaters played a crucial role as community centers.

New employment patterns, wartime dislocations and shortages, and the mixing of people in defense industries made it difficult to maintain older social boundaries, and sometimes explosive conflicts resulted. African Americans and southern whites competed for defense jobs and scarce housing. They bumped against each other in overcrowded city schools, buses, parks, and beaches. Some white workers staged walkouts to protest black hiring and promotion. Black membership in civil rights organizations such as the NAACP soared, suggesting new confidence in resisting customary forms of discrimination. Other minorities asserted themselves as well and faced ugly resentment. When Mexican-American youths in Los Angeles flaunted wartime clothing rationing by adopting zoot suits, outfits with exaggerated padded shoulders and tapered pants identified with black urban jazz culture, some white servicemen on leave responded with outrage. During a week of rioting in the summer of 1943, stripping and assaulting of zoot suiters became a major means by which servicemen attempted to claim authority over gangs of Mexican-American and African-American youth.

Sporadic clashes scarred other cities as well, including New York, Detroit, and Philadelphia. Nearly 250 racial conflicts erupted in forty-seven cities during the summer of 1943. Many of these riots stemmed from incidents in which social circumstances related to war exigencies encouraged the crossing of boundaries which previously had been assumed to be barriers. The worst riot bloodied Detroit in June, leaving twenty-five blacks and nine whites dead and more than 700 injured. White mobs, undeterred by police, roamed the city attacking blacks, who in turn hurled rocks at police and hauled white passengers off streetcars. In August, a riot in Harlem began with a confrontation between a white policeman and an African-American soldier. Rumors of an assault on the serviceman prompted blacks to respond with looting and vandalism. By war's end, tensions had eased, but new ones would emerge as economic and social change continued to reconfigure poor neighborhoods and downtowns.

Wartime sex-segregated environments, in the armed forces and, especially for women, in war jobs and housing, expanded the settings in which same-sex relationships could be pursued. These settings, working in tandem with increased mobility and the distance from "home" required by military service and industrial mobilization, drew those who had already identified themselves as homosexuals and created new opportunities for those whose desires found meaning for the first time. Many large cities already offered meeting places, especially bars, that enabled the public expression of homosexual identities. Some places encouraged mingling among a variety of patrons; others were specifically oriented to homosexual clientele. By the 1940s, there were gay-identified bars in San Francisco and Chicago, but also in smaller cities such as San Jose, Denver, Kansas City, and Buffalo. Although morals legislation and licensing laws made homosexual patrons vulnerable to legal sanctions, the bars continued to provide haven for gay culture, and by the 1950s small groups of homosexuals began organizing for political and civil rights. Other homosexual groups gathered around urban arts and cultural institutions, where they claimed a presence as part of urban cosmopolitan life.

Wartime federal intervention in the economy encouraged migration to the suburbs and the Sunbelt. Between 1939 and 1945, the federal government built an average of $2.5 billion worth of industrial buildings every year, more than double the average for private industry. Lacking adequate space in crowded cities, most of these plants located in suburbs. At war's end, these facilities were turned over to private industry, often at nominal cost. In this manner, federal construction regionalized the national economy, making southern and western metropolitan areas the locations of defense and aircraft industries. Between New Deal projects and military spending, the federal government paid for facilities in southern cities that northern cities had paid for themselves in earlier decades and on which they were still paying off debts. With help from defense industries and from research and development associated with them, the economies of Phoenix, Tucson, Albuquerque, San Diego, Los Angeles, San Francisco, Portland, and Seattle expanded substantially in the war years and after.

Political shifts accompanied these developments. The New Deal Democratic Party alliance between urban liberals and southern conservatives weakened during the war years. Republican victories in the congressional elections of 1942 hinted at a new alliance between Republicans and southern Democrats. In 1942 this new coalition had enough votes to dismantle many New Deal relief and social welfare agencies. Franklin Roosevelt's victory in the 1944 presidential election was his narrowest, and he owed his reelection almost completely to urban voters.

Population shifts explained the cities' political clout. New war workers—southern whites who had been lifelong Democrats and African Americans who had never before voted—had migrated to urban centers. But social concerns deepened after postwar layoffs pushed almost three million people off their jobs. Labor strife kindled thousands of strikes, and inflation hiked prices of everyday goods. The New Deal Democratic voting bloc was shaken after challenges from the labor-left coalition that supported Progressive party presidential candidate Henry Wallace in 1948, and from right-wing Dixiecrats who bolted the party after the adoption of a civil rights platform. Big-city voters, black voters, and most of the labor movement rallied to elect Harry S. Truman president in 1948. Still, the conservative challenge to New Deal legislation would have important ramifications for city life in the postwar years. Thomas Sugrue and Robert Self have noted that, although cities were the crucible for the New Deal focus on economic security and racial equality, in the years to come, the suburbs would constitute the crucible for the New Right's focus on propertyholders' rights and racial exclusion.[1]

SPATIAL PATTERNS OF POSTWAR GROWTH

In the postwar years, low-interest loans to military veterans combined with FHA mortgage insurance to subsidize construction of thousands of suburban real estate developments. New housing starts climbed from 326,000 in 1945 to over one million in 1946 and two million by 1950. Developers such as Arthur Levitt and Sons erected whole communities of nearly identical houses with mass-production techniques and designs. By 1948, Levitt was turning out 150 houses per week, completing one every fifteen minutes in his new community of Levittown outside New York City. Home-owning became much more possible for those with access to these developments. In 1930, less than one-third of Americans owned their homes, but nearly two-thirds would do so by 1960.

This extraordinary construction came with high environmental costs. Cities had always existed in precarious relationship with nature, gobbling up open areas and using up resources while at the same time making themselves vulnerable to adversities such as floods and storms. But as historian Adam Rome has pointed out, the new mass construction of suburban housing and related aspects of suburban growth had special environmental impact. Developers who erected hundreds of homes at a time used powerful earth-moving equipment to level hills, fill in wetlands, and clear vegetation. The result was not only lost open space but also soil erosion and disrupted wildlife. Because many new tracts lacked connection to sewage lines, homes had to be built with septic tanks to dispose of waste. Seepage of human waste and soap suds from poorly constructed septic systems polluted groundwater and fouled lakes, in addition to heightening the threat of disease. As well, the architecture of new suburban homes, many of them one-story "ranch" style with no basement, combined with the removal of trees, increased the use of energy for heating and cooling.

Much of the suburban construction would not have occurred had not federal highway construction provided access to rural land for development. In 1947, Congress authorized a 37,000-mile national highway network, including nearly three thousand miles of roads in or near major cities. Following a scheme of a hub (downtown) with spokes fanning out from the center and a beltway circling the city on the outskirts, federal roadbuilding redefined downtown as a commercial center with direct access to and from suburban areas. Cities also funded their own freeways. During the early 1950s, New York laid out the Cross-Bronx Expressway, Detroit began construction of the John Lodge and Edsel Ford superhighways, and Chicago built the Congress (later Eisenhower) Expressway. By 1956, there were an estimated 376 miles of freeways in the nation's twenty-five largest cities and at least 104 additional miles under construction.

The Interstate Highway Act of 1956 and creation of the Federal Highway Trust Fund strengthened these patterns. Justified as a means to aid intercity travel for purposes of civil defense, and to ease downtown traffic congestion, federal funds spent on highways swelled from $429 million in 1950 to $2.9 billion in 1960. Road construction leveled some older downtown neighborhoods and cut through the middle of others, in the process enabling highways to redesign racial space in cities like Atlanta and Miami by forcing massive relocations and by serving as barriers separating black and white neighborhoods. The Highway Trust Fund, supported by gas-tax revenues which could be used only to build and maintain highways, ensured that freeways would be self-supporting.

By 1950, the results of highway construction and housing policies were already clear. The suburban population, overwhelmingly white, was growing

Highway Cloverleaf. This 1962 shot of an intersection between two interstate highways in Los Angeles shows clearly the engineering feat required to build high-speed limited access freeways amidst existing neighborhoods. The freeways enabled new configurations of cross-town travel between home, work, and recreation, but the community reorientation, loss of housing and local businesses, and disruption that resulted as highways sliced between blocks permanently altered local patterns of social and economic interchange.

ten times faster than that of central cities. Between 1950 and 1970, Chicago and New York City lost population while their suburban rings grew by 117 percent and 195 percent respectively. Detroit's population fell by 20 percent as its suburban population expanded by 206 percent. Similar patterns held in Boston, Washington, D.C., Cleveland, St. Louis, Minneapolis, and Pittsburgh. The only cities that continued to grow were southern and western cities that expanded by annexation. But even in these places, suburban growth overtook

The Postwar Housing Expansion. Signs in an undeveloped section outside San Diego advertise the types of housing and government support for financing that invigorated suburbanization after World War II.

central-city increases. While Los Angeles's population grew by 43 percent from 1950 to 1970, its outer ring grew by 141 percent. Dallas's and Houston's populations grew by 94 percent and 104 percent, but their suburbs grew by 107 percent and 330 percent.

Beltway road construction and increased reliance on trucking for intercity freight traffic provided incentives for industrial relocation to suburban areas. By the 1960s, new factories lined peripheral highways, boosting tax bases of suburban communities at the cost of central cities. The decentralization of jobs began to siphon off employment from central cities. Between 1954 and 1963, in the twenty-four metropolitan areas with populations greater than one million, the central cities lost more than five hundred thousand jobs while their suburbs were gaining 1.5 million. Between 1947 and 1954, the number of manufacturing plants in Chicago suburbs doubled; there was a 220 percent rise in factor jobs in suburban Detroit. In 1957, Massachusetts completed a freeway encircling Boston, and by year's end ninety-nine plants employing seventeen thousand people had located along the highway. Some communities developed industrial parks, outlying tracts zoned exclusively for industry. Industrial Hayward and Milpitas, California, were as characteristic suburban developments as residential Lakewood, California, and Park Forest, Illinois.

Businesses followed the residential expansion and sometimes even preceded it. Malls, complete with closed arcades and sprawling parking lots, became major retail marketplaces for the metropolis, in the process replacing the public space of downtown streets with privately owned and controlled enclosed space. It became increasingly convenient for a suburban family to fill its material needs in malls rather than in old downtowns. New shopping centers featured specialty shops, department stores, drugstores, groceries, movie theaters, restaurants, banks, and, best of all, free parking. A New Mexico mall built in the early 1960s even included a bomb shelter capable of accommodating eight thousand people underground for two weeks. The shopping centers themselves, their size, and their glitter became new objects of boosterism as each year chauvinists from a different community boasted that they had the biggest. Thus outward movement energized a new multiplier effect. Access to superhighways attracted residents, who in turn lured businesses, who then brought jobs and more enticement for residential development.

The racial division between cities and suburbs was increasingly obvious—whites on the outside, people of color on the inside. The FHA refused to guarantee suburban loans to poor people, nonwhites, and other "inharmonious" racial and ethnic groups, excluding them from the tax benefits and asset value that home ownership provides. Restrictive covenants and, after these were declared illegal in 1948, unspoken agreements among realtors kept all but the most economically secure and assertive black families from buying homes in new communities. A few suburban developments sprang up to house the black middle class, but the great majority were exclusively white.

Middle Class Black Suburbanites in Parkchester Village, Richmond, California. After World War II, increased competition for scarce housing sparked tensions between blacks and whites. Parkchester Village was planned to be a model racially integrated housing development, designed to remedy both the scarcity and the tensions, but no white families moved in.

The increasingly nonwhite character of central cities had several dimensions. Approximately five million African Americans, primarily from the Deep South where they had been displaced by the mechanization of cotton harvesting, moved into cities between 1950 and 1970, while seven million white people moved out. In some cities, racial population shifts were dramatic (see Table 9–1). New York City's white population declined 7 percent

TABLE 9–1 Central-City, Black, and Metropolitan Populations for Selected American Cities, 1940 and 1970

City	1940			1970		
	Central City	Blacks	Metro Area	Central City	Blacks	Metro Area
Atlanta	302,288	104,533	558,842	496,973	255,051	1,390,164
Baltimore	859,100	165,843	1,139,529	905,759	420,210	2,070,670
Boston	770,816	23,679	2,209,608	641,071	104,707	2,753,700
Buffalo	506,775	17,694	958,487	462,768	94,329	1,349,211
Chicago	3,396,808	277,731	4,569,643	3,366,957	1,102,620	6,978,947
Cincinnati	455,610	55,593	787,044	452,524	125,000	1,384,851
Cleveland	878,336	84,504	1,267,270	750,903	287,841	2,064,194
Dallas	294,734	50,407	527,145	844,401	210,238	1,555,950
Denver	322,412	7,836	445,206	514,678	47,011	1,227,529
Detroit	1,623,452	149,119	2,377,329	1,511,482	660,428	4,199,931
Houston	384,514	86,302	528,961	1,232,802	316,551	1,985,031
Indianapolis	386,972	51,142	460,926	743,155	134,320	1,109,882
Kansas City (Mo.)	399,178	41,574	686,643	507,409	112,005	1,256,649
Los Angeles	1,504,277	63,774	2,916,403	2,816,061	503,606	7,032,075
Louisville	319,077	47,158	451,473	361,472	86,040	826,553
Memphis	292,942	121,498	358,250	623,530	242,513	770,120
Miami	172,172	36,857	267,739	334,859	76,156	1,267,792
Milwaukee	587,472	8,821	829,629	717,099	105,088	1,403,688
Minneapolis	492,370	4,646	967,367	434,400	19,005	1,813,647
Nashville	167,402	47,318	257,267	447,877	87,876	541,108
Newark	429,760	74,965	1,291,416	382,417	207,458	1,856,556
New Orleans	494,537	149,034	552,244	593,471	267,308	1,046,470
New York	7,454,995	458,444	8,706,917	7,894,862	1,668,115	11,571,899
Philadelphia	1,931,334	250,880	3,199,637	1,948,609	653,791	4,817,914
Pittsburgh	671,659	62,216	2,082,556	520,117	104,904	2,401,245
Portland (Ore.)	305,394	1,931	501,275	382,619	21,572	1,009,129
Providence	253,504	6,388	695,253	179,213	15,875	789,186
Rochester	324,975	3,262	438,230	296,233	49,647	882,667
St. Louis	816,048	108,765	1,464,111	622,236	254,191	2,363,017
Salt Lake City	149,934	694	211,623	175,885	2,135	557,635
San Francisco	634,536	4,846	1,461,804	715,674	96,078	3,109,519
Seattle	368,302	3,789	593,734	538,831	37,868	1,421,869
Washington, D.C.	663,091	187,266	967,985	756,510	537,712	2,816,123

Source: Bayrd Still, *Urban America: A History with Documents* (Boston: Little, Brown, 1974), derived from Table 4.1, pp. 356–59.

between 1950 and 1960, while its black population rose 46 percent. In Chicago the white total dropped 13 percent, while the black total rose 65 percent. In 1950, only one-sixth of the populations of Detroit, Cleveland, and St. Louis were African American; within ten years each of these cities was 29 percent black. Washington, D.C., became the first American city with a black majority. Other nonwhite groups achieved a significant presence as well. As early as 1930, Mexicans and Mexican Americans constituted more than half the population of El Paso, slightly less than half of San Antonio, and one-fifth of Los Angeles. The number of Puerto Ricans swelled in New York and Chicago, and significant numbers of Cubans settled in Miami, and Asians and Asian Americans in San Francisco, Los Angeles, and New York.

American Indians also began moving to cities. During the 1950s, the Bureau of Indian Affairs sponsored a program to induce Indians to leave reservations for cities. Relocation offices were opened in several cities, including Chicago, Denver, Salt Lake City, Oakland, and San Francisco. The program floundered, however, involving only 12,000 out of 245,000 reservation Indians. Many relocatees could not adjust to the urban environment and were disillusioned with their low-paying jobs. Rather than blend into neighborhoods as hoped, Indians were herded into all-native, low-rent districts, which only heightened their feelings of isolation. Though many returned to their reservations, reluctance to admit failure kept others in cities where they eventually found some relief in informal organizations such as all-Indian sports teams and in organizations such as Chicago's American Indian Center.

Residents of many older urban neighborhoods were increasingly likely to be either poor white ethnics, who could not afford to move out, or new nonwhite migrants. If the war and urban migration had heightened black expectations for fair housing and employment, the residents of ethnic enclaves saw their hard-won gains of home ownership and community stability threatened. Thus, though neighborhoods shifted composition, racial dividing lines became sharper.

RESHAPING DOWNTOWN: PROGROWTH COALITIONS, URBAN RENEWAL, AND THEIR CONSEQUENCES

The white exodus from central city neighborhoods, the disappearance of manufacturing investment, and an increasing impoverished, nonwhite population challenged prior assumptions about city life. As freeway suburbs grew, central city mass transit systems lost riders, downtown night clubs and movie houses lost audiences, department stores lost shoppers, and downtown hotels lost guests. City officials, business leaders, and members of Congress, all of whom connected visible urban poverty, housing shortages, and downtown decline, identified a priorty of attacking what they saw as "blight" and stimulating downtown investment under the rubric, first of slum clearance and then of urban renewal. To accomplish this goal, these leaders sought government help, with the result, according to historian Arnold Hirsch, that "government action proved remarkably successful in maintaining the color line in urban America."[2]

In 1945, Senators Robert F. Wagner of New York, Allen J. Ellender of Louisiana, and Robert A. Taft of Ohio cosponsored a bill that set a goal of 1.25 million new housing units a year to be built for all social classes during the next ten years. The proposal included government loans and subsidies for the construction of 810,000 public housing units for low-income groups in the next four years. Previously, the Housing Act of 1937, which created the U.S. Housing Authority, had committed the federal government to financing public housing. Congressional conservatives, however, had limited the appropriations, and the National Association of Real Estate Boards (NAREB) and organizations that supported private housing lobbied against any public housing at all. Instead, realtors and builders supported government subsidy for private redevelopment of what they labeled as blighted, meaning unprofitable, areas in inner cities. NAREB labeled public housing as socialist interference with the private housing market, although the real estate lobby accepted, even demanded, government intervention to acquire and clear land and sought government subsidies to redevelop land for private profit. NAREB argued that this kind of renewal would expand municipal tax bases and reinvigorate downtowns.

Champions of public housing, such as social workers, housing reformers, and labor leaders, sought government aid for public construction of dwelling units for the broadest possible range of urban residents with only so much emphasis on slum clearances as was necessary to secure sites for this housing. Conservative opponents of the 1937 Housing Act had managed to tilt its emphasis from public housing to slum clearance. In 1945, the redevelopment interests again lobbied against public housing, but public housing advocates had the votes in Congress to support their program.

After four years of debate, the legislation that finally passed as the Housing Act of 1949 was a compromise that contained several measures: slum clearance, public housing, and expanded mortgage insurance through the FHA. Title I of the bill established the principle of urban redevelopment, committing federal funds to the clearance of slums by local redevelopment agencies. The law mandated that redevelopment programs be "predominantly residential." But this term could mean *either* that areas earmarked for redevelopment had to be at least 50 percent residential in character before they were cleared *or* that new construction in cleared residential areas had to include 50 percent residential units—*but not necessarily both*. Thus redevelopment projects could level residential areas labeled as slums and replace them with office buildings, shopping complexes, luxury apartments, and parking lots—land uses intended to raise property values, assist private investment, increase tax revenues, and restore economic vitality.

Title II of the bill put public housing on a permanent basis, authorizing 810,000 units over the next six years. The AFL, CIO, U.S. Conference of Mayors, veterans' groups, and NAACP strongly supported Title II. Public housing advocates were skeptical of the redevelopment provision of Title I but believed that a compromise that included Title II was the only way public housing could be achieved. They lobbied hard for the act, countering opposition from NAREB and the Savings and Loan League.

The 1949 Housing Act committed the nation to providing "a decent home and suitable living environment" for every American family. It set public housing production targets and created a new and powerful mechanism for transforming land use in central cities. But almost immediately, the law brought disappointment to its liberal supporters. In 1951, Robert Moses, the New York City planner, park commissioner, and highway builder, showed how a local power could redirect the act's intentions. Moses wanted to build a coliseum and luxury housing at Broadway and 57th Street. Because he could show that the area included a few run-down tenements sheltering three hundred people, Moses defined it as "predominantly residential" and used urban redevelopment to gain control of more than two square blocks of thriving commercial property. With $26 million in federal assistance, Moses built an exhibition center, a parking structure, and luxury housing on the site. His action demonstrated that the 1949 Housing Act could be used to advance redevelopment agendas for downtown rather than meet housing needs of the urban poor. In 1954, Congress, backed by the Eisenhower administration, amended the 1949 provisions, and urban renewal replaced urban redevelopment.

The amended housing act recognized the need for rehabilitation of dilapidated structures rather than massive slum clearance, although provisions for clearance were retained. Subsequently, the term "renewal" came to imply both renewal and redevelopment. The amendment included a new provision that allocated 10 percent of federal grants-in-aid to projects in nonresidential areas, allowing localities to use a tenth of federal funds for projects that did not fit the loose, predominantly residential criterion. Further amendments in 1961 boosted the proportion of nonresidential funds to 30 percent, removing redevelopment further from the solution of housing problems.

Downtown revitalization became the rallying cry for mayors, who built support based on coalitions of politicians, businessmen, labor unions, and planners who favored economic growth over social reform. For example, in Pittsburgh, Mayor David Lawrence and Richard K. Mellon, heir to a huge corporate fortune, brought together local leaders and formed the Allegheny Conference on Community Development (ACCD) to develop a new central business district. Corporate executives, downtown merchants, real estate interests, and construction trades orchestrated the Pittsburgh Renaissance, a redevelopment program that cleared railroad yards and commercial

Rebuilding Downtown. While housing starts boomed in the suburbs during the 1950s, the roar of construction also vibrated through downtown areas. This view shows iron workers on the thirty-second floor of New Yorks Exxon building, built in 1954.

blight to create a park, six high-rise office structures, a luxury hotel, and underground parking garage. New Orleans mayor DeLesseps Morrison joined the business community in constructing a downtown civic center. In St. Louis, a businessmen's association known as Civic Progress allied with Mayor Raymond Tucker, labor unions, and religious groups to support a $110 million bond issue that cleared downtown areas for expressways, bridges, and hospitals. To undertake these projects, local governments lured private investment money with generous property tax abatements and reduced assessments, thereby sacrificing immediate revenue in hopes that "growth" would generate jobs and other economic benefits.

In Boston, political changes that diminished the power of inner neighborhoods and increased the input of business leaders were required before progrowth coalitions could emerge. In 1949, the Massachusetts legislature reformed the city's charter, abolishing district elections of city councilors. In 1951, the New Boston Committee, a business lobby, helped John Hynes defeat James Michael Curley as mayor. Once in office, Hynes inaugurated a redevelopment program by initiating the West End Project, which built luxury housing that displaced over twenty-six hundred families in a downtown neighborhood adjacent to government offices and major hospitals.

Then, in 1959, a group of Boston business leaders organized behind mayoral candidate John Collins. With their backing, Collins hired Ed Logue, New Haven's innovative urban renewal executive, to direct large-scale redevelopment in Boston. The program ultimately subjected 10 percent of the city's land area to redevelopment. In cooperation with Mayor Collins and the business coalition, Logue won federal funding for construction of a government center, including a new city hall and a group of towers to house federal and state agencies, plus redevelopment of the waterfront with high-rise luxury apartments. Critics charged that Boston's urban renewal was black and ethnic removal, and indeed the areas designated for slum clearance included parts of the multiethnic West End, the racially mixed South End, and Lower Roxbury, a major African-American community. The impact of urban renewal in Boston intensified the competition for a diminishing low-rent housing supply between the city's poor white ethnics and newly displaced black residents.

In Richmond, downtown businessmen and planners organized a Greater Richmond movement. A new city charter passed in 1948 provided for a city manager and small city council to be elected on a citywide basis, effectively placing local government in the hands of the white elite for the next thirty years even though Richmond had a black majority by the 1960s. The Greater Richmond plan called for freeways to be built through the city and for a larger, more exclusively commercial downtown. City leaders used federal renewal funds to remove black residents from locations desired by white businessmen. In Miami, urban renewal replaced black housing with government office and community college buildings, a sports arena, and high-rise apartments. In San Francisco, business leaders formed the San Francisco Planning and Urban Renewal Association (SPUR). In 1959, urban-renewal planner M. Justin Herman was appointed head of the city's redevelopment agency. With backing from SPUR, major city property owners, most trade unions, and future mayor Joseph Alioto, Herman undertook to redevelop large areas adjacent to the central business district. His projects disrupted the city's produce market, its Japanese neighborhood, its major African-American neighborhood, and a variety of other low-rent sites. In almost every instance, then, urban redevelopment negatively affected minority people. By the end of the 1950s, nearly 9 out of 10 families that were compelled to move because of urban renewal and redevelopment were nonwhite.

Shifting political currents influenced the fate of postwar public housing. Conservatives bent on undoing New Deal social welfare programs singled out public housing for attack. They successfully cut appropriations, and between 1949 and 1955 barely 200,000 dwelling units out of the proposed 810,000 were actually completed. The real estate lobby conducted a massive campaign to hold local referenda on public housing, defeating the issue twenty-five of thirty-eight times. In Los Angeles, Mayor Fletcher

Bowron and the city council backed a public housing plan to construct ten thousand dwelling units at a cost of $110 million. One of the largest projects was to be located in Chavez Ravine, a 315-acre area near downtown and settled by Mexican Americans and Chinese Americans. Architects designed a series of new, mostly low-rent apartments for the parcel. But real estate interests and the chamber of commerce attacked the public housing program, which was supported by local unions and various church, veterans', and citizens' groups. The antihousing forces prevailed, and by late 1951 the majority of the city council agreed to cancel the project. Mayor Bowron was defeated for reelection in 1953, and plans for over half his public housing projects were abandoned. Chavez Ravine was finally developed in 1957 when Los Angeles signed a contract with Walter O'Malley, owner of the Brooklyn Dodgers, who built a stadium on the property for his baseball team.

Where public housing was built, legal battles and neighborhood conflict over its location meant that many years passed between land clearance and the completion of new dwellings. Facing diminished financing and rising costs, 1950s housing planners had rejected the low-rise design of the 1930s in favor of high-rise towers. But there were never enough units built to house all the people who needed a place to live, and appropriations were never sufficient for adequate maintenance. In city after city, public housing became an instrument of segregation. For example, black tenants occupied two-thirds of Chicago's public housing in 1955 and 85 percent by 1959. Even when white residents in Brownsville, Brooklyn, attempted to develop an integrated neighborhood, they could not stop the uncontrollable neighborhood transformation that resulted from the influx of poor black and Latino New Yorkers displaced by Robert Moses' Manhattan urban renwal program, nor the resulting public disinvestment in the area.

Pruitt-Igoe Housing Project. Once one of the nations most acclaimed public housing complexes, the Pruitt-Igoe project in St. Louis, built in 1954, came to symbolize the unworkable qualities of poorly designed low-income housing. After futile efforts to overcome its deficiencies, the project was demolished in 1974.

Between 1950 and 1960, federal programs destroyed more homes than were built, removing mostly low-rent buildings and replacing them with high-rise apartments. Although redevelopment laws specified that housing assisted by federal funds could not discriminate by race or religion, high rents excluded most people of color from the housing erected on cleared land. Previous residents were channeled into crowded, badly maintained, segregated public housing. Experts estimated that as a result of slum clearance and urban renewal, the United States lost a total of 200,000 housing units a year between 1950 and 1956 and 475,000 a year between 1957 and 1959. Thousands of small businesses also were destroyed, and their contributions to a city's tax base lost. Other renewal projects cleared land for the expansion of tax-free universities and hospitals into black or white ethnic working-class neighborhoods. Highway construction also caused ill effects. Land in the path of highways rapidly declined in value, neighborhood shops moved away, and low-income housing became scarcer. The social costs of revitalization were high, and disproportionately born by the poor. The benefits did not adequately solve urban economic problems or stem the residential and economic flight from the city.

CURRENTS OF PROTEST

The political struggles shaping public life in the 1960s grew out of a cross-fertilization between the civil rights movement, labor militancy, and neighborhood organizing in the 1940s and 1950s. The 1941 March on Washington movement that resulted in opening defense industry jobs to black workers and establishment of a federal Fair Employment Practices Commission, and especially the victories won by the CIO labor movement reinvigorated African-American communities devastated by the Depression. Rising hopes for better jobs, housing, and schools continued to generate protest against persisting political disenfranchisement and discrimination, and critical masses in progressive trade unions agitated for fair employment and housing in cities like Detroit, Chicago, and Cleveland. CIO organizers aided the drive to register black voters in Birmingham, Alabama, in the late 1940s. In Montgomery, Alabama, the ultimately successful 1955 boycott protesting segregated seating on public transportation drew on resources of the local Brotherhood of Sleeping Car Porters, the NAACP chapter, the black women's political association, and area churches, including the leadership of the young minister, the Reverend Martin Luther King, Jr. At the same time, however, local antidiscrimination campaigns faced fierce opposition in the form of incresingly a well-mobilized conservative and anticommunist backlash. Surveillance files on civil rights activists were collected across the South by state bodies such as the Mississippi State Sovereignty Commission and the Florida Legislative Investigative

Committee, in an effort to establish links between racial unrest and communist agitation.

In Los Angeles in the late 1940s, Chicanos founded the Community Service Organization (CSO). The organization, inspired by labor-trained organizer Saul Alinsky, enrolled twelve thousand new Mexican-American voters. Politician Ed Roybal put together a coalition of Armenians, Russians, African Americans, and Jews, as well as Chicanos, to become the first Latino elected to the Los Angeles City Council since 1881. Through letter-writing campaigns and other organizing tactics, by 1960, CSO boasted thirty-seven chapters, 217,000 newly registered voters, numerous physical improvements in barrio neighborhoods, and challenges to ethnic segregation in schools and public accommodations. But opponents charged that civil rights activism was un-American, and Chicano labor leaders were vulnerable to threats of deportation.

Grass roots challenges to inadequately supported, segregated schools in several cities resulted in the legal reversal of the separate-but-equal doctrine, in effect since 1896. The 1954 Supreme Court decision, *Brown v. Board of Education,* made school segregation illegal, but southern communities balked at integration, finding various ways to circumvent the ruling, and northern communities continued to underfund and gerrymander the boundaries of nonwhite school districts. When the school board of Little Rock, Arkansas, decided in 1957 to allow a few black students to attend previously all-white Central High School, Governor Orville Faubus sent the Arkansas National Guardsmen to bar the black children from the school. President Eisenhower had to use federal troops to escort the nine black students and patrol the school's halls for the rest of the year, but the following year, local authorities shut down the school altogether. In Boston, it took concerned black parents years to overcome official denial of school segrgregation by documenting and publicizing the complex web of informal policies that consistently assigned their children to the most overcrowded and under-funded schools.

Campaigns in the 1950s and early 1960s to open up jobs, public accommodations, and schools in the North and the South coincided with the beginning of deindustrialization's impact on black economic opportunities. The multiple effects of plant relocations, the use of automation to reduce labor costs, and shifts in defense spending, combined with continuing discrimination in hiring practices and union exclusions to increase black unemployment relative to white. In factory cities like Detroit, black unemployment rates doubled those of whites. In the same years, residential segregation resulting from informal exclusionary practices, urban renewal, highway building, and red lining contributed to racial isolation, and intensified the practices of school segregation. Regional differences continued to be significant in some ways: for example, desegregation of public accommodations generated more public and well-organized white resistance in cities in southern and border states than in northern cities. Nevertheless, nonwhite urban residents faced unequal and often brutal mistreatment by the police in nearly very region.

Enough blacks now lived in cities for organized collective resistance to be effective, but many forms of racial discrimination stubbornly persisted. The civil rights campaigns spearheaded by Martin Luther King and his organization, the Southern Christian Leadership Conference, used nonviolent direct action, marches, sit-ins, and mass arrests to challenge discrimination by employers and merchants in Birmingham and Selma, Alabama, and Albany, Georgia but met with little success. Other efforts made some impact. In 1963, King keynoted a national march on Washington for civil rights, the largest political assembly in Washington to this point. The grass-roots voter registration drives led by Bob Moses and the Student Nonviolent Coordinating Committee mounted a public challenge to representation by all-white southern delegations at the Democratic National Convention in 1964. The Nation of Islam (Black Muslims), under leadership of Elijah Muhammad and his charismatic challenger, Malcolm X, proclaimed a message of religious and spiritual renewal, self-discipline, and economic self-sufficiency, militantly criticizing economic exploitation and police brutality in urban black communities. "You need somebody who is going to fight," Malcolm X once asserted in response to King's philosophy of nonviolence. "You don't need any kneeling or crawling in."

Grass roots agitation to turn national attention to the problems of poverty and racial inequality provoked some response from the Democratic adminsitrations of John F. Kennedy and Lyndon B. Johnson. Kennedy captured the attention of civic leaders with promises of federal support for urban needs such as schools, medical care, mass transit, and planning. Kennedy's Committee on Juvenile Delinquency initiated several projects that organized slum communities to work out solutions to their own problems, a tactic that later became central to the War on Poverty. However, Kennedy's attempt to create a cabinet department of urban affairs failed when southern congressmen balked at his intention to nominate a distinguished African American, housing expert Robert C. Weaver, as secretary. Creation of the Department of Housing and Urban Development was delayed until 1966, when the only way advocates of federal action in urban affairs could win support was by emphasizing housing instead of broader urban issues.

Seizing the political initiative on civil rights in the shock following Kennedy's assassination, the new president Lyndon B. Johnson prodded Congress in 1964 to pass the Civil Rights Act, outlawing racial discrimination in public accommodations, employmemt, and federal programs. In the Voting Rights Act of 1965, Congress authorized federal agents to register voters who had been illegally denied suffrage. Johnson and his advisers mounted an extensive attack against urban problems, particularly against poverty, with the

Great Society programs. In 1964, Johnson pressed Congress to pass the Economic Opportunity Act, which created the Office of Economic Opportunity (OEO) to oversee an agenda designed to end domestic poverty: Job Corps, a skill-training program; Head Start, an educational boost for preschool children with disadvantaged backgrounds; Volunteers in Service to America (VISTA), a domestic Peace Corps; and the Community Action Program, which encouraged "maximum feasible involvement" of neighborhood residents in policy planning. Other legislation expanded the food-stamp program, funded housing programs, and provided federal funds to modernize hospitals. In 1966, the Johnson administration launched the Model Cities program, a new variant of renewal that directed federal funds to special districts where locally elected boards had designed a coordinated plan to improve local housing, health, education, and employment. War on Poverty programs tended to view urban problems in terms of cultural and educational deficits of individuals rather than considering the restructuring of the urban labor market or reversing urban capital disinvestment. But the Model Cities program's emphasis on neighborhood participation in community projects opened up space for competing analyses, and often stirred conflict among community organizations, professional politicians, social workers, and planners over whose ideas should prevail.

Though federal officials tried to approve only those Model City projects that would not undermine locally elected officials, many projects had the opposite effect. For example, OEO-financed programs mobilized both black and Chicano activists in San Antonio to demand control over those projects within their own communities. Efforts by black political leaders in Oakland to utilize federally funded antipoverty programs to actively redress local black unemployment and to organize the poor put them on a political collision course with City Hall, and, as Robert Self has noted, "stretched the political capacity of the War on Poverty to its limit."[3]

Newly mobilized community groups flexed political muscles in a variety of ways. African-American and Mexican-American leaders challenged political machines through their presence on community action councils and often acquired elected posts in city and state governments. One political scientist has estimated that almost one-fourth of all blacks elected to city positions and state houses of representatives between 1964 and 1977 gained political experience from working in community action programs. Other groups organized opposition to redevelopment projects, which stood as the most visible agent of displacement and housing shortages. In San Francisco in 1967, blacks protested destruction of the thriving commercial and residential Western Addition neighborhood by forming a broad-based community organization and picketing the Redevelopment Authority office, seizing the stage at public hearings, and lying down in front of bulldozers. In Boston in 1968, community activists in renewal neighborhoods occupied redevelopment offices and built a tent city to dramatize displacement of poor families previously housed there. By the late 1960s, neighborhood activism had challenged the progrowth consensus with obstinate persistence. In Gary, Indiana, industrial pollution from steel mills vital to the city's economy engendered opposition, first from middle-class homeowners, then from unions demanding occupational health and safety, and finally from black residents who were forced by discriminatory practices into the most polluted neighborhoods and unlhealthiest jobs.

Antipoverty programs heightened awareness among the poor of their right to welfare and how to assert it. Welfare rights organizations, often led by civil rights activists, organized recipients to disrupt welfare offices and stage demonstrations in New York, Baltimore, Los Angeles, Boston, Chicago, San Francisco, and Cleveland to demand more adequate benefits. Continuing in-migration of poor rural and minority families increased the numbers on relief rolls such that by 1971, one out of ten residents in the nation's twenty largest metropolitan areas received some form of public relief. The most common forms of welfare included Aid to Families with Dependent Children, food stamps, unemployment compensation, rent supplements or public housing, and free medical care. Although state and federal agencies supported some of these programs, local governments carried most of the burden. In 1970, the welfare budget of New York City alone was $1.4 billion. The needs of the genuinely poor overwhelmed cities, straining local revenues with millions of cases like that of a nineteen-year-old New York woman who wrote on her welfare application, "I have no one to help me. I was living with my grandmother, but she put me out on the street with my two children."

As the New York applicant's case suggested, the burdens of poverty fell most heavily on women, and welfare mothers became a vocal pressure group in many big cities. These women—black and white, married and unmarried—were caught between the self-help ethic on one side and family emergency on the other. Johnnie Tillmon became a public spokeswoman for welfare mothers. Raised in Arkansas, she worked for fifteen years in a laundry before moving with her six children to California. In 1963, she became too sick to work and was forced to accept welfare. Tillmon wrote in 1972, "Welfare's like a traffic accident. It can happen to anyone, but especially it happens to women." Women like Tillmon formed the vanguard of welfare-rights and tenants' organizations, participating actively in hearings and lobbying for day-care centers, job training, fairer relief allotments, and more humane treatment by public officials.

Great Society urban spending may have attempted to attract support for the Democratic party and quiet discontent, but its actual impact neither ended poverty nor quelled protest. In spite of the achievements of legislative victories, people of color in cities continued to live in conditions that were deteriorating. By 1968, both Malcolm X and Martin Luther King were dead, and racial uprisings had repeatedly rocked scores of cities: Los Angeles, San

Segregation in Action. Throughout cities in the South, African Americans were forced by law as well as by custom into separate facilities, including, as the sign above this couples heads reveals, the rear of buses. Long-standing tensions over discriminatory treatment of black riders on the buses in Montgomery, Alabama, prompted seamstress and local NAACP chapter secretary Rosa Parks to refuse to yield her seat in to a white person, sparking the 1955 Montgomery bus boycott and resulting legal challenge to segregation in public transportation.

Francisco, Portland, Kansas City, Omaha, Chicago, Milwaukee, Atlanta, Miami, Nashville, Cincinnati, Dayton, Cleveland, Rochester, Philadelphia, New York, Boston, and many more. These uprisings took a heavy toll: during a three-week period in 1967, a riot in Newark left twenty-six dead and twelve hundred injured; an outbreak riot in Detroit killed forty-three and injured two thousand.

Nearly all the riots of these years followed the same general pattern. They began with incidents perceived by blacks as police brutality, and they provoked attacks against white-owned property and stores. Unlike most previous racial violence, these riots did not involve confrontations between blacks and whites over contested neighborhoods. Most deaths and injuries occurred in clashes between rioters and police, not from fighting between black and white citizens.

Though riots also struck smaller cities, conditions were most explosive in big cities. Investigators estimated that 10 percent or more of the ghetto

The Challenge of Civil Rights. Martin Luther King, Jr., leads a march down Columbus Avenue in Boston, Massachusetts, in 1965. Note the broad support for civil rights and integration that the banners and marchers proclaim.

populations of Detroit, Newark, and Watts (Los Angeles) participated to some extent in those cities' riots. In each case, thousands of people were involved, too many for any police force to contain. In every city conditions seemed the same: police harassment, inadequate housing, inferior schools, discriminatory courts and credit practices, and unemployment. Even blacks who had achieved some success were excluded from white neighborhoods. Thus the Kerner Commission, appointed by President Johnson to investigate the causes of the riots, speculated that "what the rioters appeared to be seeking was fuller participation in the social order and material benefits enjoyed by the majority of American citizens. Rather than rejecting the American system, they were anxious to obtain a place for themselves in it." Studies have suggested that riots were most likely to take place in cities where rapid growth was occurring in the suburbs and spatial isolation was increasing in the ghetto, where blacks felt their deteriorating circumstances were increasingly invisible to white society, rather than in cities where ghetto circummstances were the worst. Rather than referring to these as "riots," many blacks called them "revolts," a consequence of increasing and unrelenting inequality.

NEW POLITICAL ALIGNMENTS

Frustrations over the limits of legislative solutions provoked political reactions from blacks and whites, particularly in cities where numbers of African-American voters were large enough to exert significant pressure. Beginning in the mid-1960s, African-American political activism expanded, drawing on a broadened electorate and new articulations of militancy. These circumstances explain the sucessful challenge in southern cities to the at-large electoral systems and gerrymandering that had sustained white downtown rule for so many years. In many cities, blacks won representation on city councils for the first time. In 1970, fifty cities had black mayors, and by 1974, black mayors had been elected in six major cities: Atlanta, Cleveland, Detroit, Gary, Los Angeles, and Newark. Between the late 1970s and the early 1990s, black mayors were elected in New Orleans, Birmingham, Charlotte, Chicago, Philadelphia, Baltimore, New York, Denver, Tallahassee, and Memphis. Many black politicians pledged service to all races, but their positions reflected the widening of black influence on politics.

African-American urban leaders planned ways to utilize their numbers in various ways. As both black activism and expectations rose, new political spokespersons called more publicly for African Americans to make use of their numbers as "black power" rather than wait for what looked like diminsihing hopes for "blacks and whites together." The Reverend Jesse Jackson of Chicago first rose to national prominence as a fiery spokesman for black capitalism. His boycott against the A&P food chain prodded the company to hire seven hundred black workers, market black-produced goods, deposit in black-owned banks, advertise in black media, and contract with black construction firms and service companies. Jackson's Operation Breadbasket affected companies in fifteen cities by 1970. "We are going to see to it," he stated in 1969, "that the resources of the ghetto are not siphoned off by outside groups. . . . If a building goes up in the black community, we're going to build it. And we're going to stop anyone else from building it." In 1973, Lonnie King, director of the Atlanta branch of the NAACP, offered the city a plan that abandoned school integration in return for nine black appointments to the city's seventeen-member school board.

The tactics of the civil rights movement for racial equality set the terms for other kinds of urban community protest over the next decade. For example, the modern gay rights movement marked its founding moment June 27, 1969, at the Stonewall uprising in New York City, where a routine police raid on the Stonewall Inn, a gay bar in Greenwich Village serving a racially and economically mixed group of patrons, encountered sharp and unprecedented resistance from the bar patrons, as well as from a crowd gathered outside. The protests escalated into a full-scale, several-night riot in which dozens were arrested and many injured. Coming at the end of a decade and a half of civil rights agitation, Stonewall triggered a protest movement that borrowed heavily from tactics and language of radical social and political change. As news of the riot spread, groups of homosexuals in other cities organized demonstrations and organizations demanding an end to discrimination based on sexuality.

The quest for racial equality continued to stir white fears about schooling and housing. White residents in Chicago, Detroit, Boston, Philadelphia, and Los Angeles fought against both open housing and busing plans to achieve school integration. When California passed a state-wide fair housing ordinance in 1963, conservatives attacked it as abrogating the rights of property owners, and began to collect signatures for an initiative to prohibit all fair housing measures at the state and local levels. In Los Angeles, support for the initiative was strong among realty boards, taxpayers associations, and white middle class and blue collar homeowners, while defenders of fair housing included African Americans, labor and civil rights organizations, and some nonevangelical church groups. The proposition passed overwhelmingly: in the state, 65.4 percent of the voters rejected fair housing; in the white blue collar Los Angeles suburb of South Gate bordering mostly black Watts, 87.5 percent voted for propertyholders' rights of racial exclusivity.

The politics of racial division were very much an issue in the 1968 presidential race, when Alabama Governor George Wallace's campaign of segregationist rhetoric against the urban riots and the remedy of school busing garnered surprising third-party electoral support. When Republican Richard M. Nixon assumed the presidency in 1969, he adopted some of the issues that attracted Wallace voters. Though Nixon did not stem the stream of federal dollars flowing into cities (in 1960 there were forty-four federal programs allocating $3.9 billion to the nation's largest cities; by 1969, the number of programs had risen to five hundred, and annual appropriations had climbed to $14 billion), he did try to eliminate programs that emphasized neighborhood participation in policymaking. Thus in 1972, he convinced Congress to terminate Model Cities, and the next year he impounded funds from federal housing and rehabilitation.

In place of these programs, Nixon proposed "New Federalism," a transfer of policymaking decisions from federal bureaucracies to state and local levels. The keystone of this policy was revenue sharing, the distribution of federal funds directly to local governments rather than through federal agencies. Despite strong opposition, the State and Local Fiscal Assistance Act passed Congress in 1972, and during the succeeding winter checks totaling $5.3 billion were sent to thirty-eight thousand state and local governments. Two-thirds of the money went directly to cities and towns to be used in nine areas: public safety, administration, transportation, health, environmental protection, capital expenditures, libraries, recreation, and social services for the poor and aged. Beyond these priorities, the money could be spent without federal guidelines, except that discrimination by race, sex, ethnicity, or religion was prohibited.

On issues of race and poverty, the Nixon administration fomented racial polarization, including a campaign to separate the working poor from the unemployed by attacking welfare recipients and welfare programs. Moreover, Nixon consciously retreated from government intervention in issues of race and poverty. In 1970, newspapers disclosed a memo written by Daniel Patrick Moynihan, Nixon's adviser on urban affairs, recommending that "the issue of race could benefit from a period of benign neglect." Attorney General John Mitchell tried to delay school desegregation and prevent extension of the 1965 Voting Rights Act. Nixon's strategy was to attract conservative southern voters into the Republican party. Thus, in opposition to the 1971 Supreme Court decision *Swann v. Charlotte-Mecklenburg,* which upheld a school integration plan that relied on busing, Nixon proposed a moratorium on busing, denouncing it as an extreme remedy for segregation.

Racial strife in Boston dramatized tensions of the Nixon years. Boston's public schools had become increasingly segregated in the 1960s because when the city's minority population increased, the Irish-dominated School Committee used techniques of district gerrymandering and student transfers to keep white schools white. A long campaign by black parents for improved education, which involved running candidates for the school board, staging sit-ins at School Committee meetings, and organizing a voluntary busing program, culminated in a lawsuit in federal court exposing the School Committee's tactics of illegal segregation. Boston's white ethnics blamed federal intervention and black migrants for scarce jobs and housing, rising taxes and rents. When Judge Arthur Garrity ordered the School Committee to begin a program of desegregation and busing in the fall of 1974, white neighborhoods organized to protest. Action ranged from rallies and motorcades to boycotts and violent attacks on black students in white neighborhoods. The major threats of violence eventually subsided, but racial tensions continued to haunt Boston and other cities.

NEW SUBURBAN REALIGNMENTS

The 1970 census revealed that for the first time, more Americans lived in suburbs than in cities. Of the nation's two hundred million people, seventy-six million inhabited suburban areas, sixty-four million lived in central cities, and sixty million lived in nonmetropolitan areas. Almost three-fourths of the nation's total housing stock had been built since 1940, two-thirds of it single-family homes, the majority in suburbs. Suburbs continued to house both blue collar and white collar workers, but seldom in the same neighborhood. Suburban communities ranged from wealthy, exclusive towns in Marin County near San Francisco to heavily ethnic and working-class Cicero, Illinois, and Hamtramck, Michigan. But as local zoning regulations enforced plot and house size and prohibited multiple dwellings, communities stratified more than ever before along class and racial lines.

Because home ownership represented a family's most significant asset, protecting property values became a central suburban concern underlying resistance to racial integration. Although many metropolitan areas featured one model "integrated" suburb where black and white middle class families co-existed comfortably, like Mount Airy near Phladelphia, Oak Park outside of Chicago, and Freeport, Long Island, near New York, most suburbs remained determinedly racially exclusive. In 1970, only 5 percent of the nation's black population lived in suburbs.

Though suburbs varied in quality and composition, American culture celebrated an intensified vision of domesticity that presumed single-family housing in suburbia, with breadwiner fathers and homemaker mothers finding personal satisfaction in family life and the commodity purchases that enhanced it. New Deal social legislation, the GI bill, and FHA-insured mortgages subsidized the demographic trends of high marriage rates, earlier ages at marriage, and large families, with which life in the suburbs became associated. The presumption that suburban husbands would go off to the city to work, leaving wives at home to care for children, was reflected in suburban home design. Each house in Levittown was intended to be a self-contained world marked off by a white picket fence. Inside were a standardized living room with television set built into the wall and a kitchen and washing machine. The grassy lawns surrounding large house lots highlighted privacy, and the garages took car ownership for granted.

Mass culture celebrated the new suburban ideal. In *Life* magazine's special 1956 issue on American women, the most space was devoted to a suburban woman, aged thirty-two and mother of four. A high school graduate who had married as a teenager, *Life's* model mother sewed her own clothes, entertained fifteen hundred guests a year, and was supported by her husband's middle-class income. "In her daily rounds she attends clubs or charity meetings, drives the children to school, does the weekly grocery shopping, makes ceramics, and is planning to learn French," *Life* revealed as it followed the housewife from domestic chores to social events. Born in the Depression, most suburban homemakers appreciated the security and standard of living represented by a suburban lifestyle. A Gallup poll taken in 1962 reported that "few people are as happy as a housewife." But the poll also predicted future changes when most women interviewed revealed hopes that their daughters would have more education and marry later than they did.

Women's lives in the suburbs were already changing in two important ways. First, the demographics of early marriage and early childbearing meant that suburban women more quickly than their mothers would come to a point in their lives when responsibilities for childcare would lessen. More than half their adult lives would be spent neither having children nor raising them. Second, married women, particularly those with children, were more likely each year to be employed. In the 1950s, the demand for workers in sales, service, and offices grew. Clerical jobs multiplied so rapidly that by 1960 one of three women wage earners held one. At the same time, postwar inflation meant that families often needed a second income, even at the low wages that women could command, to maintain a home and cars and to save for children's education. The rising proportion of employed mothers would alter suburban lifestyles. Still, life in the suburbs was more home-centered than in urban neighborhoods, where social contacts, for better or worse, continued to occur on apartment stoops, in parks, inside saloons and beauty shops, and along streets and sidewalks.

Teenagers, who because of the baby boom were becoming a demographic force by the 1960s, were one group that made efforts to resist suburban home-centeredness, especially in their musical tastes. The most important popular cultural phenomenon of the era was the eruption of rock and roll, a new musical form building on the urban cross-fertilization of rhythm and blues, country, polka, zydeco, and Latin musics. The rock and roll shows which attracted teenage crowds to listen to the new music were the only entertainment with demonstrable capacity to fill the downtown theaters. In the Los Angeles area, even where working class neighborhoods to the east of the city continued to be divided by race and class, white, black, and Mexican-American teenagers in the 1950s and 1960s escaped on weekends to public dance halls and performance venues that featured rock and roll shows, like the El Monte American Legion Stadium, and found a rare public space enabling intercultural and interracial exchange. Similar trends occurred in other metropolitan areas. But the social mixing of black and white performers and teenagers made the live shows seem too socially explosive, and municipalities shut them down rather than capitalize on their potential for drawing crowds downtown.

Political walls reinforced the physical and social separation of cities and suburbs. In the nineteenth century, suburbs had eagerly sought annexation to the nearby city in order to take advantage of schools, water, and police and fire protection that cities could furnish. On their behalf, cities pursued annexation as a means of competitive growth; to them, bigger was better. The annexation process continued into the late twentieth century in the South and Southwest, where cities like Memphis, Jacksonville, Oklahoma City, Phoenix, Houston, and Dallas added large areas and their populations in the 1960s and 1970s. But suburban independence stifled growth of older cities of the Midwest and Northeast. Boston, New York, Philadelphia, and Cleveland were unable to annex new territory and tax bases because suburban residents worried about the taxes, troubled schools, crime, and threats to real estate values that the city seemed to harbor. As one angry suburbanite wrote to a Philadelphia newspaper in 1968, "We did not create the problems of the inner city, and we are not obligated to help in their solution." Annexation could not alone have solved cities' problems, but the inability to expand territorially has cloaked the reality that city problems are metropolitan and national problems.

SIGNPOSTS OF CHANGE

In 1973 and 1974, an Arab embargo tripled the price of oil. The resulting energy crisis, with its soaring prices for fuel and long lines at gas stations, prompted people to question the desirability of suburban life for the first time in the twentieth century. Americans, accustomed to cheap and abundant fuel, depended on big, gas-guzzling cars, and their single-family suburban houses were poorly insulated and crammed with energy-guzzling appliances. The cost of home air conditioning and heating now threatened to escalate beyond the reach of even middle-class Americans. Gas shortages momentarily revived the attractiveness of mass transit, and some people, having become wary of their commitment to automobiles, began to reconsider the advantages of downtown living.

Meanwhile in cities, information technology and services were replacing manufacturing as primary economic activities. The new downtown service

Gentrification of an Inner-City Neighborhood. The houses along Montgomery Street in Baltimore, shown here in different stages of restoration, attracted middle-class professionals to the old Federal Hill neighborhood, just one block from Baltimore's Inner Harbor. Also nearby were the newly built Maryland Science Center, National Aquarium, and the restaurant- and shop-filled Harborplace.

economy, based on banking, insurance, and communications, plus expanding medical and educational institutions, provided employment opportunities for an educated, skilled work force, whose choice to live near their jobs revived the market for downtown housing. Young urban professionals ("yuppies") remodeled inner-city apartments and townhouses, often in the name of historic preservation. A 1966 act expanded the National Register of protected historic sites to include buildings and districts of architectural and/or historic significance, and in 1976 federal tax credits were made available to owners and developers who agreed to restore buildings in historic districts.

Increasingly by the 1970s, downtown property owners were converting old apartments into condominiums and offering benefits of ownership without worries of maintenance. Condominiums in newly restored areas particularly attracted the young, often unmarried middle class. Gentrification, the process by which wealthier groups occupy and restore run-down property, propped up sagging tax bases by lifting property values, but it also exacerbated housing shortages for the poor by depleting the already low supply of inexpensive housing and pushing low-income and minority groups out of their neighborhoods. The Census Bureau confirmed these changes by reporting that 1974 migration patterns seemed to reverse the long-term trend of suburban growth at the expense of the central city. The baby-boom generation, the huge bulge of people born between 1947 and 1963, was reaching adulthood and, just as it had affected suburbanization and schools in the 1950s and 1960s, was influencing housing markets in the 1970s. Growing numbers of unmarried people living alone, childless couples, and small families were reshaping housing and consumption patterns. In 1973 and 1974, retail sales in downtown stores increased while shopping centers began to falter. City movie houses, restaurants, and hotels were increasingly well patronized.

A little-noticed but important component of downtown neighborhood revitalization was the increasing presence of gay and lesbian city dwellers. Gathering in urban centers since the early twentieth century, homosexuals composed a larger percentage of city populations than of the national population at large. Eventually they became a crucial element in communities such as North Beach and the Castro in San Francisco and Greenwich Village in New York. Such neighborhoods gave these cities a cosmopolitan image, encompassing the beat poets and artists of the 1950s and 1960s and ultimately in San Francisco, embracing the growing gay community centered around Castro Street.

Once a working-class Irish neighborhood, the Castro had been hit hard by the city's declining industrial base after World War II. A close-knit community occupying dilapidated Victorian houses began to break apart. As families moved to the suburbs or farther afield, gay men and some lesbians began moving into the cheap and available housing stock, often divided into multiunit apartments. The influx of gay residents sometimes hastened the flight of prior occupants, making more housing available at cheaper cost. As the area evolved into an established gay community, relatively affluent people with professional occupations moved in to take advantage of the safety and proximity to the city's commercial and entertainment institutions. Old houses were rehabilitated, new businesses arose to serve new clientele, and property values began an ascent that reshaped the neighborhood even more. Similar transformations occurred in cities from San Diego to Chicago to New York.

Although some urban districts experienced a revival, the 1974 boost in oil prices was detrimental to most city dwellers. High-cost fuel drove up inflation and unemployment and considerably slowed economic growth. New office towers stood empty in New York and Chicago. Housing starts dropped from 2.4 million in 1972 to 1.5 million in 1974.

As the national economy tightened, the continuing shift of businesses, jobs, and population from the northeastern and midwestern Frostbelt to the southeastern and southwestern Sunbelt had a profound impact on cities of all regions. Since World War II, the Sunbelt had captured a large share of new growth industries such as defense, aerospace, resort and retirement communities, petrochemicals, and information technology, as well as some older manufacturing such as clothing and auto parts. A band of fast-growing communities extended across the country's southern tier, among them the metropolitan areas of Tampa, Miami, Jacksonville, Atlanta, Dallas–Fort Worth, Phoenix, the southern coast of California, and up the coast to Portland and Seattle. Houston became the nation's fastest-growing city, with a population increase from two million to three million between 1970 and 1980. Meanwhile, northern metropolises such as New York, Pittsburgh, Detroit, and Cleveland grew minimally or lost population.

Partly in response, Sunbelt communities suffered their own problems of growth. Their rapid expansion left them overly dependent on automobiles, vexed by housing shortages, and threatened by crime and pollution. The media made New York a feared city for its muggings and murders, yet in the late 1970s the homicide rates of Atlanta and Houston (almost 40 per 100,000 people per year) doubled that of New York. Phoenix, once a haven for people suffering from respiratory ailments, developed atmospheric pollution caused by the cars, plants, and trash brought in by its huge influx of northern in-migrants.

Moreover, Sunbelt cities were haunted by their own forms of poverty. Northern urban poverty was characterized by unemployed people, who wanted to work but were unable to find jobs, and by discouraged workers, who were jobless because they did not believe they could find work that would pay a satisfactory wage. In the Sunbelt, rates of unemployed and discouraged workers were much lower. Instead, Sunbelt poverty consisted of involuntary part-time workers, people who wanted to work full time but could find only part-time jobs, and, more commonly, fully employed workers who were so underpaid that their earnings left them below adequate income levels. In the 1970s, El Paso, which attracted electronics firms and the garment industry with its promise of available, low-paid Hispanic laborers, had the lowest per capita income in the Southwest.

Many of the developments taking place in metropolitan America during and after World War II set the stage for events that would characterize the last quarter of the twentieth century. Changes in politics, the economy, and the environment were taking place so rapidly that governments, especially the federal government, were having difficulty crafting a coherent policy toward cities and suburbs. Cities faced crisis, yet they remained magnets for people, resources, and ideas.

BIBLIOGRAPHY

For an overview of this period, see Carl Abbott, *Urban America in the Modern Age: 1920 to the Present* (1987); Barry Bluestone and Bennett Harrison, *The Deindustrialization of America: Plant Closings, Community Abandonment, and the Dismantling of Basic Industry* (1982); Lizabeth Cohen, *A Consumer's Republic: The Politics of Mass Consumption in Postwar America* (2003); John Findlay, *Magic Lands: Western Cityscapes and American Culture After 1940* (1992); Kenneth Kusmer, "African Americans in the City Since WWII: From the Industrial to the Postindustriial Era," in *The New African American Urban History,* ed Kenneth W. Goings and Raymond A. Mohl (1996): 320–68; Christopher Silver and John Moeser, *The Separate City: Black Communities in the Urban South, 1940–1968* (1995); and Jon C. Teaford, *The Twentieth-Century American City: Problem, Promise, and Reality* (1986).

On the impact of World War II on cities, see Beth Bailey and David Farber, *The First Strange Place: Race and Sex in World War II Hawaii* (1994); Allan Bérubé, *Coming Out Under Fire: The History of Gay Men and Women in World War II* (1990); Dominic Capeci, Jr., *The Harlem Race Riot of 1943* (1977); Capeci, Jr., *Race Relations in Wartime Detroit: The Sojourner Truth Housing Controversy, 1937–1942* (1984); Dominic Capeci, Jr., and Martha Wilkerson, *Layered Violence: The Detroit Rioters of 1943* (1991); John D'Emilio, *Sexual Politics, Sexual Communities: The Making of a Homosexual Minority in the United States, 1940–1970* (1983); Marilynn S. Johnson, *The Second Gold Rush: Oakland and the East Bay in World War II* (1993); Rogber Lotchin, *The Bad City in the Good War: San Francisco, Los Angeles, Oakland, and San Diego* (2003); Lotchin, *Fortress California, From Warfare to Welfare* (1992); Mauricio Mazon, *The Zoot-Suit Riots: The Psychology of Symbolic Annihilation* (1984); and Robert Spinney, *World War II in Nashville: Transformation of the Homefront* (1998).

On the impact of federal public policy on cities, see John F. Bauman, *Public Housing, Race, and Renewal: Urban Planning in Philadelphia, 1920–1974* (1987); Ronald Bayor, *Race and the Shaping of Twentieth Century Atlanta* (1996); Adam Cohen, *American Pharoah: Mayor Richard J. Daley: His Battle for Chicago and the Nation* (2000); Arnold Hirsch, *Making the Second Ghetto: Race and Housing in Chicago, 1940–1980* (1983); Douglas Massey and Nancy Denton, *American Apartheid: Segregation and the Making of an Underclass* (1993); Wendell Pritchett, *Brownsville, Brooklyn: Blacks, Jews, and the Changing Face of the Ghetto* (2002); Thomas Sugrue, *The Origins of the Urban Crisis: Race and Inequality in Postwar Detroit* (1996); and Forrest R. White, *Pride and Prejudice: School Desegregation and Urban Renewal in Norfolk, 1950–1959* (1992).

On highway building, see Richard Longstreth, *City Center to Regional Mall: Architecture, the Automobile, and Retailing in Los Angeles, 1920–1950* (1997); and Mark Rose, *Interstate: Express Highway Politics, 1941–1956* (1979). On progrowth coalitions and urban-renewal programs in various cities, see Roger Biles, *Richard J. Daley: Politics, Race, and the Governing of Chicago* (1995); Robert Caro, *The Power Broker: Robert Moses and the Fall of New York* (1974); John Mollenkopf, *The Contested City* (1983); Jon Teaford, *The Rough Road to Renaissance: Urban Revitalization in America, 1940–1985* (1990); and David Tucker, *Memphis Since Crump: Bossism, Blacks, and Civic Reform, 1948–68* (1980). On the emergence of rock and roll from diverse musical roots, see Reebee Garofalo, *Rockin' Out: Popular Music in the USA* (1997); and George Lipsitz, *Rainbow at Midnight: Labor and Culture in the 1940s* (1994).

New work on subrbanization, black and white, includes Robert Fishman, *Bourgeois Utopias: The Rise and Fall of Suburbia* (1987); Matt Garcia, *A World of Its Own: Race, Labor, and Citrus in the Making of Greater Los Angeles, 1900–1970* (2001); Sylvie Murray, *The Progressive Housewife: Community Activism in Suburban Queens, 1945–1965* (2003); Becky Nicolaides, *My Blue Heaven: Life and Politics in the Working Class Suburbs of Los Angeles, 1920–1965* (2002); Andrew Rome, *The Bulldozer in the Countryside: Suburban Sprawl and the Rise of American Environmentalism* (2001); Andrew Wiese, *Places of Our Own: African-American Suburbanization Since 1916* (2004); and William H. Wilson, *Hamilton Park: A Planned Black Community in Dallas* (1997). On the new domestic suburban ideology, see Stephanie Coontz, *The Way We Never Were: American Families and the Nostalgia Trap* (1992); and Elaine T. May, *Homeward Bound: American Families in the Cold War Era* (1988). On the suburban origins of the New Right, see Lisa McGirr, *Suburban Warriors: The Origins of the New American Right* (2001).

On postwar civil rights activism, see Martha Biondi, *To Stand and Fight: The Struggle for Civil Rights in Postwar New York City* (2003); Albert S. Broussard, *Black San Francisco: The Struggle for Racial Equality in the West* (1993); William Chafe, *Civilities and Civil Rights: Greensboro, North Carolina, and the Black Struggle for Freedom* (1980); Gretchen Lemke-Santangelo, *Abiding Courage: African-American Migrant Women and the East Bay Community* (1996); Shirley Ann Moore, *To Place Our Deeds: The African-American Community in Richmond, California, 1910–1963* (2000); Glenda Alice Rabby, *The Pain and the Promise: The Struggle for Civil Rights in Tallahassee, Florida* (1999); James R. Ralph, *Northern Protest: Martin Luther King, Jr., Chicago, and the Civil Rights Movement* (1994); Robert O. Self, *American Babylon: Class, Race and Power in Postwar California* (2004); Jeanne Theoharis and Komozi Woodward, ed., *Freedom North: Black Freedom Struggles Outside the South, 1940–1980* (2003); Heather Thompson, *Whose Detroit: Politics, Labor, and Race in a Modern American City* (2001); and Bobby M. Wilson, *Race and Place in Birmingham: The Civil Rights and Neighborhood Movements* (2000). On the 1960s riots, see Gerald Horne, *Fire This Time: The Watts Uprising and the 1960s* (1995). See also Edward Escobar, *Race, Police, and the Making of a Political Identity: Mexican Americans and the Los Angeles Police Department, 1900–1945* (1999).

On the emergence of protest based in neighborhood organizations, see Robert Fisher, *Let the People Decide: Neighborhood Organizing in America* (1984); Ira Katznelson, *City Trenches: Urban Politics and the Patterning of Class in the United States* (1981); and Lloyd H. Rogler, *Migrant in the City: The Life of a Puerto Rican Action Group* (1986). On antihighway movements, see William E. Borah, *The Second Battle of New Orleans: A History of the Vieux Carré Riverfront Expressway Controversy* (1981) and Gordon Fellman in association with Barbara Brandt, *The Deceived Majority: Politics and Protest in Middle America* (1973).

On welfare, see Michael B. Katz, *The Undeserving Poor: From the War on Poverty to the War on Welfare* (1989) and Katz, *In the Shadow of the Poorhouse: A Social History of Welfare in America* (1986); Alice O'Connor, *Poverty Knowledge: Social Science, Social Policy, and the Poor in Twentieth Century U.S. History* (2001); and Jill Quadagno, *The Color of Welfare: How Racism Undermined the War on Poverty* (1994).

On the Sunbelt and Snowbelt, see Carl Abbott, *The Metropolitan Frontier: Cities in the American West* (1981); Abbott, *The New Urban America: Growth and Politics in Sunbelt Cities*, rev. ed. (1987); Richard M. Bernard, ed., *Snowbelt Cities: Metropolitan Politics in the Northeast and Midwest Since World War II* (1990); Richard M. Bernard and Bradley R. Rice, eds., *Sunbelt Cities: Politics and Growth Since World War II* (1983); Franklin J. James, *Minorities in the Sunbelt* (1984); Michael F. Logan, *Fighting Sprawl and City Hall: Resistance to Urban*

Growth in the Southwest (1995); Bradford Luckingham, *The Urban Southwest: A Profile History of Albuquerque, El Paso, Phoenix, and Tucson* (1982); Randall M. Miller and George E. Pozzetta, eds., *Shades of the Sunbelt: Essays on Ethnicity, Race, and the Urban South* (1988); Raymond A. Mohl, ed., *Searching for the Sunbelt* (1989); and Deborah Dash Moore, *To the Golden Cities: Pursuing the American Dream in Miami and Los Angeles* (1994).

NOTES

1. Robert O. Self and Thomas Sugrue, "The Power of Place: Race, Political Economy, and Identity in the Postwar Metropolis," in *A Companion To Post - 1945 America*, ed. Jean-Christophe Agnew and Roy Rosenzweig (New York: Blackwell Publishing, 2002): 26.

2. Arnold Hirsch, "Containment on the Home Front: Race and Federal Housing Policy from the New Deal to the Cold War," *History* 26, no. 2 (January 2000): 159.

3. Robert Self, "To Plan Our Liberation: Black Power and the Politics of Place in Oakland, California, 1965–1977," *History* 26, no. 6 (September 2000): 778.

CHAPTER
10

The Fate of the Modern American City

As the twentieth century entered its final quarter, several overlapping problems affected the fates of American cities. First, a slowdown of the national economy, the continuing effects of deindustrialization, and the dismantling of New Deal social programs dramatically increased the distance between rich and poor, and forcibly challenged city administrators to find sufficient revenues to meet their mounting needs. Second, the lack of a clear and consistent federal policy toward cities left municipalities to their own devices in dealing with problems that were basically national. Third, new immigrants reshaped urban ethnic and racial communities, unsettled prior political accommodations, and created new forms of urban culture.

Some urbanists have pointed to economic globalization as creating polarization between an emerging transnational capitalist class and its low-wage labor force, helping to explain the late twentieth century urban patterns of gentrification, immigrant enclave expansion, and the marginalization of the poor. Others point to national taxation, labor, and welfare policies as the culprits for a radically altered income distribution since the 1970s. Whatever the causes, cities were left without adequate resources to meet their needs, and political fragmentation prevented regional or metropolitan solutions. Suburbs also faced new fiscal constraints, especially after 1978 when widespread voter insistence on capping property taxes slashed local support for government services. Nonetheless, new as well as long-time urban residents continued to demand liveable cities and to devise creative solutions to improve the quality of urban life.

FISCAL CRISIS AND THE UNCERTAINTY OF FEDERAL URBAN POLICY

During the 1970s, urban administrations facing declining revenues tried to balance budgets and avoid tax increases by reducing expenses. But to meet service obligations such as road maintenance and education, and to honor union contracts, officials often had to overspend their budgets. They escaped deficits by borrowing from the city's cash flow, hoping to repay such loans from anticipated revenues due the following year. The next year, however, they found it necessary to borrow again and to postpone balancing accounts for another year. In this way, cities accumulated large internal debts. As expenses mounted and sentiment against increasing taxes persisted, it became increasingly difficult for cities to repay and eliminate these loans. A sudden emergency could collapse the system and trigger fiscal crisis. In 1979, for example, cleanup from a massive snowfall cost Chicago an unanticipated $72 million. Once this bill was paid, however, the city lacked cash to meet normal obligations, including its payroll. Only an emergency loan and sharp tax hike forestalled major catastrophe.

The most publicized fiscal crisis occurred in New York City in 1974–75. During the optimistic expansion of the 1960s, the city borrowed heavily; when economic downturn came in the 1970s, New York's budget was badly overextended. The city had been financing services that elsewhere were provided by state, county, and special-district governments, and when the Nixon administration curtailed federal aid to the city, officials were forced into budget manipulation. Postponing payment on previous debts provided temporary respite. But in October 1974 and March 1975, a number of banks pulled the plug on the city's cash supply by refusing to underwrite its municipal bonds. In the end the banks agreed to loan more money, but at high interest rates.

Conventional explanations for New York's and other cities' fiscal problems blamed excessive wages paid to municipal employees and excessive welfare doles to malingering cheaters. But the causes ran much deeper. The core of New York's fiscal crisis was the loss of 542,000 jobs when offices, plants, and stores moved to the suburbs and the Sunbelt between 1969 and 1976. Losses of tax revenue inevitably ensued. Economists estimated that if those half-million jobs were still providing income for New Yorkers, the city would have received $1.5 billion in extra tax revenues and there would have been no fiscal crisis. The suburbs and Sunbelt took similar tolls on other cities. In the late 1960s and early 1970s, Philadelphia lost 17 percent of its jobs, and New Orleans lost 20 percent. Would Washington react to cities' needs by refining a federal urban policy? The subsequent years would provide a disappointing answer.

The federal-city relationship, which had originated during the New Deal in the 1930s and tightened during the Great Society of the 1960s, began to dissolve in 1974 with passage of the Housing and Community Development Block Grant Act. This measure, which initiated revenue sharing, was signed into law by President Gerald Ford, and it signaled a shift in federal attitudes, especially a retreat from the attack on poverty. Revenue sharing merged most federal grant programs into one program and provided for single block grants totaling $8.4 billion over three years. Instead of mandating spending on specific inner-city problems, these grants gave local officials more discretion over how to spend federal funds. Pledging that the act would avoid excessive federal regulation, Ford announced that cities would have greater certainty about the level of funding they could expect and that local officials could concentrate on broad programs of community betterment rather than applying for money for small-scale, individual projects. Revenue-sharing funds could be used for almost any purpose—public works, salaries, law enforcement, housing, job training. A formula based on population density, age of housing supply, and extent of poverty would determine the distribution of funds to ensure that needy cities received proportionately more than cities that were better off.

In practice, smaller communities, especially suburbs, benefited the most from revenue sharing. Federal grants enabled suburbs to undertake new projects such as roads and sewage treatment without raising taxes. But big city officials had to spend most of their grants to avoid severe budget cuts necessitated by loss of tax revenues and to sustain Great Society programs threatened by curtailment or impoundment of federal support and by soaring inflation. As a result, cities became increasingly dependent on federal money. The percentage of local budgets funded by Washington grew from 5.1 percent in 1970 to 12.9 percent in 1975. In 1967, federal aid accounted for only 1 percent of St. Louis's budget and 2.1 percent of Buffalo's. By 1978, federal aid accounted for 54.7 percent and 69.2 percent respectively. Government aid also made up one-fourth to one-half of operating revenues of Baltimore, Philadelphia, Phoenix, Cleveland, and Detroit. Cities had set themselves up for a new and different crisis if and when federal urban policy should shift or wither—as it eventually did.

In 1976, Jimmy Carter, a rural Georgian, won the presidency by promising to help America's cities with a "comprehensive" urban program. His strategy won him a remarkably high percentage of the urban vote in 1976. Such support, however, carried with it high expectations. At first, the Carter administration fueled the appetites of America's cities. Several cabinet-level advisors spoke before the U.S. Conference of Mayors (USCM) and vowed that "no issue . . . will concern this administration more and concern the President more than the question of jobs and the question of cities." Secretary of

Finishing touches are added to a cake celebrating the reopening of historic Faneuil Hall Market in 1976 as an upscale marketplace, developed by James Rouse of restaurants, food stalls, shops, and boutiques to attract tourists and suburbanites to downtown Boston.

Housing and Urban Development Patricia Roberts Harris announced, "the White House is now in the hands of a friend of the cities."

Big-city mayors, especially the increasing numbers of African-American mayors, intended to cash in on these promises. Kenneth Gibson, mayor of Newark and chairman of the USCM, heralded "the beginning of a new relationship," and the USCM proposed that $20 billion be spent for a "national urban investment program" to address such diverse problems as employment, health care, crime, welfare, housing, and transportation. Janet Frey Hayes, mayor of San Jose, California, spoke for most urban politicians when she announced, "We come not as beggars, but as elected officials to the places where 75 percent of the people are." After being ignored for almost a decade and courted during the Carter campaign, mayors shared a sense of entitlement.

Carter, however, diverged from urban and black interests over several ideological issues. Whereas mayors focused on getting increased federal spending in inner cities, Carter, believing that federal initiative alone could not save cities, supported fiscally conservative measures to spur private investment.

Consequently, Carter's programs would revolve around tax breaks and incentives that might help coax business and industry back into the cities. In addition, the President hoped to balance the federal budget and lower taxes, a combination that would require significant reductions in spending on social welfare.

When Carter proposed a broad urban policy, it reflected his retreat from federal urban spending. Instead of extensive government assistance, he offered "a New Partnership, involving all levels of government, the private sector, and neighborhood and voluntary organizations." The government would maintain popular programs such as Urban Development Action Grants, providing fiscal relief to cities in crisis, and initiating a $1 billion public works program. It hoped to bring private capital investment back to the cities by granting tax breaks to businesses that hired the long-term unemployed or set up shop in impoverished areas, and by creating an urban development bank that could give urban businesses loans they would be unable to secure on the open market. Finally, the urban policy invited more inter-government cooperation by encouraging state governments to get involved in renewal efforts, funding neighborhood development projects directly and creating an urban volunteer corps. Once the proposals went before Congress, urban and black leaders threw support to the President in a last-ditch attempt to salvage whatever federal commitments they could find. But Congress, tilting ever more toward suburban interests, balked at Carter's initiatives.

The defeat of Carter's urban policy in Congress was indicative of an emerging trend in national politics. It marked the end of an era of significant federal spending earmarked for cities and the beginning of collective urban belt-tightening. In 1979, the National League of Cities titled one of its themes "Making do with less," and Carter warned mayors against expecting new aid in the federal budget of that year. One of his advisors told the National Urban Coalition, "We cannot hope to devote the additional resources you and I would like to rebuilding our cities."

At least two factors contributed to this new attitude. First, Carter was fiscally conservative and generally averse to massive federal aid programs. Second, many middle-class Americans, reeling from the impacts of inflation and a stalled economy, were losing faith in governmental programs. Historian Bruce Schulman has labled the 1970s as a period of southernization, when southern ideology of low taxes and limited public services began to direct national policy.

In November of 1979, Carter publicly marked the distance he had traveled from prior liberalism and from his original urban and black supporters by announcing a new policy of "urban conservatism," the goal of which was "to make sure that Federal Programs do not contribute to the economic deterioration of our cities." Almost as a response to such a plan, when the President visited riot-torn Miami in June 1980, a crowd in the

Liberty City district threw bottles at his motorcade. Carter's retreat from engagement with urban problems was eloquently illustrated in the recommendation of his presidential commission that the urban mission of the federal government was to encourage inhabitants of inner cities of the Northeast and Midwest to relocate to the Sunbelt.

RONALD REAGAN, GEORGE H. W. BUSH, AND NEGLECT AS A PANACEA

Although Ronald Reagan made a campaign stop in the South Bronx to criticize Jimmy Carter for his broken promises to urban neighborhoods, he won the presidency in 1980 without support from African-American and white urban voters. Believing in self-help and local responsibility for relieving poverty, Reagan put cuts in federal aid to cities and social programs that provided a safety net for the urban poor at the heart of his political beliefs. His supporters had been instrumental in the politics of middle-class tax revolt, white backlash, and distrust of big government, and "southernization" continued to privilege market solutions rather than federal intervention on behalf of social welfare and racial equality. Feeding on this energy, Reagan focused on bolstering the suburban upper and middle class, claiming that the economic gains that would benefit these groups would eventually "trickle down" to the urban poor. By the time he left office in 1989, deepening divisions of social and economic stratification were apparent everywhere, but nowhere were they more visible than in cities.

Reagan's budgetary measures took a sharp toll on cities. In 1981 and 1982 he proposed deep cuts in welfare, food stamps, and child nutrition. In 1983 he proposed further cuts of $14 billion in welfare, food stamps, and child nutrition. An increasingly conservative—and Republican—Congress readily approved. In 1986, the President deferred funds earmarked for Urban Development Action Grants, the most successful urban policy of the Carter Administration, in preparation for his push to abandon the program entirely. In 1987, he canceled federal revenue sharing, which had disbursed $85 billion over its fourteen-year existence and touched more municipalities than any other legislation in history. Henry Maier, mayor of Milwaukee, described the process as "the sacking of urban America." A drastic shift had taken place. As one critic observed, with this last strike, the Reagan Administration had necessitated "a basic redefinition that there is no longer any essential Federal role with cities."

Reagan's aggressive budget slashing followed from his political and economic philosophy, which called for the downsizing of government in general. The president repeatedly referred to Washington as "big brother," and he theorized that only by reducing federal intervention in the marketplace could his government reinvigorate the American economy. If he could not justify cutting programs directly, he consolidated them under block grants and let states spend federal money however they saw fit. In 1982, Reagan announced that the Department of Housing and Urban Development (HUD) would no longer monitor Community Development Block Grants to ensure that federal funds were aiding moderate and low-income people, which had always been the intent of the program. Moreover, Reagan continually lowered taxes, though the government ran huge budget deficits every year. As far as the President was concerned, small government and the free market were the keys to economic success. In his June, 1982 formulation, he emphatically praised market rather than government intervention: "The Federal government," he stated, "cannot develop the flexible, broad range of policies and partnerships needed to rebuild and revitalize urban life. Neither can it guarantee a city's long-term prosperity. All too often the promise of such guarantees has created a crippling dependency rather than initiative and independence. It will now be the responsibility of local leadership, working closely with the private sector and the city's neighborhoods, to develop a strategy for the survival and prosperity of the country's cities."

Though Reagan eventually softened some of his admonishing tone, his message remained the same. In place of federal largesse, he offered his belief that a general economic recovery would reverberate through all levels of society and benefit poor people as well as the middle class. Through a series of tax cuts, he would give the middle class more spending power with the hope that this boost to the economy would stimulate urban development through market forces.

All Reagan had to offer as an urban policy was an initiative to establish "enterprise zones," a relatively inexpensive program that was supposed to promote private sector investment in the nation's most impoverished neighborhoods. Initially proposed in Congress by Republican Jack Kemp and Democrat Robert Garcia of New York, the program would cut taxes and minimize federal regulations (such as minimum wages, pollution control, and occupational safety) in inner-city areas selected by HUD as enterprise zones. The policy aimed to encourage businesses to enter depressed slums and create prosperous commercial districts in their place. Eventually, enterprise-zone legislation died in Congress, but by 1988 several states had created similar laws, though their impact was minimal.

After eight years of "Reaganomics," urban leaders were ready to call the experiment a failure. In response to Reagan's economic policies, cities had had to cut services and raise property taxes. By 1988, the prospects for the urban poor seemed especially dim. Street crime, homelessness, joblessness, hunger, and hopelessness had been persistent problems in most inner-city neighborhoods for decades, but by 1988 urban leaders had to accept the fact that they lacked the political clout to pressure the federal government to solve these problems. According to the *New York Times,* Reagan had taught mayors two lessons: "to narrow their list of demands, and even then not to expect too much." Cities were left to search for new answers to old problems that no longer seemed to interest average people. Massive federal aid had not proved to be an urban panacea, but the Reagan administration had removed government's provision of a safety net and left a legacy of seeming disregard for poor people.

George H. W. Bush, Reagan's vice president, was elected to the presidency in 1988 by the same suburban constituency that had benefited his predecessor, and he showed few signs that he might alter Reagan's views regarding urban interests. Eight years earlier, Bush had labeled Reagan's supply-side economic theories as "voodoo economics." Once elected, his cabinet appointments, especially HUD Secretary Jack Kemp, appeared urban-friendly. Kemp even announced, "I'm going to be an activist. I'm going to be an advocate. I want to wage war on poverty." Mayors did not expect an all-out war on poverty, but they were encouraged by such aggressive rhetoric. Even the new vice president, Dan Quayle, seemed to mount the bandwagon, announcing his own commitment to combating drugs and crime and reducing the dropout rates at urban schools. African-American leaders were especially encouraged. After President Bush met with leading blacks on Martin Luther King Day, Detroit's Coleman Young observed, "In one day, he took a bigger step than his predecessor took in eight years."

When word spread late in 1989 that cities could expect a "peace dividend" resulting from the end of the Cold War, mayors believed their patience had paid off. However, the 1990 federal budget proved to be the first in a series of disappointments. It closely resembled the budgets Reagan had sent to Congress. New York's Mayor David Dinkins called it "mean-spirited." Bush's urban program, which focused on still-unfulfilled enterprise zones, languished in Congress without enthusiastic support, even from Bush himself. By the end of 1990, a *New York Times* poll revealed that 77 percent of Americans thought Bush was doing "not much" or "nothing at all" about urban problems.

The Persian Gulf crisis, which began when Iraq invaded Kuwait in the summer of 1990 and escalated into war in January of 1991, gave Bush an excuse to ignore domestic policy altogether. In addition, a recession, which gripped the country in 1991, allowed him to eschew new social spending even as cities and their inhabitants struggled to stay afloat. By mid-1991, most major cities again were being forced to deal with fiscal crisis, mostly by cutting services and raising taxes. In Philadelphia, four mayoral candidates, including the eventual victor, Ed Rendell, supported privatization of public services, and, once elected, Rendell raised taxes by $90 million. Meanwhile, the President proposed turning $15 billion in federal aid for health, education, welfare, housing, and law enforcement over to the states. Boston's mayor Raymond Flynn grumbled, "This isn't Federalism, this is fraud."

Leasing city services to private contractors offered several mayors a tempting way to effect cost-saving and efficiency. At the federal level, the U.S.

Postal Service had been privatized, and numerous schemes for turning over management of public housing, toll roads, prisons, and airports to private companies circulated at state and local levels. By contracting out services, cities could escape fast-rising employee wage, benefit, and pension costs and avoid having to purchase expensive equipment for tasks as varied as data processing and snow removal. The prospect of privatization could also force public workers to be more efficient. For example, the city of Phoenix required its own employees to bid against private firms for residential trash collecting. City workers initially lost these contracts but then streamlined their operation and won them back.

Estimates of savings to a city from privatization ranged up to 20 percent. Consequently, more and more cities began considering it. In the early 1970s, as a result of generous federal aid, Chicago, under the powerful Mayor Richard J. Daley, had over 44,000 people on the city payroll. By 1991, the payroll under his son, Mayor Richard M. Daley, had shrunk to 38,500, and the younger Daley was seeking ways to reduce it further. By contracting out jobs such as sewer cleaning, addiction treatment, towing away abandoned cars, and custodial service for city buildings, Daley hoped to prevent tax hikes and budget deficits.

But privatization did not meet with universal approval in Chicago and elsewhere. Public employee unions naturally objected, and racial minorities expressed fears that the private sector could not be prevented from discriminatory hiring practices as readily as the public sector could. Critics charged that Daley, Rendell, and other mayors too easily could award contracts to friends and campaign contributors. Others lamented the enhanced possibilities for fraud when services were released from strict public supervision. Whatever its merits, privatization received encouragement from the administrations of Ronald Reagan and George Bush, and its momentum continued well into the 1990s.

Facing empty treasuries once more, several cities considered generating new revenues through legalized gambling. Since their inception, American cities have been centers for gambling, and though it was almost always illegal, urban leaders have alternated between tolerating some modicum of gambling and trying to eliminate it. In the post–World War II era, only the state of Nevada officially allowed gambling, and Las Vegas was the only city to base its growth on gambling and the tourism that accompanied it.

By the 1970s, however, fiscal shortfalls were tempting public officials to reconsider the jobs and tax revenues gambling could create. Several states revived lotteries, which during the colonial period had been used to raise revenue. Then, states and cities began to contemplate sponsoring casino gambling. In 1978, casino gaming became legal in Atlantic City, New Jersey, and a boom in hotel building and entertainment occurred there—though not without the destruction of low-rent neighborhoods and an increase in crime. By the 1990s, other cities were moving toward legalized gambling as well. Several cities on or near waterways, such as Chicago, St. Louis, and Biloxi, benefited from gambling places, but the increased number of casinos spawned fears that there would be diminishing returns from an excess of casinos relative to the gambling population and that the economic returns hid problematic costs. Some economists estimated that for every job that legalized gambling created two were lost because consumers who lost money gambling would cut back on spending in other areas such as buying clothes or getting haircuts. Mayors, it seemed, would have to look elsewhere for a quick fix to the needs for tax revenues and unemployment relief.

If George H. W. Bush was susceptible to criticism on urban issues before the Los Angeles uprising in late April and early May of 1992, he was directly vulnerable afterward. Exposing deep-seated tensions from racism and police brutality against minority communities, the uprising's immediate spark was the acquittal of four police officers who had been videotaped violently subduing an African-American man, Rodney King, during an arrest. Abetted by youth gangs, some enraged blacks and Latinos destroyed whole city blocks in South Central Los Angeles and spread violence and fear into surrounding communities, including Hollywood. In all, more than thirty-five people were killed, most of whom were shot by the police, and $2 billion worth of property was destroyed. Like the uprisings of the 1960s, the 1992 violence renewed concern about abject poverty and anger among racial minorities in all cities as well as in Los Angeles. The conditions of economic marginalization, inadequacy of social welfare expenditures, and racial discrimination had in many ways worsened in the 1990s with the flight of capital, collapse of the welfare state, and racist backlash, but the 1990s riots also expressed complex inter-ethnic and racial tensions, as well as alienation from civic culture, among people of color.

Bush's immediate response to the rioting was to attack Great Society programs on which Reagan had effectively laid blame for most urban problems. This tactic only angered his opponents more. "It's just amazing," said presidential candidate Bill Clinton. "Republicans have had the White House for twenty of the last twenty-four years, and they have to go all the way back to the '60s to find somebody to blame." The *New York Times* was more blunt. "As if, after Los Angeles, there were any doubt; America's cities need help. So far, President Bush mainly offers them gratuitous insult." The riots jarred Americans who had mostly been content to reap the rewards of economic prosperity and to stand by as minorities and poor people suffered. According to one pollster, 61 percent of Americans now thought the nation was spending too little on inner cities, compared to just 35 percent four years earlier during the height of the Reagan Revolution.

Less than two weeks after the rioting, the President and Congress seemed on the way to forging an emergency aid package. Democrats in Congress were willing to give the President enterprise zones, public school choice, and privatization of public housing. In return, Bush would support several spending initiatives. Before the plan could pass, however, Washington again yielded to partisan squabbling. The President refused to sign any bill that included a tax increase, while Congressional Democrats held out for more spending. Meanwhile, Republicans held fast on fiscal policies. California Congressman Bill Lowery, a staunch conservative, accused Bush of "send[ing] the message that urban terrorism brings Federal largesse."

The window of opportunity had not opened very far. After some debate over how to approach issues raised by the uprising, the Bush Administration decided on middle-of-the-road themes of law and order. In May of 1992, Vice President Quayle delivered a speech in Los Angeles, essentially blaming the rioting on the immorality of its participants. Said Quayle, "I believe the lawless anarchy which we saw is directly related to the breakdown of family structure, personal responsibility, and social order." On June 18, the President and Congress agreed on a watered-down $1.3 billion aid package and promised to address urban policy needs more comprehensively at a later date. By the end of 1992, Congress had passed an urban aid and tax bill, but according to the *New York Times,* the policy was disingenuous. "Want a challenge?" an editorial asked. "Try to find urban aid in the urban aid bills just passed by . . . Congress." In the end Congress and the President could only accomplish a political standoff. Despite all the rhetoric, little actually was done to help cities, and even the measures that were passed were destined to have no lasting effect. George H. W. Bush may have paid dearly for his lack of firm response, for the legislative failures enhanced his image as a President without domestic sensitivities, an image that contributed to his defeat to Bill Clinton in 1992.

THE CLINTON YEARS: FURTHER NEGLECT

Looking more liberal than Reagan or Bush, Clinton gave mayors cause to assume he would direct his attention to urban America. But like his predecessors, he was not forced by political winds to do so. He made few attempts to reach out to urban voters, and he borrowed much of his urban policy—law and order, home ownership, welfare reform, and enterprise zones—from Reagan. Though urban America enjoyed relative prosperity during Clinton's administrations, there was no guarantee that its fortunes would remain bright.

When Clinton was elected in 1992, the urban establishment did not know how to react. Some mayors were excited by the election of a Democrat. Yet Clinton was from a mostly rural state, had no experience with urban affairs, and had ignored cities during his campaign. He had no urban agenda to speak of, but he did address urban-related issues of health care, the AIDs epidemic, and welfare reform. The USCM decided to test the President early, presenting him with a $27 billion list of seven thousand ready-to-go projects

Orioles Park at Camden Yards, Baltimore. Opened to great acclaim in 1992, this new baseball stadium represents the attempt to revive community identification with a professional baseball team by recreating the look and feel of an earlier era in which the scale of things seemed more manageable.

during his first week in office. Several weeks later, Clinton promised a "fairly sizable increase" in block grants to cities.

In May of 1993, however, mayors got their first taste of what Clinton's urban policy would be like. He announced a plan to establish 110 "empowerment zones", his name for enterprise zones. The whole program would cost only $8 billion over five years. Later that month, he explained his Community Banking and Credit Fund, which would subsidize Community Development Banks, and called for $382 million in funding, substantially less than he had led mayors to expect. It was clear that Clinton had only modest plans for cities. His philosophy resembled Carter's, but he was not burdened by the inertia of massive federal spending on cities. He could concentrate on economic development without having to appease racial minorities with social spending programs. Consequently, his urban policy closely resembled those of his conservative predecessors. Half a year after Clinton took office, Louisville Mayor Jerry Abramson had resigned himself to four more years of executive inactivity. "There was a real question of whether it was humanly possible for any individual to reach our expectations," he said.

In the fall of 1996, Clinton signed a massive welfare reform bill that possibly served as his most influential urban policy. In reality, however, it was not his policy at all. Although Clinton talked frequently about welfare reform, he chose to sign a bill sponsored mostly by conservatives that had stirred aggressive liberal opposition in Congress. The legislation dismantled the 62-year-old welfare system and turned it over to state governments, imposing only the barest minimum of guidelines. Most big-city mayors opposed the legislation, arguing that it would cause suffering among poor mothers and their children.

Based on the premise that previous welfare measures fostered dependency, the new decentralized system focused on getting welfare recipients off relief and into the workplace. It relied on two principles. The first held that limited benefits would prevent welfare from becoming a way of life. The other assumed that uneducated single mothers needed support in order to find jobs and achieve stability. The policy flowing from these principles created new work rules, penalties, and time limits for welfare payments but also expanded certain services. For example, the Wisconsin welfare system required its recipients to work thirty hours a week in order to collect benefits. Recipients who broke the rules were cut off. In addition, no one could receive benefits for longer than five years. At the same time, however, the state made a more concerted effort to find work for welfare recipients and created public service jobs for those who could not find work. Other states pursued different paths to reach the same goals.

Though a booming national economy facilitated a decline in welfare rolls, even in hard-hit inner cities, many experts criticized the plan. Some argued that the focus on work of any sort would confine welfare recipients to dead-end jobs with no hope of receiving the training to move up the occupational ladder. Others feared the penalties were too strict and the rules too hard to follow. As of June, 1997, 20,000 people had already lost benefits for failing to comply with the work rules; many of them were welfare mothers who were dropped from the rolls because their time limit ran out. Political scientist James Jennings found that welfare reform's focus on individual workforce participation had a negative impact on poor black and Latino neighborhoods, because it discouraged civic participation and burdened community-based organizations with monitoring individual compliance with regulations rather than focusing on comprehensive economic and social organizing and revitalization.

On June 23, 1997, President Clinton addressed the USCM and outlined what he called his first urban agenda. Most elements of the plan, such as giving police officers discounts on HUD-owned houses in the inner city and reducing closing costs for first-time homeowners, focused on long-time themes of law and order and promoting homeownership. Other aspects of the agenda already had been developed as part of the President's budget agreement with Congress. Conspicuously absent was any kind of social spending. Rather, Clinton focused on modest methods to promote economic development.

Even with Clinton's low-key approach to urban policy, however, cities began to share in the general health of the economy. Urban crime and unemployment were down in the late 1990s, and several big cities were achieving unparalleled fiscal stability. The seventy-two urban empowerment zones supported by the federal government had generated almost $4 billion in private investment, a 200 percent return on the federal program of $2 billion. Whether or not this trend could be attributed to Clinton's efforts, the economic recovery did not seem to be leaving poor urban dwellers as completely desperate as they had been under Reagan and Bush. What might happen when the economic boom leveled off remained uncertain.

THE SOCIAL COSTS OF WIDENING INCOME INEQUALITY AND URBAN NEGLECT

Dense concentrations of poor people in urban neighborhoods magnified the problems related to poverty: joblessness, crime, delinqunecy, drug use and trafficing, family break-up, and poor school performance. The rise in poverty concentration began in the early 1970s in cities, because of declining incomes of the poor and the exodus of middle income families leaving inner-city neighborhoods. Mixed-income neighborhoods turned into high-poverty neighborhoods, marking them as dangerous. Once this transition took place, these neighborhoods became socially and economically isolated as people tried to avoid them at all costs. Sensational journalism, fiction, and film all played their parts in popularizing high-concentration poverty areas as urban wastelands.

As a source of fear and a matter that evaded easy analysis, crime has always plagued American cities. In actuality, crime rates—the number of serious crimes per 100,000 people—fell from 1980 to the late 1990s. But the absolute numbers of robberies, assaults, and homicides increased. Two related agents intensified the sense of danger in urban society: the widespread ownership of guns and the uncontrollable use and trafficking of illegal drugs.

The temporary escape from pain promised by drugs tempted all parts of American society, including the suburbs. But in the mid-1980s, the rapid spread of crack cocaine brought severe consequences to some poverty-concentrated neighborhoods. Easily addictive, crack became an entrepreneurial bonanza, attracting youths and their gangs into dealing and provoking violent conflicts over the huge profits involved in its sale. The money and competition also prompted dealers to acquire guns, some of which had extraordinary firepower, and to use them indiscriminately. The drug epidemic amplified the AIDS epidemic. Passed to victims through infected intravenous needles as well as through infected body fluids exchanged during sexual contact, AIDS became a major urban public health concern.

The despair of homelessness also increasingly marked the urban landscape. The decline in affordable housing resulted from demolition and gentrification in downtown neighborhoods as well as from government retrenchment. In 1970, there were a few more cheap apartments than needy renters: 6.2 million renters and 6.5 million apartments. But by 1995, there were 10 million needy renters and just 6 million low-rent apartments. By 1998, for example, as many as 16,000 homeless individuals wandered the streets of San Francisco on any given day, attracted by the city's mild climate and tradition of social consciousness. More than a third of those lacking permanent housing were mentally ill people, released from homes and hospitals by the Reagan administration's cuts in federal aid and by a trend toward removing people from institutions. Increasingly, the homeless population consisted of families, especially those headed by women, unable to derive sufficient income and cast adrift by cuts in housing subsidies. The burden of the shortage of affordable housing and the resulting homelessness fell heavily on children, who composed 40 percent of the poor by the year 2000, a proportion even higher in African-American, Latino, and new Asian immigrant populations.

Gentrification's role in the decline of affordable housing has sometimes implicated a group that have themselves been recipients of discrimination: middle-class homosexuals. Because gay communities tended to form in downtown neighborhoods and to participate in the process of revitalization, this process has sometimes resulted in sharp conflict with long-time poorer residents whose access to housing has been diminished. These tensions sometimes have taken on a racial inflection when the communities affected have included African Americans, Latinos, or other people of color. Gay men and lesbians have often been the opening wedge in neighborhood gentrification, followed later by other young urban professionals whose presence helped to push out all but the wealthiest gay residents. Boston's South End, Brooklyn's Park Slope, Philadelphia's Rittenhouse Square, and Washington, D.C.'s Dupont Circle have exemplified neighborhoods where these transitions, with their attendant tensions, have occurred. When this process has managed to preserve some affordable housing, such as in Brooklyn's Prospect Heights, the resulting neighborhoods can be home to residents of diverse racial, ethnic, class, and sexual identities.

The economic boom of the Clinton years reduced unemployment, and increased the earnings of low wage workers. In 1990, 15 percent of all poor people lived in high poverty neighborhoods, but ten years later, only 10 percent did. This decline, which resulted partly from the tearing down of high rise public housing which had been allowed to fall into dangerous ill repair, was most significant in midwestern and southern cities like Detroit, Chicago, and San Antonio. Poverty concentrations remained unchanged in older northeastern cities. At the same time, poor residents moved into the inner ring of older suburbs in Chicago, Detroit, Cleveland, and Dallas. Black people were still more likely to live in high poverty neighborhoods than other poor people, although the numbers fell from 30 pecent in 1990 to 19 percent in 2000. Los Angeles was the only city to show an increase in the number of high poverty neighborhoods over this time period, but rising unemployment and individual poverty rates related to the abrupt economic decline after 2001 has caused other cities to follow the Los Angeles pattern. For example, after booming in the 1990s, Atlanta's economy crashed after 2001, losing more jobs than any other city.

NEW URBAN NEIGHBORS

In the final decades of the twentieth century, immigrants once again profoundly affected American cities. By 2000, the U.S. census recorded immigrants as constituting 11 percent of the national population, the largest proportion of foreign born since the 1930s, and 44 percent of these, 13.5 million people, arrived in the 1990s. The new immigrants came from different backgrounds than earlier waves. In 1965, Congress abolished the quota system that had restricted immigration since 1924 and instead established annual limits of 120,000 immigrants from the Western Hemisphere and 170,000 from the Eastern Hemisphere. The law gave preferential treatment to people with relatives already in the United States and to those who possessed needed occupational skills. Partly as a result of the new law and partly as a result of U.S. military engagements and the global economy's intensified linkages between industrialized and developing countries, an estimated ten million people entered the country between 1968 and 1990. Europeans represented only 10 percent of incoming immigrants, Asians and South Asians represented 40 percent, with the rest coming from Mexico, Central America, and the Caribbean. These figures do not include huge numbers of illegal immigrants, many of whom crossed into the United States over its southern borders.

Cities felt the effects immediately. Though New York continued to receive newcomers from every part of the world, large numbers of Asian immigrants helped Los Angeles replace New York as the major port of entry. Los Angeles also became the second largest Mexican city in the world. Latin Americans, especially the 900,000 who left Cuba, turned Miami into a Caribbean capital. Many immigrants were well educated and upwardly mobile; they opened shops and moved into professions. But many others had fled political repression and war-related violence, and were unskilled by U.S. standards.

Immigrants profoundly reshaped the urban racial makeup. Boston went from having a majority (67.9 percent) white population in 1980 to an evenly divided (49.5 percent) white and nonwhite city by 2000, with more than one-third of the black population coming from Haiti, Jamaica, Somalia, and Nigeria. By 2002, one-fourth of New York City's black population was from the Caribbean, and nearly 60% of the Caribbean immigrants were female. By

1990, the combined Latino groups outnumbered the native black populations in Miami, San Antonio, Houston, Phoenix, Los Angeles, and San Diego. Counting various Asians together made them a significant nonwhite presence in San Francisco, Seattle, and other West Coast cities.

The quintessential urban cultural form of the late twentieth century, rap and hip hop, was one striking product of the new racial/ethnic mixing. Rap music emerged from Jamiacan practices of using DJs, or "toasters," to add street poetry over basic instrumental dance music and using "mixing" and "sampling" sounds from turntables. Hip hop culture's use of language and sampling from a wide range of musical sources revolutionized the music business and provided a hybrid musical form that was easily and enthusiastically adopted by African-American, Puerto Rican, Dominican, Mexican, Cuban, Korean, and white musicians to speak to the urban and migrant condition.

From the 1970s onward, factors of race, ethnicity, gender, and sexuality influenced local affairs more strongly than perhaps at any time in American urban history, though these identities have been intersected by class and political differences, making community affiliation a complex process. In the 1970s, women's expanding political activism resulted in female mayors such as Kathryn J. Whitmire in Houston, Donna Owens in Toledo, Dianne Feinstein in

Hip Hop Nation in Iowa, 2003. The Puerto-Rican artist Paco, break-dancing in front of a mural which he had painted in Cedar Rapids, Iowa, on the wall of a local youth center, working with high school students as part of a fine arts summer school program featuring DJ performance, slam poetry, dance, and painting.

San Francisco, and Maureen O'Connor in San Diego. Newly registered minority voters and neighborhood campaigns brought African Americans, Mexican Americans, and white ethnics into local government as well. By the mid-1970s, six major cities—Washington, D.C., Newark, New Orleans, Baltimore, Atlanta, and Gary—were over 50 percent black, and more, including Detroit and Chicago, were approaching that proportion. The pioneer election of African-American mayors such as Richard Hatcher in Gary, Carl Stokes in Cleveland, and Kenneth Gibson in Newark had by the 1990s become commonplace as African Americans served as mayors in thirty-three cities. In some ways, blacks were a more flexible interest group than whites. A poll taken in 1992 found that 64 percent of black respondents believed that African Americans would vote for the most qualified candidate for mayor of their city, regardless of the candidate's race. Only 41 percent of whites said they would vote for the most qualified candidate.

Lawsuits charging that at-large representation discriminated against minorities and grass-roots campaigns for greater local representation revived district representation in several cities. In 1974, Albuquerque voters replaced nonpartisan, at-large representation with a district council. In San Antonio, a community organization rallied Chicano residents and challenged downtown development, urging that resources be redirected to the neighborhoods. In 1977, after a court battle that resulted in elections based on local districts, San Antonio ethnic neighborhoods elected five Mexican Americans and one African American to the city council. In Richmond, a similar court challenge redefined city council districts, enabling voters to elect a city council consisting of an African-American majority.

In San Francisco, neighborhood-oriented sentiment against urban renewal helped to elect George Moscone as mayor and to approve an initiative to elect the Board of Supervisors by district representation. In 1977, district elections brought several kinds of newcomers to the board. These included Ella Hill Hutch from the largely black Western Addition and progressive gay activist Harvey Milk, whose support came from San Francisco's sizable gay community (estimated at 20 percent of the city's population by 1970), unions, and neighborhood opponents of big development from the Haight Ashbury, Castro/Noe district. Another newcomer was Dan White, a former policeman and firefighter who represented several white, ethnic, lower-middle-class and working-class neighborhoods.

Efforts in San Francisco toward limiting high-rise development and protecting low-rent housing were cut short by the deaths of Moscone and Milk at the hand of Dan White. White, apparently troubled by personal difficulties and the pressures of his office, and disturbed by the increasing power of minorities and gays, had suddenly resigned his board position. When his constituents objected, he asked Moscone for his seat back. Moscone's liberal supporters, including Milk, urged him not to rescind White's resignation and to replace him with an appointee more sympathetic to Moscone's policies.

After weeks of vacillation, Moscone decided to replace White. The next day, feeling betrayed and humiliated, White strapped on his police revolver, snuck past a metal detector into City Hall, and shot the mayor four times. He then walked across the building and murdered Milk. White's defense, that he was temporarily insane from the ingestion of junk food, brought him a conviction only on manslaughter charges. Following the verdict, over 5,000 outraged protesters marched on City Hall and caused over $1 million of property damage. The next night, 20,000 held a block party in the Castro to mourn the deaths of Moscone and Milk and to reaffirm their strength. Gay residents continued to be a political force in San Francisco, but sky-rocketing rents and diminishing destruction of public and low-income housing forced black residents to live elsewhere. Their presence in the city fell from 13 percent of the population in 1970 to 8.6 percent thirty years later.

Meanwhile, Latinos, who by 1990 numbered twenty-two million and increased to 35 million in 2000, were searching for their own political voice. One barrier to that task has been that the variety of people—ranging from Mexican Americans to Cuban exiles to Puerto Ricans to newer arrivals from Central America—included in the ethnic group has prevented the emergence of unified leadership. Also, Latinos have had to compete with other minorities for offices opened to them by white power structures. Still, in cities such as Los Angeles, Houston, Miami, Chicago, and San Antonio, the numbers of Latinos were growing too large to overlook. Henry G. Cisneros, former mayor of San Antonio, helped establish the National Hispanic Leadership Agenda, which sought issues on which these groups could unite. Antonio Villaraigosa's bid to move from his position as Speaker of the California Assembly to be elected as mayor of Los Angeles in 2001, though unsuccessful, drew on his background in the labor movement, and especially on the "Justice for Janitors" campaign that improved wages and benefits for Latino low-wage workers in the early 1990s. Villaraigosa, echoing concerns of immigrants of a century earlier, argued that "critical issues for Latinos are the same as most Americans," but more urgent "because their neighborhoods often have the highest crime rate and the dirtiest air. It's because they often have little job security or no health insurance."

All these new actors in municipal politics inherited cities at the time when they were most stripped of financial resources and beset by fiscal burdens. Despite operating with these constraints, black mayors were able to improve public services, civic engagement, and participation in neglected neighborhoods, and increase minority access to public employment. The tensions between balancing neighborhood needs against private development and the difficulties of negotiating political coalitions across increasingly diverse communities divided by racial, ethnic, gender, class, and party differences required new forms of political negotiation. City politics in places like Atlanta, Miami, San Antonio, and Houston have entailed multiethnic coalition building. In the Elmhurst-Corona neighborhood of Queens, New

York, women activists organized politically across ethnic and racial boundaries in the late twentieth century and demonstrated a successful way to fight budget cuts, protect public services, support local businesses, and shape taxation policies to maintain the neighborhood's quality of life.

Still, racial segregation has persisted and in some places increased in the last thirty years. School segregation has intensified since 1970, as a result of large increases in African-American, Latino, and Asian enrollments, continued white flight to the suburbs, the persistence of housing patterns that isolate racial and ethnic groups, and, in recent years, the termination of court-ordered desegregation plans. In Charlotte, North Carolina, one school went from being 68% black to being nearly 100% black within one year after the end of court ordered desegregation. In Boston in 2000, most black residents were likely to live in neighborhoods that were more than 50 percent black; the large numbers of Latinos and Asians who moved to Boston have not altered the reality that most whites and nonwhites still live in separate worlds. As Latino and Asian groups increased in size, they clustered in enclaves of their own. In New York, whites were increasingly likely to live near Asians and Latinos, and blacks were more likely to live near Latinos, but the level of segregation between blacks and Asians remained almost as high as it has been between blacks and whites. According to the 2000 census, cities growing more segregated included Detroit, Milwaukee, New York, Newark, Chicago, Cleveland, Miami, Cincinnati, Birmingham, and St. Louis. There were some exceptions: proximity to military facilities helped to explain diminishing segregation in cities such as Norfolk, Charleston, Raleigh-Durham, Jacksonville, Sacramento, and San Diego.

EDGE CITY AND INNER CITY

As the twentieth century drew to a close, the spectrum of suburbs showed considerable diversity. Some suburbs were residential, some were industrial, some wealthy and some modest, some white and some black. Aging housing stock in inner suburban rings around such places as Chicago, New York, Washington, D.C., and St. Louis increasingly made these places indistinguishable from the adjacent urban core. These suburbs had begun to experience problems of crowding, an aging population, and poverty that were haunting inner cities. Even the most widely recognized feature of suburban life, commuting, underwent changes as companies that moved to urban outskirts brought thousands of both blue-collar and white-collar jobs with them and reversed commuting patterns. Pollsters in 1980 found that over 70 percent of suburban residents worked in their own or another suburb. In the New York area, one-third of suburban workers were employed in a suburb other than their own, and only one-fifth commuted to the city.

By the year 2000, the term "urban" had taken on expanded meanings. New designs and functions were altering old images of central cities, suburbs,

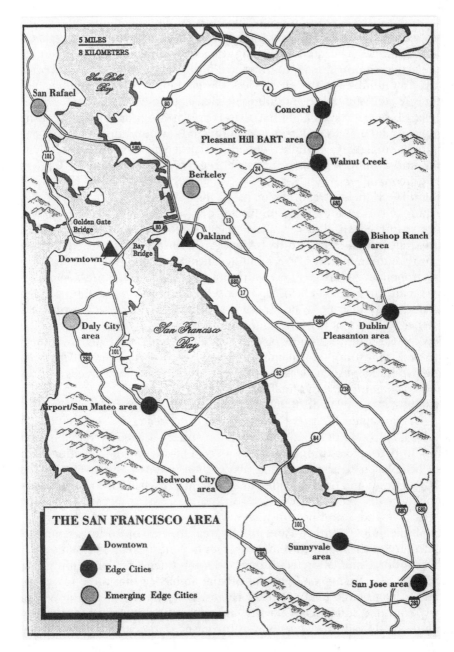

Edge Cities in the San Francisco Area. Sprinkled around the downtowns of San Francisco and Oakland, and linked by superhighways, a chain of emerging edge cities has come to represent a recent form of urban economic and residential development. According to journalist Joel Garreau, similar networks of edge cities exist around virtually every major American metropolitan area.

and various other zones of housing and business. Outside metropolitan borders, "exurbs," "out-towns," and "mall towns" had grown into major residential and commercial centers, providing residents with amenities of urban life while making it unnecessary to travel to a nearby city except for special occasions. Communities with full services of shopping, entertainment, banks, schools, water, and police and fire protection had grown up around airports such as Chicago's O'Hare and the Dallas–Fort Worth Airport, around sporting complexes such as New Jersey's Meadowlands, around malls such as the Cumberland/Galleria complex outside Atlanta and Tyson's Corner, Virginia, and around high-tech industrial regions such as southern California's Silicon Valley.

In 1988, Joel Garreau, senior writer for the *Washington Post,* gave fuller meaning to these communities in his book, *Edge City: Life on the New Frontier.* Labeling himself an observer rather than a historian, planner, or prophet, Garreau nevertheless argued that American civilization was experiencing a major revolution in how it was building cities. He asserted that the majority of metropolitan Americans now work not in brick factories and downtown skyscrapers but in glass-enclosed, low-rise buildings surrounded by parking lots, trees, and superhighways. These new urban centers, he said, owed their existence to new modes of communication over the airwaves and across the freeways. Garreau called these places "edge cities" and hailed them as centers of the postindustrial, information- and service-oriented future. Identifying some two hundred such places across the country, he defined an edge city as a place containing at least 5 million square feet of office space (more than in downtown Memphis) and 600,000 square feet of retail space.[1]

At the same time that Garreau seemed to predict a discarding of the past for a new kind of urban community, planners, architects, retailers, and community people continued to try to revive old cities by rejuvenating what they believed had been inspiring about time-honored urban life. In the 1970s, planner and developer James Rouse, already famous for developing shopping malls and the "new city" of Reston, Virginia, began renovating inner-city markets and port districts with remarkable success. His restoration of the Quincy Market–Fanueil Hall area, the hub of Boston's commercial activity in the eighteenth and nineteenth centuries, and of Baltimore's Inner Harbor district attracted throngs of local residents as well as tourists to the shops, restaurants, and general urbane ambience that these places offered. As well, large national retail chains, realizing the buying power of newly educated residents of Harlem, where by 1998 more than a third of adult residents had college degrees or higher education experience, opened shops on streets where none had existed before because of high crime rates and too many low-income residents. National and local retail stores returned to 125th Street, Harlem's main commercial strip.

Less publicized but equally noteworthy, residents of some inner-city neighborhoods tried to renovate from within. The unsung case of a group of

South Bronx inhabitants is illustrative. Formerly a blue-collar community of European immigrants, the South Bronx section of New York City experienced "white flight" in the 1960s as African Americans and Puerto Ricans moved in. A decade later, as these new residents moved out, landlords, unable or unwilling to borrow money to maintain their property because of high interest rates, allowed unfilled buildings to deteriorate. Soon South Bronx became one of the country's most devastated urban districts, racked by crime, drug use, and poverty.

Some dedicated residents did stay behind, however, and they formed a neighborhood-based nonprofit organization chartered to improve local conditions. They called their organization the Banana Kelly Community Improvement Association, named after a crescent-shaped section of Kelly Street near their homes. Formed initially to protect three buildings from demolition by the city, the association first consisted of thirty families who began working on their own to rehabilitate the neighborhood. Using the motto "Don't move, improve," they incorporated and succeeded in obtaining loans to renovate the buildings. As a result, they learned first-hand about construction, management, and financing without help from outside consultants. Their success convinced the city to turn over more abandoned South Bronx buildings to the association. Eventually, Banana Kelly built up a staff of ninety-two people and a multimillion-dollar budget. The association managed fifty-two structures, aiding thousands of residents in buying and improving apartment buildings, restoring fifty million dollars of property to the tax rolls, building a pediatric clinic, running an adult job-training program, funding a task force against crime and drugs, and providing low-interest loans for businesses locating in the community.

Local initiative was Banana Kelly's driving force. The association not only oversaw the rehabilitation of buildings but also carefully screened prospective tenants and trained them to participate in community matters. Using a grant from the Surdna Foundation, the association provided loans for residents to start their own enterprises, develop management skills, and create jobs. As one program director stated, "We invest in training local people because it builds to the capacity of the neighborhood. If our funding were cut tomorrow, the professionals would be gone, but these people would still be here." This kind of empowerment sometimes produced contentiousness when Banana Kelly professional staff made decisions without consulting neighborhood residents, but such pitfalls were built into the process of community involvement.

The Banana Kelly Improvement Association was just one of hundreds of similar community development corporations that have arisen in inner-city districts to seize the initiative for neighborhood self-improvement. Implicit in the efforts of inner-city revival, whether organized from the outside or the inside, is a challenge to Garreau's assertion that edge cities herald the nation's future. Long-time residents and new urban gentrifiers find themselves in (unequal) competition for the same urban space precisely because of the attractiveness of revitalized neighborhoods, which mix work, shops, and housing, and which nurture social and cultural interaction between neighbors, indicating a compelling challenge for the urban future.

INTO THE TWENTY-FIRST CENTURY

On September 11, 2001, airplanes hijacked by terrorists rammed and destroyed New York City's twin World Trade Center towers, killing several thousand people. Together with an almost simultaneous terrorist attack on the Pentagon, these incidents propelled the United States and its cities into a new era of uncertainty. Death and destruction were not new to American cities; the New York City draft riots of 1863, the Chicago Fire of 1871, the San Francisco earthquake of 1906 all had similar devastating effects. But the 9/11 attacks came at a time when American dwellers were feeling relatively safe and confident. The economic boom of the 1990s had not yet dissolved; race and class conflict, though still rumbling, seemed muted; crime rates were down; and the new president, George W. Bush, was focusing on sustaining prosperity and improving education. These conditions made the terrorism all the more appalling, and when a widespread electrical blackout rolled across the Northeast on August 14, 2003, plunging 50 million people in cities from New York to Cleveland to Detroit into darkness, the country had more reason to feel vulnerable even in an advanced technological age.

The foremost consequences of the 9/11 attacks were the American invasions first of Afghanistan and then of Iraq. But there were two particular effects on American cities. First, the deaths and terrible infrastructure damage in New York, coupled with the new attention to "homeland security", prompted cities and suburbs alike to worry more about protecting vital structures and services: airports, water supplies, port facilities, power plants, and the like. Many new security measures were funded in part by the federal government, but states and localities also had to expend funds in this endeavor.

Second, the extraordinary attention that President Bush now directed toward international terrorism and protecting American interests around the world with heightened defense budgets and military action overwhelmed any sort of urban-oriented domestic policy the Bush administration might have been considering. Though Bush did push Congress to pass a No Child Left Behind act that aimed to improve education, including that in cities, by mandating—but not funding—annual testing of schoolchildren among other measures, most of his actions affecting cities involved withdrawal rather than engagement of federal participation. In an extension of Ronald Reagan's goal to curtail federal commitments, Bush's domestic policy included dismantling the Head Start program for educating at-risk children, encouraging faith-based relief of poverty to replace government

Urban Resilience. On September 12, 2001, New Yorkers poured into the streets to acknowledge the heroism of the municipal firefighters, police, and rescue workers in the face of the unprecedented devastation caused by the terrorist attack on the World Trade Center buildings. In spite of incalculable losses, from the deaths of over two thousand men and women to destroyed property and jobs, the city's spirit of gratitude and determination emerged powerfully in the aftermath.

funding, weakening automobile and factory emission standards set by the Clean Air Act of 1990, and shifting more responsibility for health care to the states and private insurers. Among the measures of direct federal intervention that Bush supported were a bill to exempt gun dealers from lawsuits over crimes involving firearms, legal barriers to same-sex marriages, and the "Patriot Act" to give sweeping new powers to law enforcement and intelligence agencies. Bush made an overture to Latinos by appointing Cuban immigrant Mel Martinez to become secretary of the Department of Housing and Urban Development (HUD), but very little of his domestic agenda was directed toward cities. For example, in mid-2003, a $156 million plan to beautify parks and a $13.5 million joint HUD and Department of Labor plan to aid the chronically homeless involved budgets that fell short of what the military was spending each day in its occupation of Iraq.

As well, the emphasis on "reality" in popular media of the Bush years exaggerated the grimness of American cities. Though crime rates generally were stable if not falling, nightly news programs competed with each other to present more reports of urban violence and other malfeasance, especially by youth gangs, than ever before. Perhaps more influential, highly popular prime-time "reality" programs such as "Cops" and numerous crime-solving dramas presented multiple segments of (usually successful) urban police work, and the arrested suspects contained disproportionate numbers of poor and minority individuals. To many people, television portrayals and programs made urban neighborhoods forbidding and frightening places. The visible underclass of jobless individuals and homeless families seemed to some a permanent rebuke to the unmet promises of Great Society programs. To others, central cities provided testimony to the ravages of fiscal retrenchment and the attack on social programs. And gated suburban communities located near freeways and shopping centers enabled their residents to escape contact with many aspects of urban life altogether.

But cities, their institutions, and their people remain fonts of creativity, and the well of new ideas has not dried up. On the public level, government agencies continue to address problems such as threats to safety, poor education, lack of decent housing, low-quality health care, and the deterioration of roads, bridges, and other infrastructure. Job training, child care, and tax credits for the working poor have promised some progress in welfare and employment. At the level of individual initiatives, tenant management and ownership of public housing have been advanced as a means to empower low-income families, and community efforts such as those by the Banana Kelly Improvement Association reflect the ingenuity of strategies generated by poor urban communities themselves. Cities are recreating mixed-income neighborhoods by building affordable and subsidized housing units alongside market rate condominiums.

One of the most promising experiments in urban housing has taken place in Chicago, where the city and private developers have torn down the huge Cabrini-Green housing project, which once consisted of 3,606 dwelling units in eighty-six buildings covering seventy acres. Built between 1943 and 1962, Cabrini-Green once was home to some 40,000 public-housing residents but also was one of the most decaying, crime-ridden, gang- and drug-infested centers of any city. Instead of the grim, high-rise towers, developers have built condominiums and town houses intended to accommodate a mixed-income population, with families receiving public rent subsidies living nearby to owners of top-of-the-line residences. Low-income tenants had to pass a background check for criminal record and drug use, but families eager for better housing than the "projects" could offer worked hard to make themselves qualified for occupancy. Far fewer low-cost housing units were constructed on the site than were needed; still, the experiment of blending neighbors of differing incomes, providing at least some worthwhile public housing, and at the same time accommodating more affluent people eager to live near the shops and restaurants of the city's "Old Town" offered a more vibrant option to what had preceded it.

Mixed-Income Redevelopment in Chicago. In 1997, Chicago's Housing Authority began taking down the massive high-rise public housing of the Cabrini Green Homes, visible in this photograph in the upper right corner, and replacing them with mixed income townhouses and apartments built by private developers, thirty percent of which must be offered to low-income families. The strategy aimed to break up highly concentrated poverty areas by re-establishing mixed income neighborhoods.

A number of cities have expanded their reputations for "livability," from Portland, Maine, to Charlotte, North Carolina, to Minneapolis, Minnesota, to Portland, Oregon. Although at a high cost, historic preservation and gentrification have sparked commitments to urban life. Street fairs, concerts, public art, walking tours, running races, ethnic festivals, and many more events draw people of different classes and races to mingle in city spaces and celebrations.

Nevertheless, predictions about the future remain uncertain. It remains to be seen whether supporters of the various public sector remedies of public housing and housing subsidies, rent control, and controlled development can form effective political coalitions to challenge the direction of massive financial and corporate expansion that has reshaped American cities. It remains to be seen whether changes in social support systems, employment policies, and wage structures can keep cities from becoming a two-class society populated by the very poor and the well-off and can stem the feminization of poverty that condemns many urban women and their children to lives of deprivation. It remains to be seen whether continuing calls for combined private sector–public sector efforts to revive central city economies can succeed. It remains to be seen whether the economic downturn of the early twenty-first century, effected by federal cutbacks in urban aid, by unemployment and under-employment resulting from the nation's deindustrialization, and by government and corporate policies that have opened a deep chasm between the incomes of the rich and the poor will stifle whatever positive efforts cities and their residents are making.

The outlook for American cities, daunting and foreboding as it may seem, still has hopeful features. Better planning, neighborhood activism, and creative leadership have fueled inner-city revival in many cities as diverse as Baltimore, San Antonio, and Seattle. It is because of their viability, their appeal, and their resiliency that their history is worth studying. Cities today remain what they have always been—centers of economic, social, and cultural opportunity. As Mr. Dooley, the fictional turn-of-the-century saloon keeper and home-spun philosopher created by humorist Finley Peter Dunne, once observed,

> Ye might say as Hogan does, that we're ladin' an artyficyal life [in cities], but, by Hivins, ye might as well tell me I ought to be paradin' up and down a hillside with a suit iv skins, shootin' the antylope an' the moose, by gory, an' livin' in a cave as to make me believe I ought to get along with sthreet cars an' ilictric lights an' illyvators an' sody wather an' ice. "We ought to live where all the good things iv life comes from," says Hogan. "No," says I. "The place to live is where all the good things iv life goes to."

BIBLIOGRAPHY

Works which explore globalization's impact on cities include Carl Abbott, *Political Terrain: Washington, D.C. from Tidewater Town to Global Metropolis* (1999); Janet L. Abu-Lughod, *New York, Chicago, Los: America's Global Cities* (1999); Peter Marcuse and Ronald van Kempen, eds. *Globalizing Cities: A New Spatial Order?* (2000); Saskia Sassen, *Globalization and Its Discontents: Essays on the New Mobility of People and Money* (1998); and Sassen, *The Global City: New York, London, Tokyo* (1991). The postindustrial landscape of Los Angeles has received special attention from Mike Davis, *City of Quartz: Excavating the Future in Los Angeles* (1990). See also the essays in George Salas and Michael S. Roth, *Looking for Los Angeles: Architecture, Film, Photography and the Urban Landscape* (2001)

For works on the 1970s and 1980s urban fiscal crisis, see Ken Auletta, *The Streets Were Paved with Gold* (1979); and John Mollenkopf, *The Contested City* (1983); Mollonkopf, *New York City in the 1980s: A Political, Social, and Economic Atlas* (1993); Charles R. Morris, *The Cost of Good Intentions: New York City and the Liberal Experience, 1960–1973* (1980); Paul E. Peterson, ed., *The New Urban Reality* (1985); and Todd Swanstrom, *The Rising of Growth Politics: Cleveland, Kucinich, and the Challenge of Urban Populism* (1985).

On race, politics, and social policy since 1974, see John Hartigan, Jr., *Racial Situations: Class Predicaments of Whiteness in Detroit* (1999); James Jennings, *Understanding the Nature of Poverty in Urban America* (1994); Jennings, *Welfare Reform and the Revitalization of Inner City Neighborhoods* (2003); Michael B. Katz, *The Price of Citizenship: Redefining the American Welfare State* (2001) and Katz, *The Undeserving Poor: From the War on Poverty to the War on Welfare* (1989); George Lipsitz, *The Possessive Investment in Whiteness: How White People Benefit from Identity Politics* (1998); Alice O'Connor, *Poverty Knowledge: Social Science, Social Policy, and the Poor in Twentieth Century U.S. History* (2001); Stephen Steinberg, *Turning Back: The Retreat from Racial Justice in American Thought and Policy* (1995); William Julius Wilson, *The Truly Disadvantaged: The Inner City, the Underclass, and Public Policy* (1987) and Wilson, *The Declining Significance of Race: Blacks and Changing American Institutions,* 2nd ed. (1980).

On the Los Angeles uprising of 1992, see Nancy Ableman and John Lie, *Blue Dreams: Korean Americans and the Los Angeles Riots* (1995); Mark Baldasarre, ed., *The Los Angeles Riots: Lessons for the Urban Future* (1994); and Robert Gooding Williams, ed., *Reading Rodney King, Reading Urban Uprisings* (1993)

On new immigrants and the new racial and ethnic mix in American cities, see Rachel Buff, *Immigration and the Political Economy of Home: West Indian Brooklyn and American Indian Minneapolis, 1945–1992* (2001); Mike Davis, *Magical Urbanism: Latinos Reinvent the U.S. City* (2000); Hector Delgado, *New Immigrants, Old Unions: Organizing Undocumented Workers in Los Angeles* (1993); William V. Flores and Rina Benmayor, *Latino Cultural Citizenship: Claiming Identity, Space, and Rights* (1997); Nancy Foner, *From Ellis Island to JFK: New York's Two Great Waves of Immigration* (2000); Guillermo Grenier and Alex Stepick, eds., *Miami Now! Immigration, Ethnicity, and Social Change* (1992); James Jennings, ed., *Blacks, Latinos and Asians in Urban America: Status and Prospects for Politics and Activism* (1994); Susan Keefe and Amado Padilla, *Chicano Ethnicity* (1987); Lionel Maldonado and Joan Moore, eds., *Urban Ethnicity in the United States: New Immigrants and Old Minorities* (1985); Felix Padilla, *Latino Ethnic Consciousness: The Case of Mexicans and Puerto Ricans in Chicago* (1985); David Reimers, *Still the Golden Door: The Third World Comes to America* (1992); and Roger Waldinger, *Still the Promised City? African-Americans and the New Immigrants in Postindustrial New York* (1996).

On rap, hip hop, and immigrant youth cultures, see Joe Austin, *Taking the Train: How Graffiti Art Became an Urban Crisis in New York City* (2001); and Joe Austin with Michael Nevin Willard, ed., *Generations of Youth: Youth Culture and History in Twenteth Century America* (1998); Murray Forman, *The Hood Comes First: Race, Space and Place in Rap and Hip Hop* (2002); George Lipsitz, *Dangerous Crossroads: Popular Music, Postmodernism, and the Poetics of Place* (1994); Sunaina Maira, *Desis in the House: Indian American Youth Culture in New York City* (2002); William Eric Perkins, *Droppin' Science: Critical Essays on Rap Music and Hip Hop Culture* (1996); and Rachel Rubin and Jeff Melnick, *Immigrants and American Popular Culture* (2004);

On the emergence of African-American mayors, see Peter K. Eisinger, *The Politics of Displacement: Racial and Ethnic Tensions in Three American Cities* (1980); Steven Gregory, *Black Corona: Race and the Politics of Place in an Urban Community* (1998); James Jennings and Monte Rivera, *Puerto Rican Politics in Urban America* (1984); Paul Kleppner, *Chicago Divided: The Making of a Black Mayor* (1987); William E. Nelson, Jr., and Philip J. Meranto, *Electing Black Mayors: Political Action in the Black Community* (1977); and Adolphe Reed, *Stirrings in the Jug: Black Politics in the Post-Segregation Era* (1999). On neighborhood conflict and local initiatives, see Roger Sanjek, *The Future of Us All: Race and Neighborhood Politics in New York City* (1998).

For works on planning and new urban/suburban configurations, see Larry Bennett, *Fragments of Cities: The New American Downtowns and Neighborhoods* (1990); Edward J. Blakely and Mary Gail Snyder, *Fortress America: Gated Communities in the U.S.* (1997); Peter Dreier, John Mollenkopf, and Todd Swanstrom, *Place Matters: Metropolitics for the Twenty-First Century* (2001); Joel Garreau, *Edge City: Life on the New Frontier* (1991); M. Gottdiener, Claudia C. Collins and David R. Dickens, *Las Vegas: The Social Production of an All-American City* (1999); John Hannigan, *Fantasy City: Pleasure and Profit in the Postwar Metropolis* (1998); Dennis R. Judd and Susan S. Fainstein, eds. *The Tourist City* (1999); Jane Holtz Kay, *Asphalt Nation: How the Automobile Took Over America and How We Can Take It Back* (1998); Alexander J. Reichl, *Reconstructing Times Square: Politics and Culture in Urban Development* (1999); Michael Sorkin, *Variations on a Theme Park: The New American City and the End of Public Space* (1992); and Jon C. Teaford, *PostSuburbia: Governments and Politics in the Edge Cities* (1996).

NOTE

1. Joel Garreau, *Edge City: Life on the New Frontier* (New York: Doubleday, 1991).

Photo Credits

Chapter 1: p. 2 Cahokia Mounds State Historic Site, painting by William R. Iseminger. p. 4 Courtesy of the Library of Congress. p. 5 Archives Nationales, Section Outre-Mer, Paris, France. p. 8 I.N. Phelps Stokes Collection, Miriam & Ira D. Wallach Division of Art, Prints and Photographs, The New York Public Library, Astor, Lenox and Tilden Foundations. p. 13 Courtesy of the Library of Congress. p. 25 The Library Company of Philadelphia. p. 32 The Metropolitan Museum of Art, Bequest of Charles Allen Munn, 1924. (24.90.1566a)

Chapter 2: p. 38 Collection of The New-York Historical Society. p. 39 Courtesy of the Library of Congress. p. 41 Miriam and Ira D. Wallach Division of Art, Prints and Photographs, The New York Public Library, Astor, Lenox and Tilden Foundations. p. 47 Gore Place Society, Inc. p. 54 Courtesy, American Antiquarian Society.

Chapter 3: p. 64 "The Beauties of Street Sprinkling, NYC", by Thomas Worth, 1856, watercolor on paper, Collection of The New-York Historical Society, 1924.151 p. 67 Collection of The New-York Historical Society. p. 68 Courtesy of the Library of Congress. p. 73 Courtesy of the Library of Congress. p. 76 Collection of The New-York Historical Society, 73259. p. 79 Courtesy of the Library of Congress.

Chapter 4: p. 90 Chicago Historical Society. p. 93 Chicago Historical Society. p. 96 Picture Research Consultants & Archives. p. 100 Courtesy of the Library of Congress. p. 101 Chicago Historical Society. p. 102 Chicago Historical Society. p. 104 Courtesy of the Library of Congress. p. 105 National Archives and Records Administration. p. 107 Montana Historical Society, Helena. p. 110 "Courtesy of the Rhode Island Historical Society, Negative number RHi (x3) 487." p. 112 Courtesy of the Library of Congress.

Chapter 5: p. 120 Courtesy of the Library of Congress. p. 123 Courtesy of the Library of Congress. p. 127 Slater Mill Historic Site. p. 138 Chicago Historical Society. p. 140 Courtesy of the Library of Congress. p. 144 "Courtesy of the Boston Public Library, Print Department".

Chapter 6: p. 159 Courtesy of the Library of Congress. p. 162 Brown Brothers. p. 164 Brown Brothers.

Chapter 7: p. 183 Picture Research Consultants & Archives. p. 185 Courtesy of the Library of Congress. p. 188 Richard J. Daley Library. p. 191 Picture Research Consultants & Archives. p. 193 Courtesy of the Library of Congress. p. 199 Courtesy of the Library of Congress.

Chapter 8: p. 205 National Archives and Records Administration. p. 213 Courtesy of the Library of Congress. p. 213 Courtesy of the Library of Congress. p. 216 Chicago Historical Society. p. 218 National Archives and Records Administration. p. 219 Natural History Museum of Los Angeles County/Seaver Center. p. 224 Courtesy of the Library of Congress. p. 229 Special Collections Division, University of Washington Libraries, Photo by Lee, Negative #20102. p. 234 Franklin D. Roosevelt Library. p. 235 Courtesy of the Library of Congress. p. 239 Courtesy of the Library of Congress. p. 240 Courtesy of the Library of Congress. p. 242 Courtesy of the Library of Congress.

Chapter 9: p. 250 Courtesy of the Library of Congress. p. 255 National Archives and Records Administration. p. 256 Courtesy of the Library of Congress. p. 257 Courtesy of the Library of Congress. p. 262 National Archives and Records Administration. p. 264 Saint Louis Housing Authority. p. 264 Saint Louis Post-Dispatch. p. 270 Marion Palfi, "Somewhere in the South", 1946–49. Gelatin silver print, 24.2 x 19.0 cm. © Center for Creative Photography, The University of Arizona. p. 271 "Courtesy of the Boston Public Library, Print Department". p. 277 Courtesy Judy Smith.

Chapter 10: p. 286 AP/Wide World Photos. p. 294 Jerry Wachter Photography LTD. p. 299 AP/Wide World Photos. p. 303 From EDGE CITY by Joel Garreau. Copyright 1991 by Joel Garreau. Used by permission of Doubleday, a division of Random House, Inc. p. 307 Getty Images, Inc. p. 309 AP/Wide World Photos.

Index